ENDING IMPUNITY FOR INTERNATIONAL LAW VIOLATIONS

This open access edited collection is the first book-length academic publication on the Palestinian Bedouins at risk of forced displacement in the Central West Bank and Greater Jerusalem area.

At its core are two questions: firstly; what are the humanitarian vulnerabilities they face and how are they produced/constructed? And secondly, how does protracted impunity for international law violations drive humanitarian protection risks for them? It interweaves international law, community-based empirical research and interdisciplinary perspectives, to offer the broadest possible framework for understanding these complex and complicated questions.

Ending Impunity for International Law Violations

Palestinian Bedouins and the Risk of Forced Displacement

Edited by
Alice Panepinto
Bana Abu Zuluf
Ahmad Amara
Brendan Ciarán Browne
Munir Nuseibah
and
Triestino Mariniello

•HART•
OXFORD • LONDON • NEW YORK • NEW DELHI • SYDNEY

HART PUBLISHING

Bloomsbury Publishing Plc

Kemp House, Chawley Park, Cumnor Hill, Oxford, OX2 9PH, UK

1385 Broadway, New York, NY 10018, USA

Bloomsbury Publishing Ireland Limited, 29 Earlsfort Terrace, Dublin 2, D02 AY28, Ireland

HART PUBLISHING, the Hart/Stag logo, BLOOMSBURY and the Diana logo are trademarks of Bloomsbury Publishing Plc

First published in Great Britain 2025

A catalogue record for this book is available from the British Library.

A catalogue record for this book is available from the Library of Congress.

ISBN: HB: 978-1-50997-720-8
ePDF: 978-1-50997-722-2
ePub: 978-1-50997-721-5

Typeset by Compuscript Ltd, Shannon

For product safety related questions contact productsafety@bloomsbury.com

To find out more about our authors and books visit www.hartpublishing.co.uk. Here you will find extracts, author information, details of forthcoming events and the option to sign up for our newsletters.

Preface

THE DISPLACEMENT OF the Palestinian Bedouins evokes a synecdoche: the fate of these communities represents a piece of the bigger picture of dispossession, dispersal and attempted erasure imposed on all native, indigenous Palestinians in rural as well as urban locations. From the moment European powers embraced the Zionist movement's plan to settle Palestine, culminating in the creation of the State of Israel in 1948, the catastrophic impact on the Arab Palestinian population was apparent. One of the most prominent Zionist leaders wrote in 1923 that it would be 'utterly impossible to obtain the voluntary consent of the Palestine Arabs for converting "Palestine" from an Arab country into a country with a Jewish majority', concluding that 'Zionist colonisation must either stop, or else proceed regardless of the native population'.[1]

As this book will illustrate, the risk of forced displacement that Palestinian Bedouins face today in the Eastern Jerusalem periphery and across the Israeli-occupied West Bank – as well as within the (as yet undefined) borders of the State of Israel[2] – is steeped in a legacy of racism, colonial violence and a system of domination which normalised over time.[3] The Bedouins are one group within the broader Palestinian polity, and as such they share the plight common to their people. At the same time, their identity, as well as the opportunistic ways in which such identity has been construed by those seeking to remove them from the land they inhabit, places them in a vulnerable position due to stereotypes around their mobility and displaceability. For these reasons (among others), Palestinian Bedouins face a humanitarian emergency and a daily reality of hardship;[4] their forced displacement and urbanisation has catastrophic effects individually and collectively.[5] This vulnerability is entirely man-made and thus reversable if there is the will to hold those responsible to account in accordance with the requirements of international law. Instead, routine, almost guaranteed impunity for violations of international humanitarian law (IHL) and international human rights law (IHRL) against Palestinians is one of the drivers of the deteriorating situation of the Bedouins.

[1] Z Jabotinsky, *The Iron Wall* (1923).

[2] Amnesty International, 'Over 300 Palestinian-Bedouin face forced evictions following mass home demolitions in Negev/Naqab' (9 May 2024), www.amnesty.org/en/latest/news/2024/05/israel-opt-over-300-palestinian-bedouin-face-forced-evictions-following-mass-home-demolitions-in-negev-naqab.

[3] Amnesty International, 'Israel's Apartheid Against Palestinians: Cruel System of Domination and Crime Against Humanity' (February 2022), www.amnesty.org/en/documents/mde15/5141/2022/en.

[4] UN-OCHA, '46 Bedouin Communities at Risk of Forcible Transfer in the Central West Bank: A Vulnerability Profile', www.ochaopt.org/page/46-bedouin-communities-risk-forcible-transfer-central-west-bank-vulnerability-profile.

[5] UNRWA/Bimkom, 'Al Jabal: A study on the transfer of Bedouin Palestine refugees' (2013), www.unrwa.org/userfiles/201305293270.pdf.

From the start of the 2023 war in Gaza, in relation to which there is a case before the International Court of Justice (ICJ) on genocide,[6] attacks against Palestinians elsewhere, including Bedouin communities across the West Bank and within Israel, have intensified. In the six months following October 2023, 20 Palestinian Bedouin communities were forcibly displaced in their entirety, with many more families forced to flee their homes due to a combination of Israeli settler violence and state violence.[7] The extent of killing and devastation in Gaza cannot be compared to other contemporary situations, yet there is an evident ideological continuum with what happens in the West Bank, revealing the State of Israel's disregard for the lives and rights of all Palestinians between the Jordan River and the Mediterranean Sea.

For Palestinian Bedouins specifically, violence emerges in a coercive environment which comprises multiple factors that make life uncertain and precarious. For instance, the discriminatory Israeli permit and planning regime sees almost all buildings as illegal and thus the Israeli authorities slate properties, including homes and schools, for demolition, with devastating consequences;[8] harassment by the armed forces and Israeli settlers makes life unbearable; repeated acts of settler violence (often facilitated by armed forces), including crimes against persons and property, almost never lead to convictions;[9] the shrinking space accessible to Bedouins for grazing their flocks has a detrimental impact on their livelihood, forcing some to take low-paid and insecure jobs in Israeli settlements; and the total lack of infrastructure, including water and sanitation facilities and electricity, makes the Bedouin communities dependent on aid.[10] At the same time, over 700,000 Israelis thrive in settlements often adjacent to Bedouin communities, enjoying ample Israeli state support, despite their illegality under international law.[11]

The State of Israel maintains an official programme of acceleration of settlement activity, exacerbating 'long-standing patterns of oppression, violence and discrimination against Palestinians'; Bedouin communities are often in the metaphorical and material line of fire of settlement expansion.[12] In addition to 'official' settlements, illegal under international law but authorised and supported by the state, there are at

[6] ICJ, Order of 26 January 2024, Application of the Convention on the Prevention and Punishment of the Crime of Genocide in the Gaza Strip (South Africa v. Israel), Request for the Indication of Provisional Measures (General List No 192).

[7] Reported inter alia in Samuel Forey, 'Palestinian shepherds in the West Bank are driven off their land by settlers' *Le Monde* (20 June 2024), www.lemonde.fr/en/international/article/2024/06/20/palestinian-shepherds-in-the-west-bank-are-driven-off-their-land-by-settlers_6675284_4.html.

[8] UN-OCHA, 'Most Palestinian plans to build in Area C not approved' *The Humanitarian Bulletin* (January–May 2021), www.ochaopt.org/content/most-palestinian-plans-build-area-c-not-approved.

[9] Yesh Din, 'Law Enforcement on Israeli Civilians in the West Bank (Settler violence) 2005–2023' Data Sheet (December 2023), www.yesh-din.org/en/data-sheet-december-2023-law-enforcement-on-israeli-civilians-in-the-west-bank-settler-violence-2005-2023.

[10] UNDP, 'Bedouins in the Occupied Palestinian Territory' (March 2017), www.undp.org/sites/g/files/zskgke326/files/2022-11/internal-_resilience_series_-_bedouins_in_the_opt.pdf?ref=longroadmag.com.

[11] The prohibition of settler activities is set out in Art 49(6) Fourth Geneva Convention relative to the Protection of Civilian Persons in Time of War ('Fourth Geneva Convention'; GCIV) of 12 August 1949, and confirmed in relation to Palestine in UN Security Council Resolution 2334 (23 December 2016) – notably not vetoed by the USA.

[12] United Nations High Commissioner for Human Rights, Report A/HRC/55/72 (1 February 2024).

least 147 settler outposts which are illegal under both international law and Israeli law (despite calls from some political quarters to legalise them). As noted by the UN High Commissioner for Human Rights, outposts are 'often strategically placed and play a key role in the takeover of Palestinian land. Israel employs different financial, legal and planning mechanisms to enable the establishment and expansion of outposts'.[13] Moreover, most ideologically motivated violence by settlers against Palestinians – affecting mostly Bedouin and herding communities across the West Bank – occurs in the vicinity of outposts.[14] While this is the contemporary reality facing Palestinian Bedouins, the Israeli drive to take over Palestinian land, forcing Palestinians to flee, is nothing new. In fact, decades before the creation of the State of Israel, the Zionist movement transformed a spiritual yearning into a defined political project premised on the violent eradication and replacement of the native population with a settler society; this was endorsed by the global powers of the time and that support endures to the present day.

CONTEXTUALISING FORCED DISPLACEMENT OF PALESTINIAN BEDOUINS IN HISTORY

For over 100 years, Palestinians have been subjected to deliberate and violent attempts at displacement, resulting from the confluence between Zionist ideology and Western imperialism.[15] The first decades of the twentieth century saw an intensification of political efforts culminating in the British-sponsored Balfour Declaration of November 1917, which promised a 'national home for the Jewish people' in Palestine – the biblical Promised Land, according to proponents of that initiative.[16] Put simply by Edward Said, this document was issued '(a) by a European power (b) about a non-European territory (c) in a flat disregard of both the presences and wishes of the native majority resident in that territory', and promised that territory to a foreign group.[17] That pivotal moment set in motion a series of events that condemned Palestinians – the religiously diverse and socially composite indigenous (primarily) Arabic-speaking population of Palestine – to a position of subalternity in their homeland that continues until the present day.[18] After Britain defeated the Ottomans and occupied Palestine in December 1917, the promise contained in the Balfour Declaration became entrenched in the terms of the British Mandate in 1920, which received international endorsement by the

[13] United Nations High Commissioner for Human Rights, Report A/HRC/52/76 (15 March 2023) 5, 12.
[14] ibid 13.
[15] R Khalidi, *The Hundred Years' War on Palestine: A History of Settler Colonial Conquest and Resistance* (Profile Books, 2020).
[16] Balfour Declaration, 2 November 1917, CAB 21/58. The full text is available at avalon.law.yale.edu/20th_century/balfour.asp#:~:text=%22His%20Majesty%27s%20Government%20view%20with,religious%20rights%20of%20existing%20non%2D.
[17] E Said, 'Zionism from the Standpoint of Its Victims' (1979) 1 *Social Text* 7, 9–10.
[18] For background, see V Kattan, *From Coexistence to Conquest: International Law and the Origins of the Arab-Israeli Conflict, 1891–1949* (Pluto Press, 2009).

League of Nations (LON) in 1922.[19] Based on this arrangement, and until Britain withdrew from Palestine in May 1948,

> the colonial power allowed the Zionist movement to settle hundreds of thousands of European Jews in Palestine, to establish hundreds of settlements, including several cities, and to lay the political, economic, industrial, military and cultural foundations of the State of Israel.[20]

When the newly created United Nations (UN) inherited the 'question of Palestine' from the British, and eventually endorsed partitioning the land to create the State of Israel in most of Palestine, resulting in the displacement of approximately 750,000 Palestinians,[21] the system of Palestinian subalternity became consolidated in the international order.[22]

Britain's 'plan' for Palestine reflects both imperial history and racism throughout Europe. In keeping with its colonial mindset, British (and other European) officials believed Palestinian Arabs to be mostly primitive, displaceable bodies, whose aspirations for freedom from the colonial yoke were irrelevant in the Western corridors of power.[23] Winston Churchill himself considered Arabs as a subaltern group, and certainly as lesser to European Jews, suggesting the latter were 'a stronger race, a higher-grade race, a more worldly wise race' and as such they could replace indigenous Palestinians who, in his view, had no 'final right' to their land.[24] In keeping with this approach, Britain and other western powers embraced the Zionist movement as a *mission civilisatrice* bringing democracy to the 'Orient', and protecting Western interests in the region.[25]

At the same time, endorsing Zionist aspirations for a Jewish homeland in Palestine offered opportunistic British politicians the chance to respond to widespread anti-minority sentiments in the country, building on centuries of persecution, vilification and discrimination against Jews in England and elsewhere in Europe[26] that culminated in the horrors of the Holocaust. At the start of the twentieth century, even Balfour had been involved in promoting stringent anti-immigration laws 'meant primarily to prevent Jewish immigrants fleeing the pogroms of Eastern Europe from entering Britain' since the 1880s.[27] The racism underlying Britain's embrace of the Zionist project was patently obvious to Edwin Montagu, the only Jewish member of the cabinet at the time of the Balfour Declaration. Montagu

[19] The full text of Mandate for Palestine (2022) is available at digitallibrary.un.org/record/829707?ln=en.

[20] N Masalha, *The Palestine Nakba: Decolonising History, Narrating the Subaltern, Reclaiming Memory* (Bloomsbury, 2012) 33.

[21] This figure is taken from Rashid Khalidi, 'The Palestinians and 1948: the underlying causes of failure' in EL Rogan and A Shlaim (eds), *The War for Palestine* (CUP, 2001) 13.

[22] A Imseis, *The United Nations and the Question of Palestine: Rule by Law and the Structure of International Legal Subalternity* (CUP, 2023).

[23] R Wilde, 'Tears of the Olive Trees: Mandatory Palestine, the UK, and Reparations for Colonialism in International Law' (2022) 25 *Journal of the History of International Law / Revue d'histoire du droit international* 387.

[24] Reported in Wilde, ibid.

[25] E Said, 'The Idea of Palestine in the West' (1978) 70 *MERIP Reports* 3.

[26] G Heng, *England and the Jews: How Religion and Violence Created the First Racial State in the West* (CUP, 2018).

[27] S Sand, *The Invention of the Land of Israel* (Verso, 2012) 14–15.

condemned the British adoption of Zionism as anti-Semitic, explaining that to reconstitute a national home of the Jewish people in Palestine would result in increased hostility towards Jewish minorities in all other countries, as well as the (unjust) displacement and dispossession of the native inhabitants of Palestine to make way for Jews arriving from across the globe.[28] Despite this early admonishment, Britain's espousal of the Zionist project, the material support given by the metropole to Zionist leaders migrating to Palestine from Europe, and the international endorsement by the LON of the plan to create a 'national home for the Jewish people' in Palestine resulted in mass displacement and dispossession inflicted on the indigenous Palestinian population.

The events surrounding the creation of the State of Israel after British withdrawal from Palestine in May 1948 have been described as 'ethnic cleansing'.[29] Between 1947 and 1949, 'the Palestinian polity [was] devastated and most of its society uprooted', losing their homes, land and property in the process.[30] The newly constituted State of Israel took approximately 78 per cent of the territory of Mandate Palestine, forcing around 80 per cent of Palestinians in those parts to flee. It is estimated that at least 720,000 of a total population of 1.3 million Palestinians were made refugees.[31] The remaining Palestinians were relegated to the West Bank and Gaza Strip. The term Nakba – or catastrophe – refers to the 1948 'Zionist conquest of Palestine' and the establishment of the State of Israel, as well as capturing the reality of the 'ongoing Nakba', a structure of Israeli domination over Palestinians consolidated in the 1967 defeat by Israel of the Arab armies that gave rise to the occupation of the remaining territories (often referred to as the 'occupied Palestinian territory' (OPT), or 'Palestinian territory occupied in 1967').[32] As summed up by Rabea Eghbariah, 'the foundational violence of the 1948 Nakba has not only dispossessed and displaced Palestinians but also fractured Palestinian society and put in place a new regime that is committed to denying Palestinian self-determination in favour of the settler society'.[33]

Against this backdrop, the birth of Israel as a state and its admission as a member of the UN in 1949 seem at odds with the new international legal order set out in the 1945 UN Charter enshrining the right to self-determination (Article 1) and the prohibition of military conquest of land (Article 2(4)). For Palestinians, instead of achieving freedom and self-rule, in ways comparable to other previously colonised populations around the world, the Nakba imposed a structure of ongoing dispossession and violent denial of rights in their homeland, in which they became supplanted by a new settler colonial population.[34] This structure has

[28] Memorandum of Edwin Montagu on the Anti-Semitism of the Present (British) Government – Submitted to the British Cabinet, August, 1917, balfourproject.org/edwin-montagu-and-zionism-1917.

[29] I Pappe, *The Ethnic Cleansing of Palestine* (Oneworld, 2006).

[30] Khalidi (n 15) 58.

[31] ibid.

[32] R Eghbariah, 'Towards Nakba as a Legal Concept' (2024) 124 *Columbia Law Review* 887, 957–64.

[33] ibid 964.

[34] On settler colonialism in Palestine see inter alia O Jabary Salamanca et al, 'Past is present: Settler colonialism in Palestine' (2012) 2 *Settler Colonial Studies* 1; and T Dana and A Jarbawi, 'A Century of Settler Colonialism in Palestine' (2017) 24 *The Brown Journal of World Affairs* 197.

become constitutionally enshrined in Israel: the 2018 Basic Law 'The Nation State of the Jewish People' reaffirms the state's ongoing commitment to the development of Jewish settlements, the notable absence of an indication of territorial scope in the provision suggesting that the land in question is anywhere between the Jordan River and the Mediterranean Sea.[35] This appears to be directed at the Palestinian territory occupied in 1967, where the Bedouin communities around Jerusalem face constant violence and threats of displacement.[36] The 2018 Basic Law, and a myriad of others, corroborate what has been theorised as 'Jewishness as Property' whereby Israeli law 'enables, facilitates and mandates the ongoing dispossession of Palestinians and the redistribution of their resources in favour of Jewish-Israelis'.[37]

The Bedouin communities of Palestine were not shielded from the violence of the nascent State of Israel: thousands of families were displaced from their homes and dispersed across the region, with effects felt to the present day. Following 1948, only 13,000 out of an estimated population of 90,000 Bedouin Palestinians remained within the Beer al-Saba' area (usually referred to as 'Negev' in Hebrew, Arabised into 'Naqab' – despite this moniker reflecting the new geographies imposed by Israel and not the indigenous way of referring to those lands).[38] The forced displacement of approximately a quarter of the Bedouins of this area in 1951–52 alone reveals how the newly created State of Israel's quest for land emptied of its indigenous inhabitants superseded its commitments to citizens when these citizens were Palestinian Arabs.[39]

Early Zionist-Israeli settler colonial policies towards the Bedouin were premised on their 'nomadisation' within a colonial fantasy, which pragmatically was also a way to deny them land rights in areas that Israel wanted to control.[40] This reveals how the Zionist views of Palestinian Bedouins were distorted by Orientalist notions about the Arabs published in English, French and German, which are likely to have informed European Zionists from the late nineteenth century onwards.[41] While many Palestinian Bedouins did live a semi-nomadic life, these communities were also intimately tied to their land, with large-scale agricultural enterprises (including barley exported to Britain), a system of property ownership, and established villages offering a range of services and infrastructure. Bedouin communities that remained in what became Israel were largely concentrated in an area termed *Siyaj* (fence), northeast of Beer al-Saba', in the 1950s, and placed under military rule until 1966, despite many

[35] Israeli Knesset, *Basic Law: Israel – the Nation State of the Jewish People* (19 July 2018), Art 7: 'the state sees in the development of Jewish settlements as one of national value, and will act to encourage and advance its establishment and strengthening'.

[36] A Amara et al, 'The Bedouin communities of Eastern Jerusalem: a new locus of power in the post-Oslo battle for Palestine?' (2021) 117 *Confluences Méditerranée* 101.

[37] R Eghbariah, 'Jewishness as Property under Israeli Law' The LPA Project (7 September 2021) 2.

[38] A Kedar, A Amara and O Yiftachel, *Emptied Lands: A Legal Geography of Bedouin Rights in the Negev* (Stanford University Press, 2018) 87.

[39] G Algazi, 'Nomadizing the Bedouins: Displacement, Resistance, and Patronage in the Northern Naqab, 1951–52' (2024) 53 *Journal of Palestine Studies* 7, 27.

[40] ibid 9.

[41] See discussion of the impact of knowledge on the 'Orient' produced by European writers in multiple disciplines in E Said, *Orientalism* (Pantheon Press, 1978) 18–19.

having acquired Israeli citizenship.[42] The families that fled to the West Bank clustered mostly around Hebron and Jerusalem as refugees. It is this portion of Palestinian Bedouins – and especially the communities around Jerusalem – who are the focus of the present study.

THIS BOOK

This book presents some of the key findings of the project titled 'Palestinian Bedouins at Risk of Forced Displacement: IHL vulnerabilities, ICC possibilities' funded by the Arts and Humanities Research Council (AHRC) between 2020 and 2024 (AH/T007540/1) and its follow-on project also funded by the AHRC (AH/W006782/1). For this work, the collaboration between interdisciplinary scholars at Al Quds University (Jerusalem), Queen's University Belfast, Trinity College Dublin and Liverpool John Moores University, and a core project team of desk-based and field researchers, is complemented by contributions by an eclectic mix of authors drawing on various aspects of law, urban planning, humanitarian and development practice, politics, international affairs, and more. The work is grounded in law-in-context approaches to understanding injustice in Palestine, borrowing theories and methods from a wide range of social sciences.

Taken individually, the eight chapters shine a light on different aspects of the humanitarian vulnerabilities (and their context) in Bedouin communities, through a range of thematic, geographic and disciplinary angles and dimensions. Taken together, the suite of chapters offers the first comprehensive multidisciplinary analysis of the humanitarian vulnerabilities of Palestinian Bedouins at risk of forced displacement. While focusing primarily on communities in the Jerusalem periphery, the study connects that specific geography with other Palestinian Bedouins across the West Bank and within the state of Israel, illustrating the spatial, political and legal dis/continuities in the Israeli treatment of Palestinian Bedouins on both sides of the Green Line. This challenges the formal distinctions in international law (and accountability for violations thereof) between the displacement of protected persons living under military occupation, governed by IHL and IHRL protections, on the one hand, and the displacement of 'second class' citizens within the borders of a state described by leading international human rights organisations as enforcing an apartheid regime[43] on the other. As such, the analysis problematises the ways in which notions of Palestinian displacement, including with reference to Bedouin communities, are understood through the narrow lens of international law, and offers a broader framing to better capture these experiences through a wider lens.

Chapter one, by Ahmad Amara, Brendan C Browne and Alice Panepinto, introduces the displacement of Palestinian Bedouins and offers some of the theoretical

[42] Kedar et al (n 38) 87.

[43] Amnesty International (n 3); Human Rights Watch, 'A Threshold Crossed Israeli Authorities and the Crimes of Apartheid and Persecution' (2021), www.hrw.org/report/2021/04/27/threshold-crossed/israeli-authorities-and-crimes-apartheid-and-persecution.

framing for the rest of the book. It provides: first, an overview of the Bedouin history of Palestine focusing on the Eastern Jerusalem periphery (E1) and the West Bank; second, a note on research approaches that attempt to combat clichés; third, a reflection on the ongoing usefulness of theoretical frameworks of settler colonialism and indigeneity; fourth, a summary of the international legal framework applicable to these parts; and finally, an elaboration of the legal geography – including the notion of 'grey space' – in which Palestinian Bedouin communities exist in E1 and across the West Bank, and the vulnerability this entails. It argues that the political and legal geography of the West Bank, which includes most of E1 in the Eastern Jerusalem periphery, facilitates the Israeli efforts to displace Palestinian Bedouins, who are subjected to the sharpest edge of the occupation and violence. Like all Palestinians – urban and rural – the presence of Bedouin communities on land that Israel covets for its own use is an impediment to the realisation of Zionism's historic and contemporary *raison d'être* and the State's most recent constitutional commitment to further developing Jewish settlements on Palestinian land.

Chapter two, by Mohammed Younes, examines the socio-spatial repercussions of Israeli colonial urban planning on Palestinian Bedouin communities in the eastern vicinity of Jerusalem. It contextualises the displacement of Bedouins as a form of 'collateral damage' within the larger framework of colonial urban strategies. Utilising Henri Lefebvre's theoretical lens on the production of space, the study traces the transformation of Bedouin landscapes from lived, communal territories to abstract spaces delineated and shaped by settler colonial policies. By examining the transition from traditional pastoral practices pre-1948 to contemporary urban expansions, it unveils a pattern of indirect sedentarisation imposed on Bedouin populations. The study also explores the legal and environmental ramifications of such spatial manipulations, including the seizure of land and the destruction of Bedouin cultural identity.

Chapter three, by Bana Abu Zuluf and Ahmad Amara, investigates the displacement and threats of forced displacement of Palestinian Bedouins since 1948 on both sides of the Green Line. It reveals how shifting Israeli settler frontiers target all Palestinians, including Bedouin communities in the Beer al-Saba' region (known as the Naqab/Negev), in the southern Hebron hills of the West Bank, in the Jerusalem periphery, and elsewhere. This has resulted in direct displacement as well as displacement imposed indirectly through legal stratagems that turn the Palestinian Bedouin presence illegal, 'unseen' and 'unrecognised', and thus removable and subject to imminent displacement. Through case studies and a multidisciplinary lens of history, law and geography, the chapter unveils how Israeli policies, driven by settler colonialism, construct and manipulate borders of legality to dispossess and marginalise Bedouin communities. By highlighting connections between disparate Bedouin communities and contextualising their struggles within broader Palestinian geopolitics, the chapter calls for a holistic approach to understanding and addressing the impact of Israel's settler colonialism.

Chapter four, by Raghad Adwan and Tamara Tamimi, analyses how Israeli settler colonial policies targeting the entirety of Bedouin society have a disproportionate impact on Palestinian Bedouin women as a vulnerable and marginalised social group in two main ways. First, Israeli settler colonialism reinforces societal patriarchy and reproduces violence by the stronger social group on the weaker social group. Second, Israeli settler colonialism directly targets women through a systematic structure, rather than isolated events, due to their reproductive ability, which counters the Israeli settler colonial agenda to eliminate the indigenous population to enable the non-indigenous claim of the land. In considering the gendered dimensions of displacement and urbanisation, the chapter explores the impact on privacy, agency and psychosocial wellbeing, as well as how restrictions of mobility, due to inadequate road system and lack of public transportation, determine the economic disempowerment of women, and negate women's rights to education and healthcare.

Chapter five, by Dario Rossi D'Ambrosio, explores the complexity of foreign aid interventions in Palestine. First, it examines the condition of Palestinian communities in E1 at the frontier of Israeli settler colonialism. Second, it considers how the presence of foreign aid actors has not only coexisted with but has also at times facilitated the continuation of a colonial agenda, which in turn perpetuates the necessity for foreign aid and buries the prospects of a future in which aid is no longer needed. This, in turn, reveals how aid efforts become entangled in the very problems they seek to address and paradoxically contribute to their perpetuation. By positioning Palestinian communities as recipients of aid without adequate protection, foreign aid interventions inadvertently undermine the 'do no harm' principle. In the long run, these dynamics culminate in a 'right to temporarily stay' paradox, wherein the pursuit of temporary residence and resilience indirectly counteracts the foundational principle of the right of return of Palestine refugees. While aid provides crucial material support to vulnerable Palestinian communities including the Bedouins, these interventions contribute to entrenching the denial of the full range of rights of Palestinian communities who exist in a state of limbo.

Chapter six, by Reeda Alji, offers a poignant critique to what is understood as the Palestinian Bedouins' right to culture under Israeli settler colonial rule. Building on the development of the indigenous rights movement of the 1960s, hailed as a triumph for human rights, with current struggles for ancestral lands framed by international covenants, this chapter explores how Palestinian Bedouins have gained recognition from various UN bodies and international organisations. However, the focus on cultural rights has hindered the enjoyment of their agro-pastoralist lifestyle, which relies on vast lands for livestock herding and (having the option of) seasonal migration. The culturalisation of Bedouin indigeneity arguably essentialises their lifestyle by imposing stringent demands for cultural purity, which undermine their long-term legitimate land claims. As such, international legal protections of this type fail to consider the adaptive lifestyles of Palestinian Bedouins: instead, this narrow cultural focus perpetuates colonial racism, allowing Israel to mis-recognise Bedouins' rights and impose inadequate relocation solutions, ultimately denying their land rights and reinforcing settler colonialism.

Chapter seven, by Luigi Daniele, addresses the international legal framework governing one of the most frequent harms inflicted on Bedouin communities: demolition and confiscation of property, including homes and community buildings. After explaining the prohibition of extensive destruction and appropriation of property not justified by military necessity in international humanitarian law, the analysis considers its framing as 'grave breach' of the 1949 Geneva Conventions, and the juridical implications in the domestic legal systems of states which have ratified these treaties (which includes Israel). This chapter argues that 1) the extensive destruction and appropriation of property in the West Bank has been a constant and continuing crime of the Israeli occupation; 2) the commission of this crime has been the basis of numerous pseudo-legal titularity claims; and indeed that 3) the large-scale commission of the crime itself appears functional to alter the demographic composition of, denationalise, and maintain perpetual control over the Palestinian territory. The examination reveals the relationship between the crime of extensive destruction and appropriation of property, and the crimes of transfer and forcible transfer of civilians, as a relationship between means (removing Palestinian civilians) and ends (mobilising the infrastructure of the occupation to 'de-Palestinianise' and annex territories), which may amount to violations of international criminal law.

Chapter eight, by Giulia Pinzauti, focuses on the technical aspects of jurisdiction over international crimes committed against Bedouin communities in the Palestinian territory occupied in 1967. It argues that the alleged crimes committed against the Bedouins at risk of displacement in Area C fall within the ambit of the International Criminal Court (ICC)'s territorial jurisdiction and should be included in the scope of the ongoing investigation. The Oslo Accords do not bar ICC jurisdiction over alleged Rome Statute crimes committed on Palestine's territory: that Court's jurisdiction is not premised on the existence of a parallel jurisdictional title in the domestic legal order of the state party concerned. Thus, any prior agreements potentially limiting the enforcement of Palestine's criminal jurisdiction domestically do not affect the scope of the Court's territorial jurisdiction. Arguments on the relevance of the Oslo accords conflate a state's jurisdiction to prescribe with its enforcement jurisdiction and disregard the law of occupation. As such, failing to include alleged crimes against Bedouins within the scope of the current ICC investigation into the *Situation in the State of Palestine* would result in an artificial and unjustified separation of the Bedouin community from the broader Palestinian polity.

Acknowledgements

THIS BOOK IS the culmination of research carried out between 2020 and 2024 as part of the project titled 'Palestinian Bedouin at risk of forced displacement: IHL vulnerabilities, ICC possibilities' generously funded by the UK Arts and Humanities Research Council (AHRC) (ref. AH/T007540/1). Given the multiple obstacles faced by all colleagues writing on Palestine, we are grateful to the AHRC not only for their financial support, but also their commitment to academic freedom and holding the space for projects such as our own.

The editors wish to thank all the contributors to this volume for their time and patience throughout the lengthy process of turning ideas into a book. Each contribution offers a fascinating perspective on the topic in its own right, and taken together the chapters offer so much more than the sum of their parts in shining a light on the forced displacement of Palestinian Bedouins. We are particularly inspired by the Palestinian early career scholars who feature in this edited collection: their voices and vision are destined to shape future debates around justice in Palestine.

A special mention must go to all the Bedouins who generously gave their time to the authors carrying out fieldwork and interviews, which were made possible by the efforts of Osama Risheq and Raghad Adwan. The steadfastness and dignity of the Bedouin – and indeed of so many Palestinians – is an example for all.

Thanks also to the wonderful women looking after project finance and travel: Susan Burton in Belfast, and Nibal Kamal in Jerusalem.

A number of colleagues – some in the project advisory board, and some from other quarters – provided their intellectual and moral support over time in developing the ideas underpinning the book and looking at draft chapters: the list is long, so we will just say 'you know who you are'. We hope to return the favour when you need us.

Beyond this book, Zainah el-Haroun and our colleagues at Collage Productions and in particular Bashar Zarour must be credited for translating some of the academic findings of the project that appear in this volume into a documentary film and other audio-visual material, which complements the book and challenges the standard ways in which academics (and legal academics in particular) work.

And last but not least, we appreciate the support of Hart Publishing, in particular Sinéad Moloney, Sasha Jawed and all the production team for enabling what some might view as 'niche' research to reach more mainstream audiences in law and other disciplines. Queen's University Belfast will help turn this work into open-source material, which – we hope – will make it more accessible to readers unaffiliated to well-resourced institutions in the Global North, and to audiences outside academia.

This book is dedicated to our families.

AP, BAZ, AA, BCB, MN & TM

Contents

Author Biographies

Bana Abu Zuluf: PhD candidate in International Law at the National University of Ireland, Maynooth. Bana was previously a researcher focusing on the forced displacement of Bedouin communities in the E1 zone of the Eastern Jerusalem periphery at Al-Quds Human Rights Clinic in Jerusalem. Bana is a Palestinian interdisciplinary researcher. Her research interests are epistemic oppression, transitional justice, intersectional solidarity, decolonisation, TWAIL and international law vulnerabilities.

Raghad Adwan: holds a dual MA degree in Global Studies and International Affairs from Bard College. She completed her undergraduate degree in human rights and international law from Al-Quds Bard College, Al-Quds University. Adwan previously held the position of field researcher at Al-Quds Human Rights Clinic for two years. She also has extensive experience in the civil society sector in Palestine, having worked with several civil society organisations. Raghad is a member of the board of directors for the Alternative Information Center, Palestine and is one of the founding members of Lejan, a platform for Palestinian youth wherever they reside. Raghad is currently working as a coordinator at the Community-Based Rehabilitation programme at Bethlehem Arab Society for Rehabilitation.

Reeda Alji: PhD candidate in Law at Sciences Po in Paris, where her research focuses on the intersection of colonialism, race and labour in the Middle East. She holds an LLM from Exeter University in England and an MA in Transitional Justice and Human Rights Law from the Graduate Institute in Geneva. Reeda has previously worked at the UNHCR headquarters in Geneva and the International Center for Transitional Justice, specialising in the MENA region.

Dr Ahmad Amara: a human rights advocate and a graduate of the joint PhD programme in History and Hebrew and Judaic Studies at New York University. Before pursuing his PhD, Amara served three years as a clinical instructor and global advocacy fellow with Harvard Law School's Human Rights Program. Amara holds an LLB and LLM from Tel-Aviv University and a second Master's degree in International Human Rights Law from Essex University. Amara has a number of publications, including the co-edited volume *Indigenous (In)Justice: Human Rights Law and Bedouin Arabs in the Naqab/Negev* (Harvard University Press).

Dr Brendan Ciarán Browne: Assistant Professor of Conflict Resolution and Fellow of Trinity College Dublin, and Co-Investigator in the AHRC-funded project, 'Palestinian Bedouin at Risk of Forced Displacement: IHL Vulnerabilities, ICC Possibilities' (2020–24). His previous academic posts include as Assistant Professor of Transitional Justice at Al Quds University (Bard College), Palestine. He is the author of several books, including: *Refugees and Forced Displacement in Northern Ireland's Troubles: Untold Journeys* (with Dr Niall Gilmartin; Liverpool University Press) and *Transitional (in)Justice and Enforcing the Peace on Palestine* (Palgrave Macmillan, nominated for the 2023 Middle East Monitor Palestine book award).

Dr Luigi Daniele: Senior Lecturer at Nottingham Law School (Nottingham Trent University). He holds a PhD from Nottingham Trent University and University of the Studies of Naples Federico II, and is currently Module Leader in Laws of Armed Conflict (LLB), Comparative Law (LLB), Public International and Humanitarian Law (LLM), and International, European and Comparative Law (DL) at Nottingham Law School.

Prof Triestino Mariniello: Professor of Law at Liverpool John Moores University, and Co-Investigator in the AHRC-funded project, 'Palestinian Bedouin at Risk of Forced Displacement: IHL Vulnerabilities, ICC Possibilities'(2020–24). In addition to being an academic expert in international criminal justice and human rights, he is also a member of the legal team representing Gaza victims before the International Criminal Court.

Dr Munir Nusseibeh: human rights lawyer and academic based at Al-Quds University in Jerusalem, Palestine, where he is assistant professor in the faculty of law; the director (and co-founder) of Al-Quds Human Rights Clinic; and the director of the Community Action Center in Jerusalem. He is also the Co-Investigator in the AHRC-funded project, 'Palestinian Bedouin at Risk of Forced Displacement: IHL Vulnerabilities, ICC Possibilities' (2020–24). He holds an LLM in International Legal Studies from the Washington College of Law of the American University in Washington DC and a PhD from the University of Westminster in London, UK, for a thesis on Forced Displacement in the Palestinian-Israeli Conflict, International Law, and Transitional Justice.

Dr Alice Panepinto: Reader at Queen's University Belfast – School of Law, and Principal Investigator in the AHRC-funded project, 'Palestinian Bedouin at Risk of Forced Displacement: IHL Vulnerabilities, ICC Possibilities' (2020–24). Alice's work focuses on international law and human rights, with a regional specialism in the Middle East including Palestine.

Dr Giulia Pinzauti: Assistant Professor of Public International Law at the Grotius Centre for International Legal Studies of Leiden Law School. Prior to joining the Grotius Centre, she served as an associate legal officer at the International Court of Justice (2015–16) and in the Office of the Prosecutor of the International Criminal Tribunal for the former Yugoslavia and the Mechanism for International Criminal Tribunals (2012–14) in The Hague. She also previously worked as part of the legal staff for the pre-trial judge and the Appeals Chamber at the Special Tribunal for Lebanon (2011–12).

Dario Rossi D'Ambrosio: holds a Master of Laws from Roma Tre University (2012) and an LLM in Human Rights, Conflict and Justice from SOAS (2014). Throughout his career, he has worked on human rights issues and supported civil society initiatives in various contexts, and has many years of experience working in the humanitarian, development and peacebuilding sectors in Palestine and Israel. He has published articles on both international law and foreign aid in Palestine.

Tamara Tamimi: PhD candidate at Queen's University Belfast – School of Law, funded by the Economic and Social Research Council: Northern Ireland and North East Doctoral Training Partnership Consortium (UK). Tamara holds an MA in Human Rights Law from SOAS, University of London, where she received the Sarah Spells Prize for the best dissertation of 2015–06. Tamara was previously a researcher focusing on the forced displacement of Bedouin communities in the E1 zone of the Eastern Jerusalem periphery at Al-Quds Human Rights Clinic in Jerusalem. Tamara's academic and applied/policy research activity focuses on settler colonialism, gender equality, effectiveness of law in effectuating justice, transformative justice, forced displacement and aid effectiveness of overseas development assistance.

Mohammed Younes: researcher and urban planning engineer from Jerusalem, currently based in Paris, specialising in urban studies and spatial science. He holds a Master's degree in Urban Engineering and Habitat from École Polytechnique Universitaire de Lille, and currently serves as a Research Engineer at Gustave Eiffel University. He has engaged in diverse research projects and academic explorations within urban studies, smart cities and the social history of urban spaces, especially in Palestine. Among his research interests are Urban Modelling and Decolonisation Studies. He has worked on multiple academic projects and translated various essays and research on technology and social history into Arabic.

1

Setting the Scene: The Forced Displacement of Palestinian Bedouins

AHMAD AMARA, BRENDAN CIARÁN BROWNE AND ALICE PANEPINTO

INTRODUCTION

BEDOUIN ARABS HAVE inhabited the Middle East, including southern Palestine, since the seventh century.[1] Following the dissolution of the Ottoman Empire, and the imposition of political borders in the Middle East to establish modern nation-states, Bedouin communities were artificially divided across different polities. As a result, day-to-day life for Bedouin communities across the region has been subjected to the policies and practices of many states. Palestinian Bedouins in particular have faced a unique set of pressures from the Israeli state, both as Palestinians and as Bedouins. Waves of historic displacement and current manifestations of violence against these communities amounting to international law violations – for which nobody is ever held accountable – have resulted in serious humanitarian vulnerabilities which are entirely man-made and thus preventable. As this book will illustrate, the Palestinian Bedouin communities in the Eastern Jerusalem periphery (often referred to as 'E1') are at particular risk of forcible transfer given that they inhabit an area slated for de facto annexation by Israel – the occupying power in those parts – despite the prohibitions of international law.

This chapter frames the displacement of Palestinian Bedouins in the Eastern Jerusalem periphery by setting out the context in which it is occurring. It provides: first, an overview of the Bedouin history of Palestine focusing on the Eastern Jerusalem periphery and the West Bank; second, a note on research approaches that try to combat clichés; third, a reflection on the ongoing usefulness of theoretical frameworks of (Israeli) settler colonialism and (Palestinian) indigeneity; fourth, a summary of the international legal framework applicable to these parts; and finally, an elaboration of the legal geography – including the notion of 'grey space' – in which Palestinian Bedouin communities exist in E1 and across the West Bank.

[1] E Marx, *Bedouin of the Negev* (Frederick A Praeger, 1967).

1.1. HISTORICAL BACKGROUND

1.1.1. The History of Palestinian Bedouins

By the end of Ottoman rule, the Bedouin population of southern Palestine was estimated at about 50,000 and reached around 90,000 at the eve of the 1948 Nakba.[2] The Bedouin tribes belonged to eight main confederations (*qabīla*): Tayaha, 'Azazma, Tarabin, Jbarat, Hanajra, Jahalin, Ahiwat and S'aidiyin. The communities subsisted on an integrated agro-pastoral economy depending on their habitation areas, the size and quality of their lands, and the climatic conditions across time.[3] Bedouins, like many other tribal communities, lived with a relatively large degree of autonomy from the Ottoman state and its institutions given their geographic distance from its centres of power.[4] However, a series of political upheavals and judicial-administrative changes from the start of the twentieth century have continued to impact Bedouin lives across the Middle East, and especially in Palestine: most notably, the impact of the Ottoman Tanzimat reforms since 1839 and the decision to establish the city of modern Beersheba in 1900, making it the administrative centre of the new subdistrict of Beer al-Saba' (Beersheba). The new administration and the boundaries of the subdistrict were outlined to include most of the Bedouin confederations that previously belonged to the Gaza subdistrict. The Ottomans sought to better control the region and its inhabitants, to register Bedouin possession and cultivation of lands, to increase tax collection, and to strengthen southern Palestine as a frontier region vis-à-vis the British in Egypt.[5] Within mounting Ottoman–British political tensions, and particularly the British insistence on pushing the Ottomans away from the Suez Canal, both parties demarcated the Palestine–Egypt political border in 1906. This was the first political border of Modern Palestine, and it was the beginning of division for the Bedouin, even if it did not seriously disrupt their lives at the time.[6]

Towards the end of the First World War, Beersheba was the first Palestinian town to be occupied by the British under the command of General Allenby on 29 October 1917. After several failed attempts, Gaza fell on 2 November, the same day as the Balfour Declaration.[7] After the war, the British imposed a military administration followed by a civil one, until the establishment of the Mandate of Palestine by the League of Nations in 1922, which lasted until May 1948 when the State of Israel was founded. During the Mandate, the Beersheba subdistrict continued to enjoy large autonomy despite increasing integration and expansion of governmental and semi-governmental institutions, and the expansion of the state's judicial and administrative

[2] J McCarthy, *The Population of Palestine* (Columbia University Press, 1990) 35; Y Avci, 'The Application of Tanzimat in the Desert' (2009) 45 *Middle Eastern Studies* 973.

[3] A Kedar, A Amara and O Yiftachel, *Emptied Lands: A Legal Geography of Bedouin Rights in the Negev* (Stanford University Press, 2018) 49–55.

[4] ibid.

[5] A Amara, 'Between Imperial Subjects and Political Partners: Bedouin Borders and Protection in Ottoman Palestine, 1900–17' in Lauren Benton et al (eds), *Protection and Empire: A Global History* (Cambridge, CUP, 2017); G Biger, *The Boundaries of Modern Palestine, 1840–1947* (Routledge, 2004).

[6] Biger (n 5).

[7] E Rogan, *The Fall of the Ottomans: The Great War in the Middle East* (Basic Books, 2016).

reach. The British expanded the existing Ottoman bodies and laws in the region, alongside the local customs and traditions, some of which were recognised within the applicable law.[8]

During the 1930s – under the aegis of the League of Nations-approved Mandate, which gave material effect to the Balfour Declaration's aim to establish a Jewish national home in Palestine[9] – the Jewish National Fund joined Zionist efforts to purchase lands and establish Jewish colonies in southern Palestine. While such activities were relatively limited until 1948,[10] the region was of major interest and significance to the Zionist leadership, most notably David Ben-Gurion. Strategic geopolitical control of the region allowed a connection between Egypt and Transjordan, and access to the Red Sea, the Dead Sea and its natural resources.[11]

The Nakba of 1948 brought about vital changes in southern Palestine and beyond. With the founding of the State of Israel, most of the area came under Israeli control and about 85 per cent of the Bedouin communities, like the rest of Palestinians, were expelled from their ancestral lands, leading to social collapse as well as physical destruction of their space. Only about 13,000 Bedouin remained within Israel, many of whom were later internally displaced by the Israeli authorities, and subjected to various policies of land confiscation, concentration and forced urbanisation.[12]

Expelled from their lands, the Bedouins in Palestine became refugees in the Gaza Strip, Egypt, Jordan and the West Bank. Most of the Bedouin refugees in the West Bank, specifically in the central West Bank and the Eastern Jerusalem periphery, who are the focus of this edited collection, were displaced from the Tel-Arad area south of Hebron. After 1948, these communities lived in different localities, eventually settling more permanently around Jerusalem. While our collection focuses on the Bedouin communities in the Jerusalem area, it is important to highlight the historical continuum of Palestinian displacement within a context of settler colonial politics and practices since the 1940s. The forcible displacement of these groups, land dispossession and Israeli Judaisation policies apply to all Palestinians and all Palestinian spaces, not only to the Bedouin communities in East Jerusalem and across the West Bank. Hence, the 'E1 Plan' as well as the case of the displacement of Palestinian Bedouins should be read within this broader context of collective dispossession imposed on Palestinians by the Israeli state authorities.

1.1.2. The Eastern Jerusalem Periphery and the Central West Bank

An Ottoman 'index of the tribes', seemingly compiled before the First World War, listed the various tribes in the Ottoman Jerusalem governorate. The index listed the following tribes within the Hebron subdistrict, who lived in the Masfara lands of Tel

[8] The British Mandate for Palestine – San Remo Conference, 24 April 1920. Confirmed by the Council of the League of Nations on 24 July 1922, www.bu.edu/mzank/Jerusalem/tx/SanRemo.htm.

[9] League of Nations, Mandate of Palestine, www.un.org/unispal/document/auto-insert-201057.

[10] K Stein, *The Land Question in Palestine, 1917–1939* (Chapel Hill and London, The University of North Carolina Press, 1984).

[11] M Oren, 'The Diplomatic Struggle for the Negev, 1946–1956' (1989) 10 *Studies in Zionism* 197.

[12] For more on the Bedouin of the Negev, see Kedar et al (n 3).

Arad: Jahalin (800); Saraya'a (500); and the Kaabna (800).[13] Originally, these communities subsisted on an integrated agro-pastoralist economy; however, following their displacement from their lands they increased their reliance on animal husbandry and related activities. The displaced Bedouin communities of Tel Arad initially settled in the south-eastern edges of Bethlehem and Hebron, where they were counted and registered as refugees by the United Nations Relief and Works Agency (UNRWA).[14] Shortly after, these communities started to move further north and east, in search for new areas unused by other Palestinian Bedouin tribes, mainly in the eastern and southern hills of Jerusalem and in Jericho and the Jordan Valley, where they remain until the present day.[15]

In the Eastern Jerusalem periphery, the lands where the Bedouin communities settled belonged to (private) Palestinian landowners from the nearby towns and villages such as Jericho, Abu-Dis, Ezariya and Issawiya, who consented to such use. However, after the Israeli occupation of these areas in 1967, many were declared by the Israeli authorities as 'state lands', to be used for settlements, or as firing zones and other closed military areas from which Palestinians were banned.[16] The mid-1970s marked an increase in the risk of displacement, home demolitions and closure of pasture areas, as well as restrictions on Bedouin movement, as Israel embarked on establishing its settlements in the Eastern Jerusalem periphery, and in particular the settlement of Ma'ale Adumim, founded in 1975 and located seven kilometres to the east of Jerusalem. This was followed by the construction of additional settlements around Jerusalem, including Mishor Adumim, Kfar Adumim, Vered Yeriho, Qidar, Geva Benjamin and others.[17] Despite the illegality of settlements under international law (Article 49(6) Fourth Geneva Convention – hereafter GCIV), the settlement enterprise advanced and continues to the present day. Following the 1993–1995 Oslo Accords,[18] most of the areas inhabited by Bedouins were designated as 'Area C', falling under Israeli security and administrative control (this is discussed in more detail in section 5.1 of this chapter). Consequently, Bedouin life in these parts has fundamentally changed, and these communities have faced the constant threat of forced displacement. Over time, Bedouin communities began to settle in permanent locations out of fear that leaving their sites would bar them from returning; moreover, Israeli policies of forced urbanisation and concentration has led to these communities establishing themselves in specific places which are often not suited to their way of life.[19]

[13] A copy of the index is on file with the authors.

[14] A Heneiti, 'Bedouin Communities in Greater Jerusalem: Planning or Forced Displacement?' (2016) 65 *Jerusalem Quarterly* 52.

[15] ibid.

[16] B'Tselem, 'By Hook and by Crook: Israeli Settlement Policy in the West Bank' (July 2010), www.btselem.org/download/201007_by_hook_and_by_crook_eng.pdf.

[17] On Israeli settlements in the West Bank, see Peace Now, settlements list, peacenow.org.il/en/settlements-watch/israeli-settlements-at-the-west-bank-the-list.

[18] Israeli–Palestinian Interim Agreement on the West Bank and the Gaza Strip (Oslo II), 28 September 1995, peacemaker.un.org/sites/peacemaker.un.org/files/IL%20PS_950928_InterimAgreementWestBankGazaStrip%28OsloII%29.pdf.

[19] UNRWA/Bimkom, 'Al Jabal: A Study on the Transfer of Bedouin Palestine Refugees' (2013), www.unrwa.org/userfiles/2013052935643.pdf.

The current settlement of Ma'ale Adumim includes over 40,000 Israeli settlers living illegally on lands confiscated from Abu Dis, Al-Izzariya, Al-Issawiya, Al-Tur and Anata.[20] While its built-up area is approximately seven square kilometres, its municipal plan covers a total area of 55 square kilometres, extending almost to the Dead Sea, including to the north the E1 area (12 square kilometres).[21] Israeli spatial policies in the area seek to establish Israeli presence and control via settlements, roads, checkpoints and other infrastructure to link Jerusalem with Ma'ale Adumim, and further east to the Jordan valley, constituting what Israel envisages as 'Greater Jerusalem' and the 'Jerusalem-Dead Sea corridor'. This is also apparent in other steps taken to consolidate Israeli control over the area, including the construction of the separation Wall, 15 kilometres into the West Bank, in order to annex the entire Adumim bloc on the 'Israeli side' of the Wall.[22]

At the time of writing, it is estimated that there are over 8,200 Bedouins living in the Central West Bank in 46 different communities, most of whom (close to 6,000) are refugees.[23] All of their villages are considered illegal by the Israeli authorities and thus subject to ongoing and persistent threats of eviction and risk of demolitions. The situation for these communities is part of a broader Israeli policy of targeting Palestinians and Palestinian space, which includes land confiscation and control, zoning and planning, and access restrictions. The E1 Plan affecting the Bedouin communities in the Jerusalem area and central West Bank is one of several zoning plans seeking to control Palestinian spaces, to empty them of Palestinians, and to establish Israeli Jewish hegemony over space and demography (this is discussed in more detail by Mohammed Younes in chapter two of the present volume). For these reasons, and in light of the broader context of settler colonialism in Palestine and Israel – as discussed in section three of this chapter – the E1 plan and Israeli policies targeting the Palestinian Bedouin communities should be understood as part of the Israeli policies driven by the wider Zionist project which seeks to alter the geography and demographics of the region in violation of international law.

1.2. RESEARCH APPROACHES

As Beshara Doumani has noted, 'Of all the social groups in Palestinian society during the Ottoman period, Bedouins have been the most stereotyped'.[24] Despite the growing body of critical scholarship on Palestine and on tribal communities more generally, and more so in the case of Palestinian Bedouins of the West Bank, Doumani's statement nonetheless remains an accurate reflection of the present day. Not only have Bedouin communities been marginalised in scholarship, but they have

[20] PASSIA, *Arab East Jerusalem: A Reader* (Jerusalem, PASSIA, 2013) 132.
[21] ibid 133.
[22] ibid.
[23] UN-OCHA, '46 Bedouin Communities at Risk of Forcible Transfer in the Central West Bank: A Vulnerability Profile' (2017), www.ochaopt.org/page/46-bedouin-communities-risk-forcible-transfer-central-west-bank-vulnerability-profile.
[24] B Doumani, *Rediscovering Palestine: Merchants and Peasants in Jabal Nablus, 1700–1900* (University of California Press, 1995) 201.

also been misrepresented and studied within flawed research categories and frameworks. Bedouin communities, as Arabs and Palestinians, are usually essentialised and treated as an exceptional social group, living in a special and isolated space, and treated as passive historical and societal actors, or as warriors and savages. Although more recent academic accounts abandoned much of the negative terminology and clichés, there remains a widespread but erroneous notion of Bedouins being a solely pastoralist, nomadic and isolated tribal society that was rarely, if at all, touched by the state or by settled communities, which highlights its exceptionalities rather than commonalities with nearby communities in Palestine.[25]

Studies specifically on the Palestinian Bedouin communities of the West Bank and especially those in the central West Bank are rare, and mostly compiled by NGOs and international organisations. Most academic literature on the Palestinian Bedouin communities focus on the Naqab Bedouin, within the borders of the State of Israel. Over the past two decades this has become a distinct field, known as the Negev/Naqab Bedouin Studies, which addresses the intensifying Israeli policies of land dispossession and house demolitions.[26]

Some scholars have categorised existing scholarship on the Naqab Bedouin into three paradigms, all of which require critical scrutiny.[27] The first paradigm relates to early studies mostly produced by European travellers, and later by state bureaucrats and experts, whose research and knowledge served mostly colonial purposes aimed at governing the Bedouin. These studies have been largely ethnographic and centred on the local 'customs' and laws, and described some of the habits of the communities. Jennings Bramley, for example, toured Sinai and published a series of articles in the early 1900s in the *Palestine Exploration Fund Quarterly*.[28] Another important account was compiled by Arif Al-'Arif – an Arab amateur historian who served as Governor of Beersheba during the Mandate – and studied the Bedouin tribes and the region during that period. His seminal work, *Tarikh Bi'r al-Sab' wa Qaba'iliha* (*Beersheba and its Tribal Confederations*), which is largely an ethnographic, stereotypical survey of the region and the tribes, became a reference point for studying the Bedouins, and especially of the Naqab, and the history of the region.[29]

The second paradigm relates mainly to anthropological and geographical scholarship on the 'Negev Bedouin', mainly since the 1980s.[30] Scholars within this paradigm

[25] A Amara, 'Civilizational Exceptions: Ottoman Law and Governance in Late Ottoman Palestine' (2018) 36 *Law and History Review* 915; see also, A Amara, 'Beyond Stereotypes of Bedouins as "Nomads" and "Savages": Rethinking the Bedouin in Ottoman Southern Palestine, 1875–1900' (2016) 15 *Journal of Holy Land and Palestine Studies* 59.

[26] Kedar et al (n 3) 19–32.

[27] For some important accounts of literature review, see Mansour Nasasra et al, 'Introduction' in M Nasasra et al (eds), *The Naqab Bedouin and Colonialism: New Perspectives* (Routledge, 2015); I Shachar, 'The Accumulating Academic Literature on the Negev Bedouin in Critical View,' in G Kressel (ed), *Rishimot Binose Habedwim* (Midreshet Sdi Boker 34, Ben-Gurion University, 2002) 40–54; O Yiftachel, 'Naqab/Negev Bedouins and the (Internal) Colonial Paradigm' in A Amara, I Abu-Saad and O Yiftachel (eds), *Indigenous (In)Justice: Human Rights Law and Bedouin Arabs in the Naqab/Negev* (Harvard University Press, 2013) 289–318.

[28] See for example, WE Jennings-Bramley, 'The Bedouin of the Sinaitic Peninsula' (1907) 39 *Palestine Exploration Quarterly* 131.

[29] 'Arif al-'Arif, *Tarikh Bir al-Sab' wa Qaba'iliha* (Madbuli Library, 1934) (*History of Beersheba and its Tribes*); Jennings-Bramley (n 28).

[30] A Meir and Y Ben-David, *The Bedouin in Israel and Sinai: A Bibliography* (Department of Geography of Ben-Gurion University of the Negev, 1989). Meir and Ben-David enumerate about 700 sources.

treat the Bedouin as nomadic groups undergoing a process of sedentarisation in a modern nation-state, and examine their economic, political and social transformations over time.[31] Geographically, many of these studies have addressed the Sinai and the Beersheba area together. Temporally, most of this scholarship relates to the Israeli period and some to the British Mandate years. Notably, the Israeli government-planned Bedouin townships and later the 'unrecognized villages' spurred a great deal of such scholarship.[32]

The third paradigm, alongside the modernity paradigm, has generated a more critical body of literature in recent years, viewing the 'Bedouin-Arabs' as a peripheral minority in an ethnic state subject to multiple marginalities, and discriminatory and colonial practices.[33] This paradigm has been summarised as follows:

> The third paradigm has seen a surge in efforts to … re-Arabize (and Palestinianize) both place and community. The 'Negev Bedouin' has been increasingly challenged as a conceptual framing. In some ways this has been pioneered by the terminology of the NGO advocacy, where the 'Naqab' has become central to Palestinian iconography … and towards adding clarifying epithets, such as 'Palestinian Bedouin' or 'Arab Bedouin', or 'indigenous Palestinian Bedouin'. It is in the past decade or two that we can begin to speak of 'Naqab Bedouin studies', rather than 'Negev Bedouin studies.[34]

These paradigms have not emerged within the study of the Bedouin in the West Bank, primarily due to the scarcity of existing literature on the topic. However, comparisons and lessons learned from the study of tribal communities in general, and that of the Naqab Bedouin in particular, inform our work and this edited collection.

Linguistic choices in describing the localities of Bedouin life must also be better understood and problematised. The term 'Naqab', for example, has been used more often in the last two decades, and seeks to counterweigh the Zionist 'Negev' by seeking to (re)'Arabise' the space. However, the term 'Naqab' reproduces some of the Zionist framings of the region, given that it is merely a translation of the Hebrew term 'Negev'. This adopts the Zionist geographical formation of the region, which was mostly known as Beer al-Saba' originally, and had expansive links and networks with nearby communities, cities and regions, including Gaza, Hebron and Sinai. Most scholarship on southern Palestine and its inhabitants largely falls within the structural confines of Zionist imaginations and representations of the Negev as desert region, only scarcely inhabited by nomadic tribes.[35] In this collection we seek to transcend

[31] See, for example, A Abu-Rabiʿa, *A Bedouin Century: Education and Development among the Negev Tribes in the 20th Century* (Berghahn Books Publisher, 2001); J Ben-David, *The Bedouins in Israel – Land Conflicts and Social Issues* (Jerusalem Institute for Israel Studies, 2004) (Hebrew); E Marx, *The Bedouin of the Negev* (Praeger, 1967); A Meir, *When Nomadism Ends: the Israeli Bedouin of the Negev* (Westview, 1997).

[32] E Stern and Y Gradus, 'Socio-cultural considerations in planning towns for nomads' (1979) 277 *Ekistics* 224; J Ben-David, *The Condition of the Negev Bedouin* (Jerusalem Institute for Israel Studies, 1991); H Noach, *The Existent and the Non-Existent Villages: the Unrecognized Bedouin Villages in the Negev* (Pardes Press, 2009) (Hebrew); P Motzafi-Haller and M Feige, 'Bedouin-Arab Society in the Negev/Nageb' in Pnina Motzafi-Haller and Michael Feige (eds) (2008) 8 *Hagar: Studies in Culture, Polity, and Identity* 1.

[33] See, for example, Motzafi-Haller and Feige (n 32); G Falah, 'Israeli state policy towards Bedouin Sedentarization in the Negev' (1989) 18 *Journal of Palestine Studies* 71.

[34] M Nasasra et al, 'Introduction' in Nasasra et al (n 27) 13.

[35] A Amara and D Bir-alSabia', *Ottoman Southern Palestine, State Land and Society* (Arab Centre for Research and Policy Studies, 2024) (Arabic).

many of these common geo-social categories by stressing commonalities, connections, networks and temporal continuum, and we call for others to do the same.

Geographer Ghazi Falah's pioneering book, *The Forgotten Palestinians*, addressed the identity of these communities and the Israeli policies of land dispossession against the Arabs of southern Palestine, helping to critically unpack the importance of the Bedouin communities in Palestine. Falah stressed the Arab national identity of the Bedouin, and the role that their Palestinian identity plays in their dispossession.[36] On the same topic, Ronen Shamir's work offers an early theoretical framework, focusing on Zionism, law and questions of modernity through an analysis of prominent judgments affecting Bedouin communities.[37] The start of the twenty-first century has seen a proliferation of studies on the Bedouin communities of southern Palestine, including critical analyses and contributions by native scholars drawing on various theoretical frameworks including colonialism and settler colonialism, the national, the indigenous, and critical, legal and geographical approaches.[38] At the same time, research from an opposing political camp has emerged from scholars who deny Bedouin land rights and indigeneity, and who largely support the legal and political position of the State of Israel. According to these arguments, Bedouins are largely nomadic and pastoral communities, with no specific connection to the land, and thus not indigenous to the Negev. These authors contend that even if Bedouins had cultivated some lands, by failing to register titles in the official land registry, these communities do not have rights to the land.[39] Despite this type of literature, the legal-political geography and the land regime in southern Palestine, with its complex legal, social and territorial relations, remain understudied, with limited exceptions such as *Emptied Lands*.[40] However, to date there have been no significant studies regarding Bedouin communities across geographies and polities, comparing the Galilee, the West Bank, Sinai (Egypt), Jordan and the Bedouin communities under Israeli governance.[41]

[36] G Falah, *The Forgotten Palestinians: The Naqab Arabs 1906–1986* (Taybih, The Centre for Reviving Arab Heritage, 1986) (Arabic).

[37] R Shamir, 'Suspended in Space: Bedouin under the Law of Israel' (1996) 30 *Law & Society Review* 231.

[38] Kedar et al (n 3); I Rosen-Zvi, *Taking Space Seriously: Law, Space and Society in Contemporary Israel* (Ashgate, 2004) ch 3; O Yiftachel, 'Bedouin-Arabs and the Israeli Settler State: Land Policies and Indigenous Resistance' in D Champagne and I Abu-Saad (eds), *The Future of Indigenous People* (University of California Press, 2003); A Kedar, 'Land Settlement in the Negev in International Law Perspective' (2004) 8 *Adalah Newsletter*, tinyurl.com/johgnd3; Amara et al (n 27); Morad Elsana, *Indigenous Land Rights in Israel: A Comparative Study of the Bedouin* (Routledge, 2021); S Abu-Rabia, 'Between Memory and Resistance, an Identity Shaped by Space: The Case of the Naqab Arab Bedouin' (2008) 8 *Hagar: Studies in Culture, Polity and Identities* 93; M Nasasra, *The Naqab Bedouins: A Century of Politics and Resistance* (Columbia University Press, 2017); H Noach, *The Villages That Exist and Vanish: The Unrecognized Bedouin Villages in Israel* (Pardes, 2009) (Hebrew).

[39] For example, H Yahel and R Kark, 'Israel Negev Bedouin during the 1948 War: Departure and Return' (2015) 21 *Israel Affairs* 48; R Kark and S Frantzman, 'The Negev: Land, Settlement, the Bedouin and Ottoman and British Policy 1871–1948' (2012) 39 *British Journal of Middle Eastern Studies* 53; H Yahel, R Kark and SJ Frantzman, 'Contested Indigeneity: The Development of an Indigenous Discourse on the Bedouin of the Negev, Israel' (2012) 17 *Israel Studies* 78.

[40] Kedar et al (n 3).

[41] R Kark and S Frantzman, 'Empire, State and the Bedouin of the Middle East, Past Present: A Comparative Study of Land and Settlement Policies' (2012) 48 *Middle Eastern Studies* 487.

As mentioned, the academic literature on the Bedouin communities in the West Bank, some of whom are refugees from the Naqab, is scarce. There is no comprehensive study that focuses on their present socio-economic conditions or their history. Most available sources are reports by human rights NGOs mainly addressing the risk of forced displacement, such as those written by the Norwegian Refugee Council, the Stop the Wall Campaign, International Peace and Cooperation Center, Bimkom, 'Planners for Planning Rights', and Badil Resource Center for Palestinian Residency and Refugee Rights.[42] These reports, relying largely on field interviews, documentation and legal materials, record the major human rights violations against the Bedouin communities involving the right to tenure, housing, land, pasture, livelihood, water, food security or the right to movement.[43] Some provide an overview of the current human rights violations in light of the origins, history and social issues in Bedouin communities, such as the 2008 Stop the Wall Campaign report, 'Arab al-Jahalin: From the Nakba to the Wall', written by Hadeel Hunaiti. This was the first comprehensive report to focus on the Jahalin Bedouin, discussing the continuous displacement of the Jahalin and other Bedouin tribes since 1948 by the Israeli authorities.[44] In 2016, Ahmad Heneiti published an article on the Bedouin communities in the Jerusalem Quarterly titled 'Bedouin Communities in Greater Jerusalem: Planning or Forced Displacement',[45] which was then developed into a booklet by the Institute for Palestine Studies.[46] The first academic article focusing specifically on the situation and risk of forcible transfer of the Palestinian Bedouin communities of the Central West Bank in the post-Oslo geo-political and legal context was published in 2021, by some of the co-editors of this volume.[47]

1.3. THEORETICAL FRAMEWORK: SETTLER COLONIALISM, INDIGENEITY AND THE ROLE OF LAW

1.3.1. Settler Colonialism

The principal framework through which the displacement of Palestinian Bedouins can be understood is settler colonialism, which has been used to describe the broader

[42] Norwegian Refugees Council, 'Bedouin Rights under Occupation: International Humanitarian Law and Indigenous Rights for Palestinian Bedouin in the West Bank' (15 November 2015), www.nrc.no/resources/reports/bedouin-rights-under-occupation; International Peace and Cooperation Center, 'The Palestinian Bedouin of Barriyat Jerusalem' (2012); Bimkom, 'Planner for Planning Rights, Planning for Bedouin Communities in the West Bank' (2017), bimkom.org/eng/wp-content/uploads/Bimkom_-_Planning_for_Bedouin.compressed.pdf.

[43] ibid.

[44] H Hunaiti, *Arab Jahalin: From the Nakba to the Wall* (Palestinian Grassroot Anti-Apartheid Wall Campaign, 2008).

[45] A Heneiti, *Bedouin Communities in Greater Jerusalem: Planning or Forced Displacement?* (2016) 25 *Jerusalem Quarterly* 51.

[46] A Heneiti, *Bedouin Communities in the Middle of the West Bank as a Case Study* (The Institute for Palestine Studies, 2018) (Arabic).

[47] A Amara et al, 'The Bedouin communities of Eastern Jerusalem: a new locus of power in the post-Oslo battle for Palestine?' (2021) 117 *Confluences Méditerranée* 101.

condition imposed on all Palestinians by the Zionist movement since before 1948 and then by the State of Israel until the present day.[48] As a settler colonial movement, Zionism has advanced throughout history at different stages since its inception in the late nineteenth century.[49] The establishment of the Israeli state in 1948 embodies the realisation of settler colonialism, and the ideology of the Israeli state has been reflected in its political and legal regimes, as well as in its policies and practices, ever since. These policies and practices include the conquest and domination of Palestinians and Palestinian space, the appropriation of Palestinian land, the interruption of Palestinian growth, the control of the Palestinian economy, and the exploitation of Palestinian natural resources, all within the broader framework of the Judaisation and de-Arabisation of Palestine.[50]

In Patrick Wolfe's theorisation of the concept, settler colonialism is a condition and a structure: it is not an event that ends within a defined timeline.[51] Hence, the Nakba and the creation of Israel was not a limited and defined event that ended with the signing of the armistice agreements in 1949 between Israel and neighbouring Arab states. Rather, it instituted the settler colonial conditions imposed on Palestine and Palestinians, as Israel began to create an array of structures of colonialism and domination. Settler colonialism is dependent on the erasure and elimination of the native, ranging from physical to cultural, social, national, political, spatial and/or symbolic elimination. The aim of the settler colonial project is to exercise power to replace.[52] Since Zionism sought to create a settler colony in Palestine, and since Palestine was long populated and had its own people, communities, cultures and identities, Zionism undertook the logic of the elimination of the native, yet these policies differed from one period to another.

The Nakba unquestionably is the defining event in modern Palestinian history, leading to expulsion and dispossession, to be followed by Israeli statehood with subsequent adoption of 'legal' (in the eyes of the state, at least) acts targeting the Palestinian demography and geography. Settler colonial structures were constructed and have continued to develop to serve the broader Zionist ideology of expansion and control over Palestine. Socio-economic, geo-political, legal and military systems were all subsequently fashioned to maintain Jewish hegemony and domination in Palestine, mainly through the politics of enabling conditions for Jewish prosperity and demographic growth, at the expense of restrictions over Palestinian prosperity

[48] Some of the key literature on the topic of settler colonialism in Palestine include: O Jabary Salamanca et al, 'Past is present: Settler colonialism in Palestine' (2012) 2 *Settler Colonial Studies* 1; T Dana and A Jarbawi, 'A Century of Settler Colonialism in Palestine' (2017) 24 *The Brown Journal of World Affairs* 197; S Salazar Hughes, 'Unbounded territoriality: Territorial control, settler colonialism, and Israel/Palestine' (2020) 10 *Settler Colonial Studies* 216.

[49] E Said, *Zionism from the Standpoint of its Victims* (Duke University Press, 1979); G Shafir, *Land, Labor, and the Origins of the Israeli-Palestinian Conflict, 1882–1914* (CUP, 1989).

[50] E Zureik, *The Palestinians in Israel: A Study of Internal Colonialism* (Routledge and Kegan Paul, 1979); G Jabbour, *Settler Colonialism in Southern Africa and the Middle East* (University of Khartoum, 1970); M Rodinson, *Israel: A Settler-Colonial State?* (Monad Press, 1973).

[51] Pa Wolfe, *Settler Colonialism and the Transformation of Anthropology: The Politics and Poetics of an Ethnographic Event (Writing Past Colonialism)* (Cassell, 1998).

[52] P Wolfe, 'Settler Colonialism and the Elimination of the Native' (2006) 8 *Journal of Genocide Research* 387.

and demographic and spatial growth. Land ownership and use is central to this policy.

The Israeli legal system has provided a cloak of legality on the lands appropriated through force. Israel built a complex land regime to serve its objectives of Judaisation and land control, including the confiscation of land belonging to Palestinian refugees and internally displaced persons, lands belonging to Palestinians who became citizens of Israel, lands registered under the name of the British High Commissioner, and lands deemed by the Israeli Government as 'state lands'.[53] In parallel, Israel constructed an apparatus of governmental and semi-governmental institutions to control the sale, allocation and use of these lands. While Zionist institutions owned nearly six per cent of the land in Palestine until 1948, nowadays, roughly 95 per cent of the land in Israel is considered state and public lands: lands registered as state lands or as belonging to state organs or to the Jewish National Fund.[54] Similar policies of land appropriation and control were applied by the Israeli authorities in the West Bank and the Gaza Strip as they enacted a number of military orders and manipulative interpretations of Ottoman, British and Jordanian laws to control the Palestinian space.[55] Zoning and planning was the other major tool of Israeli hegemony and control of Palestinian land use and space, ensuring the colonisation and Judaisation of Palestinian space. As this book demonstrates, the ongoing attempts to erase Palestinian Bedouin communities in the Jerusalem periphery must therefore be seen as a continuation of the ongoing settler colonial project that undergirds Zionism and the Israeli state's logic of control and erasure in Palestine.

1.3.2. Indigeneity

While closely related to the framework of settler colonialism, the concept of indigeneity has received relatively little attention in the scholarship on the Israeli–Palestinian context. Whereas settler colonialism focuses on the ongoing Israeli structures of violence and continuous replacement of the native population with the settler population, indigeneity addresses native life before (and despite) the settler colonial process, as well as resistance, visions for liberation and future justice. Rana Barakat has argued that, whereas the settler colonial framework is important to the study of Zionism, its history and violent structures, indigenous studies offer a richer understanding of Palestine and Palestinian history.[56] The lens of indigeneity of all Palestinians is useful on different levels in approaching Palestine and its Bedouin communities: for instance, it reveals the tensions and challenges vis-à-vis

[53] H Abu-Hussein and F McKay, *Access Denied: Palestinian Land Rights in Israel* (Zed Books, 2003); Alexandre Kedar, 'On the Legal Geography of Ethnocratic Settler States' (2003) 5 *Current Legal Issues: Law and Geography* 401.

[54] See, the Israel Land Authority, www.gov.il/he/collectors/publications?limit=10&officeId=806561c8-659a-4fbb-9b8f-8ecc1e6b8164&Type=9698793e-48f5-4941-8555-b67ca738db63.

[55] B'Tselem, 'By Hook and by Crook: Israeli Settlement Policy in the West Bank' (July 2010) www.btselem.org/download/201007_by_hook_and_by_crook_eng.pdf.

[56] R Barakat, 'Writing/Righting Palestine Studies: Settler Colonialism, Indigenous Sovereignty and Resisting the Ghost(s) of History' (2017) 8 *Settler Colonial Studies* 349.

the international legal framework, including International Human Rights Law, as critically discussed in chapter six by Reeda Alji.

As noted by Siegfried Wiessner (referencing the American context):

> First, Indian freely shared, not exclusively controlled land was taken away. Second, the conqueror's way of life was imposed. Third, political autonomy was drastically curtailed. Fourth, indigenous peoples have often been relegated to a status of extreme poverty, disease, and despair.[57]

Adopting this perspective in relation to the Palestinian context, it emerges that although the 'indigenous' was invented by the colonial condition, the framework of the 'settler colonial' and that of the 'indigenous' have not been fully elaborated given the problems they reveals. Most notably, some have voiced strong criticism regarding the use of indigeneity, especially as it pertains to the Bedouin communities.[58] Lana Tatour has indicated that the culturalisation of indigeneity used to advance Palestinian Bedouin rights has in essence replicated the racialising logic of settler colonialism, which in turn makes the enjoyment of rights by these communities conditional to their 'perpetual practice of "authentic' culture"'.[59] In a similar vein, Amara and Hawari reject the emerging notion of legal discourses and categories of indigeneity in the struggles of Palestinian Bedouins: decolonisation and liberation from the violence of ongoing settler colonialism is common to all Palestinians – Bedouins and non-Bedouins alike – who face erasure because they are Palestinian.[60]

Considering these admonishments on how the lens of indigeneity engages with the context of Palestine, developments of international law should be understood more critically. The adoption of the United Nations Declaration on the Rights of Indigenous Peoples (UNDRIP) in 2007[61] has been welcomed by many, including some indigenous communities; nonetheless, UNDRIP does little to challenge the foundational injustices of existing settler colonial states, maintaining and protecting their territorial integrity and political sovereignty. Although it recognises and seeks to safeguard several significant indigenous rights (land, land use, culture), UNDRIP undermines the political aspirations of many indigenous peoples.[62] Thus, the notion of indigeneity emerging in international legal instruments assumes a rather static, almost 'post-conflict' situation, and fails to engage meaningfully with the quest for decolonisation and the initiative required to instigate such a process. For these reasons, the legalisation of indigenous struggles within the parameters of UNDRIP limits ndigenous visions and modes for liberation and decolonisation.

[57] S Wiessner, 'Rights and Status of Indigenous Peoples: A Global Comparative and International Legal Analysis' 1999 (12) *Harvard Human Rights Journal* 57, 98.

[58] L Tatour, 'The Culturalisation of Indigeneity: The Palestinian-Bedouin of the Naqab and Indigenous Rights' (2019) 23 *The International Journal of Human Rights* 1569; and A Amara and Y Hawari, 'Using Indigeneity in the Struggle for Palestinian Liberation' Al-Shabaka (8 August 2019), al-shabaka.org/commentaries/using-indigeneity-in-the-struggle-for-palestinian-liberation.

[59] ibid.

[60] Amara and Hawari (n 58).

[61] United Nations, 'The United Nations Declaration on the Rights of Indigenous Peoples' (13 September 2007), www.un.org/development/desa/indigenouspeoples/wp-content/uploads/sites/19/2019/01/UNDRIP_E_web.pdf.

[62] Amara and Hawari (n 58).

Turning to the situation of the Palestinian Bedouins, following the adoption of UNDRIP, most studies and advocacy reports have drawn on it to understand and advocate for the Palestinian Bedouin communities in the Naqab, a minoritised population within the State of Israel.[63] This approach, however, has contributed to the de-nationalisation and fragmentation of the Palestinians into several religious and cultural sub-groups, reinforcing stereotypical notions of indigenous peoples as tribal and frozen in time. Similar concerns apply to researching Palestinian Bedouin communities in the West Bank, especially as the Palestinian struggle for liberation and statehood is central and cannot be accommodated within the narrow parameters of UNDRIP. Thus, it is essential to stress that the distinct cultural identity of the Bedouin communities is an additional layer in the Palestinian national identity of these communities: the Palestinian people are an internally diverse society united by a common experience of being subjected to violent settler colonialism in many forms depending on different factors. This approach is crucial to a nuanced understanding of the struggle of the Palestinian people as a whole – based on their shared national identity – as a colonised indigenous group, which includes Palestinian Bedouins. As such, the additional theoretical framework of apartheid imposed by Israel on Palestinians has emerged in scholarship and human rights reporting to describe the overall situation of Palestine, which also applies to Palestinian Bedouins.[64] Apartheid is a mechanism through which the settler colonial state controls and manages indigenous peoples, revealing the interconnection between the frameworks of settler colonialism, indigeneity and apartheid in Palestine that describe the violence imposed on all Palestinians, including Bedouins.

1.4. INTERNATIONAL LEGAL FRAMEWORK

The international legal framework applicable to Palestinian Bedouin communities in the West Bank and the Eastern Jerusalem periphery – that is, territory occupied by Israel since 1967, which is usually referred to as the Occupied Palestinian Territory (OPT) – is determined by the ongoing occupation. This is the established position of the international community and confirmed under international law by the International Court of Justice (ICJ) in a landmark Advisory Opinion of 2004.[65] That Court reaffirmed the applicability of international humanitarian law (IHL) as well as international human rights law (IHRL) to the OPT.[66] Despite the entrenchment and permanence of the occupation, and de facto attempts to annex land (also outlined by the Independent International Commission of Inquiry in 2022[67]), Israel

[63] Amara et al (n 27) 289–318; Kedar et al 159–212.

[64] Amnesty International, 'Israel's Apartheid Against Palestinians: Cruel System of Domination and Crime Against Humanity' (2022), www.amnesty.org/en/latest/news/2022/02/israels-apartheid-against-palestinians-a-cruel-system-of-domination-and-a-crime-against-humanity.

[65] International Court of Justice, Legal Consequences of the Construction of a Wall in the Occupied Palestinian Territory, Advisory Opinion, ICJ Reports 2004, p 136 ('ICJ Wall') paras 74–78.

[66] ibid paras 101–13.

[67] Report of the UN Independent International Commission of Inquiry on the OPT, A/77/328 of 14 September 2022, paras 75–76.

cannot legally annex the OPT due to the prohibition of territorial conquest through the use of force in Article 2(4) of the UN Charter, reflected in UN Security Council resolution 242 (1967).[68] This echoes the traditional international law rule whereby, as one prominent commentator stated: there is not 'an atom of sovereignty' vested in the authority of the occupying power, who is a mere trustee of the land until the legitimate sovereign government of the Palestinian People returns to power.[69]

While not the focus of this book, it is worth noting that the Palestinian Bedouins living in the Negev/Naqab – within the Israeli state – are not usually considered to be protected by international law provisions applicable to occupations. Instead, their status as a minoritised indigenous group is generally understood through domestic Israeli law.[70] This is highly problematic for various reasons, some of which have already been discussed in the section on settler colonialism and indigeneity, and affect Palestinians living in the territory occupied in 1967 as well as 'Palestinian citizens of Israel'.[71] Moreover – as Bana Abu Zuluf and Ahmad Amara discuss in chapter three of this volume – the Israeli treatment of Palestinian Bedouins is similar on both sides of the 'Green Line', a term used to denote the 1949 armistice demarcation line between Israeli and Arab forces.[72] This empirical fact suggests that Israel's approach to Palestinian Bedouins in land it controls, either through its statehood or through its occupation, is indicative of the degree to which it sees these lands as its own.

1.4.1. International Humanitarian Law

For as long as Israel continues to occupy the West Bank,[73] IHL provisions on the legal responsibilities of the occupying power will apply.[74] Israel is bound by relevant obligations set out in treaty and custom: it ratified the Fourth Geneva Convention (GC IV)[75] on 6 July 1951,[76] extending the reach of that treaty to the OPT.[77] While Israel is not a party to the Hague Regulations (HR),[78] many of those provisions 'have become part of customary law', as confirmed by the ICJ in *Wall*;[79] these include key

[68] UN Security Council resolution 242 (1967) of 22 November 1967, which emphasises 'the inadmissibility of the acquisition of territory by war' shortly after Israel's occupation of the West Bank.

[69] L Oppenheim, 'Legal Relations Between an Occupying Power and the Inhabitants' (1917) 33 *Law Quarterly Review* 363, 364.

[70] See eg discussion in M Nasasra, 'The Politics of Exclusion and Localization: The Palestinian Minority in Israel and the Oslo Accords' (2021) 20 *Ethnopolitics* 523.

[71] H Jabareen, '20 Years of Oslo: The Green Line's Challenge to the Statehood Project' (2013) 43 *Journal of Palestine Studies* 41.

[72] See ICJ Wall, para 72.

[73] Under Art 42 HR, the law of occupation applies to territory 'actually placed under the authority of the hostile army'. Relatedly, Art 6 GCIV states that its provisions apply for as long as the occupying power 'exercises the functions of government in such territory'.

[74] A/HRC/50/21, para 17.

[75] Fourth Geneva Convention relative to the Protection of Civilian Persons in Time of War (Fourth Geneva Convention) of 12 August 1949 (GC IV).

[76] Reported also in ICJ Wall, para 91.

[77] See eg Arts 27–37 and 47–78 GC IV.

[78] The Hague Convention (IV) respecting the Laws and Customs of War on Land (Hague Convention) and its annexed Regulations respecting the Laws and Customs of War on Land (Hague Regulations) of 18 October 1907 (HR).

[79] ICJ Wall, paras 78 and 89.

humanitarian rules pertaining to occupation, such as the protection of civilian property and the prohibition of settlements.[80]

The guiding IHL principle in occupations is the protection the occupying power owes the civilian population living under occupation, ie 'protected persons' of Article 4 GC IV. This reflects HR and customary IHL norms on the distinction between civilians and combatants.[81] Protection of civilians extends to their direct environment and property, ie 'civilian objects',[82] under the control of the occupying power.[83] Additional customary norms reaffirm the illegality of settlement activities, which are known to drive Bedouin displacement: Article 49(6) GC IV is reflected in ICRC customary IHL Rule 130;[84] and the prohibition of confiscation (as well as destruction, prohibited by Article 53 GC IV) of private property of Article 46 HR, is reflected in ICRC customary IHL Rule 51(c).[85] These customary norms reaffirm the illegality of attacks on Palestinian property, including in Bedouin communities, as discussed in more detail in chapter seven by Luigi Daniele.

1.4.2. International Human Rights Law (IHRL)

Given the factual reality of occupation, and the duty to maintain public order and safety as set out in Article 43 HR,[86] Israel also has a range of human rights duties towards Palestinians. A 2013 UN fact-finding mission confirmed that 'Israel is bound to respect, protect, promote and fulfil the full range of the social, economic, cultural, civil and political human rights of all persons within its jurisdiction as a result of its being party' to IHRL treaties, and is also bound by human rights of 'customary international law' status.[87] Moreover, Palestine's accession to the seven core IHRL treaties on 2 April 2014 adds a layer of human rights protections in the OPT.[88] It is evident that all these provisions apply to all Palestinians, including Bedouins.

[80] See eg Rules 51 and 130, on the protection of civilian property in times of occupation and the prohibition of transfer of the civilian population of the occupying power in occupied territory (ie settlements), ICRC, Customary IHL Database, ihl-databases.icrc.org/en/customary-ihl/v1.

[81] See in particular Rules 5 and 6, ICRC, Customary IHL Database (n 80).

[82] ICRC, 'Protection of civilians', casebook.icrc.org/highlight/protection-civilians#:~:text=Protecting%20civilians%20during%20armed%20conflict,known%20as%20'civilian%20objects.

[83] Arts 27–34 and 53 GCIV; also Arts 46–47 HR.

[84] International Committee of the Red Cross (ICRC), Customary IHL Database, Rule 130, ihl-databases.icrc.org/en/customary-ihl/v1/rule130.

[85] ICRC Customary IHL Database, Rule 51(c), ihl-databases.icrc.org/en/customary-ihl/v1/rule51.

[86] Art 43 HR requires the occupying power to 'take all the measures in its power to restore, and ensure, as far as possible, public order and safety, while respecting, unless absolutely prevented, the laws in force in the country'.

[87] UN-HRC, Report A/HRC/22/63, 7 February 2013, para 11. The IHRL conventions are: ICCPR, ICESCR, CRC, Convention Against Torture and Other Cruel, Inhuman or Degrading Treatment or Punishment, 1465 UNTS 85 (adopted 10 December 1984 and entered into force 26 June 1987) (CAT), Convention on the Elimination of All Forms of Discrimination against Women, 1249 UNTS 13 (adopted 18 December 1979 and entered into force 3 September 1981) (CEDAW), International Convention on the Elimination of All Forms of Racial Discrimination, 660 UNTS 195 (adopted 7 March 1966 and entered into force 4 January 1969) (CERD).

[88] ICCPR, ICESCR, CRC, CEDAW, CAT, CERD and CRPD.

In addition, a key customary norm of IHRL is the right to self-determination, codified in the UN Charter as one of the core principles of the international legal order.[89] This was reaffirmed by the ICJ in *Chagos*, which clarified the 'normative character under customary international law' of the right to self-determination, and that its respect is 'an obligation erga omnes'.[90] The Palestinian people also have the right to self-determination including the right to an independent State of Palestine, as reaffirmed consistently over the years by the UN General Assembly.[91] As an integral part of the Palestinian polity subjected to erasure by the State of Israel, the Bedouins are entitled to enjoy their right to self-determination together with all other Palestinians.

1.4.3. Other International Law Provisions

Alongside IHL and IHRL provisions, it is evident that general international law applies to the OPT, which would include any treaty-based rules adopted by Palestine through the ordinary route set out in each treaty. Notably, the system of international criminal law (ICL) set out in the Rome Statute for the International Criminal Court (ICC)[92] is applicable to the OPT, as confirmed by Pre-Trial Chamber I in its 2021 decision on the ICC's territorial jurisdiction in the Situation in Palestine.[93] As a result, specific violations of international law in relation to Palestinian Bedouin communities may violate a range of treaty-based provisions that may lead to state as well as individual responsibilities, depending on the circumstances.

1.5. THE LEGAL GEOGRAPHY OF THE WEST BANK, INCLUDING THE 'E1' AREA

International law – and law more generally – interacts with people and territory in ways that shape societies and political arenas. The neutrality of law has long been questioned: uses of law reveal it to be a political tool to determine space, to form society, or to serve political ends. The lens of legal geography helps us to understand how laws vary across different geographies, and how physical and social landscapes

[89] Arts 1(2) and 55, UN Charter 1945.

[90] Legal Consequences of the Separation of the Chagos Archipelago from Mauritius in 1965, Advisory Opinion, ICJ Reports 2019, p 95, (Chagos) paras 115 and 180.

[91] Including UN General Assembly Resolutions A/RES/77/208 (15 December 2022) and A/RES/67/19 (4 December 2012).

[92] UN General Assembly, Rome Statute of the International Criminal Court, 17 July 1998.

[93] ICC PTC-I, Decision on the Prosecution Request Pursuant to Article 19(3) for a Ruling on the Court's Territorial Jurisdiction in Palestine, ICC-01/18-143 (5 February 2021). On the various stages of Palestine's engagement with the ICC, see inter alia V Azarova and T Mariniello, 'Why the ICC Needs a "Palestine Situation" (More than Palestine Needs the ICC): On the Court's Potential Role(s) in the Israeli-Palestinian Context' (2017) 1 *Diritti Umani e Diritto Internazionale* 115; and T Obel Hansen, 'Opportunities and Challenges Seeking Accountability for War Crimes in Palestine under the International Criminal Court's Complementarity Regime' (2019) 9 *Notre Dame Journal of International and Comparative Law* 3.

shape legal structures. In the socio-political context between the Jordan River and the Mediterranean Sea, Israeli laws – especially those addressing Palestinians, their rights and their land – organise space and influence realms of 'legality' and 'illegality'. Israeli political power and settler colonial objectives are distributed across the Palestinian space and advance colonisation of the West Bank through settlement activities, which in turn drives the displacement of Palestinian Bedouins. Military power is only one component of conquest: as noted by Steven Paul McSloy in relation to the United States, 'The real conquest was on paper, on maps and in laws'.[94] Something similar happened in Palestine.

1.5.1. Reshaping the OPT Through International Law Treaties: The Impact of Oslo Accords

Once the 1967 occupation of the West Bank, including East Jerusalem, and the Gaza Strip (the OPT) began, despite the international community's condemnations of the attempt to acquire territory through force as enshrined in UN Security Council resolution 242 (1967),[95] Israel's grip over the OPT consolidated over time. Countless UN reports have found that the occupation – which under international law denotes a temporary, exceptional situation[96] – has become entrenched. For instance, in late 2022, the UN Independent International Commission of Inquiry on the OPT noted

> that Israel has no intention of ending the occupation, has clear policies for ensuring complete control over the [OPT], and is acting to alter the demography through the maintenance of a repressive environment for Palestinians and a favourable environment for Israeli settlers.[97]

One of the key facilitators of this shifting socio-political geography has been the substance and uses of the Oslo Accords of the mid-1990s, specifically Oslo I[98] and Oslo II.[99] The early critiques of the Oslo Accords by Edward Said were prescient and remain pertinent.[100] As others have since noted, the Accords 'accept the Zionist consensus and, for the first time in the history of the conflict, seek to legitimize Israel as a Jewish state in historic Palestine', entrenching a 'logic of separation' between Israelis and Palestinians, and also among Palestinians based on their residency.[101]

[94] SP McSloy, 'Because the Bible Tells Me So: Manifest Destiny and American Indians' (1996) 9 *St Thomas Law Review* 38.

[95] UN Security Council resolution 242 (1967) of 22 November 1967.

[96] See discussion in A Imseis, 'Prolonged Occupation: At the Vanishing Point of the Jus ad Bellum/Jus in Bello Distinction' (2022) 58 *Texas International Law Journal* 33.

[97] See eg Report of the Independent International Commission of Inquiry on the Occupied Palestinian Territory, including East Jerusalem, and Israel, A/HRC/50/21 of 9 May 2022, paras 15–19 and 70.

[98] Declaration of Principles on Interim Self-Government Arrangements, 13 September 1993 (Oslo I).

[99] Israeli–Palestinian Interim Agreement on the West Bank and the Gaza Strip, 28 September 1995 (Oslo II).

[100] E Said, *The End of the 'Peace Process': Oslo and After* (Pantheon Books, 2000).

[101] H Eid, 'Edward Said and the Re-drawing of the (Post) Colonial Political Map of Palestine' (2017) 6 *Decolonization: Indigeneity, Education & Society* 64, 67.

Legal commentators have also indicated that certain aspects of the Accords contradict IHL, including the implicit condonation of Israel's temporary tenure in East Jerusalem and jurisdiction over settlers in the West Bank.[102] As Giulia Pinzauti discusses in chapter eight of this volume, the Oslo Accords cannot be invoked as an excuse to shield those responsible for violations of international law from accountability.

The impact of Oslo II on the legal geography of the OPT cannot be overstated. As discussed elsewhere in this volume, in 1995 this international treaty divided the West Bank into three administrative areas, A, B, and C:

> Area 'A', constituting mainly Palestinian cities and urban centres came under full Palestinian civil and military control; Area 'B' constituting mainly rural areas and villages outside Palestinian urban centres, was placed under Palestinian civil control and Israeli military control; Area 'C', comprising 59% of the area of the West Bank, and consisting of 63% of the agricultural land in the West Bank, was placed under full Israeli civil and military control.[103]

The Palestinian Bedouin communities, the subject of this collection, live almost entirely in Area C, which includes the Eastern Jerusalem periphery subject to the E1 plan, which encompasses the large settlement block of Ma'ale Adumim and close to 20 Bedouin hamlets, as illustrated in the following table (although many more in the vicinity are affected).[104]

Table 1.1 Palestinian Bedouin communities affected by the E1 plan

Communities within the E1 Plan boundaries	Communities directly impacted by the E1
Abu George Road Bedouins (Nkheila)	Khan al-Ahmar Wadi al-Sider
Abu George Road Bedouins (Kassara)	Khan al-Ahmar Abu Falah
Abu Nuwaar	Khan al-Ahmar Abu al-Helu
Wadi al-Jimel	Khan al-Ahmar Mihtawish
Jabal al-Baba	Khan al-Ahmar Makab al-Samen
Wadi Sneysel	Al-Muntar
Bir al-Maskoob B	Bir al-Maskoob A
Al-Za'ayyem Za'atreh Herders	Wadi Abu-Hindi
	Wadi al-A'awaj
	Al-Za'ayyem Bedouins

[102] A Imseis, 'On the Fourth Geneva Convention and the occupied Palestinian territory' (2003) 44 *Harvard International Law Journal* 65, 126–27.

[103] Amara et al (n 47) 105.

[104] UN OCHA, 'Tightening of coercive environment on Bedouin communities around Ma'ale Adumim settlement', www.ochaopt.org/content/tightening-coercive-environment-bedouin-communities-around-ma-ale-adumim-settlement#JabalAlBabaDemolition; see also, D Altayli, *Arab East Jerusalem: A Reader* (Jerusalem, PASSIA, 2013) 135. The vast majority of them (2,700) belong to the Jahalin tribe. UN-OCHA, 'Bedouin Communities at Risk of Forcible Transfer' (2014), www.ochaopt.org/sites/default/files/ocha_opt_communities_jerusalem_factsheet_september_2014_english.pdf.

1.5.2. Reshaping the OPT Through Israeli Laws and Planning

The impact of Oslo II on the legal geography of the OPT operates in tandem with the direct effects of Israeli laws, including planning regulations, that have shaped the West Bank including East Jerusalem from 1967 to the present day. The areas in the Eastern Jerusalem periphery inhabited by the Palestinian Bedouin communities are for the most part included in the aforementioned E1 plan, one of various Israeli zoning plans seeking to regulate Palestinian space, as discussed in more detail in chapter two by Mohammed Younes. Given its geo-political significance in connecting Jerusalem with the eastern regions in the West Bank all the way to the Dead Sea, Israel has deployed a range of measures to acquire as much Palestinian land as possible with the least number of Palestinians on it in its quest to entrench its control over the E1 area.[105] Through the parameters of Oslo II, this area is entirely under Israeli military and administrative control, exposing Palestinians, including Palestinian Bedouin communities, to the sharp end of settler colonial expansion. Against this geo-legal backdrop, Bedouin communities are at particular risk of forcible transfer, and a range of other violations of international law, as discussed throughout the rest of this book.

The impact of the E1 plan on the Bedouin communities has caught the attention of the international community. A 2021 European Union report described recent developments:

> [W]hile not part of East Jerusalem but located in the West Bank and an area known as Greater Jerusalem, another significant decision that would further hamper the contiguity with East Jerusalem and the West Bank concerned two detailed plans for the E1 area with a total of 3,401 units. This development should also be seen in the light of a plan approved by the Israeli Minister of Defence on 9 March, for a road known as the 'fabric of life road' for Palestinians, which would direct Palestinian traffic going north and south in the West Bank without passing the large Israeli settlement Maale Adumim, and the E1 area. The full scope of Israeli plans for E1 would ultimately serve to connect the Maale Adumim settlement to the Jerusalem municipality borders. *The plan for the E1 area puts 3,700 Palestinians at risk of forcible transfer.* (emphasis added)[106]

Zoning and planning have been largely treated beyond their technical aspects, as social and political tools to control societies and shape geographies. Critical scholars have tried to expose the dark side of planning, by looking at the utility of this matrix of power to exert power over specific minorities, to appropriate land and space, and to maintain power alongside class and ethnic lines.[107] Thus, the Israeli use of zoning

[105] Amara et al (n 47).

[106] European Union, Office of the European Union Representative (West Bank and Gaza Strip, UNRWA), 'Six-Month Report on Israeli settlements in the occupied West Bank, including East-Jerusalem Reporting period January–July 2020', www.un.org/unispal/document/eu-six-month-report-on-israeli-settlements-in-the-occupied-west-bank-including-east-jerusalem-jan-jul-2020.

[107] O Yiftachel, 'The Dark Side of Modernism: Planning as Control of an Ethnic Minority' in S Watson and K Gibson (eds), *Postmodern Cities and Spaces* (Blackwell, 1994); B Flyvbjerg and T Richardson, 'Planning and Foucault: In Search of the Dark Side of Planning Theory' in P Allmendinger Mr-Jones (eds), *Planning Futures: New Directions for Planning Theory* (Routledge, 2002) 44–62; M Huxley, 'Problematizing Planning: Critical and Effective Genealogies' in J Hillier and P Healey (eds), *Ashgate Research Companion to Planning Theory: Conceptual Challenges for Spatial Planning* (Ashgate, 2010) 135–57.

and planning within both Israel and in the West Bank falls largely within such realm of control and appropriation.[108] In the specific context of the Bedouin communities, spatial engineering through planning have entrapped tens of Bedouin communities in a condition of 'illegality' that is semi-permanent and constantly under the threat of demolition and displacement. This reality reveals a grey-spacing policy to produce zones of habitation where specific communities are neither completely legal (ie in white/whiteness space) nor fully erased (black/blackness space): instead, they exist in a grey space of uncertainty.[109] The Bedouin communities in Area C in the West Bank, similar to the Bedouin communities in the 'unrecognized villages' in the Negev, are entrapped within such gray space and a state of constant illegality.

CONCLUSION

Contextualising the displacement of Palestinian Bedouins in the Eastern Jerusalem periphery reveals how history, geography and politics are intertwined in shaping the vulnerabilities of these communities. While the current threats to the Bedouins and their way of life are attributable to the State of Israel's desire to remove them from the E1 area (and elsewhere in Area C of the West Bank) to expand the settlements, the legacy of the Nakba frames the constant displaceability of Palestinians, among which Bedouins are one of the most targeted groups. The political and legal geography of Area C throughout the West Bank, which includes most of E1 in the Eastern Jerusalem periphery, facilitates the displacement of Palestinian Bedouins, who are subjected to the sharpest edge of the Israeli occupation and violence. Like all Palestinians – urban and rural – the presence of Bedouin communities on land that Israel covets for its own use is an impediment to the realisation of Zionism's historic and contemporary raison d'être and the State's most recent constitutional commitment to developing Jewish (only) settlements.[110] The Palestinians who inhabit the lands slated for settlement expansion are for the most part Bedouins: by resisting displacement, these communities ensure the continuation of Palestinian presence on Palestinian territory that has been occupied since 1967. As a distinctive group within Palestinian society, the flourishing of Bedouin communities in E1, and elsewhere is the region, is intertwined with the flourishing of Palestinian life and culture in all its forms. By the same token, the displacement of Palestinian Bedouins in the Eastern Jerusalem periphery not only carries negative consequences for the families involved, but it is also detrimental for the entire Palestinian polity as a whole.

[108] O Yiftachel, *Ethnocracy: Land and Identity Politics in Israel/Palestine* (University of Pennsylvania Press, 2006); see also the work of Bimkom-Planners for Planning Rights on Israeli planning policies in the West Bank, at bimkom.org/eng/home-mobile; and Amnesty International (n 64).

[109] F Chiodelli and M Gentili, 'The Many Shades of Grey in Urban Governance: How Illegality Shapes Urban Planning, Policy and Development (2021) 84 *Political Geography* [article number 102309]; O Yiftachel, 'Critical Theory and "Gray Space": Mobilization of the Colonized' (2010) 13 *City* 246.

[110] Israeli Knesset, Basic Law: Israel – the Nation State of the Jewish People (19 July 2018), Art 7: 'the state sees in the development of Jewish settlements as one of national value, and will act to encourage and advance its establishment and strengthening'.

2

The Displacement of Palestinian Bedouins as the 'Collateral' Damage of Colonial Urban Planning

MOHAMMED YOUNES

INTRODUCTION

IN HIS SEMINAL work, *The Production of Space*, Henri Lefebvre delves into the intricate dialectics of spatial production, where old social relations dissolve to create new relations within abstract space: an utterly homogeneous space marked by uniform activities.[1] This spatial understanding, rooted in the reproduction of social relations, allows us to unravel the nuanced layers of settler colonial strategies in Israeli colonial policies.[2] Rather than a mere consequence, this displacement offers an example of Lefebvre's conceptualisation of space, becoming a vivid illustration of how colonial urban planning transforms entire communities into what might cynically be seen as 'collateral damage'. This analysis transcends the physicality of the settler colonial policies in Palestine, exploring how these spatial reconstructions not only reshape landscapes but also systematically dislocate and erode the social, cultural and psychological existence of those under occupation.[3]

Within the encompassing region of Jerusalem, Bedouin communities are exposed to the transformative logic of spatial manipulation, positioning them as poignant examples of what Lefebvre articulates as *abstract space*. These communities, under the scrutiny of colonial governance, find their lived experiences reduced to controllable fragments, sanitised for the advancement of specific settler agendas. Complementing

[1] H Lefebvre, *The Production of Space* (Blackwell, 1991) 52.

[2] The term 'abstract space' denotes a standardised, homogeneous space often utilised in scientific and social research to control variables. In urban planning, this term signifies a simplification of the multifaceted 'lived space'. Here, the unique experiences of populations are condensed into manageable details by the dominant power's planning system, turning the space into a 'clean slate' primed for restructuring in line with particular goals.

[3] See eg J Wilson, '"The Devastating Conquest of the Lived by the Conceived": The Concept of Abstract Space in the Work of Henri Lefebvre' (2013) 16 *Space and Culture* 364. Wilson explores Lefebvre's conceptualisation of abstract space and its implications for spatial theory and practice, providing background information that supports the discussion on abstract space in Lefebvre's writings.

Lefebvre, Heidegger's philosophical interpretation of space, particularly his distinction between 'space' and 'place', offers useful analytical tools in this context. In considering the spatial identity of Bedouins, their nomadic lifestyle introduces a complex dialogue concerning their connection to the land, traditionally linked to fixed habitations. For Bedouins, the mental and experiential bonds between dwellers and land bond is abstract and perceived, rather than merely tied to permanent structures, allowing colonial systems to more easily disrupt their spaces and erode their cultural identity. Consequently, when the space around Jerusalem is manipulated by the occupying power, the Bedouin identity becomes relegated to the status of collateral damage, their culturally rich practices such as grazing and cultivation dissolving under the imposition of an unfamiliar urbanity.

This analysis builds upon Lefebvre's theoretical discourse surrounding space, probing into the methodical displacement of Bedouin communities within the Palestinian territories. It posits the structured efforts to re-engineer Palestinian societal frameworks, reshaping indigenous territories through the abstraction of space. This process, under the guise of urban necessity, fortifies the settler colonial infrastructure through the elimination of the native population.

Reviewing the historic and contemporaneous impact of colonial urban planning on the Bedouin communities in Jerusalem's more expansive realm, this study employs a multidisciplinary method to examine spatial transformations within the Bedouin communities, as well as a gap in the context of Palestinian urban history from a legal perspective. This analysis is conducted through the examination of maps, urban plans and developmental projects, in conjunction with social science literature and events that are chronologically related but, seemingly, not in discernible context. The need for wide-ranging multidisciplinary research in the Palestinian context is paramount to understanding the spatial ramifications of settler colonial strategies in the Bedouin realm in Jerusalem. Therefore, comprehending the transition of a once-occupied space into an 'abstract' realm is crucial to understanding the impact of spatial manipulation of the Bedouin place. Thus, this chapter aims to reflect the native Palestinian narrative, capturing their perspective of the occupied territories at large, with a particular focus on the Bedouin domains within the eastern fringes of Jerusalem as a study area.

While numerous studies focus on overt methods of settler colonialism, this study delves into the subtle shades of the 'produced space', where urban planning amplifies the 'displaceability' of Bedouin communities adjacent to Jerusalem. Moving beyond a narrow interpretation of international law or framing what is happening in the Palestinian context as merely another 'conflict', this research explores the intricate 'lived spaces' of the Bedouins in the eastern region of Jerusalem. It illustrates how such policies intersect with their daily experiences, thereby uncovering the multifaceted dynamics of the spatial production of alien colonial spaces on an 'abstracted' original land.

This chapter's narrative unfolds across three sections. Section one retraces the steps of the Jerusalem wilderness through three pivotal periods – pre-1948, 1948–67 and post-1967 – revealing the events and plans that influenced the landscape and shaped the spatial and social fabric of the Bedouin communities. In section two, the study explores the strategies and mechanisms leveraged regulating and ensuing displacement of these communities, drawing a portrait of spatial politics and its implications. Section three examines contemporary regional plans from both the Palestinian Authority (PA) and the Israeli Government apparatus, focusing on discerning their hidden and evident implications for the future of the native Bedouin population. While distinct, each section weaves together a narrative of the past, present and potential futures, offering insights into the complexities of colonial spatial planning.

2.1. THE JERUSALEM WILDERNESS: A HISTORY OF (NON-)URBAN PLANNING

2.1.1. Jerusalem Wilderness (pre-1948)

The history of the Bedouins in Palestine has shaped and continues to influence the region's socio-economic and political landscape. Their strategic control over trade routes and involvement in political upheavals highlight their critical role beyond mere economic contributions. Particularly in Jerusalem's eastern wilderness, the Bedouins were not merely residents but were instrumental in managing the key passageway to the Dead Sea, leveraging their position to impose tolls on traversing parties. However, governmental policies towards the end of the nineteenth century drastically diminished the Bedouins' influence, leading to a period of forced sedentarisation that reshaped their social and economic structures.

As the twentieth century began, industrial activities expanded, encroaching on the grazing lands of the Bedouins near Jerusalem. These developments not only posed a threat to their water supplies but also inadvertently inflicted damage on their traditional way of life. Simultaneously, World War I highlighted Palestine's strategic importance as the southern frontier of the Ottoman Empire, leading to the creation of military and airstrip installations across the Jordan Valley and the plains of Southern Palestine.[4] These strategic installations impacted significantly upon the Bedouins' customary grazing practices.

During the British Mandate (1917–48), Zionist efforts to acquire land were strategically focused on specific areas within Palestine, aiming to geographically confine the Arab population.[5] Notably, there was minimal interest in the lands on Jerusalem's eastern outskirts,[6] where Zionist ownership barely exceeded one per cent.[7]

[4] Different military forces required flat terrain to establish temporary military bases and airfields. Such topographical characteristics were predominantly found in the Bedouin wilderness, located near the main roads to Jordan and Egypt, which were the two primary fronts with the Allied forces during the specified period.

[5] KW Stein, *The Land Question in Palestine, 1917–1939* (The University of North Carolina Press, 1984) 141.

[6] For additional information regarding the Zionist plans and proposals during the Mandate Era, see *Palestine Partition Commission: Report* (His Majesty's Stationery Office, 1938).

[7] Palestine Partition Commission, Map 5: 'Jewish Land Holdings' (His Majesty's Stationery Office, 1938) 314.

British colonial policies further transformed the Bedouin landscape, with changes emanating from infrastructure projects such as road construction, fencing and broader industrial initiatives. These efforts vividly illustrate how urban planning can significantly alter and restrict traditional Bedouin lifestyles and mobility. Despite being framed as essential infrastructure developments, these initiatives underscore the often-overlooked consequences of urban planning on indigenous and local communities.[8]

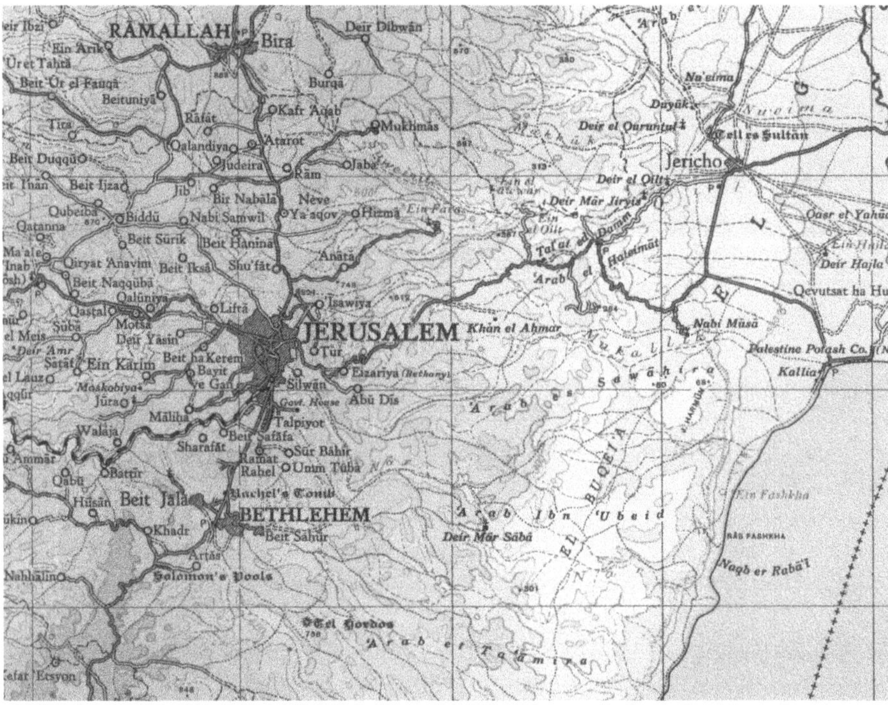

Figure 2.1 Section from the Map of Palestine showing the Jerusalem Area, including roads, the Palestine Potash Company, the Dead Sea and the distribution of the Bedouin clans in the area (Survey of Palestine, 1945, scale 1:250,000)

By the British Mandate's conclusion, key areas around Jerusalem's eastern outskirts were predominantly settled by Bedouin clans such as Al-Ta'amira, Al-Sawahira and others. This period revealed a discrepancy between the actual distribution of Bedouin communities and their representation in British maps, indicating a more fluid and less defined geographical distribution than what was officially depicted.

[8] It is worth noting that Khan al-Ahmar Bedouin area consisted of a Khan Building (inn) that provided accommodation to the travellers, and it was bombed during World War I. On this point, see RE Hammett, 'The Dead Sea – Local Soldier's Impressions' *The West Wyalong Advocate* (20 November 1941) 2.

Table 2.1 Census of nomadic population in the Jerusalem sub-district, based on official Mandate surveys[9]

Bedouin locality	**Population**
Arab el Nuseirat	520
Arab el Ka'abina	260
Arab el 'Ureinat	210
Arab es Sa'ayida	110
An-Nabi Mousa	1,330
Arab Ibn 'Ubeid, Arab er Rashayida, Arab es Sawahira and Arab et Ta'amira	7,070
Total	**9,500**

2.1.2. Jerusalem Wilderness (1948–67)

During the 1948 war, the area bridging Jerusalem and the Jordanian borders served as a crucial passageway for Arab Liberation forces, especially during the initial weeks of the war from 15 May to 11 June 1948.[10] Documentation on the ramifications of these military operations for Bedouin settlements is scarce, yet anecdotal evidence suggests their lands became temporary refuges for displaced Palestinians.[11] As hostilities expanded, numerous Bedouin tribes from southern Palestine found themselves forcibly relocated to the West Bank, Egypt and Jordan.[12] This displacement peaked by 1949, but lingered well into the late 1950s.[13]

Unlike the majority of Palestinian refugees who sought refuge in the United Nations camps, the Bedouin refugees in the West Bank preferred the wilderness between Hebron and Jerusalem, within the eastern bounds of the newly established West Bank.[14] The Al-Jahalin Bedouin tribe, originally from Tel Arad in An-Naqab, were notably resettled in the Khan al-Ahmar vicinity east of Jerusalem post-war.

Under the Jordanian governance of the West Bank (1948–67), Jerusalem was considered a secondary capital of the Hashemite Kingdom, with principal

[9] 'Village Statistics – 1945' (Palestine Government), users.cecs.anu.edu.au/~bdm/yabber/census/VillageStatistics1945orig.pdf.

[10] For a comprehensive discussion of the war incidents, see B Morris, *The Birth of the Palestinian Refugee Problem, 1947–1949*, reprint edn (CUP, 1989) 35.

[11] ibid 174, 326.

[12] A Arouri, *Palestinian Bedouins: Past, Present and Future* (Palestinian Society for the Protection of Human Rights and the Environment (LAW), 2000) 24.

[13] H Hunaiti, 'Arab Jahalin: From the Nakba to the Wall' (Palestinian Grassroots Anti-Apartheid Wall Campaign, 2008) 11.

[14] In Lefebvrian terms, the West Bank is not solely a spatial designation, but also a political product, reflective of social and colonial constructs arising from the enduring tumult of the 1948 war. This perspective illuminates how spaces are shaped and named by dominant powers, often diverging from the lived experiences and histories of its inhabitants. For a more critical appraisal of the social construction of space and its impact on geopolitical entities, refer to EW Soja, *Postmodern Geographies: The Reassertion of Space in Critical Social Theory* (Verso, 1989).

administrative functions remaining in Amman. This relegated Jerusalem to a border city status in line with the 1949 armistice demarcation. Constrained pastureland and dire economic conditions exacerbated by water scarcity and the region's overarching post-war economic tribulations forced Bedouin refugees into neighbouring lands for grazing and prompted numerous Bedouins to immigrate to Jordan in search of improved livelihoods as the foundations of their traditional existence were deconstructed/dismantled.[15]

During the two decades of Jordanian rule, Jerusalem's urban planning efforts were encapsulated in a single masterplan developed in 1964 by Henry Kendall, evolving from the 1944 plan yet focusing on the city's eastern sector.[16] This plan introduced zoning that disregarded the Bedouin population, directing its attention predominantly towards urban expansion along the north–south axis of the city. Designated zones for 'Terraced Agriculture', 'Forest Areas', and a 'Heavy Industry Area' between 'Anata and Az-Za'ayyem threatened the environmental integrity and livelihood of both peasants and Bedouins, with the 'Soak Pit' wastewater system risking contamination of Bedouin pastures and groundwater wells.[17]

Most lands classified for agricultural use were traditionally Bedouin pastures, affecting not only the eastern but also the western parts of Jerusalem, where communities like those of Beit Hanina and Bir Nabala resided. However, the onset of the Six-Day War and the subsequent occupation of East Jerusalem halted the implementation of this masterplan.[18]

The period also witnessed a reduction in pastoral lands due to both urban and rural community expansion and the settlement of Bedouin refugees, which increased livestock numbers and water demand. These developments encapsulate the complex interplay between urban planning, environmental stewardship and the traditional lifestyles of Bedouin communities under Jordanian governance, highlighting a critical aspect of the broader narrative of displacement and adaptation faced by Bedouins in the Jerusalem wilderness.

Situated within the broader discourse on colonial and post-colonial urban planning, the analysis in this section reflects on the nuanced challenges posed by zoning and land use policies that, while aiming for urban expansion and environmental management, often overlooked the socio-cultural and economic fabric of indigenous and nomadic communities, leading to significant shifts in their traditional ways of life.

[15] A Plascov, 'The Palestinians of Jordan's Border' in R Owen (ed), *Studies in the Economic and Social History of Palestine in the Nineteenth and Twentieth Centuries* (Palgrave Macmillan, 1982) 213–15.

[16] Henry Kendall, who was the last Planning Chief for Jerusalem Municipality during the British Mandate, put forth the first comprehensive zoning plan of the city during the 1940s.

[17] A soak pit system is a wastewater disposal method comprising a closed, porous chamber situated beneath a building. This chamber facilitates the seeping of waste water into the surrounding soil, potentially impacting the soil quality and the area's groundwater.

[18] A masterplan is a comprehensive planning document that outlines a conceptual framework to guide the future urban development of specific area, usually a city or a metropolitan area. It often includes analysis of the current situation, a vision for the future development, and specific measures and regulations to attain the vision, addressing different areas including land use, infrastructure services, transportation and community amenities.

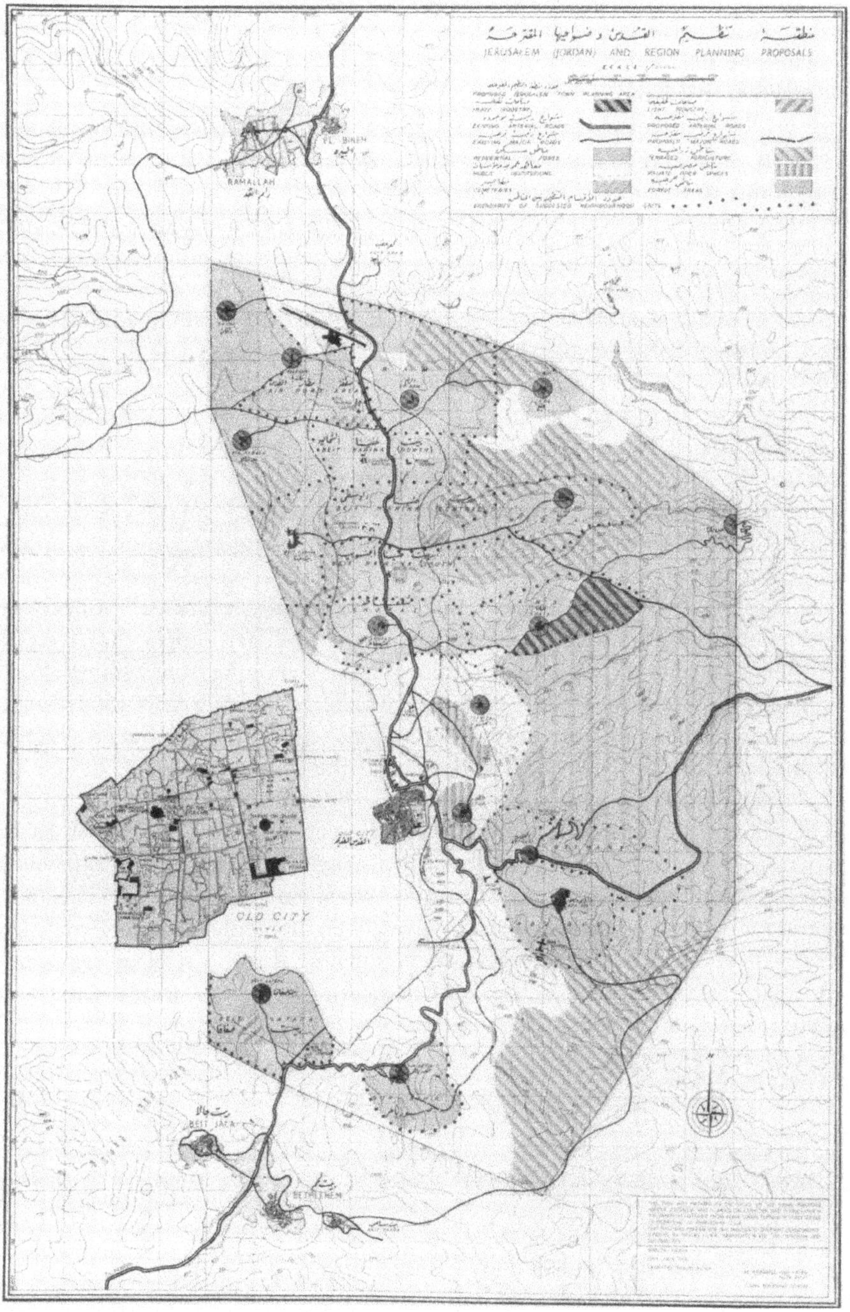

Figure 2.2 The proposed Master Plan of eastern Jerusalem (1964, scale 1:25,000)[19]

[19] H Kendall, 'Jerusalem (Jordan) and Region Planning Proposals' (The Office of the Town Planning Advisor – Jerusalem, 1964).

2.1.3. Israeli Military Orders and Land Seizures Post-1967

Following the 1967 war, the West Bank came under Israeli military rule, with every facet of life in the hands of the Military Governor of the West Bank. This marked a new era of intensified Israeli Zionist attempts to seize lands and displace the Palestinian native population using a web of military orders and legal amendments that continue to this day.[20] These orders, drawing upon existing West Bank, Gaza Strip and Mandatory Government laws and regulations, extended the legal and planning frameworks established by the Jordanian and Egyptian administrations prior to 1967.

Once in active control of the West Bank, the Israeli military administration leaned on the British Mandatory Government's emergency regulations during the first few years following the occupation, retaining the Jordanian Law where possible, in the interest of the military occupation.[21] In April 1971, military order No 418 was issued based on the Jordanian Law of 'Planning Cities, Villages, and Buildings No 79 of 1966'. The military order transferred the powers under the aforementioned law to the 'person in charge', which gave the military governor full authority in the decision-making process through the committees of the military administration.[22]

Amidst these developments, Jerusalem remained a critical concern for Palestinians, notwithstanding the enforcement of military orders that restricted their mobility within certain zones. An amendment stemming from Military Orders No 34 of 1967 and No 378 of 1970, specifically targeting access to designated regions, was promulgated in October 1971. This legislative adjustment effectively segregated the eastern part of Jerusalem from the southern expanse of the West Bank, encapsulating the Bedouin communities within its ambit.[23]

The military administration enacted orders such as Order No 544 of 1974 to tightly restrict livestock movement, requiring district office permits with defined stipulations and timings.[24] Violations, such as livestock entering restricted areas, led to penalties for owners.[25] These regulations severely disrupted the Bedouins' traditional practices of seasonal livestock migration, compelling them to relocate temporarily while leaving family members behind in their location for fear of being evicted if they vacated it.[26]

[20] M Benvenisti et al, *The West Bank Handbook: A Political Lexicon*, 1st edn (Westview Press, 1986) 196.

[21] Mandatory regulations and laws have been active since their implementation and continue to be utilised for the issuance of military orders. For instance, certain orders make use of legislation such as The Land Regulation Law (Public Purpose Acquisition) of 1943 to seize lands and authorise the occupation to restrict the use of the seized land for a duration of 17 years.

[22] Referred to as the Order of the Planning of Towns, Villages and Buildings (Judea and Samaria) (No 418) of the year 1971. West Bank, 'Publications, Commands, and Designation' (2 April 1972) 1000.

[23] West Bank, 'Publications, Commands, and Designation' (6 October 1971) 1136–37.

[24] Military Order No 544 of 1974 prohibited the movement, keeping, and grazing of livestock in several regions of the West Bank.

[25] West Bank, 'Publications, Commands, and Designation' (2 May 1974) 1325–26.

[26] A Heneiti, 'Bedouin Communities in Greater Jerusalem: Planning or Forced Displacement?' (2016) *Jerusalem Quarterly* 51, 55.

Table 2.2 presents several orders that were or are currently used to displace and control Bedouin life near Jerusalem. Military orders and amendments have been adjusted and updated to accommodate the colonisation process.

Table 2.2 Military orders impacting Bedouin communities near Jerusalem

Order No	Year	Notes
152	1967	Curfew in the Jordan Valley (lasted five years).
321	1969	Land confiscation authority for the Military Government.[27]
465	1972	Construction prohibition in place of buildings demolished by military orders.
488	1972	Restriction of movement during the night in certain areas.
489	1972	Movement restrictions in various areas of the eastern region of Jerusalem.
490	1972	Movement restrictions in various areas of the eastern region of Bethlehem.
496	1972	Movement restrictions in various areas of the eastern regions of the West Bank.
497	1973	Movement restrictions in the eastern regions of Jerusalem, Bethlehem and Hebron.
569	1974	Declaring state lands, or lands appropriated for 'security reasons'.

Military orders, incorporating spatial details via maps, were displayed in the offices of military governors, often situated in district centres, distant from the Bedouin-inhabited wilderness. Furthermore, the clarity and accessibility of these maps to those without specialised knowledge were markedly limited. The enactment of these orders and amendments took effect immediately upon their publication in the *Official Gazette* of the military administration.

In the contemporary context, military orders, amendments and plans are typically disseminated through the online platforms of the Israeli Civil Administration (ICA) or the Planning Department of Israel.[28] However, these websites often experience functionality issues. Notably, settlement plans are made available on the official website of the Israeli Ministry of Interior,[29] and can be accessed at the local office of the respective settlement.[30]

[27] This military order gave the military governor the right to confiscate lands for the 'public interest', which is not defined, and without compensation. For more information regarding the Land Confiscation, see R Shehadeh, *The West Bank and the Rule of Law* (The International Commission of Jurists, 1980).

[28] The website utilised by the Israeli Civil Administration (ICA) (www.pnim.gov.il) differs from the official publication platform of the occupation's Government (www.mavat.iplan.gov.il). It is noted that a majority of plans and orders concerning the West Bank are either unavailable or not easily accessible through the latter website.

[29] www.mavat.iplan.gov.il. This distribution mechanism for military-related information underscores the challenges posed by limited online accessibility and highlights the specific channels through which settlement plans are made public.

[30] Based on a deposit announcement for the detailed plan (510/14/1) for Kiryat Arba' settlement near Hebron.

The issuing of numerous military orders is an illustration of how these rules and their amendments are strategically and deliberately confusing, especially since sometimes these orders were not clear, and the maps were either illegible or inaccurate as they were hand-drawn. The Palestinians could do nothing to prevent the confiscation of their lands. According to a study published by the Arab Studies Society, between 1967 and 1980, about 100,000 dunams[31] were confiscated from the lands of 'Arab es-Sawahira,[32] and another 80,000 dunams from their lands near the Dead Sea.[33]

Since the beginning of the twenty-first century, the annexation wall has restricted Bedouin movement in the area. Further military orders prevented them from digging underground water wells and turned their lands into closed spaces, where their movement as nomads exposed them to displacement,[34] indirectly leading to forced sedentarisation in permanent locations, especially near the main roads where it is easier for Bedouin families to transport purchased water, which they need the ICA's permission to store in water cisterns.[35]

In summary, military orders have always played a vital role in land confiscation in the West Bank. The continuous imposition of amendments to 'The Law' is greatly revealing regarding the colonial projects to displace the Palestinians, especially the Bedouins, who live in areas designated by military orders as fire zones or natural reserves where grazing and cultivation are restricted or not allowed, even if this area has no special qualifications as a natural reserve. This has a significant impact on Bedouin economic activities.

In evaluating the challenges faced by Bedouin communities in interpreting maps, plans and military orders, it becomes evident that these documents, presented in both Hebrew and Arabic, were not inherently inaccessible due to language barriers alone. The crux of the difficulty lay in the technical language and sophisticated jargon embedded within these materials, which make the materials daunting, if not inaccessible, to individuals without the specialised knowledge necessary to interpret them. Maps, often scans of handwritten sketches, introduced a layer of ambiguity, exploited by military authorities to facilitate land confiscation and impose restrictions on Palestinian mobility. The authority and limited Arabic communication skills of Israeli officers enforcing these directives compounded the issue, creating a significant barrier for Bedouins attempting to defend their rights against land confiscations.

[31] A dunam is a unit of area measurement used in the region, equivalent to approximately 1,000 square metres, or about 0.247 acres. This traditional unit is commonly employed in land and property transactions.

[32] I Attiyah, *Musadarat al-aradi fi al-manatiq al-muhtalah 1967–1980 (Lands Confiscation in the Occupied Territories (1967–1980))* (Arab Studies Society, 1980) 40.

[33] ibid 31.

[34] Most Bedouins in the Jordan valley are prevented from digging wells, either by military orders or by the regulations imposed by Oslo Accords that prevent Palestinians in Area C from retrieving water without ICA permission, forcing them to purchase water from different resources, primarily Israeli water providers, which, notably, retrieve water from the Bedouin pastures.

[35] For background details on the colonial restrictions on water resources in Palestine, see Amnesty International, 'The Occupation of Water' (29 November 2017), www.amnesty.org/en/latest/campaigns/2017/11/the-occupation-of-water.

This practice underscores a broader strategy within the framework of settler colonialism, leveraging ambiguous or misleading maps as a tool to displace and restrict native populations, despite the existence of precise mapping technologies dating back to the British Mandate. Such methodologies not only undermined the traditional livelihoods of Palestinian families, but also posed severe constraints on Bedouin communities, necessitating vast pastures for grazing, thus exacerbating their vulnerability to land takeovers.

2.2. FROM NOMADIC ROUTES TO STRUCTURED PATHS: THE BEDOUIN JOURNEY AMIDST CHANGING PLANNING PARADIGMS

The Zionist narrative has traditionally portrayed Palestine from a spatial perspective, encapsulated in the slogan, 'A land without a people for a people without a land'. This framing suggested that Palestine was a barren wasteland awaiting development. However, from the 1970s onwards, Zionist discourse shifted to focus on the term 'Judean Desert', particularly when discussing settlements in the eastern West Bank. This reframing has been strategically adopted by Israeli authorities to promote its extensive land appropriation in the West Bank for its ongoing settlement expansion with the consequences of this appropriation shouldered disproportionately by the Bedouin populations.

In establishing these Israeli settlements, the topography and natural features of the land were altered. Often using red soil to facilitate agricultural development, many settlements also built retaining walls to prevent erosion and planted pine forests to create a closed area that restricted the movement of Bedouin livestock.[36]

The introduction of red soil in the establishment of colonial settlements in the eastern region of Jerusalem symbolises a deliberate transformation of the land, reflecting the colonial intent to assert control and permanence. Prioritising agricultural advancements over traditional Bedouin pastoral methods not only disturbs the ecological equilibrium but also leads to the economic and cultural marginalisation of the native Bedouin community. In essence, the soil becomes a tool of territorial claim, highlighting settler dominance while diminishing the Bedouin's ancestral ties to the land.

Despite efforts to plant deserted regions in Jerusalem and southern Palestine, these areas are not true prototypical deserts but rather vast wilderness areas and semi-arid regions, which means that the lands receive limited rainfall but can support some vegetation. These areas have shrubs, low-growing plants and occasionally trees, especially near water sources. The soil, while not as fertile as in more temperate regions, can be cultivated if adequately irrigated.

[36] This observation is evident in the study area, where settlements have altered the surface soil layers to agricultural soils like *Terra Rossa*, categorising the regions as agricultural (rural) from a legal perspective, thereby restricting Bedouins from grazing livestock in these designated areas. On this point, see United Nations, 'Bedouins in the Occupied Palestinian Territory – UNDP Report' (Question of Palestine, 2013), www.un.org/unispal/document/auto-insert-195392.

The notion of the Judean Desert is inaccurate and serves only to incorporate biblical elements into the colonial dialogue concerning the colonisation of the region and the ecological discourse about restoration. Historically, Bedouins have used these areas to graze their livestock, and the falsehood of Palestine being deserted and uninhabited is used as a justification and strategic misrepresentation for settler colonial objectives.

Lefebvre's spatial concepts revolve around the notion that space is a product of social processes influenced by political, social and economic dynamics. Within the framework of Zionist colonisation in Palestine, the West Bank and territories seized in 1948 are viewed as a unified spatial entity. This parallels Lefebvre's concept of 'Representational Space', characterised by a lived environment intricately embedded in the complex symbols and histories of its inhabitants.

The transformation of the existing road network exemplifies how infrastructure projects, presented as mere developmental efforts, often mask deeper political motives that adversely affect the Bedouin communities in Jerusalem's eastern wilderness. Imagine a network of roads suddenly changing: not expanding per se, but 'improving'. To an outsider, this could be perceived as merely modernisation, but under the surface, these changes are part of a bigger picture, a grand plan stitched together over the years. Fast forward a decade, and it is not just about a road in Jerusalem anymore; it is a sprawling plan linking Tel-Aviv to the Bedouin pastures near Jericho, leaving the destruction of the Bedouin lived space as a minor result, collateral damage within the process of 'urbanisation' and 'development'.

For the Bedouins, it is not just about international borders or politics; it is a matter of identity and lived experience. They remember a time when their lands spanned both sides of the 1948 boundary, long before political projects carved them up. But as their surroundings shift, their experiences, rooted in Lefebvre's spatial triad, change as well. It is not just about where they can move; it is about how they feel, how they remember, and how they live every day. In this evolving landscape, the Bedouins are not just witnesses. They are participants in a story where the setting constantly changes, altering the narrative of their very identity.

However, while the land might form a geographical continuum, international law sees these spaces differently. The Palestinian territories occupied post-1967 are distinct and separate from those taken in 1948. The international law of occupation emphasises that such an occupation does not grant sovereignty; it is temporary and provisional.[37] Israel's strategy, however, seems to blur these distinctions (as also discussed in chapter three of this volume by Bana Abu Zuluf and Ahmad Amara). Through plans and projects, the territories are blended into a single entity, an indirect form of annexation. This extends beyond being an infrastructural change; it is a reflective statement, challenging the globally accepted norms set by international law.

[37] The ICRC elaborates on the principles of international law of occupation, particularly the Geneva Conventions, which state that occupation is a temporary situation and does not transfer sovereignty over territories. See www.icrc.org/en/doc/resources/documents/misc/634kfc.htm.

Various urban plans implemented during the Israeli military occupation era were always crucial in achieving territorial control; the development of such plans depends on a hierarchical planning system to fulfil integrated and connected colonial development. These plans range from regulated plans subjected to official laws and bylaws to development programmes and governmental visions that indirectly dictate the guidelines for developing Palestinian communities. The Israeli military planning decisions for the Palestinian communities have led to zoning and planning projects that predominantly accommodate the expansion of Jewish settlements. This biased approach often indirectly influences the developmental trajectory of Palestinian communities, positioning them as secondary to the primary objective of settlement expansion.

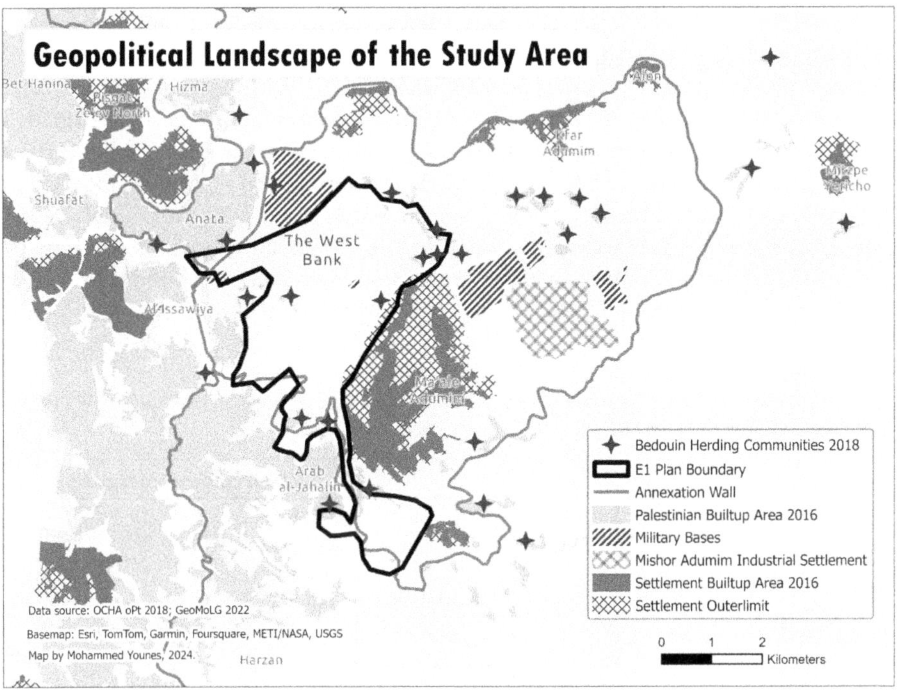

Figure 2.3 Geopolitical landscape of the research area showing the scattering of Bedouin communities within the colonial geopolitical spatial settings[38]

In the following sections, different urban plans will be discussed to analyse the displacement of Bedouin people and communities in Jerusalem's eastern region, from the regional zoning plans to the outline plans that have facilitated comprehensive colonial plans over recent decades.

[38] Author as the cartographer; data layers obtained from the Palestinian Authority's Ministry of Local Governance (MoLG); Bedouin herding communities data points collected by OCHA oPt in 2018.

2.2.1. Historical Prelude: Urban Planning under British Mandate and Jordanian Regulations

To fully grasp Palestine's planning landscape, it is essential to acknowledge the continuity of British Mandate-era zoning and planning regulations by all authorities post-1948. This discussion focuses on the West Bank, particularly the Jordanian rule (1948–67) planning framework and its evolution under Military Order No 418. This order exacerbated the marginalisation of Bedouins by embedding their rights deeper within a bureaucratic and militarised structure.[39] The Jordanian planning hierarchy mirrored the Mandatory system, structured into national, regional and local levels, governed by Law No 79. At its apex stood the Higher Planning Council (HPC), supported by District Planning Commissions (DPC) and Local Planning Commissions (LPC), the latter of which included representatives from municipal or village councils.[40]

However, this planning system was not inclusive; the Bedouin communities were conspicuously invisible as district and local planning commissions, though designated to oversee their lands, were physically distant, stationed in the heart of the district or village, and lacked the necessary insight. This geographical separation meant that the needs and realities of the Bedouins on the outskirts were not accurately represented, aggravating the marginalisation of an already sidelined population.

Table 2.3 shows a comparison between the planning stakeholders under Jordanian Law (No 79) and Israeli Colonial Occupation (Military Order No 418) in the West Bank.

Table 2.3 Comparative analysis of planning stakeholders under Jordanian Law No 79 (1966) and Israeli Military Order No 418 (1971) in the West Bank[41]

	Jordanian rule			**Israeli colonial occupation**		
	Article of Law No 79	**Number**	**Composition**	**Article of Military Order No 418**	**Number**	**Composition**
Higher Planning Council (HPC)	5	1	Minister; civil servants; representative of mayors; heads of construction and housing councils	4.A	1	Military officers appointed by the military commander

(continued)

[39] The Palestinian Authority Planning System operated under Jordanian Law No 79 until 2011 when a new planning and building system was introduced. This new system, while maintaining the fundamental planning hierarchy, addressed gaps left by the Jordanian law and introduced flexibility in handling detailed building and planning issues. However, it did not offer direct protection for the Bedouin communities.

[40] A Coon, *Town Planning Under Military Occupation: An Examination of the Law and Practice of Town Planning in the Occupied West Bank* (Dartmouth, 1992) 42.

[41] ibid.

Table 2.3 *(Continued)*

	Jordanian rule			Israeli colonial occupation		
	Article of Law No 79	Number	Composition	Article of Military Order No 418	Number	Composition
District commissions	8	3	Governor; district attorney; district representatives of Ministry of Works; Health Department and Central Planning Department; local representative	2.2	0	(Powers transferred to HPC)
Local commissions: • municipal areas	9	25	Municipal council (elected)	5	25	Municipal council (appointed or elected)
• villages		87	Village council (elected)	2.4	0	(Powers transferred to committees of HPC called planning village committees)

To comprehend the Bedouin displacement within the broader urban planning framework, it is essential to understand the types of development plans employed. The planning hierarchy is largely influenced by the plan's complexity; higher-level authorities deal with broader, less detailed visions.[42] The complexities of the planning hierarchy, with its focus on broad, strategic visions by higher-level authorities, often overlooks the specific needs and rights of Bedouin communities, leading to policies that exacerbate their displacement and marginalisation within the urban landscape.

At the regional level, land use zones are established following extensive surveys and socio-economic analyses, setting out the foundational requirements for

[42] ibid.

community development.[43] These zones inform the overarching plans for permitted developments. Progressing to the municipal level, we encounter the 'outline plan', also known as the masterplan, a term not mentioned in Law No 79 but reflecting a modern approach to more comprehensive development projects and detailed zoning to meet contemporary societal needs. This plan homes in on particular development initiatives within municipal boundaries, adhering to the broader strategies set by the regional framework. 'Detailed plans' take specificity a notch higher, evolving from the outline plans to include in-depth technicalities such as the siting of roads and allocation of facilities.

Interestingly, there are disparities across planning systems. For instance, while the British Mandatory Planning System in Palestine bypassed the concept of a regional plan,[44] which was introduced later by Jordan, the Jordanians missed out on the national plan, which the Israeli system integrated. A national plan is a macro perspective,[45] layering various national policies affecting all levels and encompassing elements like public transport frameworks or national park designs.[46] This level of planning directly impacted the Bedouin lands as they were seen as empty patches on planners' maps; they became areas easily reconstructed and reshaped by those in power, especially when marked as 'state lands'. Drawing from Lefebvre, these areas were subjected to a dominant spatial practice, often sidelining the lived experiences of the Bedouins.

The Bedouins were indirectly excluded from the Jordanian system of planning due to a discrepancy between their customary land use and the formal land ownership structure enforced by state governance. This exclusion, rooted in the absence of official recognition for nomadic land rights, allowed for the reclassification of Bedouin lands as state territory, leading to displacement and marginalisation. The impact persists today as traditional claims clash with modern legal frameworks and Bedouins continue to face challenges in asserting their rights within state-centric development plans that often disregard their nomadic lifestyle and needs.[47]

[43] The regional plans can be influenced by political agendas, whether they are local agendas focusing on specific districts or a broader national agenda aimed at guiding the country towards particular development directions such as industrial or agricultural growth. See A Abu-Ayyash, 'Israeli Regional Planning Policy in the Occupied Territories' (1976) 5 *Journal of Palestine Studies* 83.

[44] Regional plans serve as a strategic guide for the development of a specific region, considering its unique social, economic and environmental attributes. More comprehensive than local plans, it aims to harmonise development across various municipalities within the region.

[45] A national plan is the most comprehensive level of planning, incorporating the country's long-term developmental goals across all sectors, including transportation, infrastructure, economy and environmental conservation. It provides a general approach to influencing both regional and local planning to ensure consistency with national objectives.

[46] The PA's planning framework lacks a national plan as mandated by law. Nonetheless, in 2009, the PA formed a ministerial committee to initiate the Spatial National Plan project, comprising multiple layers (partial national plans) with specific emphasis on land administration and conservation of natural resources: 'Envisioning Palestine', www.undp.org/papp/publications/envisioning-palestine-2025.

[47] The Bedouins' exclusion from the Jordanian planning system, rooted in their non-registration of land and the subsequent designation of their pastures as state lands, is a legacy of Jordanian surveying practices in the West Bank during the 1960s. These practices established the basis for land ownership that continues to inform legal and planning procedures to this day, underscoring the long-term impact on Bedouin land rights and usage.

Finally, the Jordanian system included a 'detailed-outline plan' for smaller towns and villages, reducing both infrastructure specifics and broader zoning regulations.[48] There was, however, a gap in the Jordanian planning system: areas outside town boundaries did not have designated local planning authorities. Instead, they fell under broader district, or HPC, committees.[49] This absence of direct representation further marginalised Bedouin communities, leaving their concerns unaddressed and perpetuating their displacement.

Table 2.4 shows a comparison between the planning authorities under Jordanian Law (No 79 of 1966) and Israeli Colonial Occupation (Military Order No 418 of 1971) in the West Bank.

A crucial aspect of the displacement and marginalisation of Bedouin communities is how they were often caught in a jurisdictional limbo. They fell through the cracks between local and district planning authorities, as well as under direct military jurisdictions, especially in designated fire zones. The complex interplay of various planning bodies created a convoluted permit-issuing process. The preparation, approval and appeal stages of this process were fraught with ambiguities and bureaucratic hurdles, further complicating the Bedouins' ability to secure rights to their lands and maintain their traditional way of life. The absence of a tailored planning approach that recognised their unique needs led to the Bedouins being marginalised within the system, a situation that has had lasting effects on their communities.

2.2.2. The West Bank Interlude, 1967–94: Shifts in Planning Dynamics

The period spanning from 1967 to 1994 marked a critical juncture in the history of Palestine, particularly in terms of urban and spatial planning dynamics. This era was characterised by heightened Israeli military intervention, reshaping the developmental landscape and directly impacting the lives and futures of Palestinian Bedouin communities. The British Plan of 1942 (RJ/5) was a key regional plan used in the area that included Jerusalem, Bethlehem, Jericho, Ramallah and Hebron.[50] This plan designated most of the eastern regions of the planning area as 'natural reserves', which subsequently restricted the movement and activities of Bedouins.

Although the British Plan disappeared after the British withdrawal from Palestine in 1948, it was rediscovered by the Israeli military authorities shortly before 1980. However, only the plan's regulations were available at that time. It was used as a basis for Israeli military orders, and the Bedouin areas were the most affected by this matter.[51] The Bedouin communities were among the least represented in planning

[48] Coon (n 40) 45.

[49] ibid 43. Typically, detailed plans adhere to regional and district outline plans, but in cases where they do not, the HPC relies on their granted authority through law and military orders to create independent plans. However, even if a detailed plan must follow a regional plan, there are typically no provisions for the details within it.

[50] Plan RJ/5 and Plan S15 were the two regional plans issued for Palestine during the British Mandate Era in 1942, covering most of the country's built-up areas in Jerusalem and Samaria Mandatory districts.

[51] Coon (n 40) 70. The plan is noted to be used as a previous plan for a new plan (No 57/1633) approved in December 2020 for a colonial service project in Wadi Kidron near the Dead Sea in *Arab Abu-Ibaid* pastures.

Table 2.4 Comparative analysis of planning authorities under Jordanian Law and Israeli military occupation[52]

	Jordanian rule					Israeli colonial occupation				
	Development plans				Building permits	Development plans				Building permits
	Regional	Outline	Detailed	Parcellation		Regional	Outline	Detailed	Parcellation	
High Planning Council	A	A	–	–	Appeal	A	A	A	(A)[2]	(Appeal)[3]
Central Planning Department	P	(P)[1]	–	–	–	P	(P)[5]	(P)[5]	–	Grant (villages)
District Commission	–	–	A	–	Appeal	–	–	–	–	–
Local Commissions										
• municipalities	–	P	P	A	Grant	–	P	P	A	(Grant)[4]
• villages	–	P	P	A	Grant	–	–	–	–	–
Private developers	–	–	–	–	Submit	–	–	–	P	Submit

P Authority preparing the plan.
A Authority approving the plan.
1 Preparation of outline plans for municipalities 'where no such plan exists' (Law No 79 – Article 7.1).
2 Municipalities have been directed to submit parcellation plans as 'detailed plans' to HPC for their approval.
3 The theoretical duty of the HPC is to consider appeals to them by district commissions (which have been abolished).
4 Municipalities have been directed to forward most applications other than those for residential development to the Central Planning Department for their decision.
5 Villages only.

[52] ibid 44.

documents and land registrations. This oversight placed them at the mercy of military officers, which exploited the lack of comprehensive plans and accurate maps. Consequently, this gave military authorities greater latitude to 'legally' undertake new projects on Bedouin grazing lands. While the urban built-up areas had detailed plans which allowed for quicker modifications to the circumstances imposed by the military orders, the existence of any plan meant that it could be used as a basis for the population to try and object to the planned colonial projects directly to the local committee, but this was not the case for the Bedouin areas. These areas, typically situated far from regions covered by planning frameworks, faced permanent colonial limitations. These not only restricted their ability to secure building permits but also challenged their capacity to appeal proposed plans. According to Military Order No 418, final decisions in such matters rested with the high-ranking military officials in the HPC.

Under the overarching authority of Military Order No 418, regional councils were established exclusively for the Israeli settlements erected in the West Bank post-1967. The councils took it upon themselves to devise regional plans, extending beyond the immediate settlement boundaries and encroaching into areas likely owned by Palestinian villages, some of which may not even have been registered in the outdated surveying plans. Decision-making ultimately resided with the military commanders of the HPC. This was even more pronounced for the Bedouin territories, which were often overlooked in formal surveys.

These settlements functioned under regional plans formulated by these colonial regional councils. The planning committees incorporated varied stakeholders, including representatives from official Israeli governmental bodies, neighbouring settler councils in the West Bank and, in some instances during the 1980s, the Settlement Division of the World Zionist Organization (WZO). Notably, the labelling on some plans implied that these regional councils either emanated from the WZO's Settlement Division or collaborated closely with it.[53]

This approach possibly demonstrates an undeclared annexation strategy. Israel's treatment of the territories occupied post-1967 subtly integrates them into its broader developmental agenda, seemingly going beyond mere military oversight. This strategy comes to light in the specifics of these regional plans. The boundaryless approach in developmental reflections disregards international legal perspectives on the occupation. A case in point is the Jordan Valley Council Development Plan of March 1983, authored by the WZO. It envisions a comprehensive water network using the outcomes of the colonial 'Sea of Galilee – Jordan Valley' plan. This seamless integration was also evident in the infrastructural planning.[54]

In terms of impact on Bedouin communities, these plans often set aside Bedouin territories as 'available lands', primarily because they lay outside the demarcated Arab local council borders, informed by outdated mapping. Significantly, there was

[53] World Zionist Organization Settlement Division – Northern Region, Jordan Valley Regional Council, 'Jordan Valley Regional Council Development Plan' (March 1983) Israel State Archives, Archival No א-4153/10.

[54] ibid 86.

a designated category of 'Arable Lands', primarily Bedouin grazing areas, perceived as vacant Palestinian territories. These areas, spanning tens of thousands of dunams, were visualised as potential agricultural hubs to strengthen the settlers' economies. Such grand strategies, shielded by dense military orders, often concluded in new colonial projects which materialised years later.

The Bedouin communities living near Jerusalem were greatly affected by Israeli plans for the region, such as the 1967 plan to survey water resources and the Jordan Valley Regional Council Development Plan of 1983 to develop agricultural sectors in colonies.[55] The latter plan allocated a significant amount of water – 15 million cubic metres – to settlers in the Northern Dead Sea Region alone, which harmed the water sources of Bedouin pastures.[56] In a further example, the colonial tourist plan for the Jordan Valley in 1985 disrupted Bedouin communities by increasing traffic and circulation between settlements.[57] Finally, the Allon Plan (1970) and the Territorial Compromise Plan (1976) defined strips of Bedouin pastures as part of the eastern region of Jerusalem, which worsened the situation for these communities.[58]

Overall, the combination of these plans and others like them had a significant and lasting impact on the Bedouin communities living in the region. As the new plans deemed their territories as available lands under different categories, the Bedouins witnessed the gradual appropriation of their pastures for settler projects, undermining their traditional practices and imposing new colonial impositions on lands they once roamed freely.

A partial colonial plan known as Plan 1/82 was submitted for objections based on the Jordanian Law in 1982. Although the main aim of this plan was to construct Israeli settlements around Jerusalem in the West Bank areas, it cited Jordanian Law No 79 as a legal basis and defined itself as an amendment to the RJ/5 British Scheme. However, parts of the plan had already been implemented or were in the process of being implemented, and Law No 79 does not permit regional plans to be amended, let alone allow partial regional plans.[59]

The plan covered a five-kilometre belt encircling the original municipality's borders, which remains unchanged to this day. The eastern zones were designated for future development and nature reserves, which were located at the upper end of valleys flowing towards the Dead Sea and Jordan Valley. Such designation affects the movement of the Bedouin communities in nearby areas during the winter, as their mobility is curtailed by natural barriers such as water torrents from the mountains, compounded by military restrictions on access through specific wide zones

[55] World Zionist Organization Settlement Division – Northern Region, Jordan Valley Regional Council, 'Development of Water Resources in the West Jordan Valley' (1967) Israel State Archives, Archival No 4226/4- פ.

[56] World Zionist Organization Settlement Division – Northern Region, Jordan Valley Regional Council (n 53).

[57] A Niv et al, 'A Plan for Selected Projects in the Field of Tourism in Jordan Valley' (June 1985) Israel State Archives, Archival No 54137/7-גל.

[58] The Allon Plan was a colonial plan issued directly after the 1967 war to partition the West Bank between Israel and Jordan. Despite its non-implementation in a formal capacity, this strategy laid the groundwork for subsequent colonial planning actions, serving as a foundational reference in the strategic planning and territorial negotiations that followed.

[59] ibid 185.

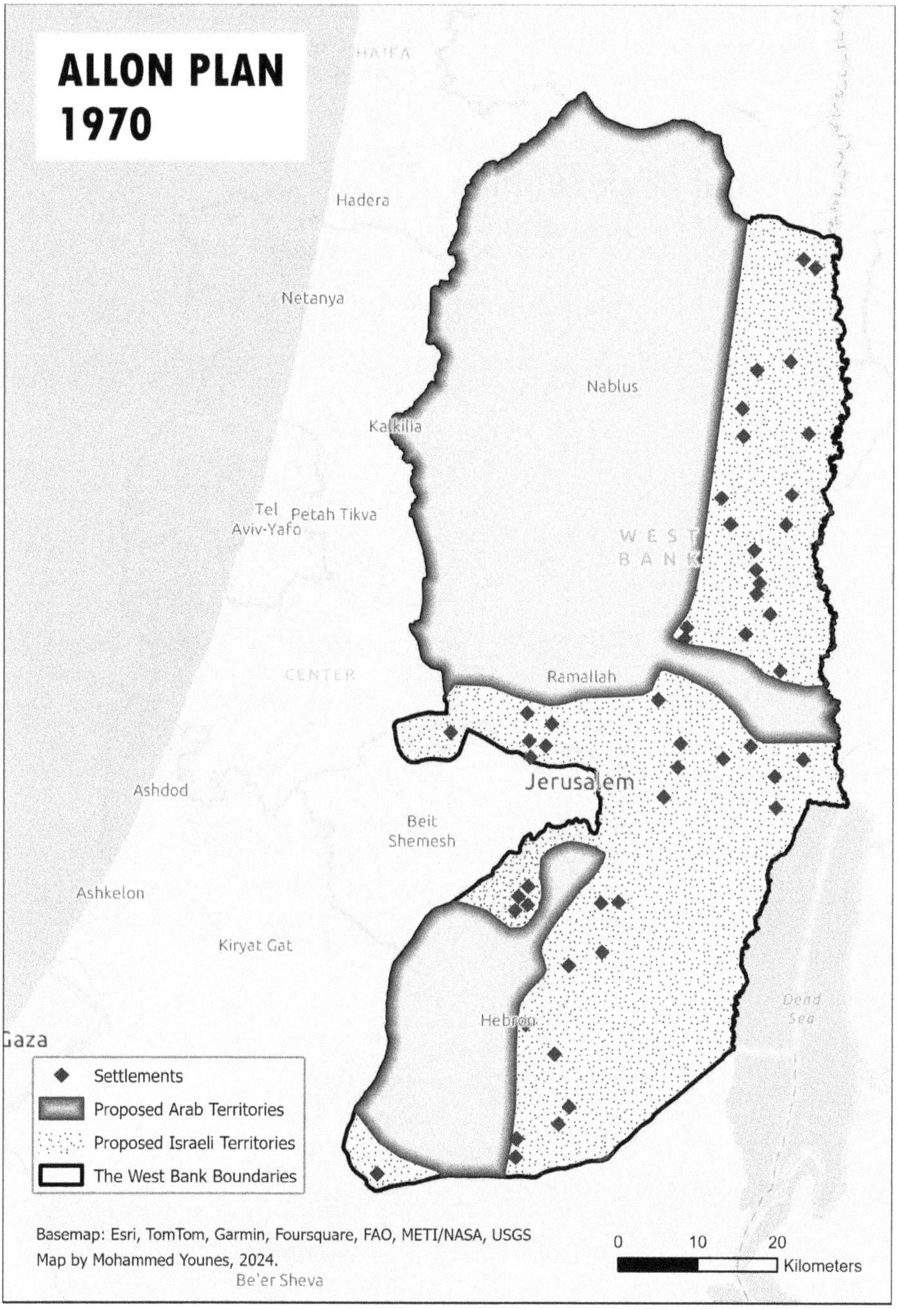

Figure 2.4 The Allon Plan (1970), outlining proposed territorial divisions in the West Bank[60]

[60] The map has been redrawn by the author based on Allon's conceptual proposals as described in Y Allon, 'Israel: The Case for Defensible Borders' (1976) 55(1) Foreign Affairs 38. Given that the Allon Plan was neither formally adopted by the Israeli government nor published with definitive borders, the plan's strategic principles have resulted in varying interpretations and representations.

or dwelling within them, thus narrowing their safe habitation options. Areas not specifically addressed in the plan were earmarked for agricultural use, albeit without explicit objectives or explanations for these designations.[61]

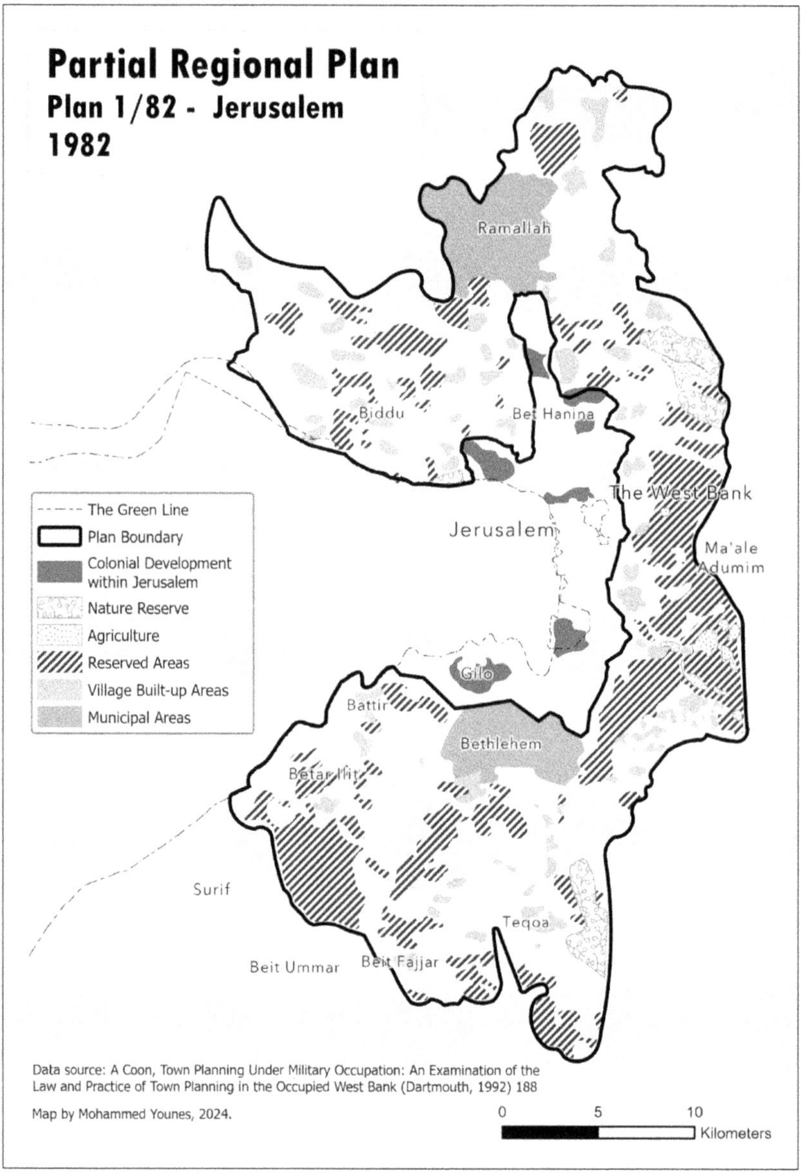

Figure 2.5 Partial Regional Plan (1/82) of 1982[62]

[61] Coon (n 40) 187.
[62] This map has been redrawn by the author, based on the depiction of the same plan in Coon (n 40) 188.

The Roads Plan No 50 (1984), proposed by the colonial authorities, aimed to connect the Israeli settlements to regional roads and provide them with easy access to the rest of the Israeli road network. Despite the massive objections to this plan over the years, none were taken seriously, as the HPC and the Israeli High Court justified the plan based on Hague Regulations that the actions of the occupation power can only be justifiable in terms of the security of its forces or the interests of the local population. These points are subject to debate when it comes to the objectives of different Israeli colonial plans.

The implementation of these plans had devastating consequences for the local population. Later, the construction works of such projects resulted in wide land confiscation, affecting the surrounding communities during the construction phases. Furthermore, these projects exposed them to continuous pollution from the planned highways when implemented, which were presented as part of detailed plans.

The plan's impact on the Bedouin communities was significant, as it disrupted their traditional way of life and movement in the region, affecting their access to water sources and grazing lands. Different colonial plans proposed during the 1970s and 1980s, including Roads Plan No 50, had no basis in town planning law as they were based on previous plans that were not approved by Jordanian rule.[63] These plans were used to restrict the movement and suspend the development of urban and Bedouin communities. Implementing these plans had long-lasting effects on the Bedouin communities in the region and their relationship with the land.[64]

For several years, Plan No 50 became a tool for the Israeli military authorities to routinely deny building and road construction permits to the Palestinians in the West Bank. One regulation applied to the proposed and 'approved' roads in the plan states that the road lines may be moved up to 1.5 kilometres, which established a vast three-kilometre buffer zone,[65] freezing and disabling the Palestinian municipalities' projects and plans for years until implementing these road sections.[66] All of this functioned within an unjust colonial planning system, geared primarily towards expanding Israeli settlements and cementing Israeli control over the occupied Palestinian territories.

In the eastern environs of Jerusalem, the plan included proposed roads in the Bedouin areas and nearby urban and rural areas. The planning policy featured a three-kilometre buffer zone, which significantly affected the development direction of the Palestinian built-up areas and their connectivity with the Bedouin areas. Moreover, this policy formed an enclave in which the Bedouins were already suffering from the Israeli-imposed restrictions on both fire zones and settlement construction.

[63] The Jordanian Town and Village Planning Law of 1966 does not deal with the creation of road system plans.

[64] For more details on the Road Plan No 50 of 1984, see A Shehadeh et al 'Israeli Proposed Road Plan for the West Bank' (West Bank Affiliate of the International Commission of Jurists, Ramallah, 1984).

[65] Coon (n 40) 195.

[66] The plan was approved without any modifications in April 1990, despite the mass objections made when the plan was placed on deposit from 1984 until 1988.

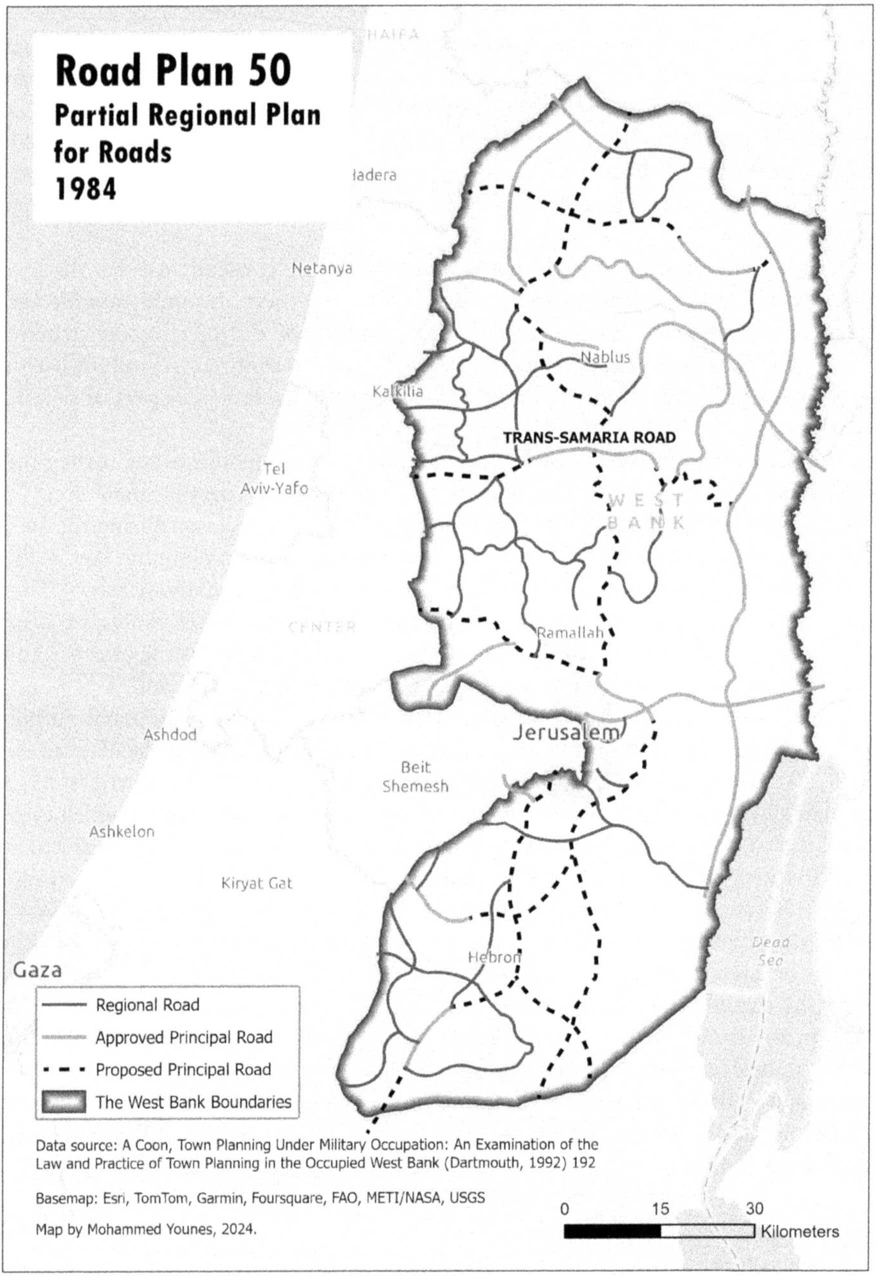

Figure 2.6 Regional Partial Plan for Roads (Road Plan 50, 1984)[67]

[67] This map has been redrawn by the author, based on the depiction of the same plan in Coon (n 40) 192.

Many zones in the plan are sparsely populated. With the implementation of planned roads, these zones were turned into spatially isolated zones. For example, the plan shows an 'approved' vertical road in the eastern regions of the West Bank, which was the basis for the colonial Highway 90 later. Most of the areas in the Jordan Valley, where the east of this road is proximate to the borders with Jordan, were declared military and firing zones through tens of military orders after 1967.

Most of these areas were populated with Bedouins, who use the land as pastures. As such, most of them were indirectly displaced to the western side of the road through military orders claiming firing zones and natural reserves, while the main goals of the firing zones were to banish the Bedouin presence and to disturb their grazing activities.[68]

These roads not only curtailed the grazing areas essential to the Bedouins but also confined the areas designated for the urban growth of the Palestinian communities in the West Bank. Additionally, the wide three-kilometre buffer zones around these roads led to the loss of tens of thousands of dunams previously used for Palestinian agriculture in the region.

In conclusion, none of these regional plans took into account or gave due consideration to the Bedouin's established presence in the region, often characterising their lands as vacant tracts. Notably, based on several of these plans and regulations, large swathes of the region were planned as natural reserves, further sidelining the Bedouin communities. Such planning policies were applied in various regions of Palestine where Bedouins have historically resided or continue to live, including areas like An-Naqab, Masafer Yatta, and the eastern outskirts of Jerusalem.

2.2.3. Metropolitan Jerusalem Plans: The Imposition of the Israeli Planning System from 1980 Onwards

In 1980, the Knesset officially approved the Jerusalem Law, which declared the city the complete and united capital,[69] consolidating its de facto control over the city for the preceding 13 years. Before that, after the occupation of the eastern part of the city in 1967, a master plan was proposed in 1968. Although this early master plan never received official ratification, it laid the groundwork for subsequent strategic planning efforts focused on extending Jerusalem's boundaries eastward. Specifically, the 1968 plan earmarked the eastern territories as open areas, effectively precluding any potential for Palestinian community expansion within these regions.

For the next three decades, colonial town planning practices did not provide any outline plan sufficient to meet the natural growth of the Palestinian built-up areas in Jerusalem. However, the military authorities and Jerusalem Municipality

[68] Military Orders No 89, 90 and 96 issued in 1972 serve as exemplars of the measures taken to regulate and curtail Palestinian activities within the Jordan Valley.

[69] United Nations, 'The Status of Jerusalem' (1997) 13,www.un.org/unispal/wp-content/uploads/2016/07/The-Status-of-Jerusalem-Engish-199708.pdf.

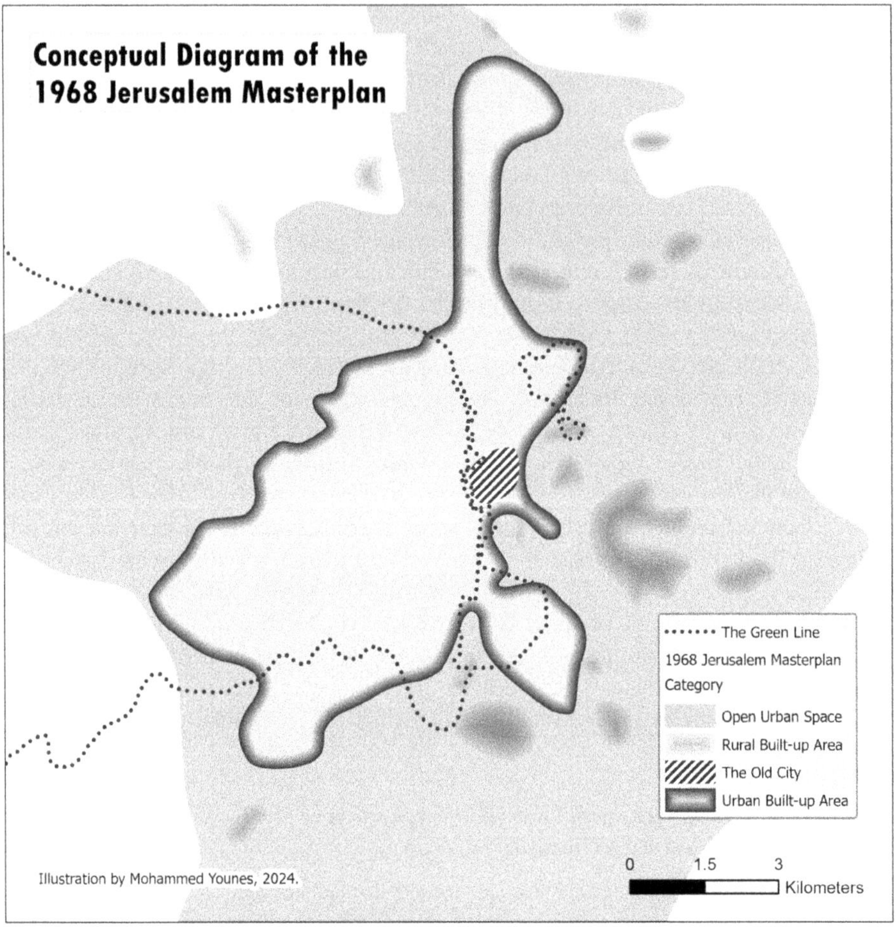

Figure 2.7 A conceptual representation of the 1968 Jerusalem Masterplan, illustrating key land use categories[70]

issued several partial detailed plans,[71] with no clear integration of these plans in the planning process between these detailed plans and the Palestinian growth, while the construction and development of their surrounding settlements continued. For Bedouins of the eastern region of Jerusalem, this approach translated into a plethora of small-scale, detailed plans aimed at facilitating colonial expansion, imposing a composition of fragmented colonial vision on Bedouin grazing lands through the

[70] Illustration based on the original 1968 Jerusalem Master Plan from the Jerusalem Municipality Archive, created by the author.

[71] A partial detailed plan refers to a targeted plan focused on a distinct section of a town, distinguishing it from comprehensive detailed plans that encompass the entire town. Such plans may or may not adhere to the broader stipulations set out in the outline plan, focusing instead on localised development objectives or specific area enhancements.

systematic limitation of traditional Bedouin activities, allowing for smoother colonial development on their territories.

Nonetheless, a metropolitan outline plan for Jerusalem was approved in 1977. It did not officially include the areas surrounding Jerusalem inside the West Bank borders. However, it provided a vision for the planned expansion and growth of the city towards the east, influencing the plans issued later for the expansion and development of the main regional roads serving the city. Later, Jerusalem's officially approved metropolitan plans remained within the same boundaries; however, the vision plans for 'Greater Jerusalem' ambitiously encompassed all neighbouring areas, including significant projected alterations in Bedouin territories.[72] These expansive visions, while not rooted in formal legal statutes, were disseminated through studies and proposals by government bodies and municipal initiatives, reflecting a strategic intent beyond the scope of ratified legal frameworks.[73]

A few years later, in 1994, the think tank Jerusalem Institute for Israel Studies and several planning and research centres released a joint study. This study involved the creation of a master plan and programme for the Jerusalem Metropolitan Area. In 1995 it was approved and supported by many government ministries and authorities, including the Jerusalem Municipality and the ICA.[74] This plan was rooted in an inter-ministerial framework with the Jerusalem Municipality that was established in 1986. This collaboration sought to legally integrate results from both the ICA and the Ministry of Interior.

Initially, a main objectives of this plan was to control the diverse landscape and water resources of the eastern areas, symbolised by connecting the urban axis from Gush Dan (the Tel Aviv metropolitan area) to Jerusalem, thereby creating an urban corridor linking the Jordanian capital of Amman and Tel Aviv.[75] However, an examination of the plan, especially when overlaying the current locations of Bedouin communities, reveals its colonial narrative. The proposal gravely impacts the Bedouin community, primarily through the annexation of their pastoral lands for new settlement development around Jerusalem. In addition to the political and military restrictions placed on the Palestinian Bedouin movement, the designation of

[72] The metropolitan plans merged projects and strategic plans from the provisions of the current and future plans at the three levels of planning equally, eg the Jerusalem Vision Plan of 2050 covered the major colonial projects of the municipality of Ma'ale Adumim settlement. Furthermore, the airport project in the 2050 Plan is based on the provisions and proposals from the Oslo Accords during the 1990s. At the same time, several projects are based on national outline plans for transportation, industry, and the economy.

[73] This approach facilitates a strategic evaluation of prospective developments, enabling a forward-looking perspective without necessitating immediate legal or policy alterations. Such a methodology is particularly relevant in a colonial context, given that it permits an exploration of expansionist strategies and urban development scenarios in contentious territories without the direct implication of state endorsement or the immediate enactment of statutory changes.

[74] S Cohen and A Mazor, Jerusalem Institute for Israel Studies, 'Jerusalem Metropolis' (December 1994) Israel State Archives, Archival No 62114/3-גל.

[75] The concept of connecting Amman and Tel Aviv is based on creating a political symbolic connection between the two large metropolitan areas to form a unique 'Conurbation'. This aims to include all the built-up areas between Tel-Aviv and Amman, including Jerusalem areas. The result is a complex form of a 'Megacity' with a combined population of around 10 million, granting it political-economic privileges, especially with the transportation plan to expand the railways from Jerusalem to Jericho near the borders with Jordan.

certain territories as protected green areas, or afforestation, further restricted developmental opportunities for the Palestinian communities. The plan's underpinning and promotion of colonial policy are evident in its prioritisation of land acquisition for colonial settlement development, clearly sidelining the needs and rights of the Bedouin community.[76]

In the map presented, construction zones are proposed, highlighting the region's physical traits. It is observed that the entry zone's development capacity is constrained in comparison to adjacent areas. Palestinian communities are labelled as 'traditional' villages, yet there is no acknowledgement of Bedouin communities.

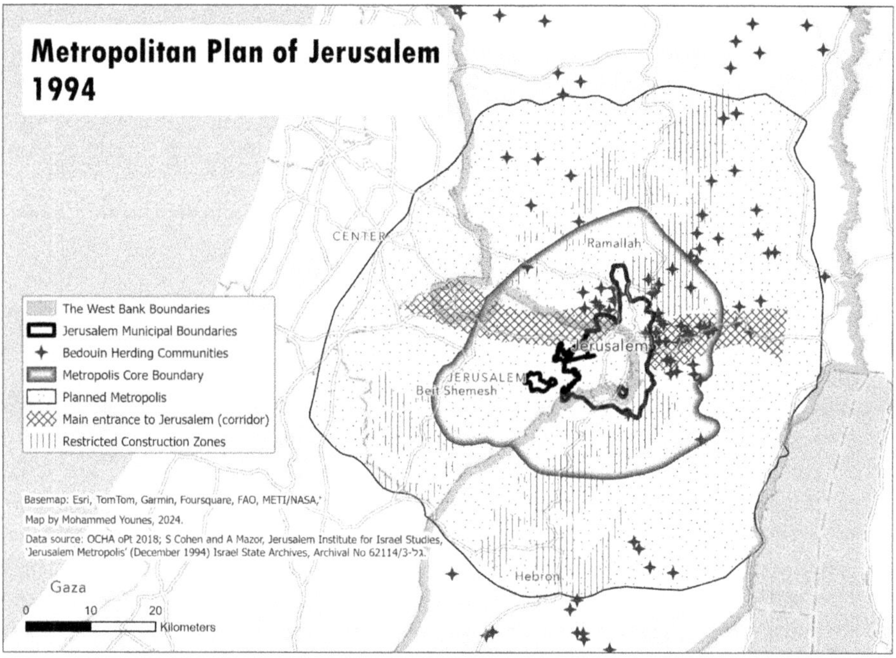

Figure 2.8 The Metropolitan Plan of Jerusalem 1994, featuring the urban corridors and the restricted construction zones, overlayed by the Bedouin communities' locations

In the next section, the application of such a proposal is elaborated on as an example of Israeli colonial policies in displacing the Bedouin population in the study area, through the expansion of the Ma'ale Adumim settlement bloc.

2.3. THE E1 PLAN AND MA'ALE ADUMIM AS 'EXHIBIT A' OF COLONIAL LAND POLICIES

In the mid-1970s, efforts to establish an Israeli settlement in Khan al-Ahmar were indicative of broader objectives to enhance military footholds and appropriate

[76] Cohen and Mazor, Jerusalem Institute for Israel Studies (n 74) גל 35.

lands near the city for colonial expansion. This initiative aligned with the Allon Plan of 1970, designed to create a link between Jerusalem and the Jordan Valley, securing the area under colonial dominion amidst concurrent discussions with Jordan.[77]

When a committee was established to study the potential sites for the settlement, it was decided to build an industrial settlement to rapidly establish Jewish existence and control over the area.[78] By March 1975, 30,000 dunams of the Bedouin pastures of the Al-Jahalin and Al-Sawahira tribes in the Khan al-Ahmar area were confiscated for the construction of the industrial area,[79] followed later in 1977 by plans to establish a work camp for the workers in the industrial zone.

This group of settlers, called Gush Emunim, was adherent to the Religious Zionism ideology, devoted to constructing Jewish settlements on the Palestinian territories captured after 1967. The Ma'ale Adumim plan was later considered part of the Jerusalem Metropolitan Development Plan.[80] The area was officially designated as a military zone, which provided grounds for the displacement of the Bedouins.[81] A new extension plan to the west of the settlement boundaries was proposed in 1982.[82]

An outline plan for the Ma'ale Adumim Bloc was approved two years later, stretching between Arab al-Jahalin communities and Wadi el-Qelt, covering an area of 35,000 dunams, most of which are Bedouin pastures and communities of Khan al-Ahmar. The plan mainly designated the confiscated lands as residential, forest, open spaces, tourism and industrial zones. In both its inception and its ongoing application, this plan serves as the basis for subsequent detailed plans, which, over time, have facilitated the extensive confiscation of lands and led to the systematic displacement of Bedouins, not only in the Jerusalem periphery but also throughout the Palestinian territories occupied post-1967.

Returning to the Metropolitan Plan of Jerusalem 1994, the eastern area of the city was dealt with as a standalone zone in the metropolis expansion, and an analysis was conducted, resulting in a plan of development for the area as shown in Figure 2.10 below. The area was designated for business and tourism development to 'protect' both the 'desert' and the corridor to the city; at the same time, moderate colonial residential activities were planned to cut the continuity of the Palestinian built-up area to the east of Jerusalem and restrict the Palestinian expansion towards

[77] For more information on the circumstances of establishing Ma'ale Adumim, see R Ranta, 'Submission to Gush Emunim' in *Political Decision Making and Non-Decisions: The Case of Israel and the Occupied Territories* (Palgrave Macmillan, 2015) 156–72.

[78] H Lifshitz, 'במעלה אדומים או במדרון הנסיגה (Up the Slope (Ma'ale Adumim) or Down the Slope)' דבר (17 January 1975) 12.

[79] Some parcels of the confiscated lands belonged to Palestinian residents of Abu Dis, Al-Issawiya and Anata, but much of the confiscated land was pastoral land for the Bedouins.

[80] A compilation of official correspondences and maps detailing the urban development in Ma'ale Adumim, Prime Minister's Office, '*מעלה אדומים*' (December 2012) Israel State Archives, Archival No 2026/9-א 42.

[81] A governmental letter dated 9 February 1979, from the Prime Minister Begin, indicated that he had no objection to declaring the area of Mishor Adumim and Ma'ale Adumim as a 'military zone'. See ibid 24.

[82] ibid 6.

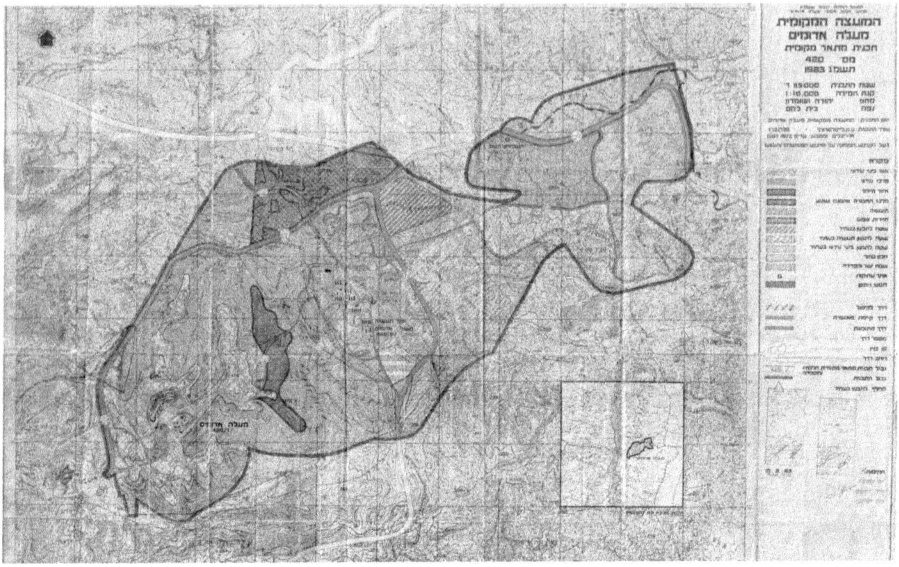

Figure 2.9 The outline plan of Ma'aleh Adumim (420) (1984)[83]

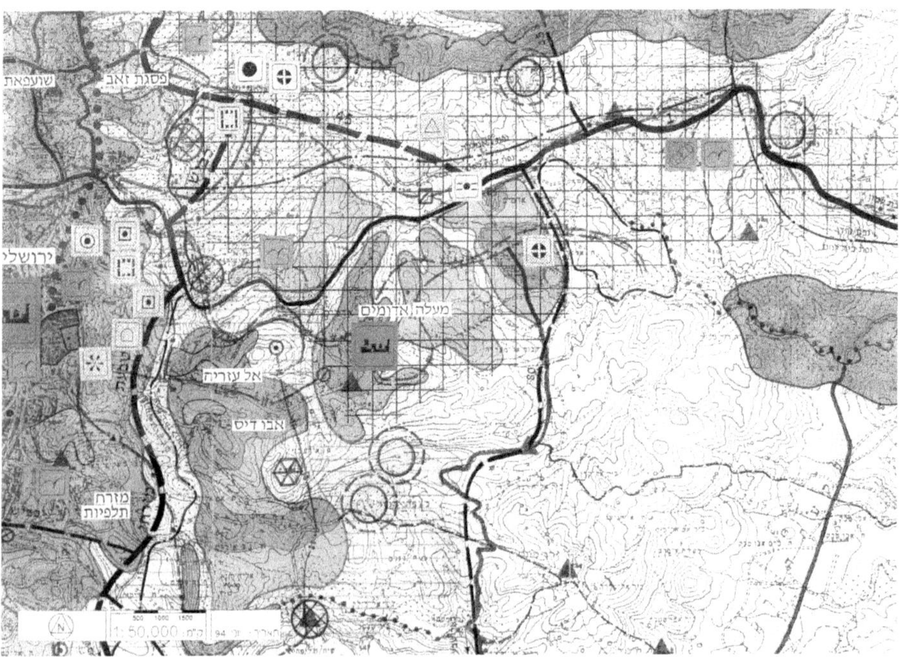

Figure 2.10 A section from the Metropolitan Proposal of Jerusalem 1994 for the Ma'ale Adumim Area

[83] Israel Land Authority: www.apps.land.gov.il/TabaSearch/#/Plans.

the Dead Sea and Jericho to terminate any future agglomeration of the Palestinians in the Jerusalem metropolis.[84] Taking into account that the planners organised for the Arab population to be concentrated in the northern and southern areas alone, they completely disregarded the existence of the Bedouin population in the planned zone.[85]

The proposed area was mainly defined and discussed as follows:

- The areas of Ma'ale Adumim, Al-Eizariya (Bethany), and Abu-Dis are included in the inner ring of the Metropolis.
- The areas located between Wadi en-Nar (Qidron Valley) and Wadi el-Qelt are the eastern entrance to Jerusalem and are considered sensitive to development.
- The area is located near both Road No 1 (Jerusalem-Amman) and Road No 9 (Ma'ale Adumim-Jerusalem), and therefore it is important to leave open areas to prevent any development near them, except at desired points.[86]

By including the two Palestinian communities in the inner ring, the Palestinian population there, including the Bedouin communities, became subject to the direct development policies of the metropolis, facilitating tighter control over Palestinian expansion in favour of the expansion of the Ma'ale Adumim settlement. Similarly, the vast region between the two valleys is home to numerous Bedouin communities, justifying any displacement operations under the guise of environmental protection.

Moreover, the plan's allowance for 'desired points' of development introduced a loophole for establishing new Israeli colonial projects. Despite its unofficial status, this document outlined a vision for future urban planning and included a calculated 'capacity' of the population of 65,000 settlers and only 17,000 Palestinians, who were 'expected' to fit in the area, despite being the existing inhabitants of these areas for decades.[87]

To achieve the proposed plan in the study, an official outline plan (420/4) was proposed in 1999, known as the E1 Plan (East-1), covering around 12,000 dunams of Anata, Al-Issawiyah, Al-Eizariya, At-Tur and Abu Dis lands, confined between Ma'ale Adumim and the western borders of the Palestinian towns. The plan aims to connect the outline plans of both Ma'ale Adumim and Jerusalem through most of the areas between Ma'ale Adumim Bloc and Jerusalem's built-up region, including those towns located outside the municipal borders, which were previously identified as part of the Metropolitan Plan's inner circle.

[84] The study indicated a fear of a scenario where the Jewish colonies are being turned into enclaves by the Palestinian urban expansion, due to the high growth in the Palestinian population. See Cohen and Mazor, Jerusalem Institute for Israel Studies (n 74) גל 126–29.

[85] Cohen (n 74) 126–42.

[86] Cohen (n 74) 185.

[87] ibid.

Table 2.5 outlines various plans related to the study area. Each of these plans serves as a foundation for subsequent detailed planning, such as afforestation projects.[88] These developments have significantly impeded the mobility of Bedouin livestock, constraining their access to their native grazing lands.

Table 2.5 Overview of plans impacting Bedouin livelihoods and grazing lands in the study area

Plan no	Year	Notes
420/2/2	1982	Development plan for Mishor Adumim's Eastern Zone
421	1989	The outline plan for Kedar Settlement
420/1/16	1993	Extension plan for Ma'ale Adumim's southern part on the land of Abu_Dis, between Abu-Nawar and Wadi al-A'awaj Bedouin communities
420/1/7	1999	The extension plan for the eastern areas of Ma'ale Adumim

These urban plans have historically functioned and continue to operate as mechanisms to displace Bedouin communities in Jerusalem's eastern territories, in conjunction with military orders and natural reserve plans. Many of these plans included developing the industrial park and connecting it to the surroundings, confiscating more land, and altering the region's natural and cultural landscapes; they have also facilitated the active displacement of the native Bedouin communities dwelling within these areas.

The following figure shows most of the original E1 outline plan. The majority of the lands in the plan are designated as open space and landscape conservation zone, while the remaining are designated for residential, tourism areas, private projects and services. The plan was never entirely approved and implemented since its proposition because of political constraints.[89] Yet, the area's landscape is undergoing a gradual transformation and reconstruction, whether through settler colonial afforestation activities or the development of new settler units in neighbouring settlements. Most significantly, the Bedouin communities that have long inhabited these lands are facing the threat of demolition and 'deconstruction' of their native space due to the (mis) application of military orders.

In April 2022, the ICA issued a colonial military order declaring a vast area of approximately 22,000 dunams of 'Wadi al-Mukalik' as a natural reserve. Located between Khan al-Ahmar and the Dead Sea on the lands of An-Nabi Mousa, this valley had been previously marked as a natural reserve in the Metropolitan Plan of Jerusalem 1994, 27 years earlier, in which it was depicted as a 'gate' leading into the city of Jerusalem.[90]

[88] Refer to the following plans: 420/1/14, 420/1/16/4/1 and 420; details available at www.apps.land.gov.il/iturTabot2/taba2.aspx?tbMerchav=712&tbMsTochnit=420.

[89] H Ofran, 'Despite Its Promise, the Government Is Promoting the E1 Plan Which Is Considered Deadly for the Future of Two States' (Peace Now, 31 May 2022), www.peacenow.org.il/en/despite-its-promise-the-government-is-promoting-the-e1-plan-which-is-considered-deadly-for-the-future-of-two-states.

[90] Military order announcement (Hebrew and Arabic): www.gov.il/BlobFolder/reports/og363/he/og%20river.pdf?utm_source=gov+il.

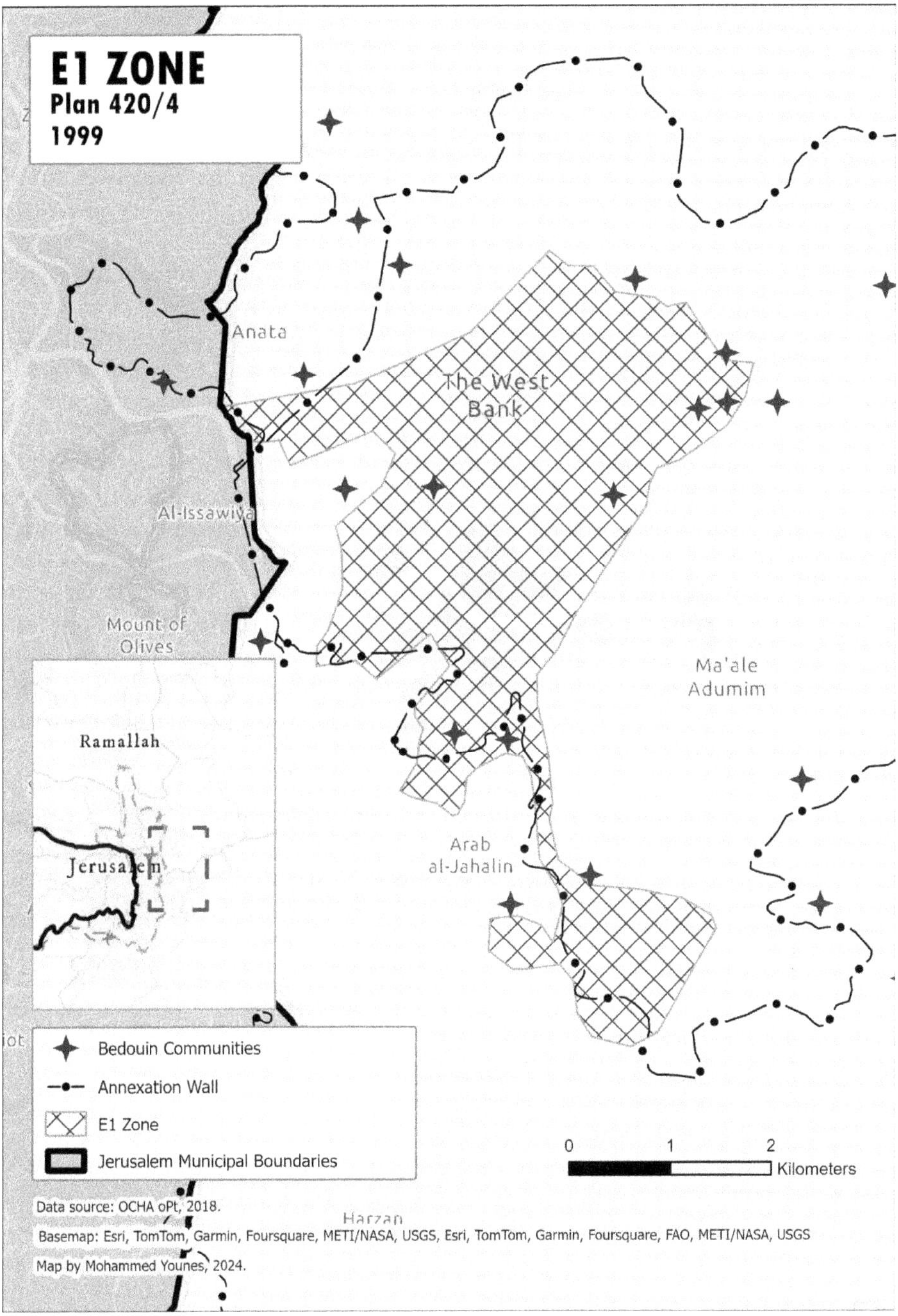

Figure 2.11 The eastern section of the E1 Plan (420), highlighting the present-day locations of nearby Bedouin communities

The declaration of Wadi al-Mukalik as a natural reserve highlights the complicated synergy between various institutions within the settler colonial framework in Palestine. The interdependence between the ICA's military orders and Israeli urban plans exemplifies the seamless integration of research, regulation and implementation within this structure. Moreover, all of these facets collectively drive the objectives of the Zionist settler colonial ideology, while in the context of international law, such practices underscore issues of state responsibility and state violence.

The idea of using natural reserves as a tool for colonial confiscation of the Bedouin pastures and a means through which to restrict their movement does not reject the idea that these areas could be, or could become, actual natural reserves for the benefit of Palestinians. However, the regulations and the bylaws used by the colonial system do not favour Palestinians, and these areas were never operated or developed as natural reserves by Palestinians themselves.

Many of these natural reserves extend past their designated boundaries. This can be evidenced by examining the topography and the hiking trails frequented by both Palestinians and colonial settlers. For example, the terrain between Wadi As-Seeq and Wadi el-Qelt has a similar topography to Wadi al-Mukalik and cannot be distinguished, yet it is not declared a natural reserve. Instead, it currently hosts a military base and a colony. This strategy suggests the land may be reserved for future colonial urban expansion while concurrently limiting Bedouin activities.

The discussion of colonial spatial usage in Jerusalem's eastern outskirts serves to elucidate the utilisation of colonial policies as a mechanism to systematically displace Bedouins. The socio-economic ramifications of these policies on the Bedouin population often remain underexplored, but the results manifest in the enforced transition towards indirect sedentariness, including the systematic destruction of Bedouin infrastructure and restrictions on their ability to settle in their lands. This effectively pushes them towards already congested Palestinian urban centres, which are squeezed between the boundaries of the Jerusalem municipality and the E1 plan.

Through their displacement strategies, the Israeli colonial authorities aim to superimpose a homogenised space, thereby eliminating the Bedouin way of life and diluting Palestinian identity into narrowly defined, controlled regions. Simultaneously, the flow of settlement activities and the backing of the Zionist colonial planning framework are shaping a distinctly colonial social realm on the outskirts of Jerusalem. In their entirety, the planning practices orchestrated by the Israeli state system strengthen its territorial encroachments in the Palestinian lands seized after 1967. This is done to strengthen its settlement enterprise, invariably and implicitly undermining the Palestinians, with the Bedouins bearing a disproportionate brunt, as they are rendered secondary to the broader Israeli expansionist objectives.

Figure 2.12 below illustrates the intense colonial urban planning practices used to confine the Palestinian Bedouins in the study area.

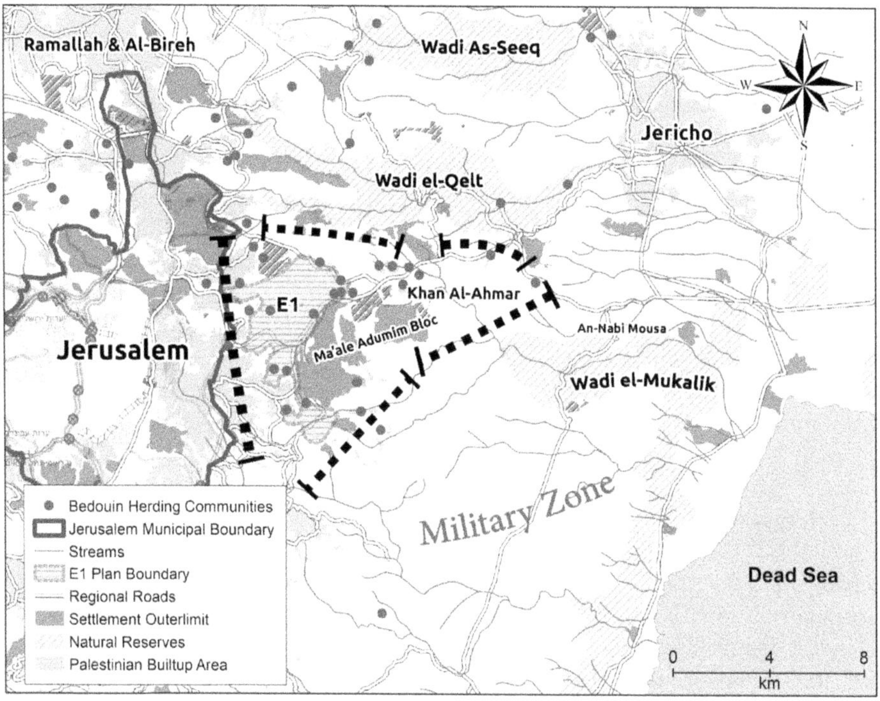

Figure 2.12 A confining triangular area formed by the existing limitations on Bedouin mobility in the eastern wilderness of Jerusalem (scale 1:130,000)[91]

2.3.1. Beyond Oslo: The Bedouin Landscape amidst Palestinian Visions

The Oslo Accords (1993–95) and the subsequent establishment of the PA (1994) did not directly affect the colonial policies in Jerusalem's eastern environs and had minimal impacts in particular on the Bedouin communities. The division of the West Bank into administrative zones, with Jerusalem's eastern environs falling into Area C under full control by the ICA, meant that the PA had no direct influence in these territories. Such administrative frameworks, combined with policies and practices, further marginalised the Bedouin communities, relegating them to the fringes of these policy decisions.

Moreover, subsequent initiatives, such as the 2014 Protection Plan for Natural Resources and Archaeological Sites, despite their broader intentions, overlooked the specific needs and rights of the Bedouin communities in Area C, not only in Jerusalem

[91] Author as the cartographer; Data Layers obtained from the Palestinian Authority's Ministry of Local Governance (MoLG); Bedouin Communities Data points collected by OCHA oPt.

but in the rest of the West Bank.[92] This neglect highlights a pattern whereby Bedouins and their lived experiences often emerge as collateral damage in larger geopolitical negotiations and policies.

In May 2020 the PA, with the assistance of the European Union and The United Nations Human Settlements Programme, prepared the Spatial Development Strategic Framework for Jerusalem Governorate 2030. The framework proposes projects that could further restrict Bedouin movement in the area, such as the establishment of solar energy projects and the designation of Bedouin lands under the 'Urban Expansion for Density' category. These planning documents may indicate the PA's direction in forcing the Bedouins to settle in their current locations, leading to the confiscation of their livestock and the restriction of their pastures by the colonial authorities.[93] This approach, seemingly in alignment with bigger Palestinian development goals, inadvertently upholds with colonial objectives, further deepening the vulnerabilities faced by the Bedouin communities in their native land.

2.3.2. Jerusalem 2050 Vision Plan: A Brief Review

'Jerusalem 5800', published in 2016, epitomises extensive colonial visioning for Jerusalem (2015–50), building upon the 1995 Metropolitan Plan's framework and extending it into a comprehensive blueprint for the city's development from 2015 to 2050.[94] This initiative – conceived by Kevin Bermeister, a Zionist South African entrepreneur who previously funded various colonial projects in Jerusalem – underscores eastward expansion, enhancing the prior plan with detailed proposals and studies that particularly impact Bedouin territories. Its implementation continues to reshape Jerusalem's landscape, exacerbating displacement issues for Bedouin communities.

The physical planning for the metropolis emphasises the area's symbolic significance, notably through the development of 'East 1' at the Jerusalem-Jericho junction, envisioned as a city gateway. This gateway aims to bolster metropolitan Jerusalem's identity by incorporating a service complex. Crucially, the plan proposes an international airport in the Ard Abu Tabaq region, traditionally inhabited by Arab es-Sawahira Bedouins. This airport, part of a collaborative initiative with the PA within the National Transport Master Plan, seeks to enhance regional connectivity.[95] It is strategically linked to Jerusalem via an extensive transportation network, including regional roads and an underground train to the city's west. However, the chosen

[92] Issued as part of the National Spatial Plan and approved by Cabinet Decree No 03/14/16 on 1 January 2014: www.info.wafa.ps/ar_page.aspx?id=9023.

[93] Spatial Development Strategic Framework for Jerusalem Governorate (UNDP, 2030), www.unhabitat.org/sites/default/files/2020/05/sdsf_2030_jerusalem_eng_1.pdf.

[94] For more details on the Jerusalem 5800 initiative, see official documentation at www.downloads-en.jerusalem5800.com/files/assets/basic-html/page-14-15.html.

[95] This location is proposed as 'Alternative 1' in the National Transport Master Plan. For further information, see the webpage of the National Transport Master Plan for Palestine at www.mot.gov.ps/ntmp.

site has been controversially designated as state land and a military zone, reflecting the complex socio-political dynamics affecting the Bedouin communities.[96]

The airport's primary impact on the local Bedouins is noise pollution. This acoustic disruption endangers animal welfare in the area, especially affecting the livestock of Bedouins residing in Jericho, Jerusalem and Bethlehem. Moreover, the region itself, which is home to diverse Palestinian wildlife in its wilderness and proximate to the Dead Sea, will also suffer the most from this disturbance. Besides, the airport will inevitably lead to heightened traffic in the area and open the door to further risks of land confiscation for subsequent development projects.[97]

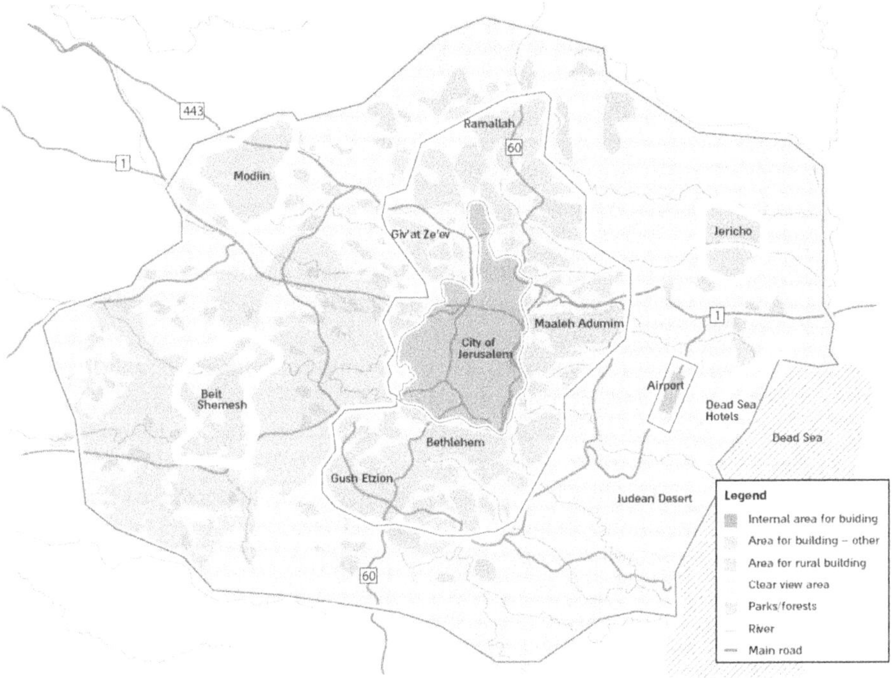

Figure 2.13 Planned zones of metropolitan Jerusalem[98]

The 1995 metropolitan plan delineates the suburban region as a key area for development, primarily advancing from existing colonial settlements like Ma'ale Adumim, with scant provisions for expanding Palestinian-populated areas. This reflects a strategic bias, anticipating a demographic shift favouring Jewish population growth due to new colonial immigration over Palestinian growth. Consequently, the E1 Plan and

[96] To view the proposal for an International Airport in Jerusalem's Horkania Valley from 2011, visit www.jerusalem5800.com/system/resources/W1siZiIsIjIwMTYvMDcvMjUvMDdfMDNfNDhfOTc4X0FpcnBvcnRfUHJvcG9zYWxfRmluYWxfLnBkZiJdXQ/Airport%20Proposal(Final).pdf.

[97] RD Alquezar and RH Macedo, 'Airport Noise and Wildlife Conservation: What Are We Missing?' (2019) 17 *Perspectives in Ecology and Conservation* 163.

[98] The Jerusalem Metropolis Master Plan 2050 (5800) (Jerusalem 5800 Initiative 2016) 21.

Ma'ale Adumim epitomise colonial land strategies, demonstrating a clear preference for settler expansion and demographically engineering the region to the detriment of Palestinian Bedouin communities. These policies not only marginalise Palestinian population growth, but also leave Bedouin communities grappling with the loss of their lands and cultural erosion, underscoring a persistent threat to their rights and heritage.[99]

CONCLUSION

This chapter has demonstrated the deep and extensive implications of the colonial spatial planning framework on the Palestinian Bedouin, both in urban and rural contexts. Such plans have consistently facilitated the depopulation of Bedouin areas in Jerusalem, leading to the entrapment of the Palestinian communities within the spatial domain of escalating colonial settlements. This urban sprawl, a concrete manifestation of these plans, is swiftly reshaping and reconstructing the native Palestinian landscape, leaving little to no space for traditional Bedouin practices such as grazing.

Drawing parallels with accomplished colonial settlements and the consequent Palestinian displacement illuminates the sustained colonial mindset: an ideology reflected in Israeli colonial policies, prolonging the displacement of Palestinians, Bedouins included, across generations. Further complicating matters, the entangled web of military orders and objection protocols within this planning framework has incrementally robbed the Bedouins of their pastures. Such tactics have systematically destabilised the Bedouin socio-cultural fabric, resulting in the diminishing of the Jerusalemite Bedouin identity. This is related to an undeniably intimidating setting. Yet, the Palestinian Bedouin spirit stands unbroken, even as they struggle with relentless pressure towards sedentarisation from Israeli colonial planning mechanisms.

Such policies of displacement and settler colonial encirclement persistently target Bedouin communities throughout historical Palestine, thus sustaining the themes of settler colonialism, territorial appropriation and relocation. Understanding the multifaceted role of urban planning in this settler colonial structure is of prime importance. Within the broader Jerusalem context, Israeli-imposed colonial urban planning operates dual-fold: as a direct instrument targeting and displacing Bedouin communities; and as an indirect catalyst fuelling the forced milieu, a lived space, that precipitates the gradual deconstruction, destruction and elimination of Bedouin traditions and presence. Given these details, the relationship between urban planning and settler colonialism merits diligent analysis – not only by urban planners and geographers, but also by international law experts, ensuring accountability for Bedouin displacement in the Jerusalem area and across Palestine.

[99] ibid 25.

3

Active Settler Frontiers: Shifting Israeli Borders and the Forced Displacement of Palestinian Bedouin Communities

BANA ABU ZULUF AND AHMAD AMARA

INTRODUCTION

As Israel continues to operate as an active settler colony and as an occupying power that has never defined its borders with the West Bank or the Gaza Strip, there is a constant emergence of new frontiers and borders for colonisation, annexation and/or demarcations of various forms of legalities.[1] The active settler project thus constantly creates active frontiers for settlement, as well as Palestinian land confiscation and displacement of Palestinians.[2] This is illustrated in the shape of Jewish settlements, military zones, nature reserves, industrial zones, walls and fences, political borders, zoning plans, highways, building and working permits, and the creation of 'illegal habitation zones' for Palestinians. These practices are continuously used to appropriate Palestinian land and spaces.

Whether in Umm al-Hiran in the Naqab (Beer al-Saba') under Israeli jurisdiction, Susya in Masafer Yatta/South Hebron Hills or in Khan al-Ahmar in the Jerusalem periphery in Area C of the Occupied Palestinian Territory (OPT), Israeli land and zoning policies are equivalent and Palestinian Bedouins face similar challenges to their presence. This chapter argues that such policies are being used on both sides of

[1] For sources on the settler colonial analytical framing in general and the study of Zionism, see: P Wolfe, 'Settler colonialism and the elimination of the native' (2006) 8 *Journal of Genocide Research* 387; E Said, *Orientalism* (Random House, Inc, 1979); G Shafir, *Land, Labor and the Origins of the Israeli-Palestinian Conflict*, 1882–1914 (University of California Press, 1996). On the Israeli Government's settler colonial policies see: N Gordon and M Ram, 'Ethnic cleansing and the formation of settler colonial geographies' (2016) 53 *Political Geography* 29.

[2] B Kimmerling, *The Invention and Decline of Israeliness: State, Society, and the Military* (University of California Press, 2001).

the Green Line (ie the pre-1967 de facto border, a demarcation line based on the 1949 Armistice Agreements) as the Israeli settler frontiers advance and are framed within a legalistic discourse that depoliticises the ideological and colonial underpinnings that guide its formation.

This chapter investigates how the borders of legalities through the use of lawfare and pseudolaws are continuously formed, what practices they entail and how they impact Palestinian Bedouins and the Palestinian geopolitical space at large. The Israeli active settler colonial frontiers have been created and recreated since the beginning of Zionist colonisation before 1948;[3] geopolitical boundaries emerged with it, both physical and imagined, which dictate Bedouin Palestinian geography. We shine a light on the E1 plan and the affected Bedouin communities who are the subject of this edited volume. The analysis diverges from the tendency to study Israeli policies in Israel and the West Bank as completely distinct; in this chapter, the Green Line is materially and discursively fluid, which becomes central to the geopolitical and legal reality. The Green Line is both invisible and existent depending on Israeli policies. For example, it is visible to West Bank Palestinians who wish to work inside Israel, while it is invisible to Israeli colonisation objectives, and to settlers. This research refers to the concept of 'grey space' as spaces between the erasure (blackness) and legality and tenureship (whiteness) – spaces 'that have neither been integrated nor eliminated'[4] to indicate the reality in which several Palestinian communities find themselves entrapped.

At the theoretical level, this chapter employs a multi-disciplinary approach of history, law and geography within the framework of settler colonialism and modern nation-states' governmentality. The following analysis is primarily based on case law of Israeli courts, maps and aerial photos to investigate how continuously shifting borders and resistance to them structure Palestinian geography and Bedouin displacement. The chapter is divided into four sections. Firstly, we provide a historical overview of Israeli colonisation efforts targeting Bedouin communities since the Nakba, tracing the establishment of frontiers and the underlying colonial logic of Israeli land systems. Secondly, we critically analyse theories of land acquisition using the lens of settler colonialism and international law, and the ways in which the Bedouin identity and lifestyle are weaponised to justify their denationalisation and displacement. In the third section, we map the establishment of new settler frontiers beginning from the Naqab, following the Israeli adoption of the 2005 Naqab Development Plan for other Bedouin communities near the Green Line – such as Susya in the South Hebron Hills – and further north in the E1 Plan and the resulting impact on Bedouin communities. Finally, we explore the concept of *Sumud* (resilience) and Bedouin agency, arguing that Bedouin communities and their social, political and

[3] Though after 1948, actions are attributed to the state of Israel, we use Zionism to indicate the dominant pre-and-post state ideology that remains the state's ideology in orchestrating and guiding Israel's policies and practices.

[4] O Yiftachel, 'Critical Theory and "Gray Space": Mobilization of the Colonized' in N Brenner, P Marcuse and M Mayer (eds), *Cities for People, Not for Profit: Critical Urban Theory and the Right to the City* (Routledge, 2011).

urban constructs create a local 'geographical dialect' that profanes Israel's colonial practices which renders them, and not the outsider, as autonomous, and thus harder to control. Employing James C Scott's concept of legibility,[5] this chapter contends that despite being under threat of displacement, Bedouin communities with their illegibility in the eyes of the Israeli authorities have managed to be resilient in creative ways.

This chapter contributes to the literature on Bedouin communities and on Palestinians, while stressing the need to explore the legalistic genealogy of displacement of the Bedouin communities and the need to draw connections between demarcated Palestinian geographies. The chapter opposes the tendency to study both the Bedouin communities as well as their space in isolation from other urban communities or other spaces and geographies in Palestine. Moreover, the chapter proves the commonalities in Israeli active frontiers policies both inside 'Israel proper' and in the West Bank, and across the invisible Green Line extending from the Jordan river to the Mediterranean sea.

***

On 4 May 2015, the Israeli Supreme Court ruled to evict the Bedouin village of Susya, located in the southern West Bank and four kilometres from the Green Line, in the Palestinian territory occupied in 1967.[6] A day later, the court ruled for the eviction of the Bedouin village of Umm al-Hiran in the Beer al-Saba' (Naqab) region, located about 20 kilometres from the Green Line, in what is now the State of Israel.[7] Tens of other Bedouin communities in both the West Bank and the Naqab are deemed illegal by the Israeli state and subject to forcible transfer, some of which face pending eviction decisions by the Supreme Court, such as Khan al-Ahmar communities. These evictions are not the first faced by these communities. Umm al-Hiran's eviction follows a history of previous displacement of the community and dozens of others carried out by the Israeli authorities after 1948 and until the late 1950s, justified by the pretext of security of frontiers.[8] These displacements are accompanied by Israeli policies of land seizure and control through the construction of Israeli settlements, and the designation of lands as industrial or military zones.

Like the Naqab, the West Bank has constituted an active settler frontier since its occupation in 1967. More specifically, after the Oslo Accords and the designation of Area C entirely controlled by Israel, Israeli settlement activity accelerated

[5] JC Scott, *Seeing Like a State: How Certain Schemes to Improve the Human Condition Have Failed* (Yale University Press, 1999).

[6] Israeli High Court of Justice (HCJ), 413/13 & 1039/13, *Muhammad Abu Aram et Al v Israel's Minister of Defense et Al*, decision 4 May 2022, available in Hebrew at supreme.court.gov.il/Pages/fullsearch.aspx.

[7] A Amara, 'Um Alhiran as a model of the displacement and re-displacement the Arabs of the Naqab' (2018) 114 *Journal of Palestinian Studies* 76 (in Arabic).

[8] A Kedar, A Amara and Oren Yiftachel, *Emptied lands: A Legal Geography of Bedouin Rights in the Naqab* (Stanford University Press, 2018).

across the West Bank, including in the Jordan Valley, alongside the Wall, and in the Eastern Jerusalem periphery.[9] In the last two decades, the area between Jerusalem and the Israeli settlement of Ma'ale Adumim has been subject to new Israeli zoning and settlement plans, the most famous of which is known as E1 (East 1), which aims to build and expand Israeli settlements, and to connect Ma'ale Adumim with Jerusalem (also discussed by Mohammed Younes in chapter two of this volume).[10] This plan led to active Israeli displacement of Palestinians, which in this area are predominantly Bedouin communities. These Israeli colonial expansionist goals constantly necessitate the creation of new borders and boundaries that structure and enable the Israeli Judaisation policies and subject the Bedouin communities to forced displacement wherever they live between the Jordan River and the Mediterranean Sea, that is, in the Naqab, in Masafer Yatta, or in the Eastern Jerusalem periphery. These boundaries are constantly changing to facilitate Israeli takeover of Palestinian land: fundamentally, the Green Line, zoning plans, highways, the border between Areas B and C, or the municipal boundaries of Israeli settlements, all dictate the geopolitical reality of the Bedouin communities and the Palestinian geography at large.

Like the rest of the Palestinian communities, Palestinian Bedouins face continuous displacement in the face of Israeli settler colonial expansion.[11] Whereas the dynamic forces and the legal-political infrastructure of displacement are common to all Palestinians, the displacement of the Palestinian Bedouin communities presents several particularities that this chapter addresses. Above all, as the conditions and structures of displacement and dispossession continue to impact Palestinians, the Palestinian Bedouin communities face the threat of 'collective' displacement as entire communities, both in the Naqab and in the West Bank. This process of displacement is part of wider policies of indigenous erasure through the application of pseudo-legalities that position the Bedouin communities in grey spaces that can render them precarious and vulnerable to forced displacement.[12] While states rely on geometrical lines and patterns to define boundaries to better control their subjects, Umm al-Hiran, Susiya and Khan al-Ahmar Bedouin communities, with their vernacular pattern of urbanism, profane these boundaries of state by becoming unrecognisable for the outsider state, and thus harder to control.[13]

The following section begins with a theoretical exploration of settler colonialism, delving into the Israeli-Zionist ideology and how it shapes evolving settler frontiers. The focus of this section will be on the resultant displacements or conditions of displacement experienced by colonised communities. Moreover, the discussion includes the uses of zoning policies and legal discourse to classify certain spaces as unrecognised or lacking legality, thereby necessitating intervention from the Israeli

[9] A Amara et al, 'The Bedouin communities of Eastern Jerusalem: A new locus of power in the post-Oslo battle for Palestine?' (2021) 117 *Confluences Méditerranée* 101.

[10] ibid 101.

[11] L Tatour, 'The Culturalisation of Indigeneity: The Palestinian-Bedouin of the Naqab and Indigenous Rights' (2019) 23 *The International Journal of Human Rights* 1569.

[12] Yiftachel (n 4).

[13] Scott (n 5).

state and military which in turn results in the displacement of Bedouin communities on both sides of the Green Line.

3.1. SETTLER COLONIAL GEOGRAPHIES AND MOVING FRONTIERS

3.1.1. Israeli-Zionist Colonisation

Since the establishment of the state of Israel in 1948, Bedouins have been the target of organised efforts to forcefully displace and remove them from their lands. Colonising the land was always an integral part of Zionist and later Israeli policies of land control and colonial expansion. On the other hand, Jewish and Israeli colonies were always strategically positioned to serve the Zionist enterprise at its different stages. Generally, the construction of pre-1948 colonies was determined by several factors including land availability, security, natural resources and economic value, and religious significance. In the early Israeli statehood years, Israeli settlements were established to solidify Israeli frontiers vis-a-vis neighbouring countries and to prevent a possible partition or allocation of areas that Israel controlled to an Arab state, such as in the Galilee. In parallel, Israeli settlements were established to interrupt Palestinian geographical contiguity and to impose Jewish dominance, demographically and geographically, as much as possible. These advancements went hand-in-hand with the erasure of Palestinian space through the expulsion and demolition of Palestinian villages, as well as the prevention of Palestinian urban growth, through for example declaring existing villages as illegal such as in the case of the Naqab, where the majority of Bedouins reside.

According to David Ben-Gurion, Israel's first Prime Minister, Jewish settlements were 'determinants of the state's security that are not any less important than establishing an army'.[14] Jewish settlement continues to be of special value in Zionist-Israeli ideology in practice and law. On 19 July 2018, the Israeli Knesset passed Basic Law: Israel – the Nation State of the Jewish People, which enshrined Israel exclusively as the 'nation state of the Jewish people' and constitutionally entrenched racial-national discrimination against non-Jews. While an Israeli civil law, it also implicitly covers the OPT, particularly in relation to settlements. Article 7 of the law stated that 'the state sees in the development of Jewish settlements as one of national value, and will act to encourage and advance its establishment and strengthening'.[15]

Over time, the Israeli state has prioritised colonial expansionism, combining military and political tools, as well as the political and regional conditions, to reach Jewish majority demographic objectives. As Zionist ideology and Judaisation policies continue to dominate the institutional politics of Israel, settler colonialism therefore continues to be active and to create new frontiers. The Naqab and the Eastern

[14] O Yiftachel, *Ethnocracy: Land and identity politics in Israel/Palestine* (University of Pennsylvania Press, 2006) 271.

[15] Basic Law: Israel – The Nation State of the Jewish People (July 2018), www.adalah.org/uploads/uploads/Basic_Law_Israel_as_the_Nation_State_of_the_Jewish_People_ENG_TRANSLATION_25072018.pdf (English translation).

Jerusalem periphery have been two active frontiers of Israeli colonisation, exhibited with higher intensity in the last two decades, as will be illustrated in section 3.2 below. Bedouin communities in the Naqab in the Eastern Jerusalem periphery are subject to policies of enclosure and isolation. Armistice borders, firing zones, Israeli settlements, the wall, nature reserves, green zones, closed military zones, seam zones, bypass roads, and discriminatory zoning and planning policies all become the driving force of Palestinian Bedouin displacement. These segmentations placed many of the Bedouin communities in entrapped geographies and heavily monitored grey spaces. Oren Yiftachel described such spaces as existing between the erasure (blackness) and legality and tenureship (whiteness), spaces 'that have neither been integrated nor eliminated; they represent semi-permanent margins of the present urban areas'.[16] Thus, their current communities are neither legalised nor completely destroyed and erased.

3.1.2. Law, Lawlessness and Frontiers

Law has been central to the Zionist enterprise prior to 1948 as Zionist leadership acted at the international level to secure a commitment for a Jewish national home, and later vis-à-vis the British Mandate Government to adopt particular legislation, such as the nullification of Ottoman prohibition on Zionist land acquisition, Jewish immigration and land title registration.[17] As the Zionist leadership pre-1948 lacked the sovereign power to confiscate lands or the military might to acquire lands through conquest, land purchase and allocations by the Mandate Government were the principal available means. However, the 1947–49 war of conquest provided the opportunity for land acquisition through violence, and after the declaration of independence, the formal sovereignty to enforce land confiscations. Thus, the first five years of Israeli statehood (1948–53) constituted the foundations of how law could be used to justify unlawful policies and violence to acquire Palestinian lands across Palestine. This included the fertile lands of Palestinian refugees, mainly in the northern parts of Israel, as well as properties that were under the ownership of the British Mandate Government such as ports, state facilities, military camps, state land and other state institutions. Whereas for seven decades the Zionist-Jewish institutions in historic Palestine (both under the Ottoman empire and under the British mandate system) managed to acquire only six per cent of Palestine's land, during the first five years of statehood Israel acquired seven times more land, making a total of 95 per cent of Israel's appropriated land to be registered as state and public lands.[18] Most notably, the adoption of the Absentees' Property Law of 1950[19] allowed the seizure of movable and immovable property

[16] Yiftachel (n 14) 293.

[17] M Bunton, *Colonial Land Policies in Palestine 1917–1936* (OUP, 2007).

[18] This includes lands registered as state lands, lands of the Development Authority (a governmental body that holds Palestinian refugees' properties), and lands of the Jewish National Fund. See www.gov.il/en/departments/israel_land_authority/govil-landing-page.

[19] Absentees Property Law (1950), www.adalah.org/uploads/oldfiles/Public/files/Discriminatory-Laws-Database/English/04-Absentees-Property-Law-1950.pdf (English); see also Adalah, 'Absentees' Property Law', www.adalah.org/en/law/view/538.

of Palestinian refugees; this was followed by the Land Acquisition Law of 1953, enabling the confiscation of land of Palestinian citizens who remained in Israel,[20] and the 1951 State Property Act, which permitted Israel to inherit the properties of the Mandate Government.[21] Such laws demonstrate what John Reynolds calls 'slow violence', which is sanctioned by 'emergency modalities' where 'Palestinian space emerges as a realm saturated by legal regulation'.[22] In other words, 'law is itself the connective tissue binding the twin colonial logic of fear and dispossession that haunts the Palestinian national and social condition'.[23] Bedouins across both sides of the Green Line in Umm al-Hiran, Susya and Khan al-Ahmar continue to experience such logic, and are subjected to it more profoundly as whole communities become targeted, mirroring how whole villages were targeted in the early days of Zionist colonisation, during the Nakba, and into the present.

In order to maintain state control over the seized lands for the advancement of Judaisation goals, Israel adopted the 1960 Basic Law: Israel Lands, which prevented the sale of these lands,[24] and then founded the Israel Land Administration (Israel Land Authority after 2009) in the same year to administer and manage state land.[25] These new laws came in addition to existing Ottoman and British Mandatory laws that remained in force after 1948 and were also utilised to enable further Israeli land appropriation on both sides of the Green Line, mainly within the framework of the Land Title Settlement process, through which Israeli authorities adopted new legal doctrines and interpretations that restricted the ability of Palestinian landholders to prove their land rights.[26] Post-1948, these laws and regulations were part and parcel of a larger attempt at denying land ownership to Palestinians and allowing for Israel's land theft and colonial expansionism to go unchallenged in the (Israeli) courts.

The Israeli land system and land-grabbing ideology were then applied with minor changes in the West Bank after its occupation in 1967.[27] The continuing use of such laws and policies until today denotes Israel's expansionist and annexationist goals in the West Bank. Moreover, the Israeli Military Government adopted military orders that enabled the appropriation of land belonging to Palestinian refugees in 1967, the appropriation and declaration of state land, and the seizure of lands for security and military purposes.[28] After the signing of the Oslo Accords (1993–95)

[20] Israel Land Authority, 'About Israel Land Authority', land.gov.il/en/Pages/AboutUs.aspx.

[21] The State Property Act (1951), www.nevo.co.il/law_html/law01/312_001.htm (in Hebrew).

[22] J Reynolds, 'Repressive Inclusion' (2017) 49 *The Journal of Legal Pluralism and Unofficial Law* 268, 270.

[23] ibid.

[24] Israel Lands Administration Law (1960), www.adalah.org/uploads/oldfiles/Public/files/Discriminatory-Laws-Database/English/08-Israel-Land-Administration-Law-1960.pdf (English translation).

[25] See Adalah, 'New Israel Land Reform Law passed by Knesset' (3 August 2009), www.adalah.org/en/content/view/6991. See also: Israel Lands Administration Law (ibid).

[26] G Forman and A Kedar, 'From Arab Land to 'Israel Lands': The Legal Dispossession of the Palestinians Displaced by Israel in the Wake of 1948' (2004) 22 *Environment and Planning D: Society and Space* 809.

[27] N Erakat, *Justice for Some: Law and the Question of Palestine* (Stanford University Press, 2019).

[28] J Rabah and N Fairweather, *Israeli Military orders in the occupied Palestinian West Bank 1967–1992* (Jerusalem Media and Communication Centre, 1995). See also B'Tselem, 'Conquer and Divide', conquer-and-divide.btselem.org/map-en.html.

and the compartmentalisation of the West Bank into Areas A, B and C, Israel's grip on Palestinian land, especially in Area C, was consolidated with the building of the separation wall and the expansion of settlements; this is especially visible in the E1 area where Bedouins became the target of displacement. As such, the Israeli legal system did not only enable the seizure of Palestinian lands, but it also enabled Israel to determine the spheres of legality and illegality, of legal ownership and trespassing, unilaterally determining what can be considered as legitimate and illegitimate, thus allowing for the establishment of frontiers targeting Palestinians, and, in particular, Bedouin communities.

Julie Evans describes settler colonial frontiers as 'the threshold space between international law and domestic law', characterised by the lack of 'international law's responsiveness to colonialism, as a necessary compliment to Europe's claim to sovereignty under the so-called doctrine of discovery'.[29] Essentially, international law's normalisation of violence against indigenous communities is the force that provided legitimacy for European colonisers to claim sovereignty worldwide, which also underpins Israeli claims to Palestine. This is, in part, reflected in the international community's inability to hold Israel accountable for its violations of international law against Palestinians as the indigenous inhabitants of Palestine. Evans discusses this process of the normalisation of violence as a shift from 'a legal space of violence (in international law) to become a space of legal violence (in domestic law)'.[30] Israeli attempts to construct pseudo-legalities aim to tighten its grip on Palestinian land and deny Palestinian ndigenous presence and ownership, and illustrate the grey area between international law and domestic law that Evans so eloquently articulates. As such, the indigenous people move between their 'unrecognised sovereignty' under international law into the domestic legal system of the colony where they experience actual dispossession; it is in the domestic legal system of the colony where violence against indigenous people becomes legalised.

Within such a legal system, the 'logic of elimination' is imperative. As such, Palestinian Bedouin sovereignty and ownership of the land are not only denied by Israel through systems of pseudo-legalities that displace Palestinians, but are also denied by international law, which fails to protect indigenous land against colonial expansion and recognises and normalises such conquest. Thus, domestic colonial frontiers may be deemed as a sovereign state matter, or as a normal urban development of such states, even when they are an expression of colonial expansion into indigenous land. Laws and boundaries are created to contain some and exclude others.[31] They are processes whereby territory and law can exist either in the form of cooperation or in the form of friction. Military laws that are applied to Bedouins in the West Bank have often taken the form of lawfare and 'friction', but for Israeli settlers in the West Bank, the application of Israeli civil law allows them a frictionless

[29] J Evans, 'Where Lawlessness Is Law: The Settler-Colonial Frontier As A Legal Space Of Violence' (2009) 30 *Australian Feminist Law Journal* 3.

[30] ibid 3.

[31] S Blandy and D Sibley, 'Law, Boundaries and the Production of Space' (2010) 19 *Social & Legal Studies* 275, 277.

existence, enjoying the ease to settle in occupied land (which is prohibited under International Humanitarian Law (IHL)) and freely operate borders with flexibility, given that borders are invisible for them.

In a similar vein, Mikko Joronen examines spaces of 'negotiated precarity', where in 'administrative zones the life of the colonised becomes prone to several flexible, negotiated use of power'.[32] These spatial compartments, Joronen argues, allow for 'several informal, indirect, and ad hoc techniques of colonial violence'.[33] Joronen introduces the concept of 'administrative violence' as a distinct type of violence that accompanies (and enhances) military violence. Administrative violence in many instances results in a stalemate. In the case of Bedouin communities on both sides of the Green Line, the ad hoc techniques of administrative violence appear in the shape of complex legislation, military orders, zoning and planning policies, and specialised state bodies to monitor Bedouins and their life and space. Hence, alongside the Zionist biblical references to the right of the Jewish people over Palestine, the Israeli Government established in 2018 a legal foundation for this right in the Basic Law Israel – The Nation State of the Jewish People.[34] At the same time, the narrative espoused by the Israeli state constructs several myths and dominant assumptions concerning Palestine and Palestinians, including the Bedouins, the Naqab and the Eastern Jerusalem periphery, part of which is referred to as the Judean Desert. These constructed representations view the Bedouin as nomadic peoples, apolitical and lacking in (Palestinian) national identity, and their space as an arid desert. Within such discursive representations and the Zionist myths of 'making the desert bloom' and of 'a land without a people for a people without land', the Bedouin were and continue to be deemed as transferrable, enabling Israeli colonial frontiers to target them and their space. Bedouin in the Naqab, Susya and Khan al-Ahmar face such policies in various ways and act to defend their space and its identity.

3.2. AT THE FRONTIERS OF NATIONALISM AND NOMADISM

3.2.1. Nomadism and the Moving Frontiers

Nomadism has always been assumed as the antipode of modern nation-states, due to mobility and non-fixity that challenges state aspiration for legibility of space and population.[35] Assumptions around nomadism were also associated with the Bedouin communities and utilised as a research category to analyse and examine Bedouin economic and social relations. Such assumptions have played a major role

[32] M Joronen, 'Negotiating Colonial Violence: Spaces of Precarisation in Palestine' (2019) 51 *Antipode* 838.

[33] ibid.

[34] Basic Law: Israel – The Nation State of the Jewish People (n 15).

[35] S Assi, *History and Politics of the Bedouin: Reimagining Nomadism in Modern Palestine* (Routledge, 2020) 74; JC Scott, *The Art of Not Being Governed: An Anarchist History of Upland Southeast Asia* (Yale University Press, 2010).

in relation to property rights, displacement and nationalism.[36] Seraj Assi introduced the concept of 'exteriority' when referring to the position of nomads as exteriors in British common law.[37] In the genealogy of modern state, most Bedouins failed to register and then prove their ownership rights over their lands. Nevertheless, the basis upon which such assumptions have been made are false: Bedouin communities are heterogeneous communities and subsisted on a combined agropastoral system. For example, in the Naqab the majority of Bedouin were settled or semi-nomadic and cultivated up to 3.5 million dunams of land until 1948, most of which was used to grow barley and wheat that was exported for the beer industry in the United Kingdom, reaching an annual export of nearly 60,000 tons in the early twentieth century.[38] Furthermore, many of these lands were registered with the Ottoman, and then the British Mandate authorities.[39] Despite ample evidence of settled Bedouin communities semi-nomadic life, assuming and placing an emphasis on their nomadic identity and denying Bedouins their Palestinian national identity offers a green light to their displacement. It can be (erroneously) argued that due to their nomadic identity they lack land ownership, and thus are movable and removable, resulting in the normalisation of their displacement. Bedouins, consequently, have been denied their connection to Palestine and Palestinians: a manifestation of the colonial divide and conquer strategy. Effectively, Bedouins on both sides of the 'invisible Green Line' have been continuously denied their connection materially and discursively to both their land and to the broader Palestinian national identity.

Within a complex set of historical, social and legal relations, Bedouin communities are an easy target for displacement and remain displaceable, even when they have been living in the same villages and communities for decades. As stated in section 3.1 of this chapter, Bedouin displacement should not be viewed as a distinct phenomenon from that of Palestinian displacement and the colonisation of Palestinian space at large.[40] However, contemporary cases of targeting an entire Palestinian village or community that is not Bedouin in the West Bank is less common. It is more frequent nowadays to colonise rural Palestinian lands and to target Palestinian houses or restrict the expansion of Palestinian localities if they fall in Area C and lack a zoning plan, which is usually the case. In the case of Bedouins, given that none of their localities are state-planned or recognised by Israel, they are deemed to be illegal under Israeli law. Therefore, these entire communities become 'legal targets' for displacement. Given that this is the case for communities across both sides of the Green Line, it is fair to argue that the Green Line is simply invisible: the same pseudo-legal pretexts for displacement are applied to both sides as long as it leads to the dislodgment of Bedouins. Nevertheless, over the years, Palestinian resilience and the steadfastness of the Bedouin communities have challenged such Israeli policies. This theme is examined in section 3.4 of this chapter.

[36] A Amara, 'Beyond Stereotypes of Bedouin as Nomads and Savages: Rethinking the Bedouin in Ottoman southern Palestine, 1875–1900' (2016) 15 *Journal of Holy Land and Palestine Studies* 59.

[37] Assi (n 35) 72.

[38] Kedar et al (n 8) 129.

[39] ibid; and Amara (n 36).

[40] Tatour (n 11).

3.2.2. Displacement and Displaceability in the Naqab

Following the Nakba, only 13,000 Bedouin Palestinians remained within the Naqab out of an estimated population of 90,000 in 1948.[41] The majority were expelled by the Zionist-Jewish paramilitary groups and the Israeli army thereafter from their lands to neighbouring countries, and to the West Bank and the Gaza Strip. Some of those expelled are from the Jahalin tribes who inhabit/inhabited lands south of Hebron and who now live as refugees in the Eastern Jerusalem periphery (discussed in section 3.2.3 below). The remaining communities, though they were granted Israeli citizenship, were placed under Israeli military rule until 1966, and in the early 1950s were forcefully displaced and concentrated in an enclosed area known as the *Siyaj* (the Arabic word for fence), north-east of Beer al-Saba' (Naqab).[42] Lands of Palestinian Bedouin refugees were appropriated through the Absentee Property Law,[43] whereas those who remained continue to face Israeli denial of their property rights to the lands that they have occupied and/or cultivated for over a century. Parallel to their displacement, Israeli authorities acted to forcefully concentrate and urbanise the Bedouin communities, and planned three townships in the 1960s for this purpose. The existing Bedouin villages and those that were re-established following their displacement in the 1950s were deemed illegal under Israeli law. In 1965, the Israeli Knesset passed the Planning and Building Law that required that building be enacted based on permits that fit with the type of zoning that applies to the land.[44] Similar laws were also applied to the Bedouins in Area C of the OPT and are discussed in detail in the following section. Bedouin communities and villages were excluded from zoning plans, making them illegal and their displacement imperative, despite applying for building permits. As such, the Israeli authorities utilised zoning as a main tool for spatial engineering in both Israel and in the West Bank, thus blurring yet again the Green Line.

In 2005, the Israeli Government adopted the Negev Development Plan (NDP), another tool used to Judaise the Naqab. The plan seeks to increase the Jewish population in the Naqab in new and existing settlements, and to that end, it seeks to 'resolve' the 'Bedouin problem', ie the unrecognised villages and the longstanding land ownership dispute between the Bedouin communities and Israel.[45] The eviction of Umm al-Hiran was due to the Israeli decision to build the Jewish settlement of Hiran instead.

Though Bedouin villages in the Naqab existed long before the enactment of the plan, and some before the founding of Israel, the Israeli planning authorities ignored the existence of these villages, turned them invisible in state maps, and zoned their lands as industrial zones, fire zones, or as open spaces where construction

[41] Kedar et al (n 8) 87.

[42] ibid.

[43] The Absentee Property Law 5710-1950, Laws of the State of Israel No 37, 20 March 1950.

[44] Israel's Planning and Building Law (1965), www.adalah.org/uploads/oldfiles/Public/files/Discriminatory-Laws-Database/English/07-National-Planning-Building-Law-1965.pdf (is available in English translation).

[45] Adalah, 'Adalah Demands Cancellation of the Government's Negev 2015: The National Strategic Plan for the Development of the Negev (Naqab) as it Ignores the Needs of the Arab Bedouin' (30 January 2007), www.adalah.org/en/content/view/6824.

is forbidden.[46] As Israeli authorities deny Bedouin ownership on both sides of the Green Line, their lands are deemed and treated as state lands, even if they are not registered under the state's name. Zoning has also been systematically utilised by the Israeli authorities for the demarcation of frontiers, legalities and grey spaces. It enables the building of new Jewish settlements and their expansion, while seeking to control Palestinian space through policies of non-zoning or active zoning that prevented the construction of new Palestinian localities and interrupted the expansion of existing ones.[47]

Forty-five Bedouin villages in the Naqab have been deemed illegal, and the only legal residence for these communities consisted of seven townships established by the state for the concentration of Bedouins. The 'illegal' villages became known as the 'unrecognised villages', resulting in the denial of all state services, and the subjecting of homes in these communities to demolition and eviction. In the 1970s, the Israeli authorities initiated the 'land title settlement' process; in this period the formal Israeli legal position towards Bedouin lands emerged. During the enforcement of the land title settlement process in the 1970s, Palestinian Bedouin claimants filed over 3,000 land claims over 1.5 million dunams. Instead of the relevant land officers considering each claim on its individual merits, in 1975 the state appointed a commission, headed by Plia Albeck from the State Attorney Office, to look into the land claims. Albeck, who was in the late 1970s part of the Israeli Government team supporting Israeli land-grabs in the West Bank for the establishment and expansion of settlements, concluded that the claimed lands were state lands.[48] According to Albeck, Bedouins have no legal rights as the lands are 'Mawat' land according to the 1858 Ottoman Land Code, meaning that they were deemed to be empty, uncultivated and unpossessed lands. The Israeli authorities utilised the Ottoman Land Code through manipulative reinterpretations and the imposition of legal standards to deny Palestinian land rights.[49] Albeck orchestrated this specific 'legalised' formula for land expropriation, and helped develop Israel's land expropriation techniques applied on both sides of the invisible Green Line.

[46] Israel's targeting of Bedouin communities with house demolition orders caused many Bedouin communities to fear building Area C, due to this instability and the trauma the families suffered with demolition. This is especially true for Bedouins in the E1 zone. Al-Quds Human Rights Clinic, among many, documented the emotional and psychological damage that children and families went through due to Israel's policy of house demolitions, noting that Bedouin are particularly precarious in such situations due to a lack of an alternative. See also, Adalah and Bimkom, 'Bedouin Communities Under Threat in the Naqab', storymaps.arcgis.com/stories/bbfbf46fb07144a68b1f62280e967a98?mc_cid=42c5df17c7&mc_eid=UNIQID; and H Noach, *The demolition of Arab-Bedouin homes in the Naqab-Naqab* (Dukium/Negev Coexistence Forum for Civil Equality, 2011), www.dukium.org/wp-content/uploads/2011/06/Demolitions_Report_2011-for-print.pdf.

[47] N Azza et al, *Forced Population Transfer: The Case of Palestine; Discriminatory Zoning and Planning* (Badil Resource Center, 2014), www.badil.org/phocadownloadpap/badil-new/publications/research/working-papers/wp17-zoninig-plannig-en.pdf.

[48] State of Israel, Ministry of Justice, Summary Report of the Team of Experts on Land Settlement in the Siyaj and the Northern Naqab (Ministry of Justice, 20 October 1975) (Hebrew) (copy with the authors) ('The Albeck Report'). See also B'Tselem, 'By Hook and by Crook: Israeli Settlement Policy in the West Bank' (2010), www.btselem.org/publications/summaries/201007_by_hook_and_by_crook.

[49] A Amara, 'The Naqab Land Question: Between Denial and Recognition' (2013) 42 *Journal of Palestine Studies* 27. See also: Kedar et al (n 8).

Albeck, and the Israeli Government, through manipulative interpretations of Ottoman and British law, argued that Bedouin lands are state lands, and that Bedouins were merely squatters on state land despite having lived on these lands for centuries. Albeck suggested going beyond the 'letter of the law' and offered Bedouins who agreed to cancel their land claim, leave their villages and move to state-planned townships, a meagre compensation.[50] The vast majority of the Bedouins refused the proposal, and most of the land claims remain pending, despite hundreds of Israeli court decisions thus far in favour of the state. In parallel, the Israeli authorities demolished – and continue to demolish – Bedouin homes and structures, displace communities, and spray chemicals on crops on these lands, all justified under the guise of 'law enforcement'.[51]

To enforce Israeli legislation, the Israeli Government established different units, some of which worked predominantly among the Bedouin communities, like the Green Patrol and Unit 101, established by Ariel Sharon. The former is a division of the Israeli Ministry of Agriculture and the latter is a unit in the Israeli army.[52] The most prominent operation by Unit 101 was the displacement of al Azazmeh tribe in 1953–54.[53] Until 1953, approximately 7,000 Bedouins had been expelled by the Green Patrol.[54] The Green Patrol, despite being part of the Ministry of Agriculture, was assigned 'to act as the executive arm of government policy' and 'to clear the land of Bedouins with as little publicity as possible'.[55] The goal of the Green Patrol was to cunningly move communities from their sites 'even if a small distance away' so that they lost the accumulated years required by 'law' to grant them prescriptive title to the land.[56] Panepinto, citing Tawil, argues that such policies of denial of Palestinian ownership of the land are proof that 'Israel enjoys a monopoly over where and how to mark and enforce the boundaries between itself and Palestinians'.[57] Clearly, these boundaries progress beyond 'borders' of the state.

In *The Naqab: Bedouin Struggles in Grey Space*, Oren Yiftachel explains how the State of Israel in theory, policy and practice aims at finding ways to fulfil the Zionist dream of control by establishing a borderless Jewish-only state.[58] This means that present-day, established borders hold little significance to Israel's expansionist objectives. The fluidity of borders is living evidence of the continuation of settler colonialism that can be achieved through 'displacement, destruction and even death'.[59] Bedouins in particular are victims of this fluidity including the functioning of peripheries on both sides of the Green Line as 'grey spaces'. Yiftachel refers to grey

[50] The Albeck Report (n 48).
[51] ibid, on the Bedouin unrecognised villages and related land disputes.
[52] G Falah, 'How Israel Controls the Bedouin in Israel' (1985) 14 *Journal of Palestine Studies* 35, 42.
[53] ibid 43.
[54] D Shmueli and R Khamaisi, 'Bedouin Communities in the Negev' (2011) 77 *Journal of the American Planning Association* 109.
[55] Falah (n 52) 43.
[56] ibid 44.
[57] AM Panepinto, 'Jurisdiction as Sovereignty over Occupied Palestine' (2017) 26 *Social and Legal Studies* 311, 332, 315. H Tawil, 'Uneven Borders, Coloured (IM)Mobilities: ID Cards in Palestine/Israel' (2012) 17 *Geopolitics* 153, 173.
[58] R Khalidi, 'It's Time to Confront Israel's Version of "From the River to the Sea"' *The Nation* (22 November 2023), www.thenation.com/article/world/its-time-to-confront-israels-version-of-from-the-river-to-the-sea.
[59] O Yiftachel, 'Critical Theory and "Gray Space": Mobilization of the Colonized' (2009) 13 *City* 246.

spaces as those which function 'outside of space' or in other ways described as 'dead zones'.[60] Spaces where Bedouins reside have been labelled 'grey spaces' to facilitate the displacement of the communities.

3.2.3. Displacement and Displaceability in the Occupied Palestinian Territory

Bedouins living within and around the E1 area between Jerusalem and the Israeli settlement of Ma'ale Adumim, which we refer to as the Eastern Jerusalem periphery, were displaced refugees from the Naqab, and face a similar fate of displacement as those who still reside in the Naqab. Their communities and villages, located in the West Bank, which has been under Israeli military occupation since 1967, are also deemed illegal by Israeli military laws. The lands where they live were designated by the Israeli authorities as firing zones, industrial or open spaces, as well as state land as reserve for Israeli settlements.[61] Their access to pasture land and open spaces is severely restricted by the Israeli military, leading to serious economic damage and impact on their Bedouin way of life.[62] The Israeli Civil Administration (ICA), a branch of the Israeli army, had also initiated forced urbanisation plans to concentrate the Bedouin communities in the Jerusalem area into three townships, and managed to relocate one of these communities in the late 1990s, with disastrous consequences for the families affected.[63]

Over the last two decades, Israeli policies to displace Bedouin in the Naqab and in Area C of the West Bank have intensified. After the original displacement of 1948, displacement, enclosure, entrapment and home demolitions have all continued at different levels, depending on the Israeli colonial frontiers established in that period. More recently, for example, the Israeli Military Government implemented draconian military orders that specifically targeted Bedouin communities. The Regulations Concerning the Transfer of Goods 1252 (Transport of Mobile Structures 1993) was enacted to target the mobile structures and makeshift housing for the Palestinian Bedouins (often provided as humanitarian aid by international donors), as they are prevented by the Israeli authorities from building concrete structures.[64] Initially, the Regulations allowed seizures to take place within 30 days of the installation of the 'mobile structure'; in 2015 the deadline was extended to 60 days, and in August 2020 it was extended to 90 days.[65] Finally, the Regulations required that a special permit be obtained in order to transport a mobile structure or parts of it, and if done without

[60] ibid 15.

[61] O Yiftachel, 'Epilogue: Studying al-Naqab/Negev Bedouins-Toward a colonial paradigm?' (2008) 8 *HAGAR: Studies in Culture, Polity & Identities* 173.

[62] UN-OCHA, '46 Bedouin Communities at Risk of Forcible Transfer in the Central West Bank: A Vulnerability Profile' (2017).

[63] UNRWA/Bimkom, 'Al Jabal: a study on the transfer of Bedouin Palestine refugees' (2013) at www.unrwa.org/userfiles/2013052935643.pdf?__cf_chl_jschl_tk__=U2_VV7yVhrdZjpj_Z4iQtwWSm3tbYR4WRWNLOHBPzoc-1638283172-0-gaNycGzNCv0.

[64] 'Regulations Concerning the Transfer of Goods (Transport of Mobile Structures) (Judea and Samaria), 1993', www.nevo.co.il/Authentication/UserLogin.aspx?ReturnUrl=%2flaw_html%2flaw65%2f666_038.htm#Seif6; www.nevo.co.il/law_html/law65/666_038.htm (in Hebrew).

[65] ibid.

a permit, an inspector, a soldier, or a police officer may seize the transporting vehicle and its licence for 14 days.[66]

Another significant legislative change is the Temporary Military Order regarding Removal of New Structures in Judea and Samaria (MO 1797), passed on 17 April 2018 by the IDF commander. This legalised the demolition/removal of new 'unlicensed' structures in Area C within a shortened timeline, granting administrative staff extensive powers, and thus eliminating most avenues for judicial review by granting the executive branch, mainly building inspectors, to issue demolition orders. Enacting such laws further limited the already-reduced ability of Bedouins to contest their displacement in court, given the already controversial issue of the jurisdiction of the Israeli High Court of Justice (HCJ) in the OPT.[67] The Israeli Supreme Court largely greenlights the Israeli military's policies and practices in the OPT. In the limited cases where Bedouins attempted to contest the zoning plans, the court functioned as a tool to buy time and postpone the demolitions, and not to resolve the question of Bedouin habitat.[68] The aforementioned MO 1797 offers an example of Israeli settler colonial frontiers and boundaries to which Palestinian communities are subjected, whereby each geography has its own legal restrictions and is accompanied by violent means of enforcement on behalf of the Israeli state. The order authorises the ICA inspector to issue a removal notice against 'new' structures within firing zones, in the proximity of main roads, in nature reserves or archaeological sites, military zones, if the structures constitute significant implications for security and public order, new Israeli construction on privately owned Palestinian lands and new Palestinian construction on privately owned Israeli land.[69] The following discussion addresses the functions of these frontiers and others on the ground during the last two decades, and how they affect Bedouin communities on both sides of the Green Line.

3.3. THE NEW SETTLER COLONIAL FRONTIERS

This section outlines the historical and political foundations of settler colonial frontiers and their movement by looking at the NDP and its impact on Bedouin communities in the Naqab by focusing on the Umm al-Hiran Bedouin community. It then proceeds with a discussion of the aftermath of the Oslo accords (1993–95), which marked the beginning of two different frontiers located, respectively, in the South Hebron Hills exemplified by the community of Susya, and in the E1 plan in the Eastern Jerusalem periphery by considering the case of the Bedouin community of Khan al-Ahmar. These two communities, among many others, face an imminent threat of forced displacement and are surrounded by Israeli settlements. This section will therefore explore the operation of the Israeli settler colonial framework across different geographies regardless of political borders, such as the Green

[66] ibid.

[67] Panepinto (n 57) 322.

[68] D Kretzmer and Y Ronen, *The Occupation of Justice: The Supreme Court of Israel and the Occupied Territories* (OUP, 2021).

[69] UN-OCHA, 'Peak in Demolitions and Confiscations amidst Increasing Denial of the Right to Justice' (2020), www.ochaopt.org/content/peak-demolitions-and-confiscations-amidst-increasing-denial-right-justice.

Line, to illustrate similar structures of Bedouin displacement. This will illustrate how Israel uses law and zoning policies to ensure the displacement of Bedouin communities. Furthermore, it demonstrates the moving frontiers and how the different boundaries that these laws and policies create dictate Palestinian geography.

3.3.1. Umm al-Hiran and the Naqab

The displacement of the residents of Umm al-Hiran in the Naqab ('Negev' in Hebrew) is part of the broader phase of reactivating the Naqab as a new settler frontier, based on the 2005 NDP.[70] The Israeli Government adopted the NDP as a 'national strategic' plan with four main objectives to be achieved within a specific timeframe (originally 10 years). These goals were: to increase the Naqab's Jewish population from 535,000 to 900,000; to increase the number of Jewish employees in the Naqab from 164,000 to 300,000; to decrease the gap in local income by 60 per cent compared with the national income; to increase the number of Jewish school students to match the national rate and that of the Bedouin students from 2.2 per cent to five per cent in the Naqab. The plan targeted five main areas: economic development (mainly investment, tourism and high-tech industry); education; housing and settlement (including the facilitation of land allocation and improving the quality of life); infrastructure; and developing the Bedouin townships to attract the 'dispersed communities' – referring to Bedouins in the unrecognized villages.[71] To achieve these ends, the NDP sought solutions for the 'Bedouin problem', to quote the language of the plan.

In the Naqab, the Bedouin and their existence are viewed by Israeli authorities as an obstacle to development and Judaisation. Turning the Naqab again into an old–new-settler frontier enables plans to displace Bedouin communities from the 'unrecognised villages', replacing them with Jewish families and policing infrastructure that is hostile towards Bedouins and their very presence in the area. The NDP included the transfer of military bases from the Tel-Aviv region to the Naqab and building settlements for soldiers serving in them. Specific plans and decisions to establish Jewish settlements in the Naqab followed.[72]

In 2005, a new Ministry for the Development of the Naqab and the Galilee was founded, and one of its main objectives was to implement the NDP. In 2018, the Israeli Minister of Housing put forward a new plan to establish new communities, expand existing ones, and to plan for 15 additional rural communities.[73] While discussing the plan at the Knesset, Housing Minister Yoav Gallant stated that:

> The south is not only exposed to attacks from Gaza, the Bedouin illegal squatting [over lands] is harming Israeli sovereignty in the Naqab …. The Naqab is under risk, and there is a serious fear of hostile control.[74]

[70] 'Cabinet Resolution 4415', the Official Site of the Israeli Ministry of Construction and Housing, 20/11/2005, www.gov.il/he/pages/2005_des4415 (in Hebrew) ('The Naqab Development Plan', 2005).

[71] ibid.

[72] In November 2022, the Israeli Government decided to build 10 new settlements in the Negev; see www.gov.il/he/pages/newdesertsettelments (in Hebrew).

[73] Israeli cabinet Resolutions no 2265 (2002), 3349 (2008), 3345 (2018), 4492 (2019) (in Hebrew).

[74] 'Minister Gallant racist statements towards the Bedouin' (The association for civil rights in Israel, 2018), law.acri.org.il/he/42653.

He added:

> [W]hat we see today on the ground is uncontrolled illegal construction. It is Palestinian and Islamist ... this is all taking place while we introduce a settlement plan to build new settlements in areas that where its crossing coincides with the risks of stone-throwing and Molotov.[75]

The statement is a manifestation of the pretext of security underpinning displacement of Bedouin communities and the building and expansion of Jewish settlements. The plan proposed that three Jewish settlements should be built on top of Bedouin villages and claimed lands, including Umm al-Hiran.[76] This is a classic move of settler colonialism, where the settler group seeks to displace and replace indigenous people.

Within this context, Umm al-Hiran was demolished in April 2018 to be replaced by the new Jewish settlement of Hiran, approved in 2002. Since then, home demolitions in Bedouin communities in the Naqab have increased steadily, as reported by the Naqab Coexistence Forum for 2015–18.[77] In 2019 alone, the Israeli authorities demolished 2,241 Bedouin structures, adding to 2,326 structures in 2018, including 604 houses; this is a sharp increase from 417 houses and 536 houses in 2016 and 2017 respectively.[78] Other practices to 'resolve' the 'Bedouin problem' undertaken by the Israeli authorities include the practice of suddenly counter-claiming against Bedouin land claims in 2004, even after the deferment of the original Bedouin land claims for over 30 years. When disputed, a claim is referred to the District Court; hundreds of claims have been contested this way. Thus far all decisions are completely in favour of the state, based on the spurious argument that the land was Mewat land according to Ottoman law, and thus the Bedouin are mere squatters on state lands.[79] As such, these courts do not uphold Palestinian Bedouins' right to land; most of the time they rule in favour of the state and Jewish settlers.

3.3.2. Susya and the Southern Hebron Hills

Much like the communities in the Naqab, Palestinian Bedouins in Area C of the West Bank suffer a comparable imminent threat of displacement. North-east of the Naqab, across the Green Line, the Bedouin communities of the South Hebron Hills, in the area known as Masafer Yatta, have been a target of Israeli eviction and demolition policies since the 1980s. The area was designated as a 'closed military zone' or Firing Zone no 918 in the 1980s. As a result, the presence of Palestinian communities within the zone became illegal according to Israeli law, and therefore any inhabitants were subject to eviction. Despite prolonged litigation and advocacy efforts against the

[75] B Frankel and Z Levi, 'Gallant presented a plan for settlements in the Naqab and attacked the planning authorities' (2018), www.ynet.co.il/articles/0,7340,L-5278439,00.html.

[76] Adalah, 'Israeli desert development plan promotes building new Jewish towns, ignores existing Bedouin towns' (7 August 2017), www.adalah.org/en/content/view/9183.

[77] Dukium/Negev Coexistence Forum for Civil Equality, 'Mechanism for Dispossession and Intimidation: Demolition Policy in Arab Bedouin Communities in Negev/Naqab (June 2019) 11, www.dukium.org/wp-content/uploads/2019/07/Demolition-Report-Eng.2018.pd.

[78] ibid.

[79] Kedar et al (n 8).

pending displacement, in 2022 the Israeli High Court of Justice ordered the eviction of eight communities from Masafer Yatta,[80] stating that there were 'no legal obstacles against the eviction', consequently making the threat of displacement imminently actionable.[81] The community of Khirbet Susiya in Masafer Yatta is trapped between the various Israeli colonisation fronts: the settlement of Susiya and plans for its expansion, a Firing Zone, and an Israeli-designated archaeological site. Thus, the targeting of Khirbet Susiya is based on the application of pseudo-legalities in the shape of military orders alongside archaeological excavations, utilised together to displace the Palestinian communities and to legitimise such displacement under the pretext of legality and paleo-historical significance. In 1986, the Israeli authorities declared Susiya an archaeological site and evicted all of its Palestinian residents. Most of the families who 'relocated to what was later designated as Area C were displaced again in the context of two waves of demolitions, in 2001 and in 2011, on grounds of lack of building permits'.[82] Similarly to Umm al-Hiran in the Naqab, the communities of Susya have faced a waves of displacement and are subject to other demolition orders based on the pretext that their homes and other structures are built without legal permits. Equivalent policies of non-recognition used in Umm al-Hiran and Susya allocate these lands in grey zones, allowing the establishment of settler frontiers that rendered the Green Line separating them invisible in the face of colonial expansion.

Since the signing of the Oslo Accords, Palestinian communities in Area C in the West Bank have become victims of various legal taxonomies and hierarchies, mainly based on Israeli military orders by the military commander who controls legislative, executive and judicial authorities pertaining to land ownership in Area C. Palestinian communities, and particularly Bedouin communities, have become the target of increasing Israeli demolition and eviction policies to enable the advancing Israeli settlement enterprise since the 1990s. In particular, Oslo II (1995) divided the OPT into Areas A, B and C and allowed Israeli control over Area C, greenlighting the displacement of many Palestinians and especially Bedouins who reside primarily in Area C.

3.3.3. Khan al-Ahmar and the Eastern Jerusalem Periphery

About 45 Bedouin communities totalling nearly 8,500 persons in the Jerusalem periphery, located between Ma'ali Adumim Settlement Bloc and Jerusalem, are under the threat of forcible displacement by the Israeli authorities. Typically, the lands in which these communities live are designated by the Israeli authorities as state lands. Given that the Israeli authorities deem these communities as having been built illegally on state lands, their residents are considered squatters and their homes are subject to demolition and eviction orders. Alongside Israeli plans for

[80] OCHA, 'Fact Sheet: Masafer Yatta communities at risk of forcible transfer' (2022), www.ochaopt.org/content/masafer-yatta-communities-risk-forcible-transfer-june-2022.

[81] ibid.

[82] United Nations Office for the Coordination of Humanitarian Affairs –occupied Palestinian, 'Susiya: A Community at Imminent Risk of Forced Displacement Territory' (2015).

building settlements and increasing land control in E1, the Israeli authorities seek to concentrate all Bedouin communities in urban centres, preferably outside Area C. Tightening Israeli grip over Area C is a catalyst for the de facto annexation of the West Bank; thus, the more Bedouins are removed from Area C, the easier it is to control Palestinian space.[83]

Alongside state authorities acting relentlessly to impose evictions, demolitions and impeding Bedouin development, Israeli settler organisations are also active. In monitoring Israeli law and zoning policies applicable to Palestinian buildings and land use, they lobby the state to take harsher action. As such, Israeli state and non-state actors play a joint role in the displacement of Bedouin communities. Regavim, for example, an Israeli NGO associated with the settler movement, monitors and targets Palestinian communities in Area C including Susiya and Khan al-Ahmar among many others. Regavim continuously lobbies the ICA for failing to enforce 'the law' and evicting communities who they claim 'live illegally' and are already facing pending eviction orders.[84] Bedouins who fall under the E1 plan are directly threatened by such organisations which leverage their resources to fight against Bedouin presence in the court system and on the ground.[85] The Israeli adoption of the E1 plan, like the NDP, is yet another tool of the Israeli active frontier of land control, leading to increased demolitions in key regions such as E1 that serve Israel's expansionist agenda. Furthermore, other geopolitical considerations and security claims mark specific frontiers and expose particular communities to higher risks of displacement than others; notably, in cases of Israeli plans for settlement expansion, or the proximity of some communities to highways linking Ma'ale Adumim and Jerusalem to Jericho. This is particularly relevant as the 'visibility' of Bedouin communities has become associated with 'security' threats, which is often the justification of ICA efforts to displace them.[86] The Khan al-Ahmar Bedouin community located in the Eastern periphery of Jerusalem is one example of several communities that are trapped within an Israeli legal and military web of grey spaces, and are facing an immediate threat of displacement, justified by several pretexts including the expansion of Israeli settlements and the proximity to the Jerusalem–Jericho highway.

As one of the most highly contested spaces in the region, East Jerusalem had been the locus of power struggles politically. Nestled in the Eastern Jerusalem periphery, Khan al-Ahmar is one of these communities facing demolition and eviction orders issued by the Israeli authorities and a court decision from 2018 confirming the

[83] See eg Israeli politicians' position on the E1 plan and the significance of controlling the lands between Jerusalem and Ma'ale Adumim: Jerusalem Center for Public Affairs, 'Israel's E1 Building Plan: The Most Strategic, Consensual – and Frozen – Project' (2022), jcpa.org/article/israels-e1-building-plan-the-most-strategic-consensual-and-frozen-project.

[84] Regavim was found to have received money from settlements' councils which amount to thousands of shekels (NIS) of Israeli taxpayers' money. Y Berger, 'How Israeli Taxpayers Are Funding a Right-Wing NGO Dedicated to Getting Palestinians Evicted *Haaretz* (18 January 2018), www.haaretz.com/israel-news/2018-01-19/ty-article/israeli-right-wing-ngo-regavim-gets-millions-of-shekels-in-public-fund/0000017f-dbf9-db22-a17f-fff992510000.

[85] See Middle East Monitor, 'Israel: racist settler group misusing charitable funds to displace Palestinians' (3 October 2023), www.middleeastmonitor.com/20231003-israel-racist-settler-group-misusing-charitable-funds-to-displace-palestinians.

[86] HCJ 2387/19, *Regavim v Israeli prime Minister et Al*, decision 7 September 2020.

intended displacement.[87] The eviction included 140 structures and a school.[88] The Khan al-Ahmar community comprises five smaller communities: Makab as Samen, Mihtawish, Abu al-Helu, Wadi al-Sider and Khirbet Abu Falah, which has received over 73 demolition orders since 2014.[89] In the eyes of the Israeli authorities, Khan al-Ahmar must be relocated due to its proximity to the Israeli highway connecting Jerusalem and the Dead Sea; in the case of nearly 20 other Bedouin communities it is the Israeli E1 Zoning Plan that drives the displacement threat.

Despite the 2018 court decision authorising displacement, residents of Khan al-Ahmar rejected the destruction of their community, arguing – inter alia – that their expulsion was in breach of international law. The Israeli court dismissed their petition, but due to international pressure, the court has granted several postponements since then.[90] Fatou Bensouda, the former ICC prosecutor, released a statement raising concern that the decision to expel the Khan al-Ahmar community may amount to a war crime.[91] It is important to note that 44 separate orders were issued since 2009 for the demolition of Khan al-Ahmar, which included a school, clinic, mosque and several inhabited and uninhabited structures, meaning that the entire village was under demolition orders.[92] Panepinto describes the Israeli High Court of Justice's jurisdiction over the Khan al-Ahmar eviction as a form of 'permanent regime of legalised control' imposed by the occupying power based solely on 'compliance with procedural standards set out in existing laws and not to substantive justice of said laws and judicial procedures.'[93] Panepinto's description pertains to the entire Israeli judicial policies and positions in the OPT, in contradiction with international law.

The Bedouin community of Khan al-Ahmar challenges what Eyal Weizman terms 'verticality' in *Hollow Land*. The concept of 'verticality' denotes a means to maximise (Israeli) control over (Palestinian) land.[94] He cites the building of settlements on top of hills as a means through which to give the impression of verticality, projecting control and power. The Bedouin community of Khan al-Ahmar challenges such 'verticality' by existing horizontally alongside a busy highway used by many settlers to commute. In other words, Khan al-Ahmar's visibility from the highway threatens the long history of Israeli colonial architecture that aims to maximise the gaps between Palestinians and settlers within a longstanding pretext of security, barely concealing its colonial expansionist motives. As Regavim continues to petition the

[87] HCJ 5193/18; HCJ 5257/18; HCJ 5410/18, *The Khan al-Ahmar residents' committee et al V IDF Commander in the West Bank et al.*

[88] OCHA, 'Tightening of coercive environment on Bedouin communities around Ma'ale Adumim settlement' (2017), www.ochaopt.org/content/tightening-coercive-environment-bedouin-communities-around-ma-ale-adumim-settlement.

[89] 'OCHA Portal, Data on demolition and displacement in the West Bank' (2022), www.ochaopt.org/data/demolition.

[90] B'Tselem, 'Communities facing expulsion: the Khan Al-Ahmar area' (2022), www.btselem.org/communities_facing_expulsion/khan_al_ahmar.

[91] UN News, 'West Bank: "Imminent" Demolition of Palestinian Village Could Be "War Crime" – ICC Prosecutor' (17 October 2018), news.un.org/en/story/2018/10/1023381.

[92] ibid.

[93] Panepinto (n 57).

[94] E Weizman, *Hollow Land: Israel's Architecture of Occupation* (Verso Books, 2012).

Supreme Court to order the ICA to carry the demolitions and the eviction of Khan al-Ahmar, at the time of writing the community remains under such threat.

3.4. BEDOUIN SPACE LEGIBILITY AND BEDOUIN *SUMUD*

As discussed throughout this chapter, Palestinian Bedouin spaces have been targeted under various pretexts. Despite efforts to prove their land ownership and right to housing, they have been unable to prove their formal legal title to land in a manner 'legible' by the Israeli authorities, thus they continue to be displaced or face threats of displacement. At the same time, being under constant threat of displacement, Bedouin spaces have been considered illegible because of their lack of 'documentation' and their 'spatial plans' were deemed unrecognised, hence movable and removable. After decades of direct and organised efforts to displace Palestinian Bedouins, the Bedouin communities continue to resist in various ways. In the face of various waves of demolitions and forced displacement, Bedouins continue to live on their land and rebuild their demolished homes and remain steadfast in their communities.[95] The communities employ various means to defy displacement, including domestic and international legal advocacy.

The logic of denying recognition/legibility as a tool of indigenous erasure is not a modern concept. Israel's monopoly over taxonomy[96] as a method used historically can define, include and exclude, create meanings and classify objects and groups into categories easily controlled and monitored by the state. Many Bedouin communities lack a centralised zoning and planning system, making their spaces harder to decipher and categorise in the hyper-legalised Israeli system of domination. The nature of Bedouin villages and structures of the many Bedouin communities make them 'illegible' to the Israeli Government, echoing what James C Scott describes as unmanageable and unreadable for state and military power whose focus is creating readable geometrical gridline infrastructure that make spaces easier to control.[97] Scott denies that illegibility is anything but a double-edged sword. While it justifies the state's interest in forced sedentarisation, it becomes the tool through which Bedouins resist the 'outsiders'. For Scott, order can be shown in the neat layouts of water pipes, sewers, electric cables, mail and roads for transportation. However, Bedouin villages lack such infrastructure, which positions them on the opposite spectrum of the definition of a modern city.

This deviation from urbanism creates two kinds of opposing knowledge about the space – the local knowledge and the outsider knowledge – thus placing external political authorities at a relative disadvantage. The local knowledge becomes more powerful than the outsider knowledge, maximising the gap between inside and outside through the inability of the outsider to familiarise themselves with the 'geographical dialect' that locals master. While the mapping and designing of cities have been the

[95] M Nasasra, *The Naqab Bedouins: A Century of Politics and Resistance* (Columbia University Press, 2017).
[96] Understood, in brief, as the process of naming and classifying things.
[97] Scot (n 5).

state's tool of control, the architecture of the disorder of Bedouin villages portrays their rebellious nature. As such, Scott argues that 'illegibility has been and remains a reliable resource for political autonomy'.[98] Therefore, despite Bedouin communities living in grey spaces in the context of active settler frontiers, this greyness provides means to assert autonomy and resilience in the face of colonial expansionist policies on both sides of the invisible Green Line.

In *Lines: A Brief History*, Tim Ingold argues that 'since the straight line can be specified by numerical values, it becomes an index of quantitative rather than qualitative knowledge. Its function is to separate, to define, to order, to measure, to express number and proportion'.[99] The straight line here owns a function to define and to express a certain number. For the Green Line, both sides are separated by lines of control and domination. The line that is strictly straight in a modern sense is a line that separates two opposites. However, the Green Line bisecting Palestine is far from a line that splits opposites. It is a line that is invisible as much as it is material in its control and power to dictate who is legal or illegal in the eye of 'the state'. Lines that are used to separate two entities become the political conditions of that area it is separating. In East Jerusalem particularly, the efforts to control space focus on the annexation of land but not the inclusion of East Jerusalemites as people. The line becomes a concept that separates, excludes and subjugates instead of including and developing. Several other lines are constantly being drawn to demarcate state 'development' plans – settlements, industry, highways and the like – and thus mark new lines of lands that need to be zones, emptied and re-built with new people and new meanings. The Bedouin communities on both sides of the Green Line thus act as a continuum to indigenous presence that resists uprooting and displacement.

CONCLUSION

For the Israeli colonial project, the Green Line is a line that separates only the formality of the type of the laws that are applied: Israeli civilian law, versus Israeli military law or Jordanian laws. Policies, ideology and practices as they apply to Palestinians, including Bedouin communities, are largely the same on both sides of the Green Line. Within these dynamic assertions of Israeli control over all Palestinian spaces and the concurrent impetus for further Judaisation of the land, there is a constant creation of frontiers, borders and boundaries to draw the 'legal' and the 'illegal', the 'inside' and the 'outside', determining races that may legitimately (in the logic of settler colonialism) flourish and races that must be dominated. Bedouins and their spaces have been targeted since 1948 by Israel in the Naqab, South Hebron hills and the Eastern Jerusalem periphery, resulting in fragmentation of communities and waves of forced displacement that continue today. The Jerusalem periphery has become the newest frontier that enables land grabs and creeping annexation, despite the prohibitions of international law. Demography has been central to Israeli colonial practices. Contrary

[98] ibid 62.
[99] T Ingold, *Lines: A Brief History* (Routledge, 2016) 153.

to the belief that land acquisition was solely for settlement purposes, declaring vast lands as military zones, nature reserves, heritage sites or state land has been a pretext to eliminate Palestinian presence on the land. Vast areas of land in Area C remain empty of settlers but are controlled by the ICA. The twin dynamic of land control for zoning purposes and Israeli colonial land control serves Israeli domination and control of the Palestinian geography from the river to the sea.

In the reflections of David Harvey, in the *Right to the City*, the right to the city is a right to development. The Bedouin communities are deprived of their right to develop in Area C, while Israel continues to find ways to exercise de facto sovereignty despite the fact that international law prohibits the annexation of the occupied West Bank by the occupying power.[100] In the words of Wolfe, 'settler colonialism is a structure rather than an event':[101] Israel's continuous policy of land expropriation and the application of draconian pseudo-legalities have increasingly blurred the Green Line, exposing the de facto annexation of the West Bank and the demise of the two-state solution. Bedouin communities are deprived of living in secured tenureship; remaining entrapped in a grey space facilitates their displacement, regardless of where they are within one of Israeli settler colonial frontiers which dissolve the Green Line. In other words, the active settler frontiers imposed by Israel create discriminatory zoning policies and practices and produce visible and invisible borders that contribute significantly to indigenous erasure of Palestinians, and particularly Bedouins, on both sides of the invisible Green Line.

[100] D Harvey, 'The right to the city' (2003) 27 *International Journal of Urban and Regional Research* 939.
[101] Wolfe (n 1) 390.

4

The Gendered Impact of Israeli Forced Displacement: The Case of Palestinian Bedouin Women in the E1 Area

TAMARA TAMIMI AND RAGHAD ADWAN

INTRODUCTION

PALESTINIAN AND WESTERN scholars largely agree that Palestinian society can be characterised as traditional, conservative and patriarchal.[1] This is seen in the assumed gender roles conferred on men and women, particularly in reference to the public and private sphere divide. Traditionally, Palestinian women are responsible for the bulk of caring responsibilities for children and extended families,[2] while men have been perceived as the primary breadwinners.[3] More recently, women have shouldered greater economic responsibilities towards the family, but without increasing their collective agency, primarily due to the perception of women's employment as an economic necessity rather than a right.[4] Furthermore, women's increasing responsibilities in the family economy have not disrupted the patriarchal system or altered the public/private divide, particularly in terms of political participation and leadership,[5]

[1] J Hilal, 'The Pauperization of Palestinian Women, Men and Children in the West Bank and Gaza Strip' in Institute of Women's Studies, Birzeit University (eds), *A Dangerous Decade: The 2nd Gender Profile of the Occupied West Bank and Gaza (2000–2010)* (Institute of Women's Studies, 2011) 60; R Giacaman, 'No Palestinian is Safe: Population Dynamics and the Well-Being of Men, Women and Children through Objective Measures and Subjective Indicators' in Institute of Women's Studies–Birzeit University (ibid) 72.

[2] J Gardam, 'The Silences in the Rules That Regulate Women during Times of Armed Conflict' in F Ni Aolain, N Cahn, D Francesca and N Valji (eds), *The Oxford Handbook of Gender and Conflict* (OUP, 2017) 41.

[3] Promundo, 'Understanding Masculinities: Results from the International Men and Gender Equality Survey (IMAGES) – Middle East and North Africa: Palestine' (UN Women, 2018) 18; L Abu Nahleh, R Hammami, P Johnson, F Labadi and J Schalkwyk, *Towards Gender Equality in the Palestinian Territories: A Profile on Gender Relations* (Women's Studies Center, Birzeit University, 1999) 29–30.

[4] T Tamimi, 'Violence Against Women in Palestine and Mediocre Accountability' (2017) 5 *Legal Issues Journal* 84.

[5] Percentage of women in decision-making positions in the Palestinian Authority ministries stands as follows: 12% as director generals, 6% as assistant deputy ministers and 7% as deputy ministers; State of Palestine, 'Atlas of Sustainable Development 2020' (State of Palestine 2021) 22, palestine.un.org/sites/default/files/2021-10/atlas_of_sustainable_development_2020.pdf. In the 18th Government (April 2019 through March 2024) only 14% of ministers are women; PCBS, 'Palestine in Figures 2020' (2021) 19, www.pcbs.gov.ps/Downloads/book2557.pdf.

as well as integration in the formal economy.[6] While women's participation in the labour force improved by five per cent[7] between 2000 and 2019, this has not corresponded with an increase in men's responsibilities in the private sphere, in caregiving and household tasks.[8]

In the case of the Palestinian Bedouins, women have always assumed both caregiving and economic responsibilities:[9] on the one hand, women are responsible for the majority of household chores, including cleaning, cooking and caring for the children and elderly; on the other hand, women are active participants in the community's economic activities and structure, primarily through tending to the herd and producing and selling dairy products. Research undertaken by Al-Quds Human Rights Clinic (AQHRC) reveals the dual caregiving and labour roles that Bedouin women shoulder; women's daily lives are described by a Bedouin female interviewee from the Jabal Al-Baba community as follows: 'Our daily routine is to wake up at 5 each day, milk the goats and sheep, produce cheese from the milk to sell it to nearby stores, then bake bread and prepare breakfast…'.[10]

Palestinian Bedouin women are among the most vulnerable people in Palestinian society given the intersection of (at least) three primary identities: as Palestinians, they are subject to Israel's settler colonial policy;[11] as Bedouins, they are marginalised in mainstream (urban) Palestinian society (as discussed throughout in this chapter); and as women, they exist within the constraints of patriarchal structures and gender roles. In line with the theory of intersectionality,[12] Palestinian Bedouin women therefore

[6] Women's participation in the labour force stood at 18.1% in 2019, compared to 69.9% for men; State of Palestine, (n 5) 23. Women's employment is confined to certain sectors, such that, as of 2018, 71% of employed women work in the service industry, particularly in education and health professions, reflecting the persistence of gender stereotypes on suitable types of work for women that enable them to continue to shoulder their caregiving and household responsibilities. This is further supported in the striking difference between men's and women's participation in the commerce, restaurants and hotels industries, which require taking night shifts and working late hours, such that men's participation stands at 24% of their total participation in the labour market, compared to 11% for women. PCBS, 'The Reality of Labour Market from a Gender Perspective' (2019) 2, www.pcbs.gov.ps/Downloads/book2457.pdf.

[7] State of Palestine (n 5) 23.

[8] C Mussida and R Patimo, 'Women's Family Care Responsibilities, Employment, and Health: A Tale of Two Countries' (2021) 42 *Journal of Family and Economic Issues* 489.

[9] Interview AQU Legal Clinic I/WG/JB/21.

[10] N Perez-Cuso, C Fogerty, C Genrot, S Cogolati, D Abu Al-Haj, O Risheq and A Arouri, 'Forced Displacement of Bedouin Communities in the Jerusalem Periphery' (Al-Quds Human Rights Clinic, 2016) 21.

[11] L Veracini, *Israel and Settler Society* (Pluto Press, 2006) 2; P Wolfe, *Settler Colonialism and the Transformation of Anthropology: The Politics and Poetics of an Ethnographic Event* (Cassell, 1999) 1; P Wolfe, 'Settler Colonialism and the Elimination of the Native' (2006) 8 *Journal of Genocide Research* 387–88; L Veracini, 'Introduction: Settler Colonialism as a Distinct Mode of Domination' in E Cavanagh and L Veracini (eds), *The Routledge Handbook of the History of Settler Colonialism* (Routledge, 2017) 3; D Lloyd, 'Settler Colonialism and the State of Exception: The Example of Palestine/Israel' (2012) 2 *Settler Colonial Studies* 67; A Amara, BC Browne, T Mariniello, Nuseibah, A Panepinto and T Tamimi, 'The Bedouin Communities of Eastern Jerusalem: A New Locus of Power in the Post-Oslo Battle for Palestine?' (2021) 117 *Confluences Méditerranée* 108; T Tamimi, A Amara, O Risheq, M Nuseibah, A Panepinto, B Browne and T Mariniello, '(Mis)using Legal Pluralism in the Occupied Palestinian Territory to Advance Dispossession of Palestinians: Israeli Policies Against Palestinian Bedouins in the Eastern Jerusalem Periphery' in N Hasan and I Schneider (eds), *International Law between Translation and Pluralism: Examples from Germany, Palestine and Indonesia* (Harrassowitz Verlag, 2022).

[12] K Crenshaw, 'Demarginalizing the Intersection of Race and Sex: A Black Feminist Critique of Antidiscrimination Doctrine, Feminist Theory and Antiracist Politics' (1989) *University of Chicago Legal Forum* 139.

face not only the adversities imposed by each of these realities, but also additional vulnerabilities due to the combination of the three. Moreover, additional factors such as disability, age, socio-economic status within the community and level of education (to name a few) also impact on the vulnerabilities of Palestinian Bedouin women.

Within the wider framework of gender roles, and despite the multiple manifestations of prevalent patriarchal social norms (elaborated on below), women, individually, in Bedouin communities enjoy a considerable degree of agency at the level of economic decision-making. Bedouin women set the household budget due to constricted finances, as a result of societal marginalisation of Bedouin communities and Israeli settler colonial expansion, as well as their ability to identify the household priorities. Many of the women involved in the production of dairy products go to the markets and sell them, purchasing household goods and keeping any remaining profits.[13] This is clearly seen in income-generating projects (explored in more detail in section 4.2.1 below) run by women, in which they keep all the profit made. This is because the economic culture of Bedouin communities expects men to be solely responsible for providing for the family, meaning that, in principle, women are allowed to make and keep their own money, and decide how to spend it. Women's direct contributions to the economic upkeep of the household through the sale and barter of dairy products reflects a dire economic situation that forces them to shoulder financial responsibilities, which are traditionally met by men, thus demonstrating that while Bedouin women have economic agency, the scarcity of finances restrict the individual enjoyment of these funds by women. Nevertheless, the fact of contributing directly to the family finances is also empowering: it enables women to control and make important decisions on financial sources, demonstrating increased agency at the economic and financial levels in comparison to women in wider Palestinian society.

As a direct result of Israel's settler colonial policy and expansion into Palestine, 18 Bedouin communities in the Jerusalem periphery commonly known as the E1 area[14] live under a constant threat of forcible displacement through both direct and indirect means, including home demolitions and forced urbanisation, and the imposition of a coercive environment to drive the indigenous community out of their localities.[15] Successive Israeli governments have pursued forced urbanisation of Bedouin communities to clear land in preparation for settlement expansion: out of the 18 Bedouin communities in the E1 area, 10 have been offered relocation sites centred around the al-Nweima area north of Jericho and other sites.[16] While Israeli settler colonial policy targets the entirety of Bedouin society, this chapter focuses on the gendered implications and argues that it has a disproportionate impact on Palestinian Bedouin women

[13] Interview by AQU Legal Clinic I/WG/Mu/21; Interview by AQU Legal Clinic I/WG/AN/21.

[14] The E1 area refers to a 12 km^2 narrow land corridor located in Area C of the West Bank that is home to 18 Bedouin communities. The E1 area is circulated by a ring of settlements as part of the infamous E1 plan. The importance of the E1 area lies in its strategic location, such that the implementation of the E1 expansion plan would complete the isolation of Jerusalem, the intended capital of Palestine, from the remainder of the West Bank and would bisect the West Bank, rendering territorial contiguity and agreement on permanent borders impossible; Amara et al (n 11).

[15] ibid.

[16] ibid.

as a vulnerable and marginalised social group in two main ways.[17] Firstly, Israeli settler colonialism reinforces societal patriarchy and reproduces violence, which is exercised by the stronger social group on the weaker social group (ie men on women and children).[18] Secondly, Israeli settler colonialism directly targets women through a systematic structure, rather than isolated events, due to their reproductive ability,[19] which counters the Israeli agenda of settler colonialism as a tool to eliminate the indigenous population in order to enable non-indigenous claim of the land.[20]

This chapter relies on a combination of primary and secondary sources, gathered through the 'Palestinian Bedouin at Risk of Forced Displacement: IHL Vulnerabilities, ICC Possibilities' project.[21] In light of the scarcity of secondary sources focusing on Palestinian Bedouin in the E1 area in general and Bedouin women in particular, primary sources will be situated within the wider literature on gender in protracted conflict and under colonial regimes. Primary sources include field research and data gathered by way of a desk review and relevant legal documents. The field research includes both targeted interviews with stakeholders and duty bearers; civil society organisations (CSOs) and official institutions,[22] and semi-structured interviews and affidavits with women from the Bedouin communities themselves conducted by AQHRC between November 2020 and August 2021.

This chapter consists of two main sections: the first focuses on the gendered implications of direct displacement and urbanisation; the second analyses the gendered impact of restriction of freedom of movement as an integral part of the coercive environment of displacement. In covering the gendered implications of displacement through urbanisation, this research shines a light on the interlocking impact of the intersection of gender and race under colonial regimes.[23] We further explore the impact on privacy, agency and psycho-social wellbeing. In doing so, this section brings to the foreground the utility of employing an intersectional analysis to capture different layers of marginalisation and exclusion.[24] In terms of restriction of mobility, we assess the disproportionate impact of an inadequate road system and lack of public transportation on Palestinian Bedouin women living in the E1 area. This discussion then addresses, in turn, women's economic disempowerment, and the infringement on their rights to education and healthcare.

[17] It is important to note that women are not the only social group that are disproportionately affected. Other groups include children, the elderly, persons with disabilities and refugees/internally displaced persons, to name a few.

[18] b hooks, *We Real Cool: Black Men and Masculinity* (Routledge, 2004) 47.

[19] N Shalhoub Kevorkian, 'Gendered Suffering and the Eviction of the Native: The Politics of Birth in Occupied East Jerusalem' in Ni Aolain, Cahn, Francesca and Valji (n 2) 564.

[20] ibid 559.

[21] The project 'Palestinian Bedouin at Risk of Forced Displacement: IHL Vulnerabilities, ICC Possibilities' [grant number AH/T007540/1] is funded by the Arts and Humanities Research Council and is jointly implemented by Queen's University Belfast, Al-Quds University, Trinity College Dublin and Liverpool John Moores University.

[22] CSOs interviewed include Palestinian Medical Relief Society (Health), Islah Charitable Society (Health), Jericho Women Charitable Society (Health), Roles for Social Change Association– ADWAR (Economic Empowerment), Sunbula (Economic Empowerment). Official institutions include Palestinian Central Bureau of Statistics (Education).

[23] Shalhoub Kevorkian (n 19) 558.

[24] E Rooney, 'Intersectionality: Working in Conflict' in Ni Aolain, Cahn, Francesca and Valji (n 2) 328–29.

4.1. GENDERING FORCED DISPLACEMENT AND URBANISATION

Palestinian Bedouin women experience forced displacement and urbanisation as Palestinians, as Bedouins, and as women – three intersectional identities, which, taken together, are more than the sum of their parts. This section will discuss the disproportionate impact on women by colonial regimes that seek to forcibly displace native populations, as is the case with Israeli displacement of Bedouin communities. Militarism and gender oppression are recognised in the literature as mutually reinforcing phenomena; both emerge from colonial European states in the nineteenth and twentieth centuries, and were imposed on colonised societies,[25] including Palestine. In the E1 area of Jerusalem, the highly militarised Israeli settler colonial regime[26] continuously seeks to displace and urbanise Bedouin communities. As this section will illustrate, the disproportionate impact on women as a vulnerable and marginalised social group affects traditional gender roles, including women's participation in the agro-pastoralist economy, familial relations, and women's agency at family and community level.[27]

4.1.1. The Gendered Impact of Relocation, Demolition and Threats thereof on Familial Relations and Household Responsibilities

The direct displacement of Bedouin communities, through their outlawing and the demolition of their homes and supporting structures such as sanitary facilities, impacts women severely.[28] Demolitions, displacement and threats thereof lead to overcrowding in Bedouin communities in multiple ways, all of which are more detrimental to women. Moreover, due to building restrictions, the discriminatory permit and planning regime, and well-founded fears that new construction will result in demolitions, many family units within the extended family live together in the same house, or closely adjacent homes. This includes repurposing outbuildings such as sheds to accommodate extended families, often used when a son marries and requires additional space for his new family. These realities carry serious gendered consequences for Bedouin women.

Firstly, land confiscation and demolitions, and threats thereof, decrease the land and areas available for construction, ultimately forcing dwellings closer together. Living in closer proximity to other families results in less privacy and space, which Bedouin women need to go about their day-to-day lives. Indeed, this diminishing space impacts women in particular because the traditional gender roles in the Bedouin community generally confine women to the domestic sphere. The domestic sphere in Bedouin encampments includes the home and surrounding open spaces, used by women who tend to flocks and make dairy products. When dwellings are too close together, Bedouin women are more exposed to meeting men from outside

[25] A Mama, 'Colonialism' in Ni Aolain, Cahn, Francesca and Valji (n 2) 265.
[26] Wolfe (2006) (n 11).
[27] Amara et al (n 11) 105.
[28] Affidavit by AQU Legal Clinic A/W/AN/21.

their immediate household, which, as a cultural norm in this community, is generally avoided, thus forcing women to spend more time indoors.

Secondly, in cases of demolitions, the family whose home is demolished usually relocates to the home of a related family until they can rebuild their house. This extends the impact of the demolition to the host family, and particularly their female members (both women and girls), who will have to carry out additional household responsibilities for their own family as well as the guests in increasingly constricted spaces.[29] In many of these cases women live in separate households from men, due to traditional norms where men do not live with women outside their immediate family (ie wives, mothers, daughters, sisters). This overcrowding and gendered division carries additional burdens for women's household responsibilities,[30] requiring different women (eg sisters-in-law) to rearrange their daily schedules and chore routines in order to avoid overlaps. Moreover, women are forced to run two households: the one in which they reside with other women and young children, as well as the one where their husbands reside with other men.[31] The presence of a large number of children in crowded and sometimes split households adds another set of challenges for women in terms of balancing their caregiving and household responsibilities within constricted spaces.[32]

Thirdly, the repercussions associated with home demolitions, including an insecure environment, an increase in poverty, displacement and the loss of home and identity is likely to increase stress and ultimately strain familial relationships. Despite their resilience and resourcefulness, the mental health of Bedouin women is fragile due to the ongoing threats of demolitions and displacement, and the worries associated with their consequences.[33] This is directly linked to parents' inability to protect and care for their children in cases of demolitions and displacement.[34] In turn, this increases the burden on women to deal with the trauma of their children and family, when they are not only unable to address their own trauma through appropriate counselling, but must also continue providing care and housekeeping despite all adversities.

4.1.2. Impact of Forced Urbanisation on Traditional Gender Roles and Women's Agency

As previously discussed, Palestinian Bedouin women have traditionally participated in the agro-pastoralist economy of herder communities living in vast open spaces; it is culturally and socially appropriate for Bedouin women to tend to flocks and make dairy products because in the wilderness it is possible for them to avoid close proximity to men outside their immediate family (ie husbands, sons, fathers, brothers).

[29] ibid.
[30] ibid.
[31] Affidavit by AQU Legal Clinic A/M3/AN/21.
[32] AQU Clinic (n 9).
[33] Interview AQU Legal Clinic I/W2/K-M/21.
[34] LC Ng and TS Betancourt, 'Risk and Resilience: The Physical and Mental Health of Female Civilians during War' in Ni Aolain, Cahn, Francesca and Valji (n 2) 360.

However, once Bedouin communities are forcibly urbanised – which is part and parcel of Israel's settler colonial policy in that it includes both land confiscation and displacement of Palestinians[35] – access to vast swathes of land is lost, and it is no longer possible for women to walk freely and safely from their homes to their flocks (which may be held in different locations, require means of transportation, male chaperones, and may expose them to settler violence). This is why forced urbanisation generally ends women's ability to actively participate in the agro-pastoralist economy, thus losing their principal source of income and consequently economic power in families and the wider community. Specifically, forced urbanisation has a disproportionate impact on women since it ruptures gender roles in Bedouin society, where traditionally women have been economically active; once confined to cramped urban spaces, with little to no space for herds, the agro-pastoralist economy is compromised. In urban settings, women cannot easily access new forms of paid employment to supplement their loss of income once they no longer can make and sell dairy products. This severely compromises women's agency and the opportunity for their fulfilment,[36] as will be elaborated further below.

The process of forced urbanisation negates Bedouin agency over how they wish to live as well as their lifestyle needs and gender roles, and thus has severe repercussions on the Bedouin community as a whole and particularly on women. While some Bedouins attend university and become doctors, engineers, teachers, etc, there are also Bedouins who prefer their original way of life as herders, living and working in open spaces. Many Bedouins choose to breed sheep and make dairy products, despite the hardships of this livelihood, exacerbated by Israeli policies and practices that continuously seek to drive them out.[37] The possibility to choose herding as a profession and a lifestyle is eliminated with forced urbanisation, as evidenced in the case of Bedouin communities that has already taken place in the Al-Naqab desert inside the Green Line and in the West Bank. The dire consequences of forced urbanisation have been documented. Take, for instance, the families from the Bir Al-Maskoob community of the central West Bank Al-Jahalin Bedouin, who were urbanised in the Al-Jabal site after a lengthy judicial process that ultimately led to their forcible transfer, resulting in the confiscation of the land, and consequently the expansion of the Ma'ale Adumim settlement.[38]

The overall impact of forced urbanisation on Palestinian Bedouin communities in E1 can be seen in the denial, erasure and gradual loss of their way of life and freedom to choose to live and work according to their wishes. An illustration of the gendered dimension of forced urbanisation is the manner through which the Israeli authorities limit access to arable and grazing land. In urban contexts, the scarcity of

[35] Wolfe (2006) (n 11); Lloyd (n 11) 67; Veracini (2006) (n 11); Veracini (2017) (n 11) 3; D Mardi and A Simry, 'The Effect of Forced Transfer on Bedouin Women' (BIMKOM, 2017) 3, bimkom.org/wp-content/uploads/The-effect-of-forced-transfer-on-Bedouin-women-Eng_DESIGN1.pdf 3; I Pappe, *10 Myths About Israel* (Verso, 2017) 141.

[36] P Petesch, 'Agency and Gender Norms in War Economies' in Ni Aolain, Cahn, Francesca and Valji (n 2) 343.

[37] Interview by AQU Legal Clinic I/M3/JB/15.

[38] UNRWA and BIMKOM, 'Al-Jabal: A Study on the Transfer of Bedouin Palestine Refugees' 16–17 (2013), www.unrwa.org/userfiles/2013052935643.pdf.

open pastures where women can tend to the herds, milk the animals and make dairy products – which can then be marketed and sold as an income-generating activity specific to women – disrupts economic opportunities for women.[39] Moreover, the lack of accessible land leads to the steady reduction of herd size, which affects the economic sustainability of entire Bedouin communities who rely on pastoral economy.[40] Before urbanisation, women's contribution to the economic sustainability of the Bedouin household and community conferred a significant degree of agency on women. In this sense, forced urbanisation compromises women's agency and decision-making powers derived from their economic activities. Bedouin women, for a range of cultural and practical reasons, do not have easy access to paid employment outside of their immediate communities (as will be demonstrated in the next section). Any loss of economic activity and financial agency increases women's dependence on men, forcing the latter to seek alternative sources of income, usually as cheap labour in Israeli settlements in the absence of minimum labour safeguards and protections.

Israeli attempts to urbanise Bedouin communities by forcing them to live in solid brick and concrete houses impact women differently, given that they are confined to constricted spaces. This is seen in the relocation of Bir Al-Maskoob Bedouin community, mentioned earlier, to the Al-Jabal site, who no longer reside in the more flexible dwellings spread out over wider spaces. In contrast, these constricted living quarters offer little access to open space, confining Bedouin women to the indoors. Women thus no longer have access to open spaces where they could move freely and meet family members in order to dispel the stress of daily life, as outdoor spaces are also considered a space to respite for Bedouin women.[41] Younger women in particular experience these constrictions more acutely due to prevalent societal perceptions that consider them to be more vulnerable than older women, who may enjoy a higher degree of independence. This underscores the impact of the intersection of age and gender,[42] and in this sense, younger women experience greater mobility restrictions. For example, the *mukhtar* (community leader) of one of the villages facing imminent urbanisation to the al-Nweima reflected: 'how should I allow my daughter to leave the house, in a crowded place, with houses close to one another, where strange men walk?'[43]

Women's loss of agency in Bedouin communities after their forced urbanisation echoes women's loss of agency at the cessation of hostilities, when traditional gender structures and roles are reinstated, and women often experience a reduction in their ability to make choices and decisions.[44] To this end, forced urbanisation also brings about a radical change in lifestyle, altering family dynamics by increasing gender asymmetry within familial relations.[45] This manifests through a decrease

[39] Mardi and Simry (n 35) 6–8; UNRWA and BIMKOM (ibid) 14.
[40] AQU Clinic (n 13).
[41] Mardi and Simry (n 35) 9.
[42] AQU Clinic (n 9).
[43] Mardi and Simry (n 35) 10.
[44] P Patten, 'Unlocking the Potential of CEDAW as an Important Accountability Tool for the Women, Peace and Security Agenda' in Ni Aolain, Cahn, Francesca and Valji (n 2) 176–77.
[45] Mardi and Simry (n 35) 8.

in women's household decision-making capabilities, encompassing economic and financial matters.

4.2. GENDERED IMPACT OF RESTRICTION OF FREEDOM OF MOVEMENT

Restrictions on freedom of movement imposed on all Palestinians affect Bedouins more severely, given that these communities live in more remote locations that are harder to reach for both geographic and political reasons. Bedouin communities are mostly located in Area C of the West Bank, where Israel retains full civil and military control. In these parts the paving of roads requires permission from the Israeli Civil Administration (ICA – the military body in charge of administering the West Bank), which is seldom granted.[46] In addition to lack of electricity, running water, educational institutions and healthcare facilities, the coercive environment that Israel imposes on Bedouin communities in an attempt to drive them out of their dwellings includes an inadequate and poorly maintained road system, coupled with a lack of public transportation.[47] Long distances separate Bedouin communities from the main roads; access routes are bumpy and unpaved, which render public transportation almost impossible. As such, accessibility to the main road becomes restricted to jumping over fences or traveling in powerful 4×4 cars, or on animals such as donkeys and horses. However, powerful cars are rarely available for Bedouin communities due to their high cost and financial constraints, and travel on animals takes longer time and exposes Bedouins to greater risks of settler violence.[48] As a result, many Palestinian Bedouin communities in the Greater Jerusalem periphery are cut off from the road network, which further isolates them. Given that most Bedouin communities do not have schools and healthcare facilities (as elaborated below), restrictions of freedom of movement also result in reduced access to education and healthcare. The lack of public transportation and inadequate road system thus infringes on several dimensions of the lives of Bedouin women, including economic disempowerment and their rights to education and healthcare.[49]

This section focuses on the restriction of freedom of movement, examining how it impacts key economic and social rights of Bedouin women in the context of a coercive environment as part of the wider settler colonial policy by Israeli Government. Women experience such restrictions in a range of unique ways. Firstly, Bedouin women's freedom of movement is impacted by the intersecting limitations of the poor road system, Israeli settler violence and gendered assumptions in their communities. Israeli settlements (which are illegal under international law)[50] tend to be established

[46] Affidavit by AQU Legal Clinic A/M2/JB/21.

[47] Amara et al (n 11) 111.

[48] AQU Clinic (n 9).

[49] UNOCHA, 'Bedouin Communities at Risk of Forcible Displacement' (2014) 1, www.unocha.org/publications/report/occupied-palestinian-territory/bedouin-communities-risk-forcible-transfer-fact-sheet; A Heneiti, 'Bedouin Communities in Greater Jerusalem: Planning or Forced Displacement?' (2016) 65 *Jerusalem Quarterly* 51, www.palestine-studies.org/sites/default/files/jq-articles/6_Heneiti_--_Bedouin_Communities_0.pdf; Interview by AQU Legal Clinic I/M1/K-H/20.

[50] International Committee of the Red Cross (ICRC), Geneva Convention Relative to the Protection of Civilian Persons in Time of War (Fourth Geneva Convention), 12 August 1949, 75 UNTS 287, Art 49.

in close proximity to existing Bedouin communities; this increases exposure to settler violence, rendering the long-distance walks to the main road dangerous. As a result, women's freedom of movement is restricted by male members of their communities, based on a combination of gendered assumptions around women's fragility and genuine concerns that the woman will be harmed. This double restriction of freedom of movement due to the risk of settler violence and gendered assumptions is exacerbated in regards to young women, who are often seen by the community as more vulnerable than older women, further reinforcing the intersectional impact of age as another factor that heightens the marginalisation of women.[51]

Secondly, in Bedouin communities, many men overcompensate by performing heightened traditional masculinities, exacerbated by their increased disempowerment due to their inability to fulfil their traditional gender roles as protectors and providers to their family.[52] Men's masculinities and patriarchal attitudes are even further exacerbated by the increase in agency that women experience in conflict-related contexts, which men widely perceive as a challenge of their decision-making roles,[53] particularly in light of the compromise of men's agency in wars and conflicts.[54] This emboldening of men's masculinities manifests in the restriction of women's freedom of movement.[55]

Thirdly, the persistence of colonisation and proliferation of donor-funded programming that employs a liberal approach to feminism, has restricted women's mobility by men under the pretext of preservation of honour.[56] Specifically, colonial powers historically sought to exploit colonised women and more recently to 'modernise' and 'liberate' women. Both of these approaches exacerbate existing men's masculinities, who respond by attempts to 'protect' and 'safeguard' women,[57] through exercising their own power and authority. In the case of Bedouin communities this is predominantly observed in the restriction of women's mobility.[58] This is aligned with postcolonial theories that postulate that dominant social groups that are oppressed (ie men) repeat and reproduce this cycle of domination and exercise their relative strength over weaker social groups (ie women) in colonial and post-colonial times.[59]

Three principal issues inform the restriction of women's mobility by men in Bedouin communities in the E1 area. First, the increased risk of settler violence, which restricts women's mobility on the availability, ability and willingness of a male relative

[51] AQU Clinic (n 9).
[52] ibid.
[53] Petesch (n 36) 346.
[54] ibid 348.
[55] ibid.
[56] R Coomaraswamy, 'Preface: Violence Against Women and "Crimes of Honour"' in L Welchman and S Hossain (eds), *'Honour': Crimes, Paradigms, and Violence Against Women* (Zed Books, 2005) xi; L Welchmann and S Hossain, 'Introduction: "Honours, Rights and Wrongs' in Welchman and Hossain (ibid) 5; Tamimi (n 4) 75.
[57] N Shalhoub-Kevorkian, 'Researching Women's Victimisation in Palestine: A Sociolegal Analysis' in Welchman and Hossain (ibid) 162.
[58] H Charlesworth, C Chinkin and S Wright, 'Feminist Approaches to International Law' (1991) 85 *American Journal of International Law* 619.
[59] hooks (n 18) 47.

of the immediate family to accompany women as they travel outside their immediate surroundings.[60] Second, the fact that Bedouin women generally do not have cars, and thus depend on men to go to urban centres and attend to daily life needs, including healthcare, education and selling of dairy products they make.[61] Third, men also restrict women's mobility, as will be demonstrated in subsequent sections, to compensate for their loss of agency in times of conflict, and as a response to a donor agenda, implemented by CSOs, that contravene traditions and customs.

4.2.1. Economic Disempowerment

Restrictions of freedom of movement impact Palestinian Bedouin women based on all three intersectional identities, as discussed above. As seen in the case of the gendered impact of forced displacement, women's economic empowerment is compromised by the Israeli settler colonial policy of land confiscation and settlement expansion affecting all Palestinians, including Bedouin communities in their entirety. In the E1 area specifically, land confiscation and access to land is restricted by the Annexation Wall that, in a number of cases such as Jabal Al-Baba, prevented the community from accessing their land.[62] Another method used by Israeli occupation is the declaration of land as state land. This is the case of Abu Nuwwar Bedouin community, who were displaced from land they dwell in into land further away from the main roads when Israeli occupation declared it state land, noting that this land is owned by Palestinians from Abu Dis town and Bedouin communities had permission from the owners to dwell there.[63]

As women are responsible for caring for the flocks, dairy production (cheese, yogurt, etc) and selling the produce, land confiscation reduces available grazing land, impacting on the quantity of dairy products that can be made and sold.[64] A reduction in pastures also leads to increasing costs, given that Bedouin women are forced to buy expensive fodder to feed the animals.[65] The decrease in quantity, and increase in cost of production, ultimately decreases the competitive edge of dairy production in urban markets, which directly contributes to women's economic disempowerment.

Consequently, financial revenue from dairy production and marketing is insufficient;[66] the reduction in Bedouin women's earning power forces Bedouin men to look for other jobs, usually in the form of low-paid and often unregulated labour in nearby illegal Israeli settlements. This compromises men's economic agency, specifically at the level of choice of labour and lifestyle, and consequently emboldens their traditional masculinities.[67] This in turn often impacts women negatively

[60] Petesch (n 36) 348.
[61] AQU Clinic (n 13).
[62] Perez-Cuso et al (n 10).
[63] ibid 22.
[64] AQU Clinic (n 9).
[65] ibid.
[66] AQU Clinic (n 13).
[67] Petesch (n 36) 347–348.

through further restriction of their freedom of movement and the reproduction of the cycle of violence in response to the degrading work conditions in settlements.[68] While only one Bedouin community out of 18 in the E1 area reports working in settlements as their main source of livelihood, 12 communities report working in settlements as their second source of livelihood.[69] Many Palestinians working in settlements, including Bedouins, report degrading and exploitative working conditions, including significantly lower pay than the Israeli minimum wage, which is NIS 271.38 per day,[70] a lack of work insurance, and discrimination compared to Jewish Israelis,[71] primarily in terms of salaries, which range from NIS 50–90 per day (USD 13–24 per day).[72]

The oppressive context that forces men to take on work that falls outside their cultural norms, as well as degrading and discriminatory work conditions, embolden men's masculinities, who may reproduce violence through controlling behaviours towards weaker social groups, namely women, children and the elderly. While this vicious cycle of men taking out the abuse and discrimination they experience on women is well-studied in other contexts, personal and cultural sensitivities, manifesting in the form of the tribal code, make it almost impossible to explore the topic with members of the Palestinian Bedouin community. Nevertheless, the extensive field-based research underpinning this chapter has revealed that Bedouin women are undoubtedly recipients of this pattern of reproduced violence, which is usually expressed through non-physical forms of control, including restrictions of movement, exclusion from family decision-making, and further economic dependency. For example, despite a CSO setting up a meeting between a Bedouin woman and the owner of a shop who buys women's products, the woman's husband prohibited her from leaving the community and going to the meeting, depriving the woman of an important opportunity for economic advancement.[73]

Obstacles facing women's economic empowerment extend to all production stages of traditional products as well as income-generating projects supported by CSOs, such as food production, beauty parlours, shirt production and embroidery. Restrictions on mobility impact women's access to markets, mainly in urban centres, primarily due to the absence of public transportation and contingency of women's mobility on the accompaniment of a male family member.[74] Also, the high cost of production, elaborated above, decreases the marketing edge of Bedouin products in the market.[75] All of this contributes to women's economic disempowerment, which

[68] hooks (n 18).

[69] UNOCHA, '46 Bedouin Communities at Risk of Forcible Transfer in the Central West Bank: A Vulnerability Profile' (2017), www.ochaopt.org/page/46-bedouin-communities-risk-forcible-transfer-central-west-bank-vulnerability-profile.

[70] https://www.btl.gov.il/english%20homepage/mediniyut/generalinformation/pages/minimumwage.aspx.

[71] I Maharmeh, 'Israel's Violations of Palestinian Workers' Rights: Covid-19 and Systemic Abuse' (Al-Shabaka: Palestinian Policy Network, 2021), al-shabaka.org/wp-content/uploads/2021/07/Maharmeh_PolicyBrief_Eng_July2021.pdf.

[72] M Samander, 'Captive Markets, Captive Lives: Palestinian Workers in Israeli Settlements' (Al-Haq, 2021) 10, www.alhaq.org/cached_uploads/download/2021/05/01/palestinian-workers-in-israeli-settlements-webversion-1-page-view-1619871735.pdf.

[73] Interview by AQU Legal Clinic I/O-S/21.

[74] Petesch (n 36) 348.

[75] AQU Clinic (n 31).

further compromises their limited agency in the family, and ability to decide on and procure household necessities using their own income.[76]

Women's marginalisation from the formal labour market constricts them to the informal economy, increasing the risks of exploitation.[77] Take, for example, the E1 area, where women produce embroidered work for private sector entities. Private shops buy an A4 embroidery piece for NIS 20 (approximately six USD) from Bedouin women, which they later sell for at least triple that price.[78] Given that women have to walk unsafe long distances to reach the main road, before commuting to urban centres on public transportation that costs them on average NIS 10 (approximately three USD), the economic feasibility of this type of work is severely reduced.[79] The long distance and challenging journey for women to access markets due to the coercive environment imposed by the Israeli occupation is thus exacerbated by private sector exploitation, which limits opportunities for Bedouin women to advance their economic empowerment.

In the case of income-generating projects by CSOs that support Bedouin women, the predominant obstacles that women face pertain to availability of equipment and necessary infrastructure. In food production projects, for example, CSOs report that Israeli restrictions on refrigerators, lack of reliable supplies of electricity, and prohibition of entry of the optimal types of fertilisers and pesticides impact both the quality and quantity of food produced.[80] Furthermore, Israeli-imposed restrictions on using refrigerators and other essential equipment prevents women from producing and storing large quantities of food to sell in the market, thus impacting the competitive edge that these women could have and contributing to their economic disempowerment.[81]

In light of mobility restrictions discussed earlier, profitable activities, such as providing beauty salon services, are aimed at local clients, which limits earning potential for the women involved and opportunities for greater economic empowerment.[82] This applies to other industries and income-generating opportunities, such as kindergarten and babysitting services and the arrangement of wedding packages. This restricts the earning potential of women, as the main clients are also economically disadvantaged Bedouins.

In addition to the obstacles imposed by the Israeli occupation and mobility restrictions affecting Bedouin women, another set of challenges is associated with patriarchal norms and mentality that confine women to the domestic sphere and adversely impact their economic empowerment.[83] There is an overall social expectation that marriage and family life should take priority over women's employment and economic empowerment.[84] This is aligned with the overall perception of women's

[76] Interview by AQU Legal Clinic I/W/K-M/21.
[77] Mama (n 25) 270–71.
[78] AQU Clinic (n 13).
[79] ibid.
[80] T Tamimi, 'A Research Study on the Impact of Israeli Military Occupation on the Access of Rural Women to their Economic Rights' (PWWSD, 2020) 22, pwwsd.org/uploads/1626009617417522025.pdf.
[81] ibid; Interview by AQU Legal Clinic I/O-S/21.
[82] Interview by AQU Legal Clinic I/O-RSCA/21.
[83] Mama (n 26) 267.
[84] E Kuttab and B Heilman, 'Understanding Masculinities: International Men and Gender Equality Survey (IMAGES) – Middle East and North Africa' (Palestine) (UN Women, 2017) 49.

employment as an economic necessity for the family, rather than a woman's choice and right,[85] as evidenced through the significant disparities between Palestinian women's and men's participation in the labour force (16.1 per cent among women compared to 65.1 per cent among men in 2020).[86]

Restrictions to women's earning potential are not limited to the physical space, but extend to the digital space as well. Bedouin women are generally not allowed to be on social media given perceptions on preservation of honour.[87] For this reason, women's marketing options remain constricted to traditional means, such as taking the products and displaying them in local markets, which come up against significant obstacles, including exploitation by the private sector and mobility restrictions discussed earlier. Consequently, women rely on CSOs supporting them in income generating projects to market their products, thereby making the sustained success of the project contingent on continued support by the CSO, thereby disempowering women's own ability to become self-reliant in the future of the enterprise.

The success of income-generating projects to benefit Bedouin women is further compromised in light of the increasing restrictions on western donor funding to CSOs.[88] Firstly, funding takes the form of restricted project funding (instead of unrestricted core funding) to thematic areas and locations that are determined by donors in a non-participatory manner with national stakeholders, including the CSOs and Bedouin communities. Secondly, project funding further compromises project sustainability and usually includes gap periods between the end of one project and the beginning of another.[89] This imposes another set of restrictions on the continuation of support to Bedouin women, particularly while projects are unable to sustain themselves.[90] These factors adversely impact the success of income-generating projects supported by CSOs and in turn are more likely to increase women's vulnerabilities. Women rely on these projects due to the limited opportunities to earn a living, and as such the termination and gaps within these projects contribute to women's economic disempowerment.[91] While women are not expected to be the primary breadwinners in Bedouin communities, the income they generate supports the family when men's earning are insufficient. Paid work increases women's economic empowerment, and in turn creates opportunities for greater social empowerment in decision-making in the home, family and wider community. Therefore, when projects experience gaps in funding, and are impacted by the Israeli occupation, women are deprived of the potential for greater economic and social empowerment.

[85] Tamimi (n 4) 84.

[86] PCBS, 'The 2020 PCBS Survey Indicators' (2021), www.pcbs.gov.ps/site/lang__en/881/default.aspx#Labour.

[87] Coomaraswamy (n 56); Welchmann and Hossain (n 57); Tamimi (n 4); AQU Clinic (n 15).

[88] O Risheq, T Tamimi, R Adwan and M Nuseibah, 'Depoliticised Humanitarianism: Critiquing the Effectiveness of International Aid for the Bedouin Communities in the Jerusalem Periphery' (2023) 33 *Development in Practice* 572.

[89] AQU Clinic (n 82); aid to Palestinian CSOs decreased from USD 286.3m in 2011 to 193.8m in 2019, compared to increase in funding to Syrian CSOs, eg, from USD 20.3m in 2011 to USD 710.3m in 2019.

[90] AQU Clinic (n 82).

[91] AQU Clinic (n 76).

4.2.2. Right to Education

The Committee on Economic, Social and Cultural Rights, the UN body mandated with monitoring fulfilment of state obligations under the International Covenant on Economic, Social and Cultural Rights, conceptualises the right to education to include the '4A' elements: availability, accessibility, acceptability and adaptability.[92] Bedouin communities face hurdles in regards to the right to education primarily with respect to availability and accessibility. Only four out of 18 Bedouin communities in the E1 area have primary schools inside the community – Abu Nuwwar, Al-Muntar, Wadi Abu Hindi and Khan Al-Ahmar Abu Al Helu[93] – all of which have outstanding demolition orders against them.[94]

The absence of schools in the majority of the communities due to the restrictions imposed by Israeli settler colonial policy means that most Bedouin children need to commute long distances to access primary education, and all children must travel to urban centres to access secondary education. These lengthy commutes on dangerous, unpaved and busy roads expose children to settler assaults and run the risk of them being run over by cars.[95] Furthermore, while walking distances vary, they remain significant in all cases. In the case of Jabal Al-Baba community, children have to walk 1.09 kilometres twice a day to reach Al- Ezzariyeh and return home; this increases to 5.56 kilometres twice a day for children from Bir Al-Maskoob 'A' community to access primary and secondary education.[96] As a result, children must start their commute very early in the morning to reach school on time, which becomes more difficult during the winter season, increasing the risk of children dropping out of schools.[97]

While walking long distances to reach primary and secondary schools affects all children in Bedouin communities, it is experienced differently by girls and young women due to restrictions on freedom of movement, particularly during the winter season and the menstrual cycle. Notwithstanding the absence of official data on school drop-out rates for Bedouin communities specifically (the Palestinian Central Bureau of Statistics does not provide disaggregated data by locality),[98] field research indicates that girls seldom finish secondary education due to the combined impact of the occupation and prevalent social norms on gender. As seen also in other contexts, during armed conflicts, targeted attacks and threats against girls prevents them from accessing education.[99] In the E1 area, this includes the risk of violence by Israeli soldiers and settlers alike. Girls' access to education in urban centres is further exacerbated by walking long distances on unpaved roads and under dangerous circumstances.[100]

[92] Committee on Economic, Social and Cultural Rights, 'General Comment 13: The Right to Education' (CESCR 1999) 2–3.
[93] UNOCHA (n 69).
[94] UNOCHA, 'Data on Demolition and Displacement in the West Bank' (2021), www.ochaopt.org/data/demolition.
[95] AQU Clinic (n 13).
[96] UNOCHA (n 69).
[97] AQU Clinic (n 9).
[98] Interview by AQU Legal Clinic I/O-PCBS/21.
[99] Patten (n 44) 177.
[100] S Abu Rabia-Queder, 'Between Tradition and Modernization: Understanding the Problem of Female Bedouin Dropouts' (2006) 27 *British Journal of Sociology of Education* 5.

A woman from the Khan Al-Ahmar Abu Falah community explained that girls access primary education in the Khan Al-Ahmar Abu Al-Helu community, but that they are not allowed to go any further to complete secondary education in urban centres. This is due to the prevalent patriarchy that is reinforced by the persistence of occupation and colonisation in the Bedouin communities, which leads girls to drop out from schools as fathers refuse to allow daughters to walk to the main road and ride in mixed public transportation, especially as they reach puberty and are considered ready for marriage.[101] Girls who drop out from schools, and their parents, emphasise the importance of maintaining family honour: accessing education where boys and girls mix signals a compromise to this crucial value.[102]

In the rare cases where girls complete secondary education, many are denied access to higher education despite achieving high marks in their matriculation exams and obtaining scholarships. This is attributed to the father or closest male family member refusing to allow young women to leave the community alone via their own transportation (eg a car) or via public transportation without the presence of a male member of the immediate family.[103] In this scenario, the occupation reinforces patriarchy and masculinity through the lack of roads and public transportation that reaches the communities, requiring Bedouin women to walk long distances to reach the main road; the risk of settler violence and patriarchal norms limit the mobility of young women, who generally only leave the community for critical issues, which do not include education. Nonetheless, given the growing importance of education among girls, as evidenced in their commitment to enrol in higher education, the number of girls in higher education is higher compared to boys, who generally enter the labour market to provide financial support for their family.

As a consequence of female drop-out rates, girls are confined to the domestic sphere,[104] where they shoulder household responsibilities from a young age and engage in the pastoral economic activity of the community (where possible). As seen earlier, due to severe restrictions by the occupation and patriarchal social norms that restrict girls' freedom of movement, the cycle of women's economic disempowerment is reproduced and prevents girls from pursuing their educational aspirations and fulfilling their potential. Furthermore, early marriage is widespread in Bedouin communities: many girls who do not complete their education marry at an early age, often between the ages of 14 and 16 years.[105] Moreover, many girls drop out of school to get married because the dominant perception in Bedouin communities is that girls are ready for marriage when they reach puberty.[106] Early marriage has significant health implications, particularly in regards to sexual and reproductive health, as these girls also have children at a very young age, thereby reinforcing structural patriarchy and reproducing this cycle that continuously marginalises women and strips them of their agency.[107]

[101] ibid.
[102] ibid.
[103] AQU Clinic (n 13).
[104] Mama (n 25) 267.
[105] AQU Clinic (n 9).
[106] Abu Rabia-Queder (n 100).
[107] NM Nour, 'Child Marriage: A Silent Health and Human Rights Issue' (2009) 2 *Review in Obstetrics and Gynecology* 53–54.

4.2.3. Right to Healthcare

In a similar way to the asymmetrical impact of Israeli settler colonial policies on the enjoyment of girls to their right to education, women's right to healthcare is also compromised. As women bear most caregiving responsibilities, the impact of Israeli mobility restrictions and hurdles extends beyond women themselves to include children and the elderly.[108] The case of healthcare typifies the interlocking impact of gender and race on Palestinian Bedouin women within a context of colonisation, dispossession and lack of protection of women.[109]

The Committee on Economic, Social and Cultural Rights conceptualises the right to the highest attainable standard of health as consisting of four elements: availability, accessibility, acceptability and quality.[110] In times of armed conflict there is a steep decline in availability, accessibility and quality of health services,[111] which directly affects Bedouin communities. This is exacerbated by the prolonged nature of colonisation and systematic denial of economic and social rights as part and parcel of the imposition of a coercive environment to drive out Bedouin communities.[112]

In terms of availability, only one of the 18 communities in the E1 area has a permanent clinic (Khan Al-Ahmar Abu Al-Helu).[113] In the rest of the communities, primary healthcare services are provided through mobile clinics operated by Palestinian Ministry of Health, United Nations Relief and Work Agency for Palestinian Refugees, and CSOs (Islah Charitable Society and Palestinian Medical Relief Society (PMRS)) that visit twice a month at best.[114] Only 14 of the 18 communities receive regular healthcare services,[115] and mobile clinics only provide basic services in terms of testing, diagnosis, and medication.[116]

The fact that there is only one permanent clinic located in the Khan Al-Ahmar Bedouin community is not surprising given the targeting of healthcare systems and facilities during armed conflict, through demolitions and limiting the availability of staff, medicines, and supplies, as well as accessibility.[117] Furthermore, the clinic in Khan Al-Ahmar lacks staff and medication. One resident of Khan Al-Ahmar observes:

> Even though a clinic was established and equipped in 2018, the presence of doctors is scarce especially after the beginning of the pandemic (Covid-19). Even in the presence of doctors, all the doctors' can do is diagnose without offering treatment, in addition to the fact that medication is never available in the clinic.'[118]

[108] Gardam (n 2); AQU Clinic (n 13).
[109] Shalhoub Kevorkian (n 19) 558.
[110] Committee on Economic, Social and Cultural Rights, 'General Comment 14: The Right to the Highest Attainable Standard of Health' (2000) 4–5.
[111] Ng and Betancourt (n 34) 357.
[112] Amara et al (n 11) 111.
[113] ibid.
[114] UNOCHA (n 69).
[115] ibid.
[116] Interview by AQU Legal Clinic I/O-PMRS/21.
[117] Patten (n 42) 176–77.
[118] AQU Clinic (n 45).

Given the extremely limited availability of healthcare services, Bedouins are forced to commute to urban centres, such as Jericho and Ezzariyeh, as well as Aqabet Jaber refugee camp, for health emergencies and to access more complex services. This inevitably has a disproportionate impact on women, primarily due to the restriction of women's mobility and its contingency on being accompanied by a male family member. In many cases, however, men are not available because they leave the community to work.[119] Therefore, women face major accessibility barriers as a result of the poor road system and infrastructure, as well as the long walking distance. For example, the distance between Abu Falah Khan Al-Ahmar community and Jericho is over 13 kilometres. Furthermore, 13 communities must travel a distance exceeding three kilometres in each direction to reach their primary healthcare service provider, while the distance for five of these communities exceeds eight kilometres in each direction.[120] The difficulty in commuting to urban centres increases the burden on women given their multiple caring responsibilities,[121] for instance in cases of sick children.

The barriers facing women in accessing healthcare services have been further exacerbated following the crackdown on the Islah Charitable Society (one of the main providers of healthcare services in Bedouin communities), after Israeli authorities imposed a ban on financial transfers to the organisation and froze bank accounts under the pretence of security.[122] Even when Islah was providing services through mobile clinics, four out of 18 Bedouin communities were not served by these clinics.[123] After the shutdown by Israel, PMRS was able to shoulder two communities previously served by Islah, raising the number of unserved communities to seven after the crackdown on Islah.[124] While this demonstrates the advanced coordination between CSOs to mitigate risks and continue to provide basic services to these communities, it is also indicative of the decrease in humanitarian funding: a major issue that exacerbates the coercive environment that Bedouin communities endure.

Moreover, pregnant women represent a unique case of gender-based and race-based violence due to Israeli occupation policies.[125] This is seen not only in the exacerbation of patriarchal norms (as already discussed), but also in the direct targeting of pregnant women by the occupation due to their birthing abilities.[126] This provides another example of the intersectional discrimination facing Bedouin women, under the framework of the logic of indigenous population elimination that is integral to settler colonialism.[127] This logic of elimination to make room for the non-indigenous claim to the land is contrasted by women's birthing abilities,[128] thus

[119] AQU Clinic (n 13).
[120] UNOCHA (n 69).
[121] Interview by AQU Legal Clinic (n 115).
[122] Interview by AQU Legal Clinic I/O-JWCS/21.
[123] UNOCHA (n 69).
[124] AQU Clinic Interview (n 116).
[125] Shalhoub Kevorkian (n 19) 559, 563.
[126] ibid 559.
[127] Wolfe (2006) (n 11) 387.
[128] A Smith, 'Queer Theory and Native Studies: The Heteronormativity of Settler Colonialism' (2010) 16 *GLQ: A Journal of Lesbian and Gay Studies* 59.

increasing the vulnerability of women and children.[129] In the Bedouin communities in E1, the targeting of pregnant women is seen in multiple facets. Firstly, the long walking distances and poor road conditions hinder the possibility of attending routine appointments necessary for pregnant women, who must often climb over fences to reach the main road. For example, one woman, who had an acute allergy, needed to have a check-up appointment every three days to protect her health and that of the foetus. Many times, she decided not to attend her check-ups due to the difficulty of commuting to Jericho (a distance exceeding 20 kilometres), and the high cost of the test NIS 70 (approximately USD 22), ultimately putting her own life and that of the foetus at risk.[130]

Many pregnant women also feel uncomfortable and dissatisfied with the quality of services provides in the public health directorate in Ezzariyeh, which pressures them to have regular check-ups with expensive private doctors in Ezzariyeh and Abu Dis. Here, we once more see how the economic disempowerment of these communities further limits their access to healthcare services, resulting in irregular and missed check-ups, putting women and their unborn babies at increased risk.[131]

As part of Israel's strategy to exert control over Jerusalem and isolate it from the rest of the West Bank, Palestinians, including many Bedouin communities, face significant challenges in accessing Jerusalem. Pregnant Bedouin women must obtain permits through a bureaucratic process involving civil coordination between the Palestinian Authority and the Israeli military to cross checkpoints and reach the nearest hospitals, which are in Jerusalem. This situation exploits the concept of 'rule by law', effectively deeming Palestinian society, especially pregnant women, as 'illegal', and simultaneously legitimising exterminatory violence to the advantage of settler colonial endeavours.[132] Unfortunately, the permit process is often marred by delays and refusals by Israeli authorities. Consequently, pregnant women may have to travel to more distant hospitals in Bethlehem or Ramallah, which involves crossing at least one checkpoint, often with traffic jams, increasing health risks for both mothers and babies, and forcing women to endure prolonged pain. In (at least) one extreme case, where civil coordination was significantly delayed and entry to Jerusalem was refused, a woman gave birth in the unequipped emergency centre of Abu Dis, since there was not enough time to transport her to Bethlehem or Ramallah.[133]

CONCLUSION

As part of a marginalised and vulnerable social group, Palestinian Bedouin women in the E1 area are under the continuous threat of forced displacement through Israeli-imposed outlawing of entire communities, home demolitions and the imposition of a coercive environment. Women are disproportionately affected by the Israeli

[129] Shalhoub Kevorkian (n 19) 560.
[130] Interview AQU Legal Clinic I/W2/K-M/21.
[131] ibid.
[132] Shalhoub Kevorkian (n 19) 565.
[133] AQU Clinic (n 13).

Government's settler colonial policy: they are equally targeted by demolitions and displacement, but these practices undoubtedly reinforce existing conservative and patriarchal social norms. This reverberates and manifests in several key areas of life, including the right to privacy, women's decision-making agency, economic disempowerment, right to education and right to healthcare.

Israeli Government settler colonial policy, namely land confiscation, displacement and threats thereof, infringes the right of Bedouin women to privacy, an integral part of Bedouin tradition which is essential to ensure women's autonomy. Cutting land off using the annexation Wall, declaring land as (Israeli) state land, outlawing communities, demolishing structures and imposing a coercive environment all contribute to the reduction of the private space that Bedouin women once enjoyed. Furthermore, displacement has a profound impact on women's ability to fulfil their household and caregiving responsibilities: home demolitions can force families made homeless to live with relatives, and force women who have not (yet) lost their homes to host other families that have been subjected to home demolitions.

Despite prevalent gender-based discrimination within Bedouin society, clearly seen in their lack of enjoyment of right to education, conventional employment and protection from violence, women traditionally held a significant degree of economic agency in their communities, due to their active participation in community's economic activity. Nevertheless, the forced urbanisation of Bedouin communities has disrupted the traditional Bedouin lifestyle and consequently their traditional gender roles, leading to a decline in women's economic agency: in urban settings Bedouin families are forced to give up their herds due to limited space, meaning that women can no longer rely on the sale of dairy products as a means to earn an income, and other opportunities for women to join the paid workforce remain extremely limited.

As an integral part of the imposition of a coercive environment to drive Bedouins out of their land, the poor road system and infrastructure severely restrict women's economic empowerment and enjoyment of their rights to education and healthcare. Additionally, settlement expansion and wider violence perpetrated by Israeli settlers and the army reinforces traditional masculinities and patriarchal mentality in Bedouin men. This further restricts women's mobility in the absence of a male member of the immediate family to accompany her and impacts negatively on her autonomy and ability to access opportunities.

Israeli Government policy against Bedouin communities is part and parcel of its expansionist settler colonial policy that is directed against the Palestinian people as a whole. However, Palestinian Bedouin women are trapped between the hammer and the anvil, as a result of their intersectional identities as female, Palestinian and Bedouin, discussed throughout this chapter. On one side, women are subjected to Israeli Government settler colonial policy, but on the other side, their enjoyment of rights is further compromised by prevalent patriarchal attitudes in Palestinian Bedouin communities that is reinforced and exacerbated under Israeli settler colonialism. As such, all efforts to address the vulnerabilities of Palestinian Bedouin communities must embed an intersectional gender analysis at its core.

Ultimately, if Bedouin displacement and land-grabbing policies continue in a climate of a total lack of accountability for the Israeli state, this will encourage the persistence of attempts to forcefully urbanise Bedouin communities, which signals the violation of a myriad of human rights including shelter, health and education, apart from perpetrating international crimes of destruction of property and unlawful transfer as war crimes, and forced displacement as a crime against humanity. These measures further diminish the quality of life of women as well as the little agency that they still enjoy. Thus, as this chapter has argued, in efforts to bring about accountability for Israeli crimes and gross human rights violations, it is crucial to include the specific experiences of Palestinian Bedouin women in the (long) list of Israeli violations against Palestinians, in order to ensure proper accountability and reparations. This is particularly crucial when gender-based harm occurs in the context of the private sphere, which all too often goes 'unseen' in mainstream international law.

5

Scrutinising Foreign Aid to Palestinian Bedouin Communities at the Frontier of Israeli Settler Colonialism

DARIO ROSSI D'AMBROSIO

INTRODUCTION

THIS CHAPTER CONTRIBUTES to the problematisation of foreign aid in Palestine, with a specific focus on the Palestinian communities in the Eastern periphery of Jerusalem (often referred to as the 'E1' area) and across the West Bank. It investigates existing critiques of foreign aid interventions that form part of the decades-long involvement of foreign donors. Without a focus on the root causes of humanitarian and development needs and concerted political actions, foreign aid fails to deliver on its promises. This perpetuates a cycle of dependency and vulnerability for Palestinian communities, making them susceptible to repeated colonial violence without proper protection and recourse. Although aid projects meet immediate humanitarian needs and aim to ensure a minimum standard of living for Palestinians, they function within a depoliticised framework that does not address the fundamental structural violence of settler colonialism which creates the need for aid in the first place.

As discussed by Reeda Alji in chapter six of this volume (and other contributors), although Palestinian Bedouins have distinct cultural practices that differentiate them from non-Bedouin Palestinians, Palestinian Bedouins are an integral part of the Palestinian polity. In this chapter, Bedouins are not treated as a special or separate group for two main reasons. First, as the focus of this chapter is on the role and intervention of foreign aid actors in the context of Israeli[1] settler colonialism, the Bedouin communities in Areas C and E1 are taken as examples from within a broader structure. Secondly, treating Bedouins as a distinct group separate from the

[1] The adjective 'Israeli' is used to refer to Israel as a state, which is responsible for the policies it implements on the territories under its control. Broadly, these are a continuation of the Zionist movement ideology and can be described as Zionist in their political nature, though they are ascribed to the State of Israel as a legal entity.

rest of the Palestinian population could also contribute to their essentialisation and racialisation,[2] and indirectly support the multiple fragmentations imposed on Palestinians in the context of settler colonialism. As such, this chapter considers the entire Palestinian population, including Bedouin communities, as a single yet internally diverse group of people indigenous to Palestine who face the same larger system and ideology of Israeli settler colonialism.

The chapter is divided into three parts. First, it examines the main features of the State of Israel's colonial policies in E1 and the condition of the Palestinian (including Bedouin) communities in that area. In positing that E1 represents a frontier of Israeli settler colonialism, currently perpetuating the logic of elimination[3] of the native population through strategic erasure, the displacement of the indigenous Palestinian populations and the re-engineering of geography and demography in the Palestinian territory occupied by Israel in 1967 ('occupied Palestinian territory', or 'OPT') emerges as a key practice to further consolidate Israeli territorial control. It is in this context that foreign aid is deployed to provide relief to the communities affected. However, as much as these interventions are essential and important, this chapter will illustrate that they do not fully address the root causes of the need for this aid which is driven by a range of international law violations for which there is very limited accountability.

The next section of this chapter draws from existing literature on foreign aid in Palestine[4] to consider how the presence of foreign aid actors has not only coexisted with, but also at times facilitated, the continuation of a colonial agenda, which in turn perpetuates the necessity for foreign aid. Since the 1993–95 Oslo Accords there has been a tension between how foreign aid has been deployed and the political context which exacerbates the need for aid. Despite the passage of time since the signing of the Oslo Accords, the vision of an independent and sovereign Palestinian state remains elusive. Israel's persistent expansion of its settler colonial project has rendered this aspiration more akin to a myth than a tangible reality.[5] By implanting a growing settler population and supporting settlement activities (despite their illegality under international law, confirmed in UN Security Council Resolution 2334 (2016)), the consolidation of Israeli presence across Area C of the West Bank and in East Jerusalem is driving the displacement of Palestinian communities.

The impact of initiatives implemented within a humanitarian and development aid framework is limited, because they are generally divorced from human rights and social justice aims, and most importantly are not accompanied by parallel political initiatives that challenge structural power relations underpinning the needs. As such, although essential for the survival and basic well-being of marginalised communities, donor-funded aid projects usually offer a form of depoliticised routine assistance to

[2] L Tatour, 'The Culturalisation of Indigeneity: The Palestinian-Bedouin of the Naqab and Indigenous Rights' (2019) 23 *The International Journal of Human Rights* 1569.

[3] P Wolfe, 'Settler Colonialism and The Elimination of The Native' (2006) 8 *Journal of Genocide Research* 387.

[4] Including works by E Dabed, T Haddad, O Jabary Salamanca, S Roy, O Schweiki, S Taghdisi-Rad, M Turner, J Wildeman and A Tartir.

[5] A Abunimah et al, 'Focus On: 25 Years of Oslo' (Al-Shabaka, 13 September 2018), www.al-shabaka.org/policy-focus/focus-on-25-years-of-oslo.

Palestinians. This chapter will discuss how foreign aid initiatives may also contribute to the consolidation of the dominance of Israeli interests over Palestinian rights. The provision of aid to Palestinian Bedouins living in Area C of the West Bank, for example, demonstrates inherent contradictions of prolonged involvement of foreign aid donors and providers in Area C in a context of settler colonialism.[6] Bedouin communities are provided with foreign aid by a mix of actors, such as Palestinian NGOs, international NGOs, and UN Agencies, all funded by international state donors.

Finally, the chapter discusses how foreign aid in Palestine presents several paradoxes: while it offers vital assistance to vulnerable Palestinian communities like the E1 Bedouins, it is also hindered by the constraints of Israel's settler colonial policies and practices. By analysing the *modus operandi* of aid projects, this chapter explains how donor interventions indirectly contribute to the normalisation of violations and acquiesce to the colonial order established by Israel in the West Bank. In particular, without demanding accountability via diplomatic means and/or in combination with appropriate forums for violations of international law and other Israeli policies and practices that harm Palestinians, international donors end up providing basic humanitarian aid and services in substitution of the occupying power, who is primarily responsible for under international humanitarian law (IHL) and international human rights law (IHRL).[7] This paradox is particularly evident in the absence of an international response, or in the timidity of international responses, which normally amount to statements[8] or, at best – and very rarely – official letters or private phone calls at ministerial level demanding monetary compensation when donor-provided (and thus foreign taxpayer-funded) aid is confiscated, demolished or rendered unusable by Israeli forces.[9]

Furthermore, this chapter contends that aid donors and providers recognise a 'right to temporarily stay' for marginalised Palestinian communities, such as the Bedouins in Area C and the Greater Jerusalem periphery. However, by providing aid in specific locations, and thus implicitly and explicitly affirming the right of Palestinians to remain in their current locations, without providing legal or political protection,

[6] O Risheq et al, 'Depoliticised humanitarianism: critiquing the effectiveness of international aid for the Bedouin communities in the Jerusalem periphery' (2023) 33 *Development in Practice* 572.

[7] Convention Relative to the Protection of Civilian Persons in Time of War (adopted on 12 August 1949, entered into force 21 October 1950) 75 UNTS 287 (IV Geneva Convention), Arts 55, 56, 59–60; ICJ, *Legal Consequences of the Construction of a Wall in the Occupied Palestinian Territory* (Advisory Opinion) 2004, ICJ Rep 136, paras 106–13; ICJ, *Case Concerning Armed Activities on the Territory of the Congo* (Judgement) 2005, ICJ Rep 168, paras 216–18.

[8] Office of the European Union Representative (West Bank and Gaza Strip, UNRWA), 'One Year Report on Demolitions and Seizures in the West Bank, including East Jerusalem Reporting Period: 1 January – 31 December 2022' (EEAS, 28 March 2023) 10–12, www.eeas.europa.eu/sites/default/files/documents/2023/One%20Year%20Report%20on%20Demolitions%20and%20Seizures%20in%20the%20West%20Bank%20including%20East%20Jerusalem%20-%201%20January%20%E2%80%93%2031%20December%202022.pdf.

[9] P Smolar, 'Des Pays d'Europe Se Retournent Contre Israël Après Des Destructions En Cisjordanie' *Le Monde* (17 October 2017), www.lemonde.fr/international/article/2017/10/17/des-pays-d-europe-s-appretent-a-demander-compensation-a-israel-apres-des-destructions-en-cisjordanie_5201945_3210.html; B David, 'In Unprecedented Move, Eight European Countries to Demand Compensation From Israel for West Bank Demolitions' (Haaretz, 19 October 2017), www.haaretz.com/israel-news/2017-10-19/ty-article/.premium/in-first-eu-states-to-demand-compensation-for-w-bank-demolitions/0000017f-db3a-df62-a9ff-dffffcdf0000.

aid actors may inadvertently expose them to Israeli violence – the root cause of their vulnerability – both when it is perpetrated by state actors (such as the army or police) and by private actors such as settlers. In espousing this 'right to temporarily remain', aid donors and providers also uphold a two-state vision, which may implicitly deny the Bedouins' right of return to their ancestral homeland in present-day Israel.[10]

Indeed, as discussed by Bana Abu Zuluf and Ahmad Amara in chapter three of this volume, the Bedouin tribes living in what is now referred to as Area C of the occupied West Bank were originally displaced from their ancestral homes in the Naqab (Arabic) or Negev (Hebrew) (hereinafter Naqab) region of present-day Israel after its establishment, and became refugees in what was then the Jordanian-controlled West Bank. This situation underscores the complexity and paradoxes of aid provision in perpetuating political dynamics while addressing immediate humanitarian needs.

5.1. FRAMING THE NEED FOR AID: THE SETTLER COLONIAL GEO-DEMOGRAPHIC RE-ENGINEERING OF E1 AND THE IMPACT ON PALESTINIAN BEDOUINS

As also discussed by Mohammed Younes in chapter two of this volume, and Ahmad Amara and others in chapter one, successive rulers in Palestine have coveted Bedouin lands and acted in ways to displace and settle them, at least since the nineteenth century.[11] The dispossession of Palestinian Bedouin land dates back to Ottoman land policies that forced Bedouins to register their land in the *tabu* system at the beginning of the 1900s, which reduced the areas under their control and triggered a sedentarisation process.[12] Case studies show pre-1948 Bedouin land expropriation (by the British mandate authorities occupying Palestine) in northern historical Palestine and in the Naqab.[13] The process of dispossession and transfer continued across Palestine throughout the twentieth century, which culminated in what the Palestinians refer to as the Nakba (catastrophe).[14] The dispossession of land continues to this day,[15] manifesting itself in different forms and to varying degrees of intensity. During and after 1948, Bedouins in the south of historic Palestine were stripped of their lands in a

[10] Seminal works on the right of return of displaced Palestinians under international law are RI Khalidi, 'Observations on the Right of Return' (1992) 21 *Journal of Palestine Studies* 29; WT Mallison and SV Mallison, 'The Right of Return' (1980) 9 *Journal of Palestine Studies* 125; K Lawand, 'The Right to Return of Palestinians in International Law' (1996) 8 *International Journal of Refugee Law* 532; J Quigley, 'Displaced Palestinians and a Right of Return' (1998) 39 *Harvard International Law Journal* 171.

[11] E Marx, 'Land of the Negev Bedouin' in E Hertzog et al (eds), *Perspectives on Israeli Anthropology* (Wayne State University Press, 2010) 489.

[12] I Pappe, *A History of Modern Palestine* (CUP, 2022) 46.

[13] G Falah, 'Pre-State Jewish Colonization in Northern Palestine and Its Impact on Local Bedouin Sedentarization 1914–1948' (1991) 17 *Journal of Historical Geography* 289; T Mazarib, 'Bedouin on the Borders: The Impact of Political-Geographical Borders on Settlement of Bedouin in the Galilee During the British Mandate, 1918–1948' (2022) 42 *Geography Research Forum* 70.

[14] For a detailed account of the depopulation of Palestinian villages in 1948, see W Khalidi, *All That Remains* (Institute for Palestine Studies, 1992).

[15] M Nasasra, 'The Ongoing Judaisation of the Naqab and the Struggle for Recognising the Indigenous Rights of the Arab Bedouin People' (2012) 2 *Settler Colonial Studies* 81.

manner similar to that outlined in policies enacted during the Ottoman Government[16] and forcibly settled by Israeli policies and authorities.[17]

The Bedouins, along with other sections of the Palestinian population, were the target of expulsion plans, one example being in the area of the town of Bisan (today the Israeli town of Beit Shean) in the Jordan Valley.[18] In 1948, there were approximately 75,000–90,000 Bedouins living in the Naqab in southern Palestine,[19] whereas after the 1948 war and expulsions, the 11,000–13,000 Bedouin who remained were resettled in the Sayig region, located in the northeastern portion of the Naqab Desert, which is the area between Beer al-Saba' and what are today the Israeli Jewish towns of Arad, Dimona and Yeruham.[20] In the 1960s some of the tribes were resettled in the north of Israel.[21] Throughout time, many Palestinian Bedouin progressively abandoned previous ways of life and found employment as unskilled workers in agriculture, construction and maintenance.[22]

In general, this seems to be the case both for those Bedouin communities living in the Naqab as well as for the Bedouin living in the West Bank. Case studies of E1 Bedouin communities conducted by UNRWA and Bimkom[23] show that by the mid-1990s, increased restrictions on mobility, economic insecurity stemming from limited access to natural resources and the persistent threat of administrative demolitions due to a lack of building permits led to heightened social instability and hindered community investment in long-term plans. Despite verbal notifications from Israeli authorities in the late 1980s to vacate the Ma'ale Adumim area, the Salamaat Jahalin Bedouin groups remained steadfast in their resistance to relocation, sustaining their traditional livelihoods through innovative strategies such as intensive livestock management and ad hoc employment in nearby colonies.[24]

Despite efforts to convey their desire to remain in their rural communities, the Bedouin faced bureaucratic hurdles and were denied access to essential resources and infrastructure by the Israeli Civil Administration (ICA). As Bedouin communities sought assistance from international and local organisations for rural recovery

[16] S Frantzman and R Kark, 'Bedouin Settlement in Late Ottoman and British Mandatory Palestine: Influence on the Cultural and Environmental Landscape, 1870–1948' (2011) 1 *New Middle Eastern Studies* 1.

[17] A Amara, 'The Negev Land Question: Between Denial and Recognition' (2013) 42 *Journal of Palestine Studies* 27.

[18] N Masalha, *Expulsion of the Palestinians – The Concept of Transfer in Zionist Political Thought 1882–1948* (Institute for Palestine Studies, 1992) 185.

[19] Amara (n 17).

[20] S Swirski and Y Hasson, 'Invisible Citizens: Israeli Government Policy Toward the Negev Bedouin' (ADVA Center, February 2006), adva.org/wp-content/uploads/2014/09/NegevEnglishSummary.pdf.

[21] Pappe (n 12) 170–71.

[22] ibid. On the issue of stereotypes about the Bedouin, see A Amara, 'Beyond Stereotypes of Bedouins as "Nomads" and "Savages": Rethinking the Bedouin in Ottoman Southern Palestine, 1875–1900' (2016) 15 *Journal of Holy Land and Palestine Studies* 59.

[23] Bimkom and UNRWA, 'Al Jabal: A Study on the Transfer of Bedouin Palestine Refugees' (28 May 2013), www.unrwa.org/userfiles/201305293270.pdf.

[24] In line with growing literature on the topic, the usual and neutral term 'settlement' is substituted in this chapter with 'colony', considered to be more accurate in the description of the settler-colonial character of their establishment and expansion. See the use of the word *colonie* in the French version of official documents, for example: UNSC Res 2334 (23 December 2016) Un Doc S/RES/2334.

initiatives, including shelter rehabilitation and solar power projects in Area C, they faced demolition and eviction orders from the ICA.[25] Attempts by Bedouin communities to undertake development initiatives requiring the construction of infrastructure have been deemed illegal by the Israeli authorities due to the lack of building permits issued by the ICA, which are virtually impossible to obtain,[26] leaving them with no viable alternatives other than, at best, unspecified compensation and relocation to concentrated environments unsuitable for their pastoral economy and social customs.

Specific forms of demographic engineering have been and continue to be implemented throughout historical Palestine and take the shape of ethnic dilution, consolidation and ethnic cleansing in the sense of expelling people (in this case, Palestinians) from an area to rid it of 'undesirables'.[27] Emerging from the conflict in former Yugoslavia, the term 'ethnic cleansing' is defined by the Commission of Experts established through Security Council Resolution 780 (1992) to examine and analyse information on alleged grave breaches of international humanitarian law committed in former Yugoslavia as 'rendering an area ethnically homogenous by using force or intimidation to remove persons of given groups from the area'. It is described as 'a purposeful policy designed by one ethnic or religious group to remove by violent and terror-inspiring means the civilian population of another ethnic or religious group from certain geographic areas'.[28] Pappe uses the concept in the sense of 'an effort to render an ethnically mixed country homogeneous by expelling a particular group of people and turning them into refugees while demolishing the homes they were driven out from'.[29] Against the backdrop of settler colonialism, the entire Palestinian population has been affected by demographic engineering from the Nakba onwards. The Bedouins are no exception, and their current geopolitical presence in the E1 area places them at the sharp end of Israeli attempts to cleanse greater Jerusalem of Palestinians.

The dual dimension of settler colonialism, as is currently happening in E1, is described by Wolfe through the notion of the 'logic of elimination' as part of a larger Israeli settler colonial pursuit:

> Settler colonialism has both negative and positive dimensions. Negatively, it strives for the dissolution of native societies. Positively, it erects a new colonial society on the expropriated land base – as I put it, settler colonizers come to stay: invasion is a structure not an event. … Settler colonialism destroys to replace.[30]

[25] B'Tselem, 'Civil Administration Continues Demolition Sweep: 14 Bedouin families left homeless in the Ma'ale Adumim area today' (17 August 2015), www.btselem.org/planning_and_building/20150817_demolitions_in_maale_adumim_area; UN OCHA, 'West Bank Demolitions and Displacement, July 2018' (16 August 2018), www.ochaopt.org/content/west-bank-demolitions-and-displacement-july-2018; UNHRC, 'Israeli Settlements in the Occupied Palestinian Territory' in 'Report of the United Nations High Commissioner for Human Rights' (28 April 2022) Un Doc A/HRC/49/85.

[26] Peace Now, '(Dis)Approvals for Palestinians in Area C – 2009–2020' (31 January 2021), peacenow.org.il/en/approvals-for-palestinians-in-area-c-2009-2020.

[27] MZ Bookman, 'Demographic Engineering and The Struggle for Power' (2002) 56 *Journal of International Affairs* 25, 38.

[28] Letter of the Secretary-General containing 'Final Report of The Commission of Experts Established Pursuant to Security Council Resolution 780 (1992)' (1994) UN Doc S/1994/674, paras 129–30.

[29] I Pappe, *The Ethnic Cleansing of Palestine* (Oneworld, 2006) 3.

[30] Wolfe (n 3) 387, 388.

In the E1 dynamics, both dimensions happen on the intertwined levels of geography and demography. The 'negative' dimension of this process is a slow but steady ethnic cleansing of Palestinian communities residing in areas designated for settler implantation through destruction, dispossession and displacement.[31] The 'positive' dimension is the creation of a new Jewish colonial society in place of the Palestinian one. Importantly, what is observed in E1 is not a new phenomenon; rather, it posits itself in historical continuity with the alienation, Israelisation, Judaisation, shrinking and in Palestinian colloquial terms robbery or plunder of Palestinian land.[32] In other words, its transformation into Jewish-controlled territory that started between the late nineteenth century and the beginning of the twentieth.[33] The expansion of Israeli colonies in E1, across the Jerusalem periphery and in the West Bank has long been recognised by specialised United Nations agencies as a key driver of Palestinian, including Bedouin, vulnerability and displacement.[34] As such, the dynamics of settler colonialism and the ethnic cleansing of Palestinians to make way for colony expansion appears to be the root cause of the humanitarian vulnerabilities of the Bedouin communities.

Both of Wolfe's negative and positive dimensions of settler colonialism are also reflected in the ideological and material construction of a territory that on the one hand breaks the links of the Palestinian population to the land, and on the other connects the Israeli settlers to that same territory. Palestinian communities of E1 (and Area C generally) are excluded from the same services that colonisers have easy and subsidised access to. As Jabary Salamanca puts it, infrastructure such as roads, electricity, water and telecommunications serve as crucial material and symbolic tools for the territorialisation of the settler community, while simultaneously contributing to the de-territorialisation of 'native outsiders'.[35] In this sense, the past and current process of Judaisation of several areas of historical Palestine, such as the Galilee, the Naqab and greater Jerusalem, happens by impeding spatial development of

[31] International Crisis Group, 'Reversing Israel's Deepening Annexation of Occupied East Jerusalem' (12 June 2019), www.crisisgroup.org/middle-east-north-africa/eastern-mediterranean/israelpalestine/202-reversing-israels-deepening-annexation-occupied-east-jerusalem; B'Tselem, 'The Hidden Agenda' (December 2009), www.btselem.org/download/200912_maale_adummim_eng.pdf; Amnesty International, 'Land Day 2017: Israel's Relentless Land Grab Continues' (30 March 2017), www.amnesty.org/en/latest/news/2017/03/land-day-2017-israels-relentless-land-grab-continues/; UN OCHA, '46 Bedouin Communities at Risk of Forcible Transfer in the Central West Bank: A Vulnerability Profile', www.ochaopt.org; see also, N Shragai, 'Understanding Israeli Interests in the E1 Area: Contiguity, Security, and Jerusalem' (JCPA, 2013), jcpa.org/understanding-israeli-interests-in-the-e1-area; N Shragai, 'Demography, Geopolitics, and the Future of Israel's Capital: Jerusalem's Proposed Master Plan' (JCPA, 2010), jcpa.org/wp-content/uploads/2012/04/Jerusalem-Master-Plan.pdf.

[32] G Falah, 'Dynamics and Patterns of The Shrinking of Arab Lands in Palestine' (2003) 22 *Political Geography* 179, 181.

[33] Pappe (n 12).

[34] UN OCHA, 'Communities In The Jerusalem Periphery At Risk Of Forced Displacement' (June 2013), www.ochaopt.org/sites/default/files/ocha_opt_communities_jerusalem_factsheet_june_2013_english.pdf; UN OCHA, 'The Humanitarian Impact of Israeli Settlement Activities' (2017), www.ochaopt.org/sites/default/files/israeli_settlement_activities.pdf; UN OCHA, 'Humanitarian Needs Overview OPT' 24, 41 (16 December 2021), www.ochaopt.org/content/humanitarian-needs-overview-2022.

[35] O Jabary Salamanca, 'Assembling the Fabric of Life: When Settler Colonialism Becomes Development' (2016) 45 *Journal of Palestine Studies* 64, 65.

Palestinian villages and towns[36] constructed and enacted through notions of illegality/legality and (misused) human rights discourse.[37]

In essence, the E1 plan (discussed in more detail by Mohammed Younes in chapter two of this volume) can be interpreted as part of the historical multifaceted process of subjugation of the Palestinian population and the rupture of its relationship with the land by way of expropriation of property and demographic engineering.[38] The Eastern Jerusalem periphery (E1) nowadays represents a frontier[39] of Israeli settler colonialism,[40] where the ethnic cleansing is incomplete. Ethnic cleansing is nearly complete in other areas that have reached a more advanced form of conquest and normalisation, such as the Golan Heights.[41] Accordingly, the places inhabited by Bedouin and other Palestinian communities of E1 have increasingly become one of the current 'loci of power' in Palestine–Israel for the struggle against displacement and the related consolidation of Israeli control.[42]

Similarly to other segments of the Palestinian population and reflecting historical continuity with the displacement and restrictions they have faced for decades, the E1 communities have been severely affected by the Israeli closure system, consisting of physical checkpoints, roadblocks and other kinds of barriers which began as temporary measures in 1991. These include, most notably, the Wall – shorthand for a system of walls, fences, ditches, checkpoints, military posts and barriers that Israel started building in 2002 in occupied Palestinian territory (OPT) on and beyond the 1949 armistice line, including in and around East Jerusalem. Later, movement restrictions were crystallised throughout the Oslo years[43] and intensified after the eruption of the second or Al Aqsa Intifada in 2000, both through the aforementioned hard and soft infrastructures, such as the permit system and access policies.[44] Hard infrastructure such as physical barriers and checkpoints increases the disintegration and fragmentation of Palestinian territory.[45] On the other hand, soft infrastructure such as the permit system governed by the Israeli army, results in a systematic segregation

[36] Pappe (n 12) 294.

[37] N Perugini and K Rabie, 'The Human Right to the Colony' in S Jacoviello and T Sbriccoli (eds), *Shifting Borders: European Perspectives on Creolisation* (Cambridge Scholars Publishing, 2012).

[38] UNSR, A/HRC/49/87, para 57; UNSR, A/HRC/47/57, para 30.

[39] E Weizman, *Hollow Land* (Verso, 2012) 1–17; S Salazar Hughes, 'Unbounded Territoriality: Territorial Control, Settler Colonialism, and Israel/Palestine' (2020) 10 *Settler Colonial Studies* 216.

[40] L Veracini, '"Settler Colonialism": Career of a Concept' (2013) 41 *The Journal of Imperial and Commonwealth History* 313; L Veracini, 'The Other Shift: Settler Colonialism, Israel, and the Occupation' (2013) 42 *Journal of Palestine Studies* 26; Wolfe (n 3).

[41] N Gordon and M Ram, 'Ethnic Cleansing and the Formation of Settler Colonial Geographies' (2016) 53 *Political Geography* 20.

[42] A Amara et al, 'The Bedouin communities of Eastern Jerusalem: a new locus of power in the post-Oslo battle for Palestine?' (2021) 117 *Confluences Méditerranée* 101.

[43] A Hass, 'Israel's Closure Policy: An Ineffective Strategy of Containment and Repression' (2002) 31 *Journal of Palestine Studies* 5.

[44] E Zureik, 'Constructing Palestine through Surveillance Practices' (2001) 28 *British Journal of Middle Eastern Studies* 205; N Parsons and MB Salter, 'Israeli Biopolitics: Closure, Territorialisation and Governmentality in the Occupied Palestinian Territories' (2008) 13 *Geopolitics* 701; see also, Amnesty International, 'Israel's Apartheid against Palestinians' (1 February 2022) 96–97, www.amnesty.org/en/documents/mde15/5141/2022/en/.

[45] O Jabary Salamanca (n 35) 66; UNCHR, 'Report by Special Rapporteur Francesca Albanese – Situation of human rights in the Palestinian territories occupied since 1967' (2022) Un Doc A/77/356, 14.

between Jews and Palestinians enforced through legal(istic) and institutional tools,[46] which curtail geographic and economic mobility for Palestinians while allowing and enhancing uncontrolled Jewish-Israeli mobility.[47] These material and legal infrastructures impact heavily upon the lives of all Palestinians and contextualise the man-made humanitarian vulnerabilities of Palestinian Bedouins in E1 and across the West Bank. The Israeli closure regime in E1, including physical barriers and permit systems, exacerbates Palestinian fragmentation and segregation, impacting Bedouin communities and creating humanitarian vulnerabilities.

As illustrated in the previous paragraphs, the process of colonisation, which aims simultaneously at the implantation of settlers and the displacement of indigenous peoples, is implemented through a complex and multilayered system of hard and soft infrastructures that annex land and restrict the movement of people and goods.[48] This results in an economic reality whereby Israeli authorities and Israeli-authorised businesses control and exploit natural resources in the OPT. At the same time, Palestinian communities, including Bedouin communities who are under constant threat of displacement, become dependent on the Israeli economy and international aid.[49] The Bedouins, as discussed by Tamara Tamimi and Raghad Adwan in chapter four of this volume, are particularly vulnerable to economic disempowerment.

In essence, the E1 plan and corresponding colony construction has a clearly stated geo-demographic engineering goal of Israelisation, which seeks to create a Jewish majority in and around the Israeli municipal boundaries of Jerusalem (positive dimension of the process of settler colonialism, corresponding to ethnic consolidation) by excluding the Palestinian population (negative dimension corresponding to ethnic cleansing).[50] As of January 2023, the United Nations Office for the Coordination of Humanitarian Affairs estimated that there were 7,000 Bedouin people living in 46 small communities in the Jerusalem periphery.[51] As such, the impact of the E1 project on Palestinian Bedouin communities cannot be overstated.

Evidently, then, the impact of Israelisation of the E1 area on all Palestinians, including the Bedouin communities, carries severe humanitarian and development

[46] Y Berda, *Living Emergency* (SUP, 2018) 109; B'Tselem, 'A Regime of Jewish Supremacy from The Jordan River to The Mediterranean Sea: This is Apartheid' (12 January 2021), www.btselem.org.

[47] H Tawil-Souri, 'Uneven Borders, Coloured (Im)mobilities: ID Cards in Palestine/Israel' (2012) 17 *Geopolitics* 153.

[48] Restrictions to Bedouin mobility and land expropriation are also to be seen in historical continuity with the British Mandate ordnance and laws in Palestine; see T Mazarib, 'Bedouin on the Borders: The Impact of Political-Geographical Borders on Settlement of Bedouin in the Galilee During the British Mandate, 1918–1948' (2022) 42 *Geography Research Forum* 70.

[49] UNCHR, 'Report by Special Rapporteur Francesca Albanese – Situation of human rights in the Palestinian territories occupied since 1967' (2022) Un Doc A/77/356, 15.

[50] I Mattar, 'From Palestinian to Israeli: Jerusalem 1948–1982' (1983) 12 *Journal of Palestine Studies* 57; ICJ, *Legal Consequences of the Construction of a Wall in the Occupied Palestinian Territory* (Advisory Opinion) 2004, ICJ Rep 136, paras 119, 122 and 133; International Crisis Group 'Reversing Israel's Deepening Annexation of Occupied East Jerusalem' (12 June 2019) 5, www.crisisgroup.org/middle-east-north-africa/eastern-mediterranean/israelpalestine/202-reversing-israels-deepening-annexation-occupied-east-jerusalem; see also, N Shragai, 'A Jerusalem Solution: One Sovereignty, Multiple Local Authorities (including for the Arab Neighbourhoods)' (JCPA, 20 February 2018), jcpa.org/a-jerusalem-solution-one-sovereignty-multiple-local-authorities-including-for-the-arab-neighborhoods.

[51] UN OCHA, 'Humanitarian Needs Overview OPT' (25 January 2023) 33, www.ochaopt.org/content/humanitarian-needs-overview-2023.

consequences that constitute the foundation of the ongoing and intensifying emergency in the area. It is against this backdrop that international donors operate in identifying humanitarian needs and delivering aid.[52] The socio-economic consequences of Israeli settler colonialism create a vicious cycle of humanitarian vulnerabilities. These vulnerabilities include de-development[53] and economic reorientation towards neoliberal globalisation since the Oslo Accords of 1993–95.[54] In addition to humanitarian and crisis relief interventions aimed at fixing basic needs on the basis of universal moral principles, other paradigms of foreign aid chaperoned by Western donors and international financial institutions provide the formal legitimacy for international actors to intervene in Palestine. In principle, justifications for development aid interventions include its usefulness for the peace process (so-called aid for peace model),[55] budget support to the Palestinian Authority (PA), including for its financial solvency, and the creation of a stabilised Middle East region focused on mutual security and prosperity.

These humanitarian and development interventions progressively became inevitably entangled with the settler colonial reality that they coexist with (at best) and actively sustain (at worst). The following section will problematise foreign aid against this backdrop, specifically in the case of the E1 Palestinian communities.

5.2. FOREIGN AID IN PALESTINE DETACHED FROM REALITY

While aid provides crucial material support to vulnerable Palestinian communities such as the E1 Bedouins, and the importance of this aid should not be underestimated, it is hampered by the constraints imposed by Israel's settler colonial policies and practices, which reduce the effectiveness of the aid provided and buries the prospects of a future in which aid is no longer needed. The models of foreign aid implemented in Palestine operate within a framework of settler colonialism, rather than in opposition to it. It could be further argued that foreign aid is even delivered in parallel and in a manner that is complementary to the absence of a political track of initiatives that oppose colonisation and transform conflict. This exposes the contradictions arising from the need for foreign aid, its preventability and its actual ineffectiveness. Without addressing the underlying causes of humanitarian and developmental needs, foreign aid therefore falls short of fulfilling its commitments,[56] whether it be peace and security, poverty reduction, development, economic prosperity, state-building, or democracy.

[52] ibid.

[53] See the next section for the concept introduced by Sara Roy in the 1980s.

[54] Whilst it falls outside the scope of this chapter, notable discussions of this topic include the works of M Turner and O Schweiki; A Tartir, T Dana, T Seidel and T Haddad. See also the next section for a summary of political economy dynamics and consequences of the Oslo Accords and interventions of foreign institutions.

[55] Declaration of Principles on Interim Self-Government Arrangements (Oslo Agreement) (13 September 1993).

[56] Inter alia, see Risheq et al (n 6).

In essence, the operational framework of international aid in Palestine, including for Bedouin communities, embodies the aims of providing humanitarian and development assistance, as well as delivering peace. On a formal level, this is the focus of Western donors (members of the OECD Development Assistance Committee) and UN agencies (who are part of the Inter Agency Standing Committee), who all recognise the importance of 'effectively reducing people's needs, risks and vulnerabilities, supporting prevention efforts and thus, shifting from delivering humanitarian assistance to ending need'.[57] As virtually all state donors and aid organisations maintain, the needs to which foreign aid delivered in Palestine responds do not result from inevitable natural disasters: what donors often avoid saying explicitly is that the needs are the product of deliberate and systematic policies and actions that could be reversed mainly by Israel. Thus, the underlying causes are entirely man-made and policy-driven, implying that there is ample potential for redress, including through concerted political initiatives at local level and through international pressure from third states and the international community.

Critiques and studies on the failings of foreign aid interventions in Palestine are not new. In the late 1980s Sara Roy originally described the economic situation of the OPT as de-development, defined as 'a process which undermines or weakens the ability of an economy to grow and expand by preventing it from accessing and utilizing critical inputs needed to promote internal growth beyond a specific structural level'.[58] The definition of de-development was later narrowed down to 'the deliberate, systematic and progressive dismemberment of an indigenous economy by a dominant one, where economic – and by extension, societal – potential is not only distorted but denied'.[59] This influential analysis of the context in which Palestinians are denied the opportunity to flourish economically (and across all areas of life) has become central to understanding development and humanitarian needs in Palestine to this day. Other scholars, such as Turner and Schweiki confirm that the colonial political economy in historic Palestine imposed by Israel, supported by foreign donors and facilitated by the PA, has mainly achieved de-development, including the effective elimination of a Palestinian economy independent from Israel and sustainable on its own terms.[60] In this context, because of the complex system of closures and restrictions described earlier – crucially the lack of access to land and movement as fundamental economic assets – the E1 Bedouins find themselves at the receiving end of an oppressive political

[57] OECD, DAC Recommendation on the Humanitarian-Development Peace Nexus (Adopted on 22 February 2019) OECD/LEGAL/5019; OECD and INCAF, Report on the implementation, dissemination and continued relevance of the DAC Recommendation on the Humanitarian-Development-Peace Nexus (11 March 2024) DCD/DAC/INCAF (2023)1/FINAL.

[58] S Roy, 'The Gaza Strip: A Case of Economic De-Development' (1987) 17 *Journal of Palestine Studies* 56; S Roy, 'De-Development Revisited: Palestinian Economy and Society Since Oslo' (1999) 28 *Journal of Palestine Studies* 64; later increasingly and widely used in the literature to describe the situation of the Palestinian economy as a whole, eg United Nations Conference on Trade and Development 'Developments in the economy of the Occupied Palestinian Territory' (10 July 2017) UN Doc TD/B/64/4; A Tartir, T Dana and T Seidel (eds), *Political Economy of Palestine* (Palgrave Macmillan, 2021).

[59] S Roy, *Failing Peace: Gaza and the Palestinian-Israeli Conflict* (Pluto, 2007) 33.

[60] M Turner and O Schweiki (eds), *Decolonizing Palestinian Political Economy: De-development and Beyond* (Palgrave Macmillan, 2015).

and economic system and have become increasingly marginalised in terms of access to services, making them progressively reliant on insecure jobs in nearby colonies and on international aid.

Since the signing of the Oslo Accords, there has been a persistent disconnect between the delivery of foreign aid and the complex political realities that exacerbate the need for such assistance. Despite 30 years having passed since the signing of the Oslo Accords, the realisation of an autonomous and sovereign Palestinian state remains elusive. Israel's continued advancement of a settler colonial agenda, characterised by the displacement of Palestinian communities and the implantation of settler populations, has cast doubt on the feasibility of any aspiration to a state, relegating it to the realm of myth rather than an achievable reality.[61]

The Oslo Model, developed in 1993, is a depoliticised aid-for-peace framework created by international donors and financial institutions. The model focused on open markets and trade, as well as economic integration with Israel, with the PA functioning as the principal local apparatus to implement the model and maintain the 'status quo'.[62] Within the model, donor aid is framed as an 'investment in peace'.[63] In addition to the broader context of settler colonialism, the internal political situation of Palestine exacerbates the need for aid. This is because, on its part, the Fatah leadership of the Palestinian Liberation Organization gained control of the position of being the default local partner for foreign aid interventions through the PA, having historically chosen 'state before liberation' over the opposite and practically renounced all forms of resistance. As Dabed notes, this gradually transformed the Palestinian national movement into a colonial administrator with dictatorial tendencies, creating an indirect rule regime, which 'reproduced three main colonial patterns, namely, the non-sovereign status of Palestinians, authoritarian forms of domination, and the division of the colonized/occupied population in social groups with different legal statuses and antagonistic interests'.[64] Indeed, most critics of the so-called Oslo Model note that Western donors have formally supported the peace process and provided substantial amounts of aid 'to make the (Oslo) agreement work',[65] but that the goals of the agreement, including the promotion of economic growth and the establishment of an independent (politically and economically) Palestinian state, have not been met.[66] This highlights a significant discrepancy between any of the goals formally set by Western donors (ie state-building, peace and economic development) and the actual results achieved at the macro level. Despite decades of significant financial and political involvement by the international community in the

[61] Abunimah et al (n 5).

[62] T Haddad, *Palestine LTD* (Bloomsbury, 2018); similar arguments in J Wildeman, 'Neoliberalism as Aid for the Settler Colonization of the Occupied Palestinian Territories After Oslo' in A Tartir and T Seidel (eds), *Palestine and Rule of Power* (Palgrave Macmillan, 2019).

[63] World Bank, ''Developing the Occupied Territories: An Investment in Peace' (World Bank, 1993).

[64] E Dabed, 'The Oslo Agreements and The Palestinian Authority: Or How to Convert Freedom Fighters into Docile Colonial Administrators' (2021) 117 *Confluences Méditerranée* 161, 164–65. See also, E Dabed, 'Decrypting the Palestinian Political Crisis: Old Strategies Against New Enemies: Chile 1970–73, Palestine 2006–09' (2010) 32 *Arab Studies Quarterly* 73.

[65] R Brynen, *A Very Political Economy* (US Institute of Peace Press, 2000) 73.

[66] J Wildeman and A Tartir, 'Can Oslo's Failed Aid Model Be Laid to Rest?' (Al-Shabaka, 18 September 2013), www.al-shabaka.org/briefs/can-oslos-failed-aid-model-be-laid-to-rest.

region, critics argue that the intended goals of peace remain elusive. Furthermore, the support provided to the Fatah-led PA has not resulted in the establishment of a sovereign Palestinian state. Economic conditions and production capacities in Gaza, the West Bank and East Jerusalem continue to deteriorate steadily (even before the recent round of conflict escalation). On their part, rather than prioritising the real needs of the population, donor actions have been driven primarily by their own foreign policy agendas,[67] which leave little room for a contextualised and comprehensive response that is appropriate and coherent with the requests of the relevant population. As a result, foreign aid initiatives have largely failed to deliver on their goals because they do not adequately address the entrenched power dynamics inherent in settler colonialism, rendering their analyses and proposed solutions largely ineffective.[68]

Although colonisation and the Oslo paradigm offer some context and background to foreign aid interventions, their impact vary according to different areas. For instance, Ramallah and other localities have become more middle class, East Jerusalem and Area C have become poorer, and the Gaza Strip endures a humanitarian crisis caused by a blockade, which as of late 2023 has turned into total devastation. Western donors have not only played a major role in shaping this reality by essentially acquiescing to the colonisation of Palestinian land and the socio-economic fragmentation of Palestine, but they have also tried to mitigate or manage the dire impacts of Israeli colonisation on all aspects of Palestinian life.[69] In other words, donor states have allowed Israel's policies to largely continue undisturbed for decades, choosing instead to intervene with an aid model that is seemingly detached from the reality of the occupation being the driver of ongoing humanitarian need and entrenched de-development. This results in aid programmes, including humanitarian and development projects, which are incoherent and ineffective, and only attempt to manage the crisis stemming from Israeli colonisation and a depoliticised foreign aid model.

The paradox of aid models that address needs on the surface without acknowledging that the structural causes of humanitarian and development gaps are premised on Israeli colonisation of Palestine emerges clearly from ongoing practices. As Wildeman and Tartir claim, Israel and the US have been able to work alongside all international financial institutions and major Western donors because the latter do not question existing colonial structures and relations of power,[70] but rather adopt a shallow understanding of a two-state solution based on Western tenets of democracy and governance. This can partially explain why interventions by US, EU and international institutions such as the World Bank resemble each other and work in the same manner on the ground, even though policy underpinnings may be theoretically different.[71]

[67] S Taghdisi-Rad, *The Political Economy of Aid in Palestine* (Routledge, 2011).

[68] Inter alia, L Tabar and O Jabary Salamanca, *Critical Readings of Development Under Colonialism: Towards A Political Economy for Liberation in The Occupied Palestinian Territories* (Birzeit, 2015); A Hanieh, 'Development as Struggle: Confronting the Reality of Power in Palestine' (2016) 45 *Journal of Palestine Studies* 32.

[69] M Turner, 'The Political Economy of Western Aid' in Turner and Schweiki (n 60) 47.

[70] J Wildeman and A Tartir, 'Political Economy of Foreign Aid in the Occupied Palestinian Territories: A Conceptual Framing' in A Tartir, T Dana and T Seidel (eds), *Political Economy of Palestine* (Palgrave Macmillan, 2021) 240–41.

[71] ibid.

For instance, a typically European approach promoting a two-state solution and a neo-colonialist approach promoting stabilisation and control of different forms of Palestinian resistance, could practically work towards the same goal. That is, both approaches translate into the advocacy of institution-building, different kinds of financial support, and the provision of humanitarian aid to meet the basic needs of underserved or marginalised communities, such as the Bedouin communities of E1.

A further consideration of the detachment of foreign aid models from the political context and underlying power dynamics is found in the terminology used in the aid sector. For instance, by invoking the often-used term 'resilience', aid projects in E1 and Area C fall into the category of projects that aim to reduce or manage the impact of settler colonial policies by maintaining a minimum standard of living and take a rather depoliticised approach to survival despite ongoing harm inflicted.[72] These interventions, labelled as 'humanitarian' or 'developmental', rather than opposing or constraining the structural violence of colonialism, manage the short-term needs of Palestinians while allowing settler colonialism to expand and become more entrenched, thus condemning Palestinians to rely further upon aid.[73]

In this context, the adoption of the resilience rhetoric by international organisations and NGO projects – divested of any reference to the notions of resistance against oppression or *sumud* – may in practice promote coping with colonial realities rather than challenging or overcoming them.[74] This is apparent in relation to aid given to Bedouins in E1 and across the West Bank: donors attempt to respond to the dire humanitarian needs of these communities with a range of ad hoc projects, including emergency relief, resilience building (community-based protection; basic and social infrastructure; legal aid) and advocacy,[75] but when foreign-funded items are confiscated or destroyed by Israeli forces, donor states generally do little more than issue statements of discontent or lodge official complaints. As a result, the realities of settler colonialism and the essential acquiescence to the status quo, in which Israel can continue to render foreign aid useless, prevail over prioritising the effectiveness of aid interventions.

The intersection of foreign aid projects with the reality of settler colonialism, the contradictions inherent in the necessity and ineffectiveness of such aid, and the absence of concerted political efforts generate paradoxes that are illustrated in the next section.

5.3. PARADOXES STEMMING FROM THE ENTANGLEMENT OF FOREIGN AID PROJECTS WITH REALITIES

A closer look at aid projects reveals several paradoxes. In the absence of comprehensive initiatives that directly challenge settler colonial policies, these aid efforts become

[72] Risheq et al (n 6).
[73] Jabary Salamanca (n 35) 64.
[74] EP Keelan and BC Browne, 'Problematising Resilience: Development Practice and the Case of Palestine' (2020) 30 *Development in Practice* 9.
[75] Openaid, 'West Bank Protection Consortium – Resilience Program' (4 April 2024), www.openaid.se/en/contributions/SE-0-SE-6-14571.

entangled in the very problems they seek to address. Their ostensible goal of mitigating the ramifications of military occupation and settler colonialism paradoxically contribute to their perpetuation, notably by avoiding to ensure accountability for perpetrators of violations of international law, and instead by assuming a surrogate role in the provision of basic services for communities living within the oppressive environment of settler colonialism. Moreover, by positioning Palestinian communities as primary recipients of aid within a framework lacking adequate protective measures, foreign aid interventions may inadvertently undermine the tenets of the 'do no harm' principle, derived from the Hippocratic oath, which – at a minimum – prescribes that any aid project must avoid causing unintended harm.[76] Further, over the medium-to-long term, these dynamics, to which aid projects contribute directly, culminate in what may be termed the 'right to temporarily stay' paradox, wherein the pursuit of temporary residence and resilience indirectly counteracts the foundational principle of the right of return of Palestine refugees to their ancestral homes in what is now called the Naqab in present-day Israel.

Aid projects in Area C, including E1, therefore present a particular set of contradictions. The main aim of aid projects is to address the short-term humanitarian needs of Palestinians and in E1 to also keep the two-state solution alive by avoiding the bisection of the West Bank, though in a manner that preserves the imperatives and respects the limits set by Israeli settler colonialism. In doing so, donors contribute to ensuring that Palestinians can cope with their current reality imposed by Israeli authorities, rather than contest it or rebel against it. In practice, these initiatives contribute to the maintenance of the military occupation: while they address humanitarian needs, they also relieve the Israeli authorities of legal accountability to ensure civilian populations living under occupation enjoy an adequate standard of living and are able to access key services (such as education, health and essential utilities including water and power) required by the Hague Regulations and Fourth Geneva Convention. As such, foreign donors discharge Israel's responsibility to respond to the material needs of the occupied population, essentially funding a status quo in which international donors are the ones paying for the damage caused by Israel's military occupation and colonial expansion. Thus, as the growing literature on this topic reveals, emergency assistance helps to sustain the occupation in different ways.[77]

Ongoing violations of international law by the Israeli authorities and settlers at the expense of Bedouin communities are a key factor in their need for aid. Such violations are seldom met with any genuine attempt to hold those responsible to account; partly because of a lack of deterrence, Israel has no reason to put an end to such violations or to reverse its effects. Despite the widely reported patterns of home demolitions, destruction of private and community property – including animal pens,

[76] For an evolution of the principle of 'do no harm' in the humanitarian, development and peacebuilding sectors, see M Anderson, *Do No Harm: How Aid Can Support Peace – Or War* (Lynne Rienner, 1999); H Slim, *Humanitarian Ethics: A Guide to The Morality of Aid in War and Disaster* (Hurst & Co, 2015); S Schmeidl, A Ware and C Alberti, 'Conflict Sensitivity/Do No Harm (DNH) in Development, Humanitarian, and Peacebuilding Practice – Reflections and Emerging Trends' (2023) 33 *Development in Practice* 517.

[77] Taghdisi-Rad (n 67) 77; T Tamimi and O Risheq, 'Palestinian Bedouins in the E1 Corridor: A Critique of Donor Aid' (Al-Shabaka, 18 July 2022), al-shabaka.org/briefs/palestinian-bedouins-in-the-e-1-corridor-a-critique-of-donor-aid.

water facilities and solar panels essential for their economic survival and basic living standards – harassment of Bedouins by Israeli settlers and military, and a range of other harms, there is widespread impunity for the perpetrators of these abuses.[78] The lack of accountability in an appropriate domestic and international forum for violations of international law – including IHL and IHRL – is contributing directly to the conditions of the Palestinian Bedouins in E1 and across the West Bank. If there are no legal or political consequences for breaking international law, perpetrators are emboldened, and there is no end in sight for these abuses. This means that material aid for these communities is more needed than ever, despite the fact that the need arises from a man-made emergency that could be prevented by decisive legal and political action forcing the occupying power to uphold the basic requirements of IHL and IHRL in relation to the civilian population living under occupation it controls. Put simply by Tamimi and Risheq, 'In the absence of requisite accountability, aid thus fuels a vicious and mutually reinforcing cycle: donors help Bedouin communities rebuild after Israeli demolitions, only to have Israel destroy donor-funded projects, necessitating further aid'.[79]

Another factor that sustains ongoing Israeli colonial efforts is the substitution of the occupying power in the provision of basic services. Rather than requiring Israeli authorities to put an end to their attempts to ethnically cleanse large swathes of E1 from Palestinians (including Bedouins) and to provide basic services to the occupied population, donor countries cyclically provide material support and some of the services that Israel has an obligation to provide according to international law.[80] This means that, in line with the earlier critique of the failure of donor interventions at the economic (sustainable growth), institutional (statehood) and political (peace) levels, donor-sponsored aid projects are again failing to address the root causes of the needs of Palestinian communities, and are in turn helping to perpetuate a cycle of dispossession that continually serves Israel's colonisation efforts and traps those communities in need of foreign aid in a vicious circle. This is particularly visible in the context of the Bedouin communities constantly at risk of displacement in E1 and across the West Bank, whose position at the frontier of settler colonialism exposes them to the sharper end of dispossession by Israeli state and non-state actors.

Perhaps material assistance to communities at the frontier of Israeli colonisation may be considered instrumentally useful to endure and oppose the settler colonial process of land grabbing and displacement. However, in the absence of accountability

[78] Yesh Din, 'Mock Enforcement' (May 2015), www.yesh-din.org/en/mock-enforcement-law-enforcement-on-israeli-civilians-in-the-west-bank/; Yesh Din, 'Settler crime and violence inside Palestinian communities, 2017-2020' (May 2021), www.yesh-din.org/en/position-paper-settler-crime-and-violence-inside-palestinian-communities-2017-2020/; Yesh Din, 'Law Enforcement on Israeli Civilians in the West Bank (Settler violence) 2005–2022' (1 February 2023), s3.eu-west-1.amazonaws.com/files.yesh-din.org/law+data+dec+22/Law+data+22+ENG.pdf.

[79] Tamimi and Risheq (n 77).

[80] Risheq et al (n 6); Convention Relative to the Protection of Civilian Persons in Time of War (adopted on 12 August 1949, entered into force 21 October 1950) 75 UNTS 287 (IV Geneva Convention), Arts 55, 56, 59–60; ICJ, *Legal Consequences of the Construction of a Wall in the Occupied Palestinian Territory* (Advisory Opinion) 2004, ICJ Rep 136, paras 106–13; ICJ, *Case Concerning Armed Activities on the Territory of the Congo* (Judgement) 2005, ICJ Rep 168, paras 216–18.

and deterrence for violations, this mechanism directly or indirectly places the 'beneficiaries' of aid projects at the front lines and receiving end of settler colonial violence, creating another paradox in terms of the 'do no harm' principle. The ones who pay the price of demolitions and dispossession are exactly the same communities that the aid projects aim to assist. By assisting them at specific locations without tackling the root causes of their humanitarian vulnerability and de-development, Palestinian communities who receive aid are left at the receiving end of repeated cycles of violence. The E1 Bedouin communities such as Al Khan Al Ahmar, Jabal Al Baba and Abu Nuwar are merely examples of a broader phenomenon where Israeli authorities demolish, force people to demolish, or seize Palestinian structures, including foreign-funded ones.[81]

Furthermore, because of their political underpinnings and structural features, aid projects often only operate within a present and provisional reality, with little regard for the historical patterns and power dynamics that have led to the present situation of need. In this way, aid projects can contribute to spatial and temporal fragmentation. For example, projects in E1 do not focus on the return of Palestinians to the region of Tel Arad from which they were displaced, although this would be in line with a common interpretation of the right of return of Palestine refugees enshrined in international law. Rather, aid projects focus on maintaining a minimum standard of living for the communities despite the violence of the ongoing occupation and efforts to consolidate Israeli colonisation. This contingent approach could be described as the 'right to remain' in their current place of residence, as refugees have been since the early 1950s. Thus, by looking at the *modus operandi* of aid projects, I argue that aid donors and providers recognise a temporary 'right to remain' of marginalised Palestinian communities living in geopolitically relevant areas, including the Bedouin in Area C of the West Bank and the Greater Jerusalem periphery. Consequently, by providing aid to the Palestinian Bedouin, international donors are contributing to the survival of these communities on their current lands in the West Bank, which is both a positive outcome and potentially a larger paradox.

Thus, by providing aid to ensure that Palestinian Bedouin communities remain on their non-original lands, international aid projects are indirectly contributing to the Palestinian communities' 'right to temporarily remain' in their current limbo. This indirectly contradicts a process that realises their full rights, including the right of return to their ancestral homes or the exercise of their right to freedom of movement, which, combined with the right of return and according to one of the possible interpretations, should mean a right to reside anywhere in historic Palestine.[82] Indeed, the

[81] eg UN OCHA, 'West Bank demolitions and displacement, January-March 2023' (3 May 2023), www.ochaopt.org/sites/default/files/Demolition-report_Jan-Mar_2023.pdf; UN OCHA (n 31); UN Special Rapporteur OPT Michael Lynk, 'Israel's proposed demolition of Palestine village Khan al-Ahmar could result in war crime, warns UN rights expert' (UN OHCHR, 24 July 2018), www.ohchr.org/en/press-releases/2018/07/israels-proposed-demolition-palestine-village-khan-al-ahmar-could-result-war; Office of the European Union Representative (West Bank and Gaza Strip, UNRWA), 'Local EU statement on the demolition by Israeli authorities of parts of the school of the Bedouin community of Abu Nuwar' (EEAS, 6 February 2018), www.eeas.europa.eu/node/39422_en.

[82] International Covenant on Economic, Social and Cultural Rights (adopted 16 December 1966, entered into force 3 January 1976) 993 UNTS 3 (ICESCR), Art 11.1; Committee on Economic, Social and Cultural Rights, 'General comment 4' (1991) UN Doc E/1992/23.

demands of this group of Palestinians include returning to their previous homeland now in present-day Israel, which they are banned from accessing.

The picture of aid projects is therefore complex. Given that aid projects are not part of comprehensive initiatives that counter settler colonial policies and actions in the OPT as the root cause of humanitarian and development needs, they become entangled in the reality in which they operate, creating several paradoxes as explored throughout this contribution. Importantly, they seek to mitigate the humanitarian consequences of military occupation and settler colonialism while, paradoxically, making them more sustainable in the long term, despite the range of international law violations that occur within that framework. For example, by taking responsibility for remedying violations committed by Israeli state authorities and non-state actors such as settlers (often times backed directly or indirectly by the state), and by substituting for the occupying power in the provision of basic services, foreign aid donors and providers contribute to further entrenching Israel's settler colonial project in Palestine, which is driving the displacement of Bedouins from E1 and other parts of the West Bank. Moreover, by placing Palestinian communities at the forefront of violence without adequate legal or political protection, foreign aid actors indirectly undermine a 'do no harm' approach. In the medium-to-long term, these dynamics create another paradox that we have described as the 'right to temporarily stay', which, by upholding a two-state vision, in turn negates the right of return.

CONCLUSION

In conclusion, international aid projects in E1 and Area C exemplify a complex interplay between the need for humanitarian assistance, foreign donors' political agendas, and the perpetuation of past and current colonial structures. Continued reliance on foreign aid without substantive political action by donor states to address the root causes of humanitarian needs – or, in legalistic terms, ensure the application of, and accountability for violations of basic norms of international law, including IHL and IHRL – perpetuates a cycle of dependency and vulnerability for Palestinian communities, leaving them exposed to recurrent colonial violence without adequate protection and recourse. While it is important to note that these projects address immediate humanitarian needs and aim to maintain a minimum standard of living for Palestinian communities, they also operate within a depoliticised framework that fails to challenge the underlying structural violence of settler colonialism that creates the need for aid in the first place. By addressing short-term needs without confronting the root causes of Palestinian vulnerability and displacement, these initiatives inadvertently sustain the military occupation and relieve Israeli authorities of accountability. Furthermore, these interventions contribute to entrenching Palestinian communities in a state of limbo without realising their full rights, including the right of return.

6

Beyond Physical Destruction: Palestinian Bedouins' Right to Culture under Israeli Colonial Rule in the Jerusalem Periphery

REEDA ALJI

INTRODUCTION

THE INDIGENOUS RIGHTS movement in the 1960s was welcomed in the human rights community as a triumph for indigenous agency and human rights.[1] Nowadays, it is hard to imagine any indigenous struggles for ancestral lands outside the indigenous rights framework, underpinned by the International Covenant on Economic, Social and Cultural Rights (ICESCR),[2] the International Covenant on Civil and Political Rights (ICCPR),[3] the UN Declaration on the Rights of Indigenous Peoples (UNDRIP),[4] the International Labour Convention concerning Indigenous and Tribal Peoples[5] and the UN Declaration of Human Rights (UNDHR).[6] Various international bodies have recognised the indigeneity of Palestinian Bedouins, including the UN Special Rapporteur on the rights of indigenous peoples,[7] the UN Permanent Forum on Indigenous Issues, the UN Working Group on Indigenous Populations, and the Expert Mechanism on the Rights of Indigenous Peoples, with Bedouin activists routinely attending relevant sessions since 2005.[8] Other UN

[1] CJ Christie, *A Modern History of Southeast Asia: decolonization, nationalism, and separatism* (IB Tauris, 1996).

[2] International Covenant on Economic, Social and Cultural Rights 1966, 993 UNTS 3.

[3] International Covenant on Civil and Political Rights 1966, 999 UNTS 171.

[4] United Nations Declaration on the Rights of Indigenous Peoples, GA Res 61/295, UN GAOR, 61st sess, 107th plen mtg, Supp No 49, UN Doc A/RES/61/295 (13 September 2007).

[5] International Labour Organization, International Labour Convention concerning Indigenous and Tribal Peoples in Independent Countries (adopted 27 June 1989, entered into force 5 September 1991) ILO Convention No 169.

[6] Universal Declaration of Human Rights, GA Res 217A (III), UN GAOR, 3rd sess, 183rd plen mtg, Supp No 16, UN Doc A/810 (10 December 1948).

[7] James Anaya, 'Annex VI: Israel: Situation of Unrecognized Bedouin Villages in the Negev Desert', in Cases Examined by the Special Rapporteur (2011), unsr.jamesanaya.org/casos-2011/06-israel-situation-of-unrecognized-bedouin-villages-in-the-negev-desert.

[8] As reported in SJ Frantzman, H Yahel and R Kark, 'Contested Indigeneity: The Development of an Indigenous Discourse on the Bedouin of the Negev, Israel' (2012) 17 *Israel Studies* 78.

human rights bodies, such as the UN Committee on the Elimination of Racial Discrimination,[9] the Human Rights Committee, the Committee on Economic, Social and Cultural Rights, the European Parliament[10] and other international human rights organisations,[11] have also acknowledged the Bedouin as indigenous. Although the discourse on Bedouin indigeneity has assisted Bedouins in gaining international recognition and widespread attention from the international community to advocate for their rights, the focus on the right to culture has contributed to preventing rights-based enjoyment of the Palestinian Bedouins' lifestyle. Bedouins are agro-pastoralist communities[12] whose lifestyle is based on the 'pastoral economy', which relies on accessing vast space to raise livestock and herding in search of fresh pastures. Recent research on nomadic culture denotes that the Bedouin way of life 'operates along a continuum of economic and social activities'[13] that changes throughout the year and sometimes includes agriculture,[14] a key component of their lifestyle.

This chapter problematises the culturalisation of Bedouin indigeneity in international law, arguing that it marginalises the Bedouin lifestyle by subjecting Palestinian Bedouins – as agro-pastoralist communities – in the West Bank to repressive demands for cultural purity, which in turn risks compromising their long-term claims to land by conditioning them upon the perpetual practices of an imagined 'authentic' culture. Throughout this chapter, culturalisation is understood as the various international legal mechanisms through which indigenous peoples' rights are recognised based on their culture, whereby liberal multiculturalism's racial and colonial agenda is intertwined with the international indigenous rights regime.[15]

The chapter is divided into three sections. Section 6.1 provides background on the Bedouin lifestyle focusing on land and cultural activities. Section 6.2 analyses what international law offers Palestinian Bedouins to protect their lifestyle, including seasonal migration, land requirements and title. Section 6.3 examines the challenge to the culturalisation of Bedouin indigeneity that mobilises an essentialist framework which misconceptualises Palestinian Bedouins on two levels. The first level is that it overlooks that the Bedouin lifestyle is agro-pastoralist, but adaptive to modernity. It therefore includes Bedouins' integration into nearby villages and urban life and the practice of *seasonal* migration. The second level is that the emphasis on the discourse of the right to culture instead of the right to self-determination of the Palestinian Bedouins as part of the wider Palestinian people (who are all indigenous to Palestine) is a mere illusion which forces Bedouins to assimilate into Israeli colonial policies.

[9] UN Committee on the Elimination of Racial Discrimination, Concluding Observations: Israel, 14 June 2007, UN Doc CERD/C/ISR/CO/13; UN Committee on the Elimination of Racial Discrimination, Concluding Observations: Israel, 3 April 2012, UN Doc CERD/C/ISR/CO/14-16.

[10] EU Resolution calling Israel to stop the Prawer Plan (2012/2694(RSP)).

[11] Human Rights Watch, 'Off the Map: Land and Housing Rights Violations in Israel's Unrecognized Bedouin Villages' (2008); D Vinding (ed), *The Indigenous World 2002–2003* (IWGIA, 2003).

[12] R Bartlett, 'An obsession with traditional laws and customs creates difficulty establishing native title claims in the south: Yorta Yorta' (2003) 31 *University of Western Australia Law Review* 35.

[13] HA Al-Zubaidi, 'Agropostalism and International Law: The Case of Palestinian Agriculture' (2015) 21 *The Palestine Yearbook of International Law* 95.

[14] Bartlett (n 12).

[15] L Tatour, 'The Culturalisation of Indigeneity: The Palestinian-Bedouin of the Naqab and Indigenous Rights' (2019) 23 *The International Journal of Human Rights* 1569.

Consequently, the discussion of the second level of misconceptualising Palestinian Bedouin communities will argue that the settler colonial framework, without duly accounting for the broader current and historical colonial policies, has constructed an essentialised and depoliticised understanding and meaning of the right to culture by focusing on culture in isolation from self-determination. This understanding of culture is part of the sustained liberal and colonial racism that aims to prevent any discourse regarding Bedouin's right to self-determination – both political and cultural – and the ability to practise their culture freely. It also widens the possibilities for Israel to seek alternative ways to annex lands and marginalise Bedouins. For instance, it provides Bedouins with Israeli-proposed relocation sites that prima facie might seem to fulfil the requirements of international law, but, in reality, ignore the needs of Bedouins. Furthermore, the culturalisation of Bedouin indigeneity allows Israel to uphold its intentional misrecognition of the Bedouin lifestyle as an agro-pastoralist community. This enables Israel to unjustly consider Bedouins as nomadic and use this as a pretext to deny their land rights.

Section 6.1 below offers a background on Bedouin culture, focusing on seasonal migration, land use, registration and title. This background is critical to understanding the relationship between Bedouins, land and the scope of protection that should be provided for them.

6.1. BEDOUIN CULTURE

The agro-pastoralist lifestyle of the Palestinian Bedouins involves raising livestock and cultivating crops in a semi-nomadic manner.[16] For centuries, Bedouin communities in Palestine have relied on sheep, camels and goats for meat, milk, wool and growing crops, such as olives, barley and wheat.[17]

The Bedouin lifestyle is intertwined with the land and the seasons: Palestinian Bedouins' activities and movements are dictated by water availability and spacious land for grazing.[18] In the winter, they tend to move to the lowlands to cultivate crops and enjoy milder weather. During the summer, they move to higher elevations to find cooler temperatures and better grazing land for their herds.[19]

Palestinian Bedouin have developed a rich culture and traditions intrinsically tied to their agro-pastoral way of life.[20] They have a deep knowledge of the land, its flora and fauna, and the natural cycles that govern it.[21] They have also developed skills and practices for managing their herds, including rotational grazing, which involves moving herds from one grazing area to another in order to avoid overgrazing, so that the land can regenerate.[22]

[16] D Grossman and S Shalev, 'Bedouin Herders in Palestine: The Dispossession of the Jahalin Tribe' *The New York Review of Books* (21 April 2016) 12.

[17] M Nasasra, *The Naqab Bedouins: A Century of Politics and Resistance* (Columbia University Press, 2017) 288.

[18] Tatour (n 15).

[19] Nasasra (n 17).

[20] ibid.

[21] ibid.

[22] ibid; M Nasasra et al (eds), *The Naqab Bedouin and Colonialism: New Perspectives* (Routledge, 2014).

For the Bedouins, the significance of the land extends beyond economic factors. The land is crucial to the community's social structure and cultural identity.[23] Bedouin communities in the West Bank have a traditional social structure based on extended family networks and clan relationships; land ownership plays a crucial role in defining these relationships.[24] Moreover, spacious lands are important to women, giving them freedom, autonomy and agency. Given that women traditionally manage the household and their families' livestock, the spacious land enables women to move independently and freely without repression.[25]

However, the Bedouin communities in Palestine face significant challenges to their way of life and culture.[26] The Israeli occupation and settlement policies have led to confiscation of their lands, demolishing their structures (including homes), and restricting their movements and access to necessary natural resources. This results in the loss of their traditional grazing lands and leads to the destruction of their crops and displacement of their communities.[27]

Against this contextual backdrop, the section 6.2 below assesses what international law offers to Bedouins in light of repeated Israeli human rights violations affecting them, including forced displacement and urbanisation. This section is critical in evaluating whether international legal instruments, including the UNDRIP, ICESCR, ICCPR and IHL, adequately protect the Bedouin lifestyle regarding the activity of seasonal migration, land requirements and title.

6.2. INTERNATIONAL LAW AND BEDOUIN INDIGENOUS RIGHTS

6.2.1. Land

Land constitutes a significant component of cultural preservation for indigenous people. Article 25 UNDRIP recognises the strong relationship between indigenous peoples, their lands, territories, resources and their cultural heritage, stating that:

> Indigenous peoples have the right to maintain and strengthen their distinctive spiritual relationship with their traditionally owned or otherwise occupied and used lands, territories, waters and coastal seas and other resources and to uphold their responsibilities to future generations in this regard.[28]

The UNDRIP thus recognises the cultural and spiritual linkage that indigenous communities have with their ancestral lands and natural resources, including water. Article 25 highlights that such a connection is vital for maintaining Indigenous peoples' cultural identity and well-being. Although the wording of Article 25 sets

[23] UNRWA/Bimkom, 'Al Jabal: A study on the transfer of Bedouin Palestine refugees' (2013) 21 and 33, www.unrwa.org/userfiles/201305293270.pdf.

[24] ibid 21.

[25] ibid.

[26] Nasasra et al (n 22).

[27] Nasasra (n 17).

[28] United Nations Declaration on the Rights of Indigenous Peoples (adopted 13 September 2007) GA Res 61/295, UN Doc A/RES/61/295, Art 25.

out the foundation for preventing forced displacement and ensuring that indigenous people have access to adequate housing, its language is ambiguous; in particular, it fails to provide clear guidance on how states or authorities should implement the right to guarantee and strengthen the relationship between indigenous peoples, their land and their culture.

Similarly, the connection between culture and land has been articulated in the ICESC.[29] For example, Article 11 of the Covenant, which addresses the right to secure adequate housing and prohibits forced displacement and eviction, is thoroughly interrelated to the realisation of the right to culture, which is acknowledged in Article 15 of the Covenant.[30] The Committee on Economic, Social and Cultural Rights, in its General Comment No 21 (2009) on the Right of Everyone to Take Part in Cultural Life, articulated the relationship between the right to an adequate standard of living and the right to culture. According to the Committee, cultural life is integral to human existence. It includes the enjoyment of cultural heritage, participation in cultural activities, and producing artistic and intellectual works.[31] The United Nations Committee on Economic, Social and Cultural Rights (CESCR, 'the Committee') in General Comment 21, concerning the right to culture, states that as indigenous people rely heavily on the use of lands to practise their culture and lifestyle,[32] they must not be subject to forced displacement, systemic discrimination and marginalisation.[33] Thus, when their culture is threatened, this right is undoubtedly breached.

Culture encompasses social as well as political and socio-economic components upon which people who inhabit the land depend in order to survive and develop. While the relationship to land is an essential factor of indigenous sovereignty, sacredness and existence the CESCR limits the value of land to its role in maintaining indigenous people's culture and the community's ability to practise it without restrictions. The CESCR denotes that culture is a broad concept that is comprised of traditions that represent indigenous culture[34] and that entails norms, social relations and production methods for sustaining a living. The CESCR also affirms 'the need to consider, as far as possible, cultural values attached to, among other things, the way housing is designed and constructed'.[35] The Committee views the understanding of culture as interconnected to the group's attachment to their ancestral lands which sustain their cultural survival. As the Committee states, 'The strong communal dimension

[29] S Borelli and F Lenzerini, 'Preliminary Material' in S Borelli and F Lenzerini (eds), *Cultural Heritage, Cultural Rights, Cultural Diversity* (Brill | Nijhoff, 2012).

[30] International Covenant on Economic, Social and Cultural Rights (ICESCR) (adopted 16 December 1966, entered into force 3 January 1976) Art 15.

[31] ICESCR, Art 11.

[32] Committee on Economic, Social and Cultural Rights, 'General Comment No. 21: Right of Everyone to Take Part in Cultural Life (Art 15, Para 1(a), of the International Covenant on Economic, Social and Cultural Rights)' (21 December 2009) UN Doc E/C.12/GC/21.

[33] ibid.

[34] Committee on Economic, Social and Cultural Rights (16th Sess. 1997), General Comment 7: The Right to Adequate Housing (Art 11.1): Forced Evictions, [9], UN Doc E/1998/22, annex IV, 1997. This is discussed in T Abu-Ras, 'Land Disputes in Israel: The Case of the Bedouin of the Naqab' (2006) 24 *Adalah's Newsletter* 2.

[35] ibid.

of indigenous peoples' cultural life is indispensable to their existence, well-being, and full development. It includes the right to the lands, territories, and resources they have traditionally owned, occupied, otherwise used or acquired'.[36] This discussion is essential for understanding the relationship between land and culture, implemented from the perspective of the CESCR, which forms a foundational interpretation of the right to housing.[37] In the same vein, the emphasis on land and the protection against forced displacement is integral to various human rights under different human rights instruments, such as the rights to freedom of movement,[38] privacy,[39] family,[40] food and housing.[41]

The association between the right to culture with land occupation and traditional activities limits the understanding of culture as something that is static.[42] The right to culture as a basis to access lands for indigenous peoples makes the threshold of attaining specific standards for Bedouins high.[43] It freezes culture in time by questioning the continuity of cultural activities on a specific territory.[44] The concept of culture invokes notions of tradition and continual and repetitive social activity that offer expression to a community bounded by a collective character and, therefore, considered authentic.[45] This particular understanding of culture requires lifestyles to remain fixed and unchangeable, neglecting how various environmental, political and social factors play a role in reshaping culture in indigenous (and other) communities. The analysis of how different UN committees have understood the UNDRIP and ICESC with reference to ICCPR seems to present culture as a fixed artefact, which does not take into account the dynamic nature of culture amongst indigenous groups.

A further set of laws applicable to the relationship between land and Palestinian Bedouin communities in the Jerusalem periphery and across the West Bank (occupied by Israel since 1967) is found in international humanitarian law (IHL). Forced displacement of protected persons, such as civilians living in occupied territories, is prohibited under IHL.[46] This may also constitute a war crime and a crime against

[36] ibid.

[37] Committee on Economic, Social and Cultural Rights (n 34).

[38] ibid.

[39] See, on an international level, Art 12 of UDHR; Art 17 of ICCPR; Art 8(16) CRC. At the regional level, Art 10 of AfCRWC; Art 11 of AmCHR; and Art 8 of ECHR.

[40] See Art 16 of UDHR; Art 10 of ICESCR; Arts. 17 and 23 of ICCPR, Arts. 16 and 18 of CRC and at the regional level, Art 18 of AfCHPR; Art 17 of AmCHR; Art 38 of ArCHR; Art 5 of the Cairo Declaration on Human Rights in Islam; Arts 8 and 12 of ECHR; and Art 16 of the revised ESC. See also Principle 17 of the Guiding Principles on Internal Displacement.

[41] See eg Art 25 of UDHR; Art 11 of ICESCR; Art 5(e)(iii) of ICERD; and Art 14(2)(h) of CEDAW; and Art 27 of CRC; and on a regional level, Arts 15 and 16 of the Protocol to the AfCHPR on the Rights of Women in Africa. See also General Comments of the Committee on Economic, Social and Cultural Rights No 4 (1991) on the right to adequate housing and No 7 (1997) on forced evictions; and Principle 18 of the Guiding Principles on Internal Displacement.

[42] JR Baldwin et al (eds), *Redefining culture: perspectives across the disciplines* (Lawrence Erlbaum Associates, Routledge, 2006).

[43] ibid.

[44] S Goggin, 'Human rights and "primitive" culture: misrepresentations of indigenous life' (2011) 15 *The International Journal of Human Rights* 873.

[45] ibid.

[46] Art 49, Geneva Convention Relative to the Protection of Civilian Persons in Time of War (adopted 12 August 1949, entered into force 21 October 1950) 75 UNTS 287 ('Fourth Geneva Convention');

humanity under the Rome Statute of the International Criminal Court (ICC).[47] Forcible transfer is broadly considered a threat to the Bedouin way of life across historic Palestine, including in the Naqab/Negev and the West Bank. However, IHL applies only in the latter parts, as this territory has been considered by international law as occupied by Israel since 1967 (as confirmed inter alia by the ICJ Advisory Opinion on the Wall),[48] while the rest of historic Palestine that now falls under the jurisdiction of Israel, such as the Naqab/Negev, is paradoxically outside the scope of IHL, despite the displacement that Bedouins in that area too.

This artificial distinction made in international law is problematic, because it does not account for the similarities between Palestinian Bedouin communities targeted for displacement by the Israeli authorities on both sides of the Green Line. Nevertheless, Bedouins in the West Bank are protected persons under international law. As such, any violent acts that directly target them with the intention of removing them from their lands are considered a breach of international law. IHL obliges Israel, as the occupying power and temporary administrator of the West Bank, to protect the interests of the protected persons,[49] except for specific instances of military necessity only when it is legitimate and proportionate.[50] However, by misusing the pretext of military necessity to justify derogations,[51] Israel continues to displace Bedouins in order to replace the Palestinians with Jewish settlers in illegal settlements.[52] Furthermore, as the occupying power, Israel must safeguard the protected persons' interests and not carry out any forcible transfer nor destroy their property.[53] The current Israeli permit and planning regime[54] in the West Bank does not effectively recognise the rights of Palestinian Bedouins as protected persons under IHL; their unlawful deportation and transfer is considered a grave breach of IHL,[55] and listed as a crime in the Rome Statute of the ICC.[56]

Planning and construction in Area C[57] in the West Bank are regulated by the 1966 Jordanian Law, modified by an Israeli Military Order (1971) (this is discussed in more

Art 17, Protocol Additional to the Geneva Conventions of 12 August 1949, and Relating to the Protection of Victims of Non-International Armed Conflicts (Protocol II) (adopted 8 June 1977, entered into force 7 December 1978) 1125 UNTS 609.

[47] Art 8(2)(e)(viii) and Art 8(2)(e)(viii); Art7(1)(d) of the Rome Statute of the International Criminal Court (adopted 17 July 1998, entered into force 1 July 2002) 2187 UNTS 90 ('Rome Statute' or 'ICC Statute').

[48] International Court of Justice, Legal Consequences of the Construction of a Wall in the Occupied Palestinian Territory, Advisory Opinion, ICJ Reports 2004, 136 ('ICJ Wall').

[49] Art 3, Fourth Geneva Convention.

[50] Art 51, Protocol Additional to the Geneva Conventions of 12 August 1949, and relating to the Protection of Victims of International Armed Conflict ('Protocol I'), 8 June 1977.

[51] ibid.

[52] Tatour (n 15).

[53] Art 53, Fourth Geneva Convention.

[54] S Thawaba, 'Building and planning regulations under Israeli colonial power: A critical study from Palestine' (2018) 34 Planning Perspectives 133.

[55] Art 53, Fourth Geneva Convention.

[56] Arts 8(2) and 7(1), Rome Statute.

[57] The term 'Area C' is used to refer to the lands of the West Bank, which are under full Israeli military and civil control, according to the Oslo Accords of 1993. The Oslo Accords divided the West Bank into three areas – A, B and C – with each area having a different level of Palestinian self-governance and Israeli control. Area C comprises about 60% of the total area of the West Bank, and it is the only area where Israel has full control over both security and civilian matters. This entails a full control over land use,

detail in chapter two of this volume by Mohammed Younes).[58] Through its changes to the law, Israel aimed at precluding Palestinian development and continuing to dispossess Palestinians, including Bedouins, from their lands. The Israeli agenda of depriving Palestinians of land access is always masked by applying the same legal terms to developing the illegal settlements in the West Bank and Israel proper. This once more highlights the main challenge: although the remaining portion of historical Palestine – currently under Israeli jurisdiction and legally regarded as the State of Israel, including the Naqab/Negev region – seems to be excluded from the purview of IHL, the Bedouin communities residing there still face displacement. This arbitrary separation in international legal frameworks poses a problem as it fails to recognise the shared experiences of Palestinian Bedouin communities, who are targeted for displacement by Israeli authorities irrespective of their location on either side of the Green Line. While Israeli (Jewish) settlers benefit from the Israeli laws that regulate development and balance their various needs, the same laws are designed to be disadvantageous for Palestinians in the West Bank.[59]

The Israeli state authorities administering the occupation prevent development through systematic demolitions and by preventing Palestinians, including Bedouins, from obtaining permits to build on their lands.[60] Such policies are part and parcel of the continued Israeli agenda in the West Bank to maximise and exploit the use of Palestinian resources for the exclusive benefit of Israeli (Jewish) citizens while minimising Palestinians' access to their lands.[61]

Having outlined the applicable international legal framework for indigenous peoples, including the UNDRIP and ICESCR, supported by the ICCPR, UDHR, IHL and ICL, and demonstrated how these legal instruments emphasise the importance of land in protecting lifestyles and cultures, the next step is to examine the concept of cultural activities in international law and the challenges faced by Bedouin communities due to the way these laws are articulated.

6.2.2. Cultural Activities

The emphasis on the links between lands and culture has been expanded by the ICCPR, and its treaty body, the United Nations Human Rights Committee (UNHRC), has also discussed cultural activities. Article 27 of the ICCPR states that:

> In those States in which ethnic, religious or linguistic minorities exist, persons belonging to such minorities shall not be denied the right, in community with the other members of their group, to enjoy their own culture, to profess and practice their own religion, or to use their own language.[62]

planning and construction, water resources, and movement of people and goods. See generally: United Nations Office for the Coordination of Humanitarian Affairs (OCHA) 'The Humanitarian Impact of Israeli-Imposed Restrictions on Access to Land and Water in the West Bank' (2012).

[58] Towns, Villages and Buildings Planning Law no 79 of 1996, amended by Israeli military order, Order Concerning Towns, Villages and Buildings Planning Law (Judea & Samaria) 1971.

[59] Thawaba (n 54).

[60] ibid.

[61] ibid.

[62] ICCPR, Art 27(1).

Article 27 strengthens religious, ethnic, and/or linguistic minorities' rights to enjoy cultural uniqueness and arguably helps to link together cultural rights and land rights. It is noteworthy that Article 27 does not refer to land rights per se; however, its understanding should be extended to the connection between land rights and culture because land is a prerequisite for the practice of culture, as the committee has noted.[63] The UNHRC's interpretation of Article 27 has taken a limited bent regarding the discourse of culture; its approach relies heavily on land occupation by indigenous populations for *traditional activities* such as agriculture and fishing.[64] The UNHRC has influenced the interpretation of culture through Article 27 of the ICCPR. That is, the UNHRC's interpretation of the culture of indigenous peoples recognises that the importance of land stems from the fact that indigenous people need land to practise traditional activities such as hunting, fishing, gathering and harvesting food.[65]

As discussed by Yupsanis in 2013, it can be argued that the Human Rights Committee's examination of culture and traditional lifestyles opens space for flexibility in interpretation.[66] For example, the case *Ilmari Länsman et al v Finland* indicates a significant development of the right to culture,[67] which held that a group's practice of its traditional activities is essential to the collective cultural identity. In that case, the UNHRC Committee further claimed that various economic activities can still fit within Article 27 as long as they signify indispensable elements of the culture of an ethnic community.[68] Moreover, the UNHRC asserted that Article 27 does not necessitate the culture to be unchangeable, nor is the Article limited to safeguarding ancient cultures, traditions and customs.[69] Put differently, Yupsanis denotes that the UNHRC's interpretation considers culture changeable and unstable, given that adjusting traditional activities to modern techniques does not prevent such actions from falling under the concept of culture.[70]

Furthermore, the UNHRC affirms that 'measures that have a certain limited impact on the way of life of persons belonging to a minority will not necessarily amount to a denial of the right under Article 27'.[71] In relation to Palestinian Bedouins, the UNHRC's interpretation is crucial as it acknowledges that coercive circumstances, such as relocation schemes that reduce communal areas and hinder Bedouins' access

[63] Human Rights Committee, 'General Comment No 23: The rights of minorities (Art 27)' (8 April 1994) CCPR/C/21/Rev.1/Add.5, para 6.

[64] *Ivan Kitok v Sweden* (Communication No 197/1985), Supplementary No 40 A/50/40.

[65] *Chief Bernard Ominayak and Lubicon Lake Band v Canada*, HRC Communication No 167/1984 (26 March 1990).

[66] A Yupsanis, 'Article 27 of the ICCPR Revisited – The Right to Culture as a Normative Source for Minority / Indigenous Participatory Claims in the Case Law of the Human Rights Committee' (2013) 26 *Hague Yearbook of International Law* 359.

[67] C Tavani, *Collective Rights and the Cultural Identity of the Roma: A Case Study of Italy* (Brill, 2012) 92; Human Rights Committee, 'General Comment No 23: The rights of minorities (Art 27)' (8 April 1994) CCPR/C/21/Rev.1/Add.5; *Ominayak and Lubicon Lake Band v Canada*, HRC Communication No 167/1984 (26 March 1990); Human Rights Committee, 'General Comment No. 23: The rights of minorities (Art 27)' (8 April 1994) CCPR/C/21/Rev.1/Add.

[68] *Ilmari Länsman et al v Finland*, Communication No 511/1992, UN Doc. CCPR/C52/D/511/1992, para 9.2.

[69] ibid, para 9.3.

[70] Yposanis (n 66).

[71] *Ilmari Länsman et al v Finland* (n 68) para 9.4.

to land for sustenance, demonstrate a lack of regard for the Bedouin way of life.[72] The cultural changes in the Bedouin lifestyle resulting from forced urbanisation do not deprive Bedouins of their indigenous status and protection under international law. Forced urbanisation, in the context of Palestinian Bedouins, includes the Israeli plans to resettle the entire Bedouin population in the West Bank into urban-style towns to modernise Bedouin communities regardless of their wishes.[73]

Although there is some flexibility in interpreting the notion of culture,[74] the UNHRC still limits culture to land and the continuity of practising outdated activities.[75] Article 27 of the ICCPR ensures ethnic, linguistic and religious minorities' right to enjoy their culture, which requires continuing conventional activities including land resources for different purposes, such as fishing and hunting.[76] Their lands can thus be protected by Article 27.[77] The UNHRC's understanding of culture seems to be limited to nature-based connections with conventional activities, which require physical occupation on the land.[78] Considering the outlined discussion in the context of forced urbanisation, Bedouins' right to land is tied to cultural authenticity and performativity principles, essential to sustain their cultural survival.[79]

The UNHRC has taken a traditional approach in *Yakye Axa Indigenous Community v Paraguay*. The UNHRC confirmed that the Paraguayan Government's failure to protect the Yakye Axa indigenous community's land rights was considered a violation to the right to culture under Article 27 of the ICCPR.[80] The UNHRC found that the community's traditional lands had been confiscated by the Government, causing poverty to the affected community, which did not have access to services.[81] The UNHRC forced the Government to take measures to return the community to its traditional lands or to provide it with alternative lands, where it would be able to practise its cultural activities.[82]

The UNHRC's interpretation of culture in cases where indigenous people face similar violations of forced displacement like the Palestinian Bedouins fails to

[72] A Amara and M Nasasra, 'Bedouin Rights under occupation: International Humanitarian Law and Indigenous Rights for Palestinian Bedouin in the West Bank' (Norwegian Refugee Council, 2015) 43.

[73] ibid.

[74] ibid.

[75] J Anaya and L Rodríguez-Piñero, 'The Making of UNDRIP' in J Hohmann and M Weller (eds), *The UN Declaration on the Rights of Indigenous Peoples: A Commentary* (OUP, 2018) ch 2, 7.

[76] ibid.

[77] ICCPR, Art 27; UN Commission on Human Rights, Report of the Special Rapporteur on the situation of human rights and fundamental freedoms of indigenous people (16 February 2006) E/CN.4/2006/78 (5).

[78] Anaya (n 7).

[79] ibid.

[80] *Yakye Axa Indigenous Community v Paraguay*, Communication No 137/1983, UN Doc CCPR/C/41/D/137/1983.

[81] ibid para 2.

[82] ibid. The same interpretation was also made by the HRC in *Kichwa Indigenous People of Sarayaku v Ecuador*, Inter-American Court of Human Rights (IACtHR), Judgment of 27 June 2012, Series C No 245; *Sawhoyamaxa Indigenous Community v Paraguay*, Inter-American Court of Human Rights (IACtHR), Judgment of 29 March 2006, Series C No 146; A Xanthaki, *Indigenous Rights and United Nations Standards: self-determination, culture and land* (CUP, 2007) 91; C Courtis, 'Notes on the Implementation by Latin American Courts of the ILO Convention 169 on Indigenous Peoples' in K Henrard (ed), *The Interrelation between the Right to Identity of Minorities and their Socio-economic Participation* (Brill | Nijhoff, 2013).

recognise their right to choose their way of life and to decide how to express their identity, whether by integrating into modern society, practising traditional customs, or both. This oversight undermines indigenous peoples' autonomy and their ability to shape their own destinies.[83] In the case of Palestinian Bedouins, confining the cultural survival to land potentially enables the legitimisation of the Israeli policies of forced urbanisation because the relocation plans offer Bedouins alternative lands where they are given opportunities to enjoy physical and effective occupation on a piece of land.[84] In other words, the rigid requirement of land allows Israel to create alternative channels of displacement embedded through relocation plans that still include access to land that fall, nominally, within the logic of UNHRC. However, these relocation plans are not meant to protect Palestinian Bedouins but to displace them for the creation and expansion of settlements. In the case of Palestinian Bedouins in the Jerusalem periphery, Israel aims at establishing a linkage between Ma'ale Adumim and Jerusalem, ultimately viewing the Palestinian Bedouin communities in that area as an obstacle to their desired result.[85]

The UNHRC's interpretation of Article 27 has been adopted by the UN Special Rapporteur on the Rights of Indigenous People in 2011, who commented on the injustices against Bedouins in the Naqab, pertinent to Bedouins in East Jerusalem facing similar challenges.[86] The UN Special Rapporteur emphasised the right to access lands to allow Bedouins to sustain their traditional agriculture, animal grazing and livestock.[87] The Special Rapporteur also refers to Article 10 of the United Nations Declaration on the Rights of Indigenous Peoples (UNDRIP), stressing that

> Indigenous peoples shall not be forcibly removed from their lands or territories. No relocation shall occur without the free, prior and informed consent of the Indigenous peoples concerned and after agreement on just and fair compensation and, where possible, with the option of return.[88]

Denial of land and forced displacement infringe on Bedouin culture. Therefore, the land is necessary for sustaining their living, which signifies a central component of their cultural identity and its survival.

However, the right to culture as maintained in international law overlooks the shape of land offered to Bedouin communities. The land needed for Bedouins to sustain their cultural survival must be vast in order to facilitate seasonal migration, which is a cornerstone of the Bedouin way of life.

The proposed lands for relocation do not facilitate the seasonal migration and grazing that are defining characteristics of the Bedouin way of life. Bedouins, including communities in the Jerusalem periphery, rely on vast areas of land to let their animals graze; moreover, given that a key component of their culture is privacy, living

[83] UN HRC, General Comment 23: The Rights of Minorities (Article 27) (n 63), para 12; Tatour (n 15).
[84] Tatour (n 15).
[85] ibid.
[86] A Heneiti, 'Bedouin Communities in Greater Jerusalem: Planning or Forced Displacement?' (2016) 65 *Jerusalem Quarterly* 51.
[87] Anaya (n 7).
[88] J Anaya, 'Report of the Special Rapporteur on the Rights of Indigenous Peoples' (2011) 4–31. UNGA Doc A/HRC/18/35/Add.1.

too close to others in the resettlement sites proposed by the Israeli authorities is incompatible. In addition, large spacious areas are essential in Bedouin's social fabric because space plays a role in maintaining healthy relationships between the kinships, and it also allows Bedouin women to maintain their traditional roles as economically and socially active members of the community. This means that the buildings proposed in the relocation sites must ensure the distance between the families based on kinship degree.[89] Spacious areas guarantee that no strangers from other families trespass into the family's private area unless they have prior approval from that family. Consequently, women can conduct their domestic and other activities freely according to their community's traditions and their individual comfort. Such spatial characteristics guarantee their groups survival.[90]

6.3. THE IMPEDIMENTS OF RIGHT TO CULTURE DISCOURSE IN INTERNATIONAL LAW

6.3.1. The Right to Culture Discourse Prevents Bedouin Lifestyle from being Dynamic and Adaptable to Modernity

One implication of considering culture as static – as evident in international law instruments discussed in the previous section – is that it overlooks that the Bedouin lifestyle changes throughout the year due to economic necessities as agro-pastoralist communities.[91] The origin of the Bedouin way of life is found in the pastoral economy, which relies on vast space to raise livestock and herding in search of fresh pastures. Although economic activities including seasonal migration might be considered traditional according to Article 27 of the ICCPR, they cannot be regarded as *ongoing* activities because they are not practised year-round. Article 27 requires cultural activities to be practised continuously in order to be protected under international law.[92] According to Tatour, Article 27 offers a narrow scope of the notion of cultural activities, which is problematic because it does not take into consideration the fact that, due to economic necessity, Bedouin communities are usually integrated into nearby villages and urban life instead of living in isolation. For Bedouins in the Jerusalem periphery, economic interdependence and opportunities for trade and employment have resulted in the development of close relations with farmers and landowners based in Al-Izariyya and Abu Dis.

These relations are vital in order to facilitate the exchange services that can be mutually beneficial to each community and are suitable for shared benefit. Some family members participate in the seasonal movement of livestock whilst the rest remain in their location to avoid displacement by the Israeli authorities. For the Abu Nuwar community, their seasonal mobility in the 1970s started in June and lasted until October.[93] They moved their livestock to the villages in the northern Jerusalem

[89] ibid.
[90] ibid.
[91] Tatour (n 15); Bartlett (n 12).
[92] Tatour (n 15).
[93] Heneiti (n 86).

periphery. They had longstanding links with agriculturalists, herding their livestock after harvesting fields in exchange for support in hay harvest.[94]

The systematic Israeli violations, including forced displacement, which restricted Bedouins' right to movement and access to the Jerusalem markets due to the segregation wall, caused Bedouin families in the Jerusalem periphery to sell their livestock to survive.[95] For example, in 2013, 'only about 30% of the residents at the alternate site still earn a living from raising livestock'.[96] The remaining animals are used only for the production of dairy products to meet personal needs.[97] The example of Abu Nuwar community demonstrates how the Bedouin lifestyle was forcibly changed because of the systematic violations of international law by the Israeli military occupation of the Jerusalem periphery. Thus, the Bedouin lifestyle has become adaptive to sustain economic needs.

Another problem with essentialising culture in international law is that it ignores the fact that Bedouin lifestyle can adapt to modernity, which suggests that economic activities do not always maintain what is understood to be a traditional character. Although migration is a cornerstone of traditional Bedouin culture, some Bedouins choose to settle in order to pursue opportunities in education and employment. Their choice stems from the fact that they lack certain essential urban services to support their living. Also, their right to move freely is infringed as they are forced to settle in certain locations and are always under the threat of displacement.[98] As such, they are forced to move to other places to guarantee their survival.

For instance, not all of the permanent population of Al Jabal were livestock-dependent before 1997, nor were they physically transferred to Al Jabal.[99] Twelve families resided on the sporadically populated hillside before Al Jabal was selected by the Israeli occupation as a transfer site.[100] These families had reduced their ownership of livestock years before the forced transfer, mostly because they sought to move closer to urban centres to pursue higher education and formal employment. The arrival of more than 100 families to the Bedouins' hillside disrupted their shift away from traditional ways of life, such as a reliance on livestock, all while preserving the social structures guided by Bedouin kinship.[101]

It is noteworthy that the Bedouins' shift from animal grazing to labour in illegal settlements does not mean that Bedouins lost their lifestyle. Many Bedouins are compelled to work in illegal Israeli settlements in the West Bank due to systematic land confiscation committed by the Israeli occupation which deprives the communities of traditional livelihoods, leaving them with few alternatives for sustenance. This discussion affirms that the essentialisation of culture to what is presumed to be a traditional, authentic and nomadic life does not reflect the realities of Bedouin

[94] B'Tselem, 'Civil Administration Plans to Expel Thousands of Bedouins from Homes, Concentrate Them in Inadequate Settlement' (17 September 2014).

[95] OCHA, 'Bedouin Communities At Risk of Forcible Transfer' (September 2014), www.ochaopt.org/documents/ocha_opt_communities_jerusalem_factsheet_september_2014_english.pdf.

[96] B'Tselem, 'Ma'ale Adumim Area' (November 2013).

[97] Heneiti (n 86).

[98] ibid.

[99] ibid.

[100] B'Tselem (n 94).

[101] ibid.

lifestyle today, which does not necessitate having traditional activities, but rather is flexible and adapts to modernity as required without dissolving the group's identity.

Although some Bedouins have adopted a mostly sedentary lifestyle, they still adhere to semi-nomadic values and are connected to 'a persistent nomadic identity even in the context of residential stability'.[102] Bedouins have been undergoing a process of transformation in which 'they are adjusting their material and political life to rapidly changing modern conditions, and yet they continue to respect and adhere to a range of traditions that help them define and perpetuate their ethnic integrity, their Bedouin-ness'.[103] Some, such as Israeli academic Hubert Law-Yone, argue that 'since almost all the true nomadic population[s] in Israel has become sedentarised, it is technically incorrect to call them Bedouins.'[104] Law-Yone's argument fails to recognise however, that the Bedouin lifestyle incorporates elements of modernity without necessarily negating their semi-nomadic identity.

6.3.2. The Right to Culture Discourse and the Denial of the Bedouins' Right to Self-determination

Positioning the right to culture as a main aspect of indigeneity upholds liberal and colonial racism, diverting attention from the key right to self-determination. This right to self-determination would enable Bedouins, as indigenous peoples, to freely practice their culture.[105] Despite the narrow understandings of the right to culture in relation to land in IHRL, as well as the longstanding contempt and disregard of the Israeli authorities for the Bedouin customary system of land law, the relationship between this indigenous group, the land they inhabit and use, their right to culture and their right to self-determination is clear. The most recent General Comment 26 (2022) of 24 January 2023 of the UN Committee on Economic, Social and Cultural Rights is a step in the right direction.[106] In the opening paragraph, it recognises that land 'constitutes the basis for social, cultural and religious practices and the enjoyment of the right to take part in cultural life'. This is expanded in the fifth principle:

> [L]and is closely and often intrinsically related to the enjoyment of the right to take part in cultural life owing to the particular spiritual or religious significance of land to many communities, for example, when land serves as a basis for social, cultural and religious practices or the expression of cultural identity. This is particularly relevant for Indigenous

[102] Heneiti (n 86).

[103] ibid.

[104] H Law-Yone, 'From Sedentarization to Urbanization: State Policy towards Bedouin Society in Israel' in D Champagne and I Abu-Saad (eds), *The Future of Indigenous Peoples: Strategies for Survival and Development* (UCLA American Indian Studies Center, 2003) 175–83, discussed in Tatour (n 15).

[105] GJ Coulthard, *Red Skin, White Masks: Rejecting the Colonial Politics of Recognition* (University of Minnesota Press, 2014) 15–16 (emphasis in original), discussed in Tatour (n 15); EA Povinelli, *The Cunning of Recognition: Indigenous Alterities and the Making of Australian Multiculturalism* (Duke University Press, 2002) 5, discussed in Tatour (n 15); P Wolfe, *Traces of History, Elementary Structures of Race* (Verso Books, 2016) 271.

[106] United Nations Economic and Social Council, Committee on Economic, Social and Cultural Rights, General comment No 26 (2022) on land and economic, social and cultural rights (24 January 2023).

> Peoples and for peasants and other local communities living traditional lifestyles (paragraph 10).

The document also addresses the right to self-determination:

> Sixth, land is also closely linked to the right to self-determination, enshrined in article 1 of the Covenant, the importance of which was emphasized in Declaration on the Right to Development (1986). The realization of self-determination is an essential condition for the effective guarantee and observance of individual human rights and for the promotion and strengthening of those rights. Indigenous Peoples can freely pursue their political, economic, social and cultural development and dispose of their natural wealth and resources for their own ends (paragraph 11).

There are limits to articulation of self-determination; the same paragraph indicates that indigenous people can enjoy the rights listed 'if they have land or territory in which they can exercise their self-determination', which 'has to be exercised in accordance with international law and respecting the territorial integrity of States'. In applying these provisions to the Palestinian Bedouins in the Jerusalem periphery and across the West Bank more generally, it is clear that these groups do indeed have land in which they can exercise self-determination in accordance with international law. In particular, their self-determination would fully respect the territorial integrity of the state of Palestine – to which Palestinian Bedouins belong – because Bedouins do not seek to establish their own Bedouin micro-state, but to decolonise Palestine and free it from Israeli control.

In this regard, the self-determination of Palestinian Bedouins therefore operates as part of the collective right to self-determination of all Palestinians who are indigenous to Palestine. In this frame, Bedouins are an indigenous group within the wider Palestinian population (urban and rural) who are in their entirety politically indigenous to Palestine and are thus entitled to the right to self-determination collectively. The Bedouins, therefore, have rights vis-à-vis the Israeli occupiers as Palestinians who seek self-determination, ending the occupation and colonialism. They also have special rights vis-à-vis the State of Palestine, who – once decolonisation of colonised land occurs – must ensure that the cultural rights of an indigenous group within the broader Palestinian polity are protected, respected and fulfilled. Colonial rule, in Palestine and elsewhere, has been transformed from an 'unconcealed structure of domination to a mode of colonial governmentality that works through the limited freedoms afforded by state recognition and accommodation.'[107]

Multiculturalism therefore becomes a central component of racist, colonialist and patriarchal state power.[108] The notion of multiculturalism in the context of settler colonialism which is defined as 'an ideology and practice of governance of the settler state'[109] is associated with depriving indigenous people of their rights to self-determination and sovereignty and is part and parcel of the colonial agenda.[110] According to Patrick Wolfe, multiculturalism is a strategic response by the modern

[107] Coulthard (n 105).
[108] ibid 3.
[109] Povinelli (n 105) 5.
[110] Tatour (n 15).

settler state;[111] it aims to 'de-politicise Indigenous difference by reducing it to the detoxified arena of cultural variety, a sovereignty-free zone'.[112] Compromising land rights for cultural survival confines indigenous self-determination and land rights to the colonial regime's centric terms. As such, settler-colonial states, including Israel, are able to manipulate what indigenous self-determination means and how it can be practised. Hence, the discussion of the right to culture as a means for achieving indigenous rights, in Palestine and elsewhere, produces an illusion that diverts attention from the fact that no culture can be practised freely if the indigenous groups are denied the right to self-determination and sovereignty.[113] In other words, no culture can be preserved if the people of that culture do not have a sense of self-determination and sovereignty over their lands. The focus on culture therefore reinforces the domination of the settler colonial system and forces indigenous people to co-adapt to the state agenda and become subject to assimilation.[114] For these reasons, the right to culture in its current form does not protect the Bedouin lifestyle. Instead, it shifts the focus away from the need to obtain self-determination for Bedouins in order to practise their lifestyle, and instead promotes ways in which they may practise their culture under the Israeli colonial regime imposed on both sides of the Green Line.

Moreover, the focus on the right to culture allows hegemonic colonial regimes to sustain normative control over cultural expression and contribute to Bedouin marginalisation.[115] The discourse on the right to culture in international human rights law affects indigenous rights by setting narrow parameters on what is considered suitable for the modern regime: the focus is on basic rights instead of how state power controls the lands and denies the indigenous group of the full enjoyment of human rights. Regarding indigenous communities' rights, Povinelli uses the term 'invisible asterisk', which is a condition that reads cultural customs against the 'skeletal structure of state law'.[116] It also assesses if the cultural practice is different from prevailing cultural standards as required by the majority.[117]

In this respect, the invisible asterisk in IHRL is recognised in the narrow scope of indigenous peoples' rights, such as their claim to land, property and political autonomy based on static concepts of culture.[118] For instance, the invisible asterisk is evident in the HRC's General Comment 23, which reinforced the linkage between the right to culture, Article 27, and other rights mentioned within the ICCPR. As the Committee observes, 'none of the rights protected under article 27 of the Covenant may be legitimately exercised in a manner or inconsistent with the other provisions of the Covenant'.[119] Although these words recognise cultural rights in international

[111] Wolfe (n 105) 271.

[112] ibid.

[113] G Hingangaroa Smith, 'Indigenous Struggle for the Transformation of Education and Schooling' (paper presented at the Alaska Federation of Natives Convention, Anchorage Alaska, October 2003).

[114] J Corntassel, 'Re-envisioning Resurgence: Indigenous Pathways to Decolonization and Sustainable Self-Determination' (2012) 1 *Decolonization: Indigeneity, Education and Society* 86.

[115] K Engle, *The Elusive Promise of Indigenous Development: Rights, Culture, Strategy* (Duke University Press, 2010).

[116] Povinelli (n 105) 176.

[117] ibid 177.

[118] Engle (n 115).

[119] UN HRC, General Comment 23: The Rights of Minorities (Article 27), UN Doc CCPR/C/21/Rev.1/Add.5 (8 April 1994) para 8.

law, the wording indicates the limits of this right, and burdens indigenous people to preserve and practise their cultural customs. In this sense, the invisible asterisk is the rigid requirement for cultural rights to be recognised in the human rights system. This has ultimately resulted in an essentialisation of culture and alienation, placing a heavy burden on indigenous communities to demonstrate their authenticity, which is always subject to approval by the dominant authority.

The essentialisation of culture and the role of the dominant authorities is evident in how Israel takes advantage of the Bedouins' changeable lifestyle to deny their rights to land. Israel used the changeable lifestyle of Bedouin as a pretext to deny the continual connection of Bedouin to land. As the occupying power in the West Bank, Israel has always justified the seizure of Palestinian lands for constructing settlements such as Ma'ale Adumim by proclaiming that the confiscated lands constituted 'empty' state land, where no Palestinians lived or would be impacted by the settlement.[120] This justification is based on the Israeli Government's claim that uncultivated lands cannot fall under individual ownership, which stands in opposition to local land laws and customary practices of Bedouin groups. Indeed, established records demonstrate that much of this land was cultivated by Bedouins.[121] Moreover, even the Israeli Ministry of Construction and Housing recognised that many of the expropriated lands of Ma'ale Adumim were cultivated, which made it necessary to 'evacuate an agricultural area and a small number of families'.[122]

Another argument the Israeli state uses to deny the Bedouins' connection to land is the nomadism narrative. According to this narrative, constant mobility does not establish a close enough connection to a particular land. The limitation of the right to culture and how it impacts Bedouins is demonstrated in the *Al-Uqbi* case in the Naqab, which falls within the jurisdiction of the Israeli state. The case addressed the legality of a 1954 Israeli requisition of land in Al-Araqib, an unrecognised village under Israel's Land Acquisition Law 1953. The Supreme Court established that the tribe of Al-Uqbi had no rights in the requisitioned land, and thus they did not have the right to remedy.[123] A similar approach has been taken in the Israeli authorities' current dealings with Bedouins in the Jerusalem periphery and across the West Bank.

In the *Al-Uqbi* case, the Israeli courts did not recognise the established customs of the Bedouins community pertaining to land use and ownership in proving the claims of ownership. The customary ownership system is not based on official paper registration of individual titles to the land; this is in contrast to the legal systems of modern states with regards to the registration and proof of property rights.[124] Most contemporary and western states, including Israel, usually only uphold formalised land registration systems and specific legislative frameworks; as such, Israeli courts

[120] B'Tselem, 'Under the Guise of Legality, Israel's Deceleration of State Land in the West Bank' (February 2012) 26.

[121] A Muhammad, 'Abd al-Rahman, al-Tawtin wa al-tanmiya fi al-mujtami'at alsahrawiyya: dirasat fi 'ilm al-ijtima' al-badawi [Resettlement and Development in the Desert Communities: Studies in Bedouin Society] (Dar al-Ma'rifa al-Jami'iyya, 1991) 67; B'Tselem (n 20); A Kedar, A Amara and O Yiftachel (eds), *Emptied Lands: A Legal Geography of Bedouin Rights in the Negev* (Stanford University Press, 2018) 37.

[122] O Yiftachel, *Ethnocracy: Land and Identity Politics in Israel/Palestine* (University of Pennsylvania Press, 2006) 188–210.

[123] ibid.

[124] Amara and Nasasra (n 72).

only apply formal property and land laws as colonial tools to allow Israel to claim Palestinian land as state lands by 'unseeing' the customary rules of property used and recognised by the indigenous community.[125] In the *Al-Uqbi* case, the Israeli Supreme Court requested the Bedouin community to provide proof of land use based on non-Bedouin traditions and customs.[126]

While *Al-Uqbi* dates back to the 1950s and the ICCPR was established in 1966 – preventing the retroactive application of human rights mentioned in the covenant – the inclusion of the ICCPR in this analysis nevertheless illustrates how the Zionist project, rooted in colonial ambitions, aligns with the liberal framework of international human rights law, in particular Article 27.[127] The ICCPR focuses and limits the use of land to agriculture and not the broader range of pastoral activities of Bedouin groups. The Court's request for formal documentation proving title to land is a serious impediment for semi-nomadic Bedouins, because it denies their right to lands as grounded on their pastoral culture and semi-nomadic lifestyle.

Article 27's misinterpretation of pastoral culture mirrors the way in which Israeli courts reaffirm basic western theories of land rights by considering cultural activities as a static framework wherein land is a prerequisite for any cultural practice.[128] That is, cultivation and agriculture tests are the only available means for indigenous people, such as Palestinian Bedouin people, to prove their indigeneity and their belonging to the land. The requirement of *effective occupation* in Article 27 of the ICCPR, Article 15 of the ICESCR, and Article 8 of the UNDRIP, has been considered a prerequisite to land ownership and usage.[129] The arguments of agriculture and cultivation place a heavy burden on Bedouins as they do not occupy the land in terms of what Article 27 requires, and therefore they are most likely to fail in proving their possession[130] through the parameters of formal law accepted in Israeli courts. For these reasons, it is complicated to prove Bedouins' possession of land through the formal legal system.

Despite the difficulty in proving possession of land according to settler standards, it is important to highlight that the burden is not limited to the proof of cultivation, but since 1858 it has also included providing a proof of residence in a 'village' in a proximity of less than 1.5 miles.[131] The problem with such a requirement is that a 'Bedouin encampment' does not constitute a village in the eye of the Israeli courts.[132] As Amara notes, given that the Bedouin way of life is often/largely characterised by pastoral activities, the Israeli courts do not regard Bedouin communities/families/people/groups as legal occupiers of any land because they do not have a fixed and defined territory belonging to the group by whom these lands are occupied.[133]

[125] ibid.
[126] ibid.
[127] ICCPR, Art 27.
[128] ibid.
[129] G Ulfstein, 'Indigenous Peoples' Right to Land' (2005) 8 *Max Planck Yearbook of United Nations Law* 1, 26.
[130] ibid.
[131] ibid.
[132] ibid.
[133] ibid.

The Israeli courts therefore take advantage of the inability of Bedouin inhabitants to prove their land ownership and classify them as nomads, thus assuming they never cultivated their lands.

Although the intention of Article 27 is not to create discrimination, its narrow formulation does, which eventually results in the Israeli courts discriminating against Bedouins. This discrimination is evident in Israel's failure to recognise Bedouins as land right-holders.[134] The nomadism narrative has been central to keeping Bedouins outside the liberal regime of property, which does not recognise collective ownership nor accept ownership based on customary systems of land law not recorded in writing.[135] Palestinian Bedouins have traditionally lived in structures whose ownership was passed down orally without an official registration. The Israeli narrative enables Israel to label Bedouin communities as peoples who lack 'the fundamental and constructive bond with the soil that marks the transition of humans in nature to humans in society'.[136] The rigid understanding of culture in terms of land occupation and cultivation and the requirement of official registration make it difficult for Bedouin people(s) to stop their forced displacement and subjection to Israeli relocation plans.

CONCLUSION

This chapter examined the problematic, narrow focus of the right to culture in ICCPR, UNDRIP and ICESC[137] when understood in isolation from self-determination. It questioned the universality of cultural rights in international law, uncovering the colonial policies underpinning them in their current guise, especially in relation to the Bedouin communities in Palestine. The culturalisation of Bedouins' rights has contributed to preventing rights-based enjoyment of the Palestinian Bedouin lifestyle in all areas controlled by the Israeli state (either through sovereign jurisdiction or through military occupation).[138] The discourse of multiculturalism and the universal understanding of culture fail to take into consideration the particularity of Bedouins' lifestyle, and as such they are fundamental components of colonialism and racism which omit self-determination and only allow indigenous people to practise their culture within the narrow confines of the colonial system. The culturalisation of the rights of indigenous peoples thus creates an illusion and re-victimises Palestinian Bedouins by diverting attention from the mere fact that no culture can be practiced freely without fulfilling the right to self-determination and sovereignty for all Palestinians. Limiting the indigeneity of Palestinian Bedouins to that particular group is a claim used by the Israeli state

[134] M Elsana, 'Indigenous people's Land: The Case of Bedouin Land in Israel' (2019) 49 *California Western International Law Journal*, Art 4.

[135] ibid.

[136] H Yahel, R Kark and S Franzman, 'Are the Negev Bedouin an Indigenous People? Fabricating Palestiian History' (2012) 19 *Middle East Quarterly* 3.

[137] ICCPR, Art 27; UNDRIP, Art 25; ICESC, Art 15.

[138] Tatour (n 15) 34.

to further deepen the division of Palestinian society, which threatens the collective right to national self-determination and instead enables co-adaptation under the Israeli colonial rule, which is clearly detrimental to Bedouin rights. Endorsing the decolonisation of cultural rights may serve as a parallel endeavour to liberating Palestine from colonial oppression. Moreover, it encompasses efforts to ensure adequate recognition and inclusion of Palestinians belonging to minority community, such as the Bedouins, who possess distinct and protected characteristics.

7

Denying the Cornerstone of Jus in Bello *in Palestine: Bedouin Communities and the War Crimes of Extensive Destruction and Appropriation of Property not Justified by Military Necessity*

LUIGI DANIELE

INTRODUCTION

BEDOUIN COMMUNITIES ARE one of the most vulnerable groups in the multifaceted processes of civilian victimisation in the occupied Palestinian territory (OPT).[1] The humanitarian vulnerabilities of Palestinian Bedouins include routine demolitions affecting homes, community spaces such as schools and health clinics, key infrastructures such as wells and generators, and structures needed for their economic survival. In the protracted occupation of the OPT, Israeli authorities intervene in the space between internationally protected rights and the possibility of their enjoyment, without explicitly denying their existence, but appropriating full legislative authority to control all the conditions for their exercise. As such, the occupying power (and its judiciary) routinely upholds the validity of military orders, endorsing the de facto *potestas* of the occupier in deciding which structures are lawful and which must be destroyed, based on its visions of military necessity that fail objective tests. This chapter argues that the appropriation of sovereign prerogatives, distorting exceptional derogations strictly limited by international humanitarian law (IHL), is justified by Israel through spurious declinations of the concept of military necessity devoid of plausible and legally admissible grounds.

A high-profile example of the international law violations associated with the routine attacks on Bedouin property can be found in the Khan Al-Amar village 'saga'. In 2009 Israeli authorities issued demolition orders, claiming that village structures

[1] See eg UNDP, 'Bedouins in the Occupied Palestinian Territory' (Infocus, 25 October 2013), www.undp.org/papp/publications/bedouins-opt.

violated Israeli planning laws. However, given the delays in the actual demolition, the Israeli settler NGO Regavim petitioned the authorities demanding the immediate implementation of the orders. After several developments, in May 2018 the Israeli High Court of Justice (HCJ) endorsed the implementation of the demolition orders and eviction of residents.[2] Shortly after that decision, the (former) Prosecutor of the International Criminal Court (ICC) issued a statement confirming that she was 'following with concern the planned eviction of the Bedouin community of Khan al-Ahmar, in the West Bank', underlining that 'extensive destruction of property without military necessity and population transfers in an occupied territory constitute war crimes under the Rome Statute'.[3] However, no further developments have been registered since then in the ongoing ICC investigation in relation to these potential crimes,[4] despite the prohibition of extensive destruction and appropriation of property not justified by military necessity being a cornerstone of IHL.

This chapter begins with an overview of the origins, development and consolidation of the prohibition of extensive destruction and appropriation of property not justified by military necessity in IHL. This prohibition epitomises a fundamental, overarching rationality of contemporary *jus in bello*, that is the aspiration to strike a balance between imperatives of humanity and civilian protection on the one hand, and considerations of military necessity on the other, representing opposing polarities (and competing paradigms) of the law of armed conflicts. At the same time, this discussion illuminates the evolution of the prohibition as one that mirrors crucial historical and normative shifts of the law of occupation. In particular, the prohibition reflects the evolution of law of occupation from an intermediate regime preceding territorial conquest (until the early nineteenth century) to a temporary, exceptional regime of authority without sovereignty (since the Hague Conventions of 1899 and 1907), reflecting the prohibition of acquisition of territory by force in contemporary international law, established in Article 2(4) of the UN Charter. The new regime no longer bestows on occupying powers any of the prerogatives of domestic governments over the economies, demographics and legislative frameworks of occupied territories. This shift, in fact, emerges in parallel to the prohibition against the use of force and the affirmation of the principle of self-determination as peremptory norms of international law.

The analysis then proceeds to the contemporary scope of the prohibition of destruction and appropriation of property not justified by military necessity under

[2] See *Kfar Adumim Cooperative Village for Community Settlement LTD et al v Minister of Defence et al*, 25 April 2018, HCJ 3287/16, tr by B'Tselem, www.btselem.org/sites/default/files/201806/20180524_hcj_ruling_3287_16_khan_al_ahmar_eng.pdf.

[3] 'Statement of the Prosecutor of the International Criminal Court, Fatou Bensouda, regarding the Situation in Palestine' The Hague, International Criminal Court (17 October 2018), www.icc-cpi.int/pages/item.aspx?name=181017-otp-stat-palestine.

[4] On 17 November 2023 and 18 January 2024, the Office of the Prosecutor received a referral of the Situation in the State of Palestine from South Africa, Bangladesh, Bolivia, Comoros and Djibouti, followed by the Republic of Chile and the United Mexican State. As stated on the Court website, 'On receipt of the referral, the Prosecutor confirmed that it is presently conducting an investigation into the Situation in the State of Palestine, which remains ongoing and extends to the escalation of hostilities and violence since the attacks that took place on 7 October 2023' (see *Situation in the State of Palestine*, ICC-01/18, www.icc-cpi.int/palestine).

international criminal law (ICL). After analysing the most important jurisprudence of international criminal tribunals on the crimes of 'plunder' and 'spoliation', the chapter discusses the current, three-fold criminalisation of unjustified destruction and appropriation of property under Article 8 of the Rome Statute (RS) of the International Criminal Court (ICC), and the analogies and differences between the offences. The analysis will highlight how IHL and ICL set out complementary legal frameworks in this area. This complementarity is both normative, since the relevant ICL war crimes were drafted using the prohibitions previously defined by IHL treaties as models, and interpretative, since these war crimes require cross-referencing to IHL notions to be correctly understood. Once the main features of the interplay between IHL and ICL are clarified in relation to destruction and appropriation of protected property, the chapter assesses whether the practices of dispossession of Palestinian land and demolitions of Palestinian property carried out by Israeli authorities over the last decades of the occupation meet the criteria of the specific crimes under the Rome Statute. Considering the factual reality of the West Bank that frames the situation faced by Bedouin communities, this chapter thus critically engages with the core elements of the discourses mobilised to justify the systematic nature of the practices of dispossession and demolition developed by the infrastructure of the Israeli occupation and supported by the HCJ.[5]

In light of the above, this chapter builds on the former ICC Prosecutor's statement on Khan al Ahmar by highlighting the reasons why the ICC should closely scrutinise facts amounting to crimes of unjustified destruction and appropriation of property perpetrated by the Israeli authorities in Bedouin communities in the West Bank. As watermarks of an institutional project employing systematic, large-scale, and interdependent *jus in bello* violations, the extensive destruction of property without military necessity supports objectives outlawed and criminalised by *jus ad bellum*: conquest and annexation resulting from an unlawful use of force, as the discussion that follows illustrates.[6]

7.1. THE ORIGINS OF THE PROHIBITION OF EXTENSIVE DESTRUCTION AND APPROPRIATION OF PROPERTY, IN THE NORMATIVE SHIFT FROM THE LAW OF CONQUEST TO THE LAW OF OCCUPATION

To understand the evolution of the normative prohibition of destruction and appropriation of property not justified by military necessity, we must consider its early formulations in the codification of the laws and customs of war of the late nineteenth

[5] See N Hishaq and P Haqala, 'Area C: More than 60 % of the occupied West Bank threatened by Israeli annexation' European Parliament Directorate-General for External Policy (Policy Brief) (April 2013), www.europarl.europa.eu/RegData/etudes/briefing_note/join/2013/491495/EXPO-AFET_SP(2013)491495_EN.pdf.

[6] See R Wilde, 'The International Law of self-determination and the use of force requires an immediate end to the occupation of the Palestinian West Bank and Gaza' UCL Policy Brief (July 2022), www.ucl.ac.uk/laws/sites/laws/files/ralph_wilde_palestine_policy_brief.pdf. More extensively, see R Wilde, 'Using the Master's Tools to Dismantle the Master's House: International Law and Palestinian Liberation' (2021) 22 *Palestine Yearbook of International Law* 1.

century.[7] From a scholarly perspective, one domestic codification is conventionally regarded as decisive in the historical journey of modern international humanitarian law (IHL): the 1863 Lincoln's General Order No 100, which contains the 'Instructions for the Government of Armies of the United States in the Field', more commonly known as Lieber Code.[8] While taking stock of the fundamental problems associated with western-centred approaches to legal history,[9] the Code is commonly identified as 'the first attempt to set down, in a single set of instructions for forces in the field, the laws and customs of war'.[10] Some authors describe it as the 'the final product of the eighteenth-century movement to humanise war through the application of reason', offering the 'greatest theoretical contribution to the modern law of war'.[11] Lieber, however, had no strong sympathy for the universalism of Enlightenment ideals,[12] nor for Kantian pacifist globalism.[13] Moreover, legal histories beyond the global north offer numerous examples of greater protection of civilians in times of war.[14] Nonetheless, the Code was *sui generis* in its attempt to provide a comprehensive catalogue of rules spanning: from martial law to the protection of persons, religion, arts and sciences; from the treatment of prisoners of war to deserters, and spies; from battlefield booty to the parole.[15] However, the Code was infused with the Clausewitzian views of its author,[16] resulting in a rather broad and all-encompassing declination of the concept

[7] See F Kalshoven and L Zegveld, *Constraints on the Waging of War: An Introduction to International Humanitarian Law*, 4th edn (ICRC, 2011) 8–15.

[8] See JF Witt, *Lincoln's Code, The Laws of War in American History* (Free Press, 2012); RS Hartigan, *Lieber's Code of the Law of War* (Precedent Publishing, 1983).

[9] See M Koskenniemi, 'Histories of International Law: Dealing with Eurocentrism' (2011) 19 *Rechtsgeschichte* 152; A Orford, *International Law and the Politics of History* (CUP, 2021) 215–48; A Roberts, *Is International Law International?* (OUP, 2017) 209–29; A Anghie, *Imperialism, Sovereignty, and the Making of International Law* (CUP, 2004) 17–64; N Tzouvala, 'The Specter of Eurocentrism in International Legal History' (2021) 31 *Yale Journal of Law & the Humanities* 413, 427–31.

[10] In these terms, see C Greenwood, 'Historical Development and Legal Basis' in D Fleck (ed), *The Handbook of International Humanitarian Law*, 2nd edn (OUP, 2008) 116, 21. Similarly, see eg M Howard, 'Constraints on Warfare' in M Howard, G Andreopoulos and M Shulman (eds), *The Laws of War: Constraints on Warfare in the Western World* (Yale University Press, 1994) 6.

[11] BM Carnahan, 'Lincoln, Lieber and the Laws of War: The Origins and Limits of the Principle of Military Necessity' (1998) 92 *American Journal of International Law* 213.

[12] See M Curti, 'Francis Lieber and Nationalism' (1941) 4 *Huntington Library Quarterly* 263, 265.

[13] See E Kant, *Perpetual Peace. A Philosophical Project*, 3rd edn (George Allen & Unwin Ltd, 1917) and F Lieber, *Manual of Political Ethics*, 2nd edn (J.B. Lippincott Company 1890) vol 2, 430, cited in S Moyn, *Humane. How the United States Abandoned Peace and Reinvented War* (Macmillan, 2021) 48–49.

[14] Relatedly, and as sample of the prevalence of Eurocentrism in international laws of war history, see A Gurmendi, 'Latin Lieber: Uncovering the History of the Treaty on the Regularisation of War' *Opinio Juris* (10 June 2022), opiniojuris.org/2022/06/10/latin-lieber-uncovering-the-history-of-the-treaty-on-the-regularisation-of-war, which illuminates the advanced humanitarian approach of some of the solutions identified in the 1820 treaty object of the enquiry, often overlooked by European scholarship (with few exceptions; see J Basdevant, 'Deux conventions peu connues sur le droit de la guerre' (1915) 21 *Revue Générale de Droit International Public* 5. More extensively on this treaty, see A Valencia, *La humanización de la Guerra: Derecho Internacional Humanitario y Conflicto Armado en Colombia* (Ediciones Uniandes, 1992) 25–37. See also, for the Islamic tradition, A Al-Dawoody, *The Islamic Law of War: Justifications and Regulations* (Palgrave Macmillan, 2011).

[15] Instructions for the Government of Armies of the United States in the Field, General Order n.100 ('Lieber Code'), adopted 24 April 1863. See D Schindler and J Toman, *The Laws of Armed Conflicts* (Martinus Nihjoff, 1988) 3–23.

[16] S Moyn, *Humane. How the United States Abandoned Peace and Reinvented War* (New York, 2021) 163.

of military necessity – that is, 'necessity of those measures which are indispensable for securing the ends of the war' – still far from the humanitarian constraints typical of the contemporary laws of war, and standing out as overarching protected good of the codification.

The pre-eminence afforded to 'securing the ends of the war' is evidenced by several emblematic articles, such as those explicitly declaring starvation (included of the 'unarmed') a legitimate weapon of war,[17] or that citizens or natives of a hostile country were 'thus an enemy',[18] or that 'all direct destruction of life or limb of armed enemies, and of other persons whose destruction is incidentally unavoidable in the armed contests of the war'.[19] As noted in contrast to the emerging vision of European authors and jurists such as Dunant and Moynier, the Lieber Code 'shared almost nothing of the aspiration for humane war that Swiss gentlemen breathed deeply across the ocean at the same time'.[20] Despite this distance from the spirit, ideals and aspirations of other early codifications, the Code stated that 'private property, unless forfeited by crimes or by offenses of the owner' could be 'seized only by way of military necessity' for the 'support or other benefit of the army'.[21] Military necessity therefore already emerged as the exception to the general protection of, and duty to respect, private property.

On opposite sides of the Atlantic these legal concepts took different historical trajectories. While for Lieber the notion of military necessity was open-ended, and functionally identified as set of means to secure the 'ends of the war', only five years later, the 1868 St Petersburg Declaration adopted the notion of military necessity in a different and stricter teleological manner, proclaiming that 'the only legitimate object which States should endeavour to accomplish during war is to weaken the military forces of the enemy'.[22]

The intellectual difference between these two approaches becomes even more apparent through the 1874 Project of an International Declaration Concerning the Laws and Customs of War (Brussels Declaration; see below),[23] particularly in relation

[17] 'War is not carried on by arms alone. It is lawful to starve the hostile belligerent, armed or unarmed, so that it leads to the speedier subjection of the enemy' (Art 17 Lieber Code; n 15).

[18] 'The citizen or native of a hostile country is thus an enemy, as one of the constituents of the hostile state or nation, and as such is subjected to the hardships of the war' (Art 21, ibid).

[19] 'Military necessity admits of all direct destruction of life or limb of armed enemies, and of other persons whose destruction is incidentally unavoidable in the armed contests of the war; it allows of the capturing of every armed enemy, and every enemy of importance to the hostile government, or of peculiar danger to the captor; it allows of all destruction of property, and obstruction of the ways and channels of traffic, travel, or communication, and of all withholding of sustenance or means of life from the enemy; of the appropriation of whatever an enemy's country affords necessary for the subsistence and safety of the army, and of such deception as does not involve the breaking of good faith either positively pledged, regarding agreements entered into during the war, or supposed by the modern law of war to exist. Men who take up arms against one another in public war do not cease on this account to be moral beings, responsible to one another and to God' (Art 15, ibid).

[20] Moyn (n 16) 163.

[21] And adding 'If the owner has not fled, the commanding officer will cause receipts to be given, which may serve the spoliated owner to obtain indemnity' (Art 38 Lieber Code; n 15).

[22] Declaration Renouncing the Use, in Time of War, of Explosive Projectiles Under 400 Grammes Weight (Saint Petersburg, 11 December 1868), ihl-databases.icrc.org.

[23] Project of an International Declaration concerning the Laws and Customs of War (Brussels, 27 August 1874), ihl-databases.icrc.org.

to occupation. The Lieber Code openly admitted that occupation, and the martial law maintaining it, could operate as temporary regime functional to complete 'conquest'. The consequence of this approach was that titularity over public property could ultimately pass from the ousted sovereign – through abeyance during the *interregnum* of occupation – to the conqueror.[24]

A key draft treaty in the early modern developments of *jus in bello* was redacted under the auspices of Czar Alexander II and the representatives of 15 European states in Brussels in 1874. While the draft was never adopted, it signals an emerging shift in the international legal conception of property in occupied territory. In contrast with the Lieber Code, the Brussels Declaration offered a reconfiguration of the international legal regime governing occupation. It recognised the possibility for the occupying power to seize 'all movable property belonging to the State which may be used for the *operations of the war*',[25] further restricting the boundaries of military necessity. More importantly, the Declaration stated for the first time that 'the occupying State shall be regarded only as *administrator and usufructuary* of public buildings, real estate, forests, and agricultural estates belonging to the hostile State, and situated in the occupied country. It must safeguard the capital of these properties, and administer them in accordance with the rules of usufruct'.[26] An occupier, then, is considered a *pro tempore* administrator and usufructuary of public immovable property, which it cannot appropriate in preparation of conquest and annexation, foreshadowing the affirmation of self-determination as a pivotal value of contemporary international law.[27] This provision was later codified in Article 55 of the Regulations annexed to the 1907 IV Hague Convention (Hague Regulations/HR).[28]

Another novelty of the Declaration pertains to private property: it was 'especially prohibited' to 'destroy or seize the enemy's property', unless 'imperatively demanded by the necessities of war'.[29] The exception is thus limited to when military necessity 'imperatively' requires the seizure or destruction of the property itself. The reference to the 'necessities of war' suggests that the drafters were aware of the compelling needs related to active hostilities. The protection of private property is reaffirmed in Article 38, which unequivocally states that 'the lives and property of persons … must be respected', and that 'private property cannot be confiscated'.[30] These provisions in

[24] 'A victorious army appropriates all public money, seizes all public movable property until further direction by its government, and sequesters for its own benefit or of that of its government all the revenues of real property belonging to the hostile government or nation. The title to such real property remains in abeyance during military occupation, and until the conquest is made complete' (Art 38 Lieber Code; n 15.

[25] Art 6, Project of an International Declaration concerning the Laws and Customs of War (n 23) (emphasis added).

[26] ibid Art 7 (emphasis added).

[27] On the normative shift from conquest to occupation see A Gross, *The Writing on the Wall. Rethinking the International Law of Occupation* (CUP, 2017) 17–23; and E Benvenisti, *The International Law of Occupation*, 2nd edn (OUP, 2012) 59.

[28] Convention (IV), Respecting the Laws and Customs of War on Land and its Annex: Regulations concerning the Laws and Customs of War on Land (The Hague, 18 October 1907, entered into force 26 January 1910) in D Schindler and J Toman, *The Laws of Armed Conflicts* (Martinus Nijhoff, 1988) 69–93.

[29] Art 13(g) Project of an International Declaration concerning the Laws and Customs of War (n 23).

[30] ibid Art 38.

relation to private property were later adopted, respectively, as Articles 23(g) and 46 of the Regulations annexed to the IV Hague Convention.[31]

The protection of private property of civilians under occupation is hailed as one of the fundamental shifts in the history of the law governing these situations, and of international law more generally;[32] the emergence of this protection accompanies the development and consolidation of the principle of humanity,[33] a legacy of the Enlightenment ideals, and related new theories framing war as a relationship between states rather than people. Consequently, private property began to be included in the protected space, based on the principle of distinction between civilians and combatants, which is a cornerstone of IHL.[34]

Hague Regulations Articles 55, 23(g) and 46, in sum, defined the position of the occupying state as: 1) legally permitted only to administer temporarily public property as usufructuary; 2) barred from confiscating private property; and 3) able to seize or destroy property only if forced to do so by imperative necessity of strictly military character. These provisions consolidated customary IHL in this three-fold direction,[35] and also continue to apply today as customary rules.[36] They are therefore binding for Israel and provide protection for the property in Bedouin communities in the West Bank.

7.2. THE CONTEMPORARY IHL PROHIBITION OF EXTENSIVE DESTRUCTION AND APPROPRIATION OF PROPERTY NOT JUSTIFIED BY MILITARY NECESSITY

7.2.1. Article 53 of the Fourth Geneva Convention

The legality of demolitions and demolition orders affecting private and public property in Bedouin Communities in the West Bank is determined by the legal framework applicable in those areas. Today, the IHL prohibition of destruction of property by occupying authorities is set out in Article 53 of the 1949 Geneva Convention IV (GCIV):

> Any destruction by the Occupying Power of real or personal property belonging individually or collectively to private persons, or to the State, or to other public authorities,

[31] Convention (IV) Respecting the Laws and Customs of War on Land and its Annex: Regulations concerning the Laws and Customs of War on Land (n 28).

[32] See Benvenisti (n 27) 20–25.

[33] See H Slim, 'Sharing a Universal Ethic: the Principle of Humanity in War' (1998) *International Journal of Human Rights* 28; R Coupland, 'Humanity: What is it and how does it influence International Law?' (2001) 844 *IRRC* 969; and T Meron, 'The Humanization of International Humanitarian Law' (2000) 94 *American Journal of International Law* 239.

[34] See eg B Jia, '"Protected Property" and Its Protection in International Humanitarian Law' (2002) 15 *Leiden Journal of International Law* 131.

[35] Convention (IV) Respecting the Laws and Customs of War on Land and its Annex: Regulations concerning the Laws and Customs of War on Land (n 28) 69–93. On the function of the Hague Regulations provision for customary IHL, see JM Henckaerts and L Doswald-Beck, *Customary International Humanitarian Law. Volume I: Rules* (CUP, 2005) 175–82.

[36] See IMTFE, *In re Hirota* (12 November 1948), 15 ILR 356, 366; see also ICJ, Advisory Opinion Concerning Legal Consequences of the Construction of a Wall in the Occupied Palestinian Territory, 2005, ICJ Rep 36, para 89.

> or to social or cooperative organizations, is prohibited, except where such destruction is rendered absolutely necessary by military operations.[37]

This norm applies to both private and public property, irrespective of the extent of the destruction; the absolute necessity for military operations operates as *extrema ratio* justification.

The drafting history of this provision shows that the initial formulation in the 1948 Stockholm Draft only included private property to protect essential civilians' possessions against any destruction 'not absolutely necessary' for military operations.[38] At the 1948 Geneva Diplomatic Conference, the Soviet delegation requested for the Article to include state and collective properties. Article 23(g) of the Hague Regulations – that prohibits destruction and seizure as previously discussed – referred generically to 'enemy property', not to property of enemy nationals. Nonetheless, to take into account different types of property, several delegations (including the United States) supported the expansion of the text to include public property, as well as property of collective and cooperative organisations,[39] and this reflects the historically shifting burden of war from the people to belligerent states.[40] As a result, the present contours of this provision outlaw the destruction of both public and private property in occupied territory, with the strictly construed exception as will be discussed in the following section.[41] The protection of the two typologies of property appears particularly relevant for Bedouin communities, as the Israeli practices of extensive destruction not justified by military necessity involve both.

7.2.2. A Typical IHL 'Vulnerability': The Military Necessity Exemption

A crucial aspect of Article 53 of GC IV is the 'absolute necessity' for 'military operations' which allows for exceptionally admissible destructions. Unlike numerous other articles of the Convention,[42] this provision does not precisely reference the general concept of military necessity, but one of its specific iterations, qualifying what type of military necessity might allow limited derogations to the relevant prohibition. In other words, absolute necessity for military operations is a more stringent

[37] Art 53 Convention (IV) relative to the Protection of Civilian Persons in Time of War (Geneva, 12 August 1949, entered into force 21 October 1950) 75 UNTS 287 ('Fourth Geneva Convention').

[38] 'No protected person may be punished for an offence he has not himself committed. Collective penalties are forbidden. Measures of reprisal against protected persons or their property are forbidden. The destruction of movable property or real estate, which military operations do not make absolutely necessary, is forbidden, as are all measures of intimidation, or of terrorism' (Art 30, Revised or New Draft Conventions for the Protection of War Victims, Texts Approved and Amended by the XVII International Red Cross Conference, ICRC, 1948, Stockholm, Annex III at 160).

[39] See Final Record of the Diplomatic Conference Convened by the Swiss Federal Council for the Establishment of International Conventions for the Protection of War Victims, ICRC, Geneva, 21 April–12 August 1949, Vol I, 118; Vol II-A, 719–21, 829, 856; Vol II-B, 417–18; Vol II, 134.

[40] See H Dichter, 'The Legal Status of Israel's Water Policies in the Occupied Territories' (1994) 35 *Harvard International Law Journal* 565, 578.

[41] See J Pictet (ed), *Commentary to IV Geneva Convention* (ICRC, 1958) 301–02; Y Arai-Takahashi, 'Protection of Private Property' in A Clapham, P Gaeta and M Sassòli (eds), *The 1949 Geneva Conventions: A Commentary* (OUP, 2015) 1517.

[42] See Arts 108, 143 and 147 Fourth Geneva Convention (n 37).

requirement than general military necessity. At the Geneva Diplomatic Conference, several delegations voiced concerns over the *verbatim* reproduction of Article 23(g) of the Hague Regulations, referring to destructions 'imperatively demanded by the necessities of war'. The concerns anticipated the possibility of broad interpretations of the 'necessities of war' by military commanders, who would inevitably and unduly over-expand the scope of the exception. The term 'military operations' was preferred in order to minimise these risks. The qualifier was also slightly reworded, from 'absolutely required' to 'made absolutely necessary'.[43]

The precise meaning of the notion of 'military operations' is unclear, as are the specific instances when military operations may lawfully be invoked to impose an absolute necessity of destruction of property. This lack of precision in the wording of the Article results in broad interpretations of the notion, threatening the cogency of the relevant prohibitions in Palestine and elsewhere. However, as specific iterations of the broader principle of military necessity, the requirements for the operativity of military necessity as an IHL exception apply, namely that: the action was undertaken in pursuit of a legitimate military purpose; the action itself was in conformity with it; the action is not otherwise prohibited by IHL.[44] It therefore appears indispensable to align the interpretation of the concept of 'absolute necessity for military operations' to the IHL principle of the protection of civilian objects in case of active hostilities. In other words, this protective framework must integrate the assessment of the necessity evoked by Article 53 GC IV. As noted by Pertile 'The relationship between Articles 53 IV GC and 23(g) HR demonstrates that the concept of "military operations" relates to combat activities and the active operations that an army may have to carry out also in occupied territories'.[45] This means that destruction of property is only admissible as a last resort, in pursuit of lawful objectives not achievable by other, less harmful means.[46] As Oppenheim had noted already in 1912, 'What may be ignored in case of military necessity are not the laws of war, but only the usages of war. *Kriegsraeson geht vor Kriegsmanier*, but not *vor Kriegsrecht!* [reason for war comes before manners of war, but not before the laws of war]'.[47]

7.2.3. The IHL Discipline Governing Seizure of Movable Property

While destruction of property by occupying powers appears to be strictly limited to cases of exceptional and absolute necessity, in compliance (rather than in contrast to)

[43] See Final Record of the Diplomatic Conference Convened by the Swiss Federal Council for the Establishment of International Conventions for the Protection of War Victims (n 39) Vol II-A, 730.

[44] See M Sassòli, A Bouvier and A Quintin, *How does Law Protect in War? Cases, Documents and Teaching Materials on Contemporary Practice in International Humanitarian Law*, 3rd edn (ICRC, 2001) vol I 8.

[45] M Pertile, '"Legal Consequences of the Construction of a Wall in the Occupied Palestinian Territory": A Missed Opportunity for International Humanitarian Law?' (2004) 14 *Italian Yearbook of International Law* 121, 135.

[46] See JF Quéguiner, 'Precautions Under the Law Governing the Conduct of Hostilities' (2006) 88 *International Review of the Red Cross* 793.

[47] LFL Oppenheim, *International Law. A Treatise. Vol. 2: Disputes, War and Neutrality* (Longmans, Green & Co, 1912) 84, 69. See also S Horton, '*Kriegsraison* or Military Necessity?' (2007) 30 *Fordham International Law Journal* 576.

with IHL, other provisions deal with the separate, but related, issue of appropriation. An overview of the relevant IHL norms is necessary to understand and correctly interpret the prohibitions enshrined in the Rome Statute war crimes sanctioning both destruction and appropriation of property.

Notwithstanding the clear general prohibition against confiscation of private property in Article 46, the Hague Regulations allow – within specific limits – requisitions and seizure of movable property for compelling military needs. Under Article 52, 'requisitions in kind and services' of movable private property can be demanded 'for the needs of the army of occupation'.[48] The notion of requisition is only applicable in case of payment, compensation or restoration. According to the provision, these requisitions should 'as far is possible be paid for in cash; if not, a receipt shall be given and the payment of the amount due shall be made as soon as possible'.[49] Some commentators have noted that in consideration of the military necessity requirements mentioned above, the title of the requisitioned goods does not validly pass to the occupying authorities when the range of legally admissible needs of the occupying army do not justify the requisition.[50] Furthermore, under Article 53, after specifying that 'An army of occupation can only take possession of cash, funds, and realizable securities which are strictly the property of the State', the Regulation affirms in paragraph 2 that military equipment and all kinds of 'munitions of war' can be 'seized' even if they 'belong to private individuals'. In these cases, however, they 'must be restored and compensation fixed when peace is made'.[51] This provision, however, is clearly confined to equipment employable in active hostilities. No Geneva or Hague law article provides legal basis for the requisition of any private immovable property.

7.2.4. Objects Indispensable for the Survival of the Civilian Population in Additional Protocol I, and their Functional Nexus with the Prohibition of Forcible Transfer

Two other norms complete the IHL framework protecting property: Article 54 of the first 1977 Additional Protocol to the Geneva Conventions (AP I), and Article 147(2) GC IV. First, in stark opposition to the Lieber Code provision allowing starvation, the fundamental prohibition contained in Article 54(2) AP I is considered a reflection of customary IHL.[52] This norm not only prohibits attacking and destroying, but also removing and rendering useless objects 'indispensable to the survival of the civilian population'. It specifies a requirement of intent, consisting of 'the specific purpose of denying' the use of these objects 'for their sustenance

[48] Art 52, Convention (IV) Respecting the Laws and Customs of War on Land and its Annex (n 28).

[49] ibid.

[50] G Schwarzenberger, 'The Protection of Private Property in the Law of Belligerent Occupation' (1960) 1 *Indian Journal of International Law* 212.

[51] Art 53(2) Convention (IV) respecting the Laws and Customs of War on Land and its Annex (n 28).

[52] Henckaerts and Doswald-Beck (n 35) 189–93, and JM Henckaerts and L Doswald-Beck, *Customary International Humanitarian Law. Volume II: Practice* (CUP, 2005) 3463–70.

value to the civilian population or to the adverse Party'. The Article adds that this denial of means of subsistence is relevant 'whatever the motive', included – crucially – 'to cause them *to move away*'.[53] This prohibition thus unequivocally outlaws the destruction, removal of objects, or depletion of resources that are fundamental for the livelihood of the civilian population. Paragraph 3(a)–(b) specifies that the prohibition does not apply only in case of objects used 'solely' for the sustenance of the armed forces of the adverse party or in direct support of their military action. However, it is specified in subparagraph (b) that 'in no event shall actions against these objects be taken which may be expected to leave the civilian population with such inadequate food or water as to cause its starvation or *force its movement*'.[54] This provision, therefore, repeats twice that compromising objects indispensable for the adequate sustenance of civilians is prohibited in all cases expected to put civilians in such dire conditions that they are forced to move away. It therefore appears that the Article should be read in conjunction with the prohibition of forcible transfer, underpinning the latter in those situations where belligerents could be tempted to impel civilians to relocate elsewhere by indirect means, by denying them fundamental means of adequate subsistence.[55]

This prohibition is directly relevant to the Bedouin communities in the West Bank, whose livelihoods and survival depend on a semi-pastoral and agricultural economy based on the integrity of their flocks (and the structures that keep them, such as animal pens and shelters) and access to pastures.[56] The United Nation Office for the Coordination of Humanitarian Affairs' (OCHA) datasets detailing the specific vulnerabilities of Bedouin communities in Area C illustrates the risks to their agro-pastoralist economy.[57] OCHA documents almost 700 episodes of demolitions carried out by the occupying authorities against the Bedouin communities, including more than 200 incidents of dismantling donors-funded structures,[58] in addition to policies of appropriation of natural resources such as water.[59] The combined effect of these unlawful policies, exacerbated by settlers' attacks on property indispensable for the

[53] Art 54(3) Protocol Additional to the Geneva Conventions of 12 August 1949, and relating to the Protection of Victims of International Armed Conflicts ('Protocol I'), adopted 8 June 1977, entered into force 7 December 1978, 1125 UNTS 3 (emphasis added).

[54] ibid (emphasis added).

[55] See eg S D'Cunha, 'The First Plague: The Denial of Water as a Forcible Transfer under International Humanitarian Law' (2015) 24 *Michigan State International Law Review* 279.

[56] 'Bedouin are guardians of desert, their culture built around sustainable living in those deserts. In days of climate change, with increasing scarcity of water already apparent in droughts, heatwaves, soaring summer temperatures extending throughout autumn, and regularly raging forest fires, the criminalisation of the sustainable lifestyle of Bedouin is a sign of arrogance and short-sightedness' (A Godfrey-Goldstein, 'Foreword' in Balfour Project, 'Bedouin Communities in Area C: Contemporary Realities, Indigeneity and British Historical Responsibility' (November 2021) 4, balfourproject.org/bp/wp-content/uploads/2021/11/Bedouin-Communities-in-Area-C-NEW-FINAL.pdf.

[57] UN OCHA, '46 Bedouin Communities at Risk of Forcible Transfer in the Central West Bank: A Vulnerability Profile' ('Land and Livelihood'), www.ochaopt.org/page/46-bedouin-communities-risk-forcible-transfer-central-west-bank-vulnerability-profile.

[58] ibid ('Demolitions 2009-2017).

[59] See the references to Bedouin communities deprived of access to water in Amnesty International, 'The Occupation of Water' (29 November 2017), www.amnesty.org/en/latest/campaigns/2017/11/the-occupation-of-water.

survival of the Bedouin communities,[60] results factually in a constant denial of the protection granted by Article 54(2) AP I, and by its corresponding customary rule.[61]

7.2.5. Extensive Destruction and Appropriation of Property not Justified by Military Necessity as a Grave Breach

The second key norm of the IHL framework protecting property in occupied territories is crucial. Destruction and appropriation of property, in fact, are explicitly mentioned in Article 147(2) of the GCIV, listing 'extensive destruction and appropriation of property, not justified by military necessity and carried out unlawfully and wantonly' as a grave breach.[62] Qualified as a grave breach, this violation of the law of international armed conflict is considered of the highest gravity, triggering duties of criminalisation and prosecution by state parties.

Leaving aside the analysis of the military necessity exception and mental element requirements (discussed in section 7.4 below), it is however important to note the discrepancy between this provision and the structure of the Hague Regulations and Geneva Convention IV norms analysed so far. Article 147 does not differentiate between types of property, nor between destruction and appropriation, and requires both to be extensive to qualify as grave breaches. As noted, the provision 'cover[s] a number of very different offences'. A correct interpretation of the provision is therefore bound to systematic readings of relevant IHL norms, providing supplementary indications.

Firstly, the extensiveness requirement seems to indicate that isolated episodes would not meet the threshold to qualify as a grave breach. However, leading commentators suggest that if the episodes in question were 'intentional' acts of destruction, it would be inadmissible to draw the inference that the act does not constitute a grave breach.[63] For acts of destruction or appropriation carried out amidst or in proximity of active combat, the principles governing the conduct of hostilities[64] offer supplementary guidelines to evaluate the extensiveness, and therefore support the possibility to decide over dubious situations on a case-by-case basis. As already discussed, almost 700 demolitions devastated Bedouin communities in Area C between 2009 and 2017;[65]

[60] See eg Al Jazeera, 'Palestinian Bedouins in Hebron face demolitions, settler attacks' (6 November 2021), www.aljazeera.com/news/2021/11/6/palestinian-bedouins-in-hebron-face-demolitions-settler-attacks; Z Al Tahhan, 'Settler attacks wreak havoc on Palestinians during olive harvest' Al Jazeera (17 October 2021), www.aljazeera.com/news/2021/10/17/settler-attacks.

[61] 'Rule 54 – Attacks against Objects Indispensable to the Survival of the Civilian Population' in Henckaerts and Doswald-Beck (n 35) 189.

[62] See A Van Engeland, 'Protection of Public Property' in A Clapham, P Gaeta and M Sassòli (eds), *The 1949 Geneva Conventions: A Commentary* (OUP, 2015) 1549–50; and Y Arai-Takahashi, 'Protection of Private Property' (ibid) 1530–31.

[63] J Pictet (ed), *Commentary to IV Geneva Convention* (ICRC, 1958) 601.

[64] Particularly in relation to proportionality assessments, see E Cannizzaro, 'Proportionality in the Law of Armed Conflicts' in A Clapham and P Gaeta (eds), *The Oxford Handbook of International Law in Armed Conflict* (OUP, 2014) 332.

[65] See references at nn 59–60.

the reports therefore suggest that these are intentional, not isolated episodes of destruction.

In occupied territory, evaluating the extensiveness of the unlawful destruction, or appropriation, requires instead a systematic reading of the framework protecting public and private property under the law of occupation. Articles 55, 23 and 46 HR, as well as Article 53 GCIV and Article 54 API, should be considered together to assess the scope of the grave breach of extensive destruction and appropriation of property not justified by military necessity.

In conclusion, the qualification of these conduct as grave breaches when carried out unlawfully and wantonly assumes particular significance under both IHL and ICL and should be of topical focus for the current ICC investigation. The Geneva Conventions, in fact, did not provide any international criminal liability for the violations listed therein. Nonetheless, the grave breaches – pertaining exclusively to international armed conflicts – enumerated include the destruction and appropriation of property, and are considered to be of such gravity that state parties to the Convention, upon ratification, agreed to enact domestic penal legislation to prevent them, as well *aut dedere, aut iudicare* obligations.[66] Importantly, there is an argument that the grave breaches regime has acquired customary status.[67] This means that destruction and appropriation of property presenting the features described in Article 147 GCIV already evokes a legal duty under IHL for all states to criminalise the conduct domestically.

Failing this criminalisation and the states' duty to prosecute such conduct, this grave breach provides a model for the corresponding war crime offences in the statutes of international criminal tribunals, including the Rome Statute of the ICC,[68] discussed in section 7.4 below. Since Israeli authorities fail to prosecute such conduct domestically – despite being legally bound to do so under IHL – and instead adopt it as a regular, long-standing practice in the maintenance of the prolonged occupation of the West Bank – these war crime offences should invite specific attention from the ICC investigators currently examining the situation in Palestine.

7.3. EXTENSIVE DESTRUCTION AND APPROPRIATION OF PROPERTY NOT JUSTIFIED BY MILITARY NECESSITY AS WAR CRIME

7.3.1. The Three Offences of Destruction and Appropriation/Seizure of Property under Article 8 of the Rome Statute

The Rome Statute (RS) norms on the destruction and appropriation of property not justified by military necessity are articulated in three distinct provisions: on the one hand, Article 8(2)(a)(iv), criminalising the analysed grave breach ('extensive destruction

[66] Art 146 Fourth Geneva Convention (n 37).

[67] J Henckaerts, 'The Grave Breaches Regime as Customary International Law' (2009) 7 *Journal of International Criminal Justice* 683.

[68] See M Divac-Oberg, 'The Absorption of Grave Breaches into War Crimes Law' (2009) 91 *International Review of the Red Cross* 163.

and appropriation of property, not justified by military necessity and carried out unlawfully and *wantonly*'[69]); and on the other, Article 8(2)(b)(xiii) and 8(2)(c)(xii), which respectively punish those 'destroying or seizing the property' of an enemy in an international armed conflict, or of an adversary in an armed conflict not of an international character, 'unless [in both cases] such destruction or seizure be imperatively demanded by the necessities of war'.[70] These three offences are distinct from the crime of pillage, characterised by a *dolus specialis* of appropriation for private or personal use by the perpetrator.[71]

While the objective elements of these offences largely correspond to the elements of the conduct prohibited under IHL analysed earlier, their distinctive ICL discipline emerges from the subjective elements of the crimes. Regarding the mental element of the three offences against property, Article 8(2)(b)(xiii) and 8(2)(e)(xii) do not specify a mental element requirement for unjustified destruction and seizure. The subjective element for these offences thus remains governed by the general *mens rea* discipline provided by Article 30 RS,[72] requiring at least 'intent' to engage in the conduct and 'knowledge' that can be interpreted as an awareness that the prohibited consequence of the action 'will occur in the ordinary course of events'. This awareness of the occurrence of the consequence was construed in a rather restrictive manner in terms of threshold of foreseeability: it requires that the perpetrator foresees the occurrence of the prohibited consequence with virtual certainty.[73] The conduct of dispossession and demolition perpetrated at the expense of Bedouin communities seem to meet this threshold in full: it is undisputable that alleged perpetrators would not be aware that such conduct would lead to prohibited outcomes, or that such outcomes were not foreseeable. These practices, in fact, are part of institutionalised procedures aimed at acquiring control of territory and structures, as well as disposing of the property rights of the population under occupation.

Article 8(2)(a)(iv) specifies a different mental element, affirming that extensive destructions and appropriations are criminal when committed 'wantonly'. The 'wanton' requirement in Article 8(2)(a)(iv), reproducing the text of Article 147 GC IV, was identical in Article 2(d) of the Statute of the International Criminal Tribunal for the Former Yugoslavia (ICTY). The ICTY jurisprudence stated in several leading cases:

> With regards to the *mens rea* requirement for destruction of property the perpetrator must have acted with the intent to destroy the protected property or in reckless disregard of the

[69] Emphasis added.

[70] Rome Statute of the International Criminal Court (last amended 2010), adopted 17 July 1998, entered into force 1 July 2002, UNTS 2187.

[71] Since this offence has a much lower incidence among the Bedouin communities in area C, it will not be discussed in this chapter. In relation to this crime, see inter alia Y Nuzban, '"For private or personal use": The meaning of the special intent requirement in the war crime of pillage under the Rome Statute of the International Criminal Court' (2002) 102 *International Review of the Red Cross* 1249.

[72] See G Werle and F Jessberger, '"Unless Otherwise Provided": Article 30 of the ICC Statute and the Mental Element of Crimes under International Criminal Law' (2005) 3 *Journal of International Criminal Justice* 35.

[73] 'The 'virtual certainty' test was also upheld by the Appeals Chamber, which maintained that 'The verb "occur" is used with the modal verb "will", and not with "may" or "could". Therefore, this phrase conveys, as does the French version, certainty about the future occurrence. However, absolute certainty about a future occurrence can never exist; therefore the Appeals Chamber considers that the standard for the foreseeability of events is virtual certainty' (ICC, *Prosecutor v Thomas Lubanga Dylo*, Appeal Judgement, ICC-01/04-01/06 A 5, 1 December 2014, para 447).

likelihood of its destruction. With regard to the *mens rea* requisite of appropriation of property, the perpetrator must have acted intentionally, with knowledge and will of the proscribed result.[74]

While the reference to recklessness does not seem reconcilable with the virtual certainty standard adopted by the ICC, most cases of unjustified destruction and appropriation in occupied Palestinian territory are undoubtedly characterised by direct intent, since a whole military infrastructure, in the absence of active hostilities but in the context of protracted occupation, mobilises with the clear purpose of causing the prohibited consequence.

7.3.2. Analogies and Differences of the Three Offences against Property

To fall under the scope of application Article 8 of the RS, these offences need to satisfy two elements common to all the crimes under the Article. These common elements anchor each offence in the contextual sphere of war crimes, distinguishing them from domestic crimes which might happen on a territory caught up in an armed conflict but unrelatedly to the conflict itself. These elements are: 1) that the conduct in question took place in the context of and was associated with an armed conflict; and 2) that the perpetrator was aware of factual circumstances that established the existence of an armed conflict.[75] These common elements reflect scholarship and jurisprudence on the 'war nexus'.[76] As summed up by the ICTY in the *Kunarać* Appeal Judgement: 'what ultimately distinguishes a war crime from a purely domestic offence is that a war crime is shaped by or dependent upon the environment – the armed conflict – in which it is committed.'[77] These common elements are satisfied by all the potential crimes committed in the context of the Israeli occupation of the Palestinian territory.

An initial comparison between the offences discussed shows that Article 8(2)(a)(iv), other than being applicable only in international armed conflicts as it is the case for

[74] *Prosecutor v Brdanin*, Trial Chamber Judgement, IT-99-36-T, 1 September 2004, paras 489–90. Similarly, see *Prosecutor v Prlić et al*, Trial Chamber Judgement, IT-04-74-T, 29 May 2013, para 127; *Prosecutor v Naletilić and Martinović*, Trial Chamber Judgement, IT-98-34-T, 31 March 2003, para 577; *Prosecutor v Kordić and Cerkez*, Judgement, Trial Chamber, IT-95-14/2-T 26 February 2001, para 341. See also K Dörmann, 'Paragraph 2(a)(iv): "Extensive destruction and appropriation of property"' in O Triffterer and K Ambos (eds), *The Rome Statute of the International Criminal Court: A Commentary* (Hart-Nomos, 2015) 339–42.

[75] *Elements of Crimes*, *Official Records of the Assembly of States Parties to the Rome Statute of the International Criminal Court*, First session, New York, 3–10 September 2002, ICC-ASP/1/3 (Pt II-B), as amended in 2010, *Official Records of the Review Conference of the Rome Statute of the International Criminal Court*, Kampala, 31 May–11 June 2010 (ICC, RC/11) 13–42. For the second element, it is specified that there is no requirement for the perpetrator to carry out a legal evaluation on the existence, or typology of the armed conflict under international law. It is sufficient awareness of the conflict as contextual element of the conduct.

[76] See inter alia HG van Der Wilt, 'War Crimes and the Requirement of a Nexus with an Armed Conflict' (2012) 10 *Journal of International Criminal Justice* 1113.

[77] ICTY, *Prosecutor v Kunarać at. al*, Appeals Chamber Judgement, IT-96-23, 12 June 2002, paras 57–61. More recently, on the territorial dimension of the nexus in NIACs, see ICC, Situation in the Islamic Republic of Afghanistan, *Prosecutor's Request for authorisation of an investigation pursuant to article 15*, ICC-02/17 20 November 2017, para 251.

all grave breaches, stands out for three elements not shared by the other two offences of destruction and appropriation. Firstly, it sets a higher threshold of punishability, since it requires extensiveness of the prohibited conduct, which is absent in Articles 8(2)(b)(xiii) and 8(2)(e)(xii). Secondly, it affirms that the prohibited conduct must be carried out wantonly, whereas the other offences do not add specific mental element requirements. Thirdly, it makes use of the term 'appropriation', rather than 'seizure' which is used in Articles 8(2)(b)(xiii) and 8(2)(e)(xii). All these aspects require closer analysis. To analyse the differences, we must first identify the protective purpose of each of them, in order to clarify whether the notion of protected property in international criminal jurisprudence corresponds to the notion of protected property under IHL (section 7.4.3 below). On this basis, it then becomes possible to identify the *actus reus* of destruction, as well as that of appropriation (section 7.4.4 below). Subsequently, it must be determined whether unjustified destruction and appropriation can be criminal even when not extensive (section 7.4.5 below). Finally, it is necessary to enquire to what extent, according to the law, military necessity – as notion with requirements and limits set out in IHL – can exceptionally justify destruction and appropriation of property (section 7.4.6 below).

7.3.3. The Notion of 'Protected Property' in the Jurisprudence of International Criminal Tribunals

An important, preliminary point to clarify is how international criminal tribunals have interpreted the notion of protected property as emerging from the IHL framework. The aforementioned incidents of dispossessions and demolitions against Bedouin properties, in fact, often concern community-owned objects or donor-funded structures such as solar panels, schools or healthcare facilities, raising the question of what type of property qualifies for the relevant crimes.

The jurisprudence of the ICTY adjudicating this specific war crime identified protected property as classifiable under two categories: the first, constituted by 'real or personal property in occupied territory, belonging individually or collectively to private persons, or to the state, or to other public authorities, or to social or cooperative organisations (except where such destruction is rendered absolutely necessary by military operations)'; the second, by 'property that carries general protection under the Geneva Conventions of 1949 regardless of its location'.[78] This two-fold classification was followed by the ICTY in several leading cases,[79] further highlighting the specific protection enjoyed by property, be it public or private, in occupied territory.

Thus, the whole IHL discipline governing protected property in occupied territory (analysed above) is applicable, and integrates the framework provided by

[78] ICTY, *Prosecutor v Radoslav Brdjanin*, Trial Chamber Judgement, IT-99-36-T, 1 September 2004, para 586.

[79] ICTY, *Prosecutor v Tihomir Blaškić*, Trial Chamber Judgement, IT-95-14-T, ICTY, 3 March 2000, para 148; *Prosecutor v Naletilić and Martinović*, Trial Chamber Judgement, IT-98-34-T, ICTY, 31 March 2003, para 575; *Prosecutor v Jadranko Prlić*, Case No. IT-04-74-T, Trial Chamber Judgement, 29 May 2013, paras 106–18.

Article 8 RS. As noted in the scholarship, this offence 'refers to an extensive and detailed law contained in other rules of the GC and the 1907 Hague Regulations. Therefore, the determination of what constitutes conduct that is *unlawful* under international law must be carried out in light of specific provisions of the GC and Hague Regulations.[80]

7.3.4. What Constitutes Prohibited Destruction and Appropriation?

Given that Article 8(2)(a)(iv) covers both destruction and appropriation of protected property, once the protected property is identified in consideration of IHL rules, the two conducts need to be analysed separately. As such, we must distinguish between destruction and appropriation, as well as identify cases where the two prohibited conduct occur cumulatively.

7.3.4.1. Case Law on Prohibited Destruction

In relation to punishable acts of destruction, it is necessary to define what kind of actions may amount to destruction. In the *Mbarusihmana* case it was declared that 'the destruction may be carried out through acts such as setting fire to, pulling down, or otherwise damaging the adversaries' property'.[81] Dormann similarly suggests that 'to set fire to property, to destroy, pull down, mutilate or damage' are all conduct which could amount to prohibited destruction.[82] Werle, on the contrary, considers that 'only destruction of property, not merely damage to it, is covered by the wording'.[83] However, in the *Katanga* case, judges stated that 'destruction entails acts such as setting ablaze, demolishing, or otherwise damaging property', adding that 'badly damaged property may be akin to partial destruction and thus fall under the definition of destruction', depending on the circumstances of each case.[84] It therefore does not seem compatible with the protective scope of the provision to exclude from the concept of destruction damage compromising protected property, causing serious consequences for large groups of civilians, such as forcing them to relocate. This appears extremely relevant in relation to the destruction of property in Bedouin communities, which negatively impacts the possibility for these communities to live in the areas where properties, infrastructures and objects indispensable for their survival are found.

Another problematic aspect is the scale of the prohibited destruction. The wording of the provision ('extensive destruction and appropriation') might be erroneously understood as suggesting that only large-scale destructions of protected property

[80] K Dörmann, *Elements of War Crimes Under the Rome Statute of the International Criminal Court: Sources and Commentary* (ICRC / CUP, 2003) 82 (emphasis added).

[81] ICC, *Prosecutor v Mbarushimana*, PTC I Decision on the Confirmation of Charges, CC-01/04-01/10, 16 December 2011, para 171.

[82] Dörmann (n 80) 83.

[83] G Werle and F Jessberger, *Principles of International Criminal Law*, 4th edn (OUP, 2020) 526.

[84] ICC, *Prosecutor v Katanga*, Trial Chamber Judgement, 7 March 2014, ICC-01/04-01/07, para 891.

could meet the requirement of extensiveness. However, in different cases ICTY judges supported a different reading. In the *Blaškić* case, the Trial Chamber affirmed that:

> To constitute a grave breach, the destruction unjustified by military necessity must be extensive, unlawful and wanton. The notion of 'extensive' is evaluated according to the facts of the case – a single act, such as the destruction of a hospital, may suffice to characterize an offence under this count.[85]

In the *Naletilić and Martinović* judgment, it was reaffirmed that 'a single act may, in exceptional circumstances, be interpreted as fulfilling the requirement of extensiveness'.[86] In the *Prlić* case, the judges stated 'the criterion that the destruction be extensive in scope must be evaluated in light of the facts of the case, and a single incident … may suffice to constitute an offence under this count'.[87] In all these decisions, it appears that the extensiveness requirement should not be interpreted merely as the number of objects destroyed. The consequences of the destruction on the needs and fundamental rights of the victims (as the example of the bombed hospital indicates) seem to be the key factors to consider. The specific vulnerabilities of the Bedouin communities exacerbated by prohibited destruction should therefore provide the basis for a case-by-case assessment, taking into account the impact of the unjustified destruction on the affected community.

7.3.4.2. *Case Law on Prohibited Appropriation*

The problem of prohibited appropriation, and the distinction with the prohibited seizure of Article 8(2)(b)(xiii) and 8(2)(e)(xii), raise further issues. IHL, in fact, does not provide guidance to interpret the notion of appropriation, with other provisions preferring terms such as 'requisition', 'confiscation' or 'seizure'.[88]

Historically, international criminal tribunals have discussed the issue in relation to the offence of 'plunder', including acts of 'spoliation' and 'exploitation'. Post-World War II, the *IG Farben* case judges held that in relation to 'the widespread and systematized acts of dispossession and acquisition of property in violation of the rights of the owners' that took place under the Germany belligerent occupation by Germany, 'spoliation' was 'synonymous with the word "plunder" as employed in Control Council Law 10'. The tribunal added that the consent of the owner could not validly exclude liability when 'obtained by threats, intimidations, pressure, or by exploiting the position or power of the military occupant under circumstances indicating that the owner is being induced to part with his property against his will'.[89] In the *Krupp* trial, the charge of plunder and spoliation included 'offences against

[85] ICTY, *Prosecutor v Tihomir Blaškić*, Trial Chamber Judgement, IT-95-14-T, 3 March 2000, para 157.

[86] ICTY, *Prosecutor v Naletilić and Martinović*, Trial Chamber Judgement, IT-98-34-T, 31 March 2003, para 576.

[87] ICTY, *Prosecutor v Jadranko Prlić*, Case No. IT-04-74-T, Trial Chamber Judgement, 29 May 2013, para 126.

[88] See eg Articles 23(g) and 53(2) Hague Regulations.

[89] United Nation War Crimes Commission, *Law Reports of Trials of War Criminals*, Vol X, *The I.G. Farben and Krupp Trial* (1949) 44–45.

property and civilian economies of countries and territories' under belligerent occupation. The tribunal affirmed:

> Spoliation of private property, then, is forbidden under two aspects; firstly, the individual private owner of property must not be deprived of it; secondly, the economic substance of the belligerently occupied territory must not be taken over by the occupant or put to the service of his war effort-always with the proviso that there are exemptions from this rule which are strictly limited to the needs of the army of occupation insofar as such needs do not exceed the economic strength of the occupied territory.[90]

Many years later, in the *Čelebići* case, the ICTY, substantially considering plunder, spoliation and pillage (today criminalised autonomously) as manifestations of the same category of crimes, claimed that 'prohibition against the unjustified appropriation of public and private enemy property is general in scope and extends ... to the organized seizure of property undertaken within the framework of a systematic economic exploitation of occupied territory'.[91]

Considering this long-standing jurisprudence, commentators indicate that taking, obtaining and withholding property, as well as theft, requisition, plunder and spoliation, even without a definite transfer of title as to the property seized or exploited, can all amount to prohibited appropriation under Article 8(2)(a)(iv).[92] The same applies to confiscation, which constitutes a specific IHL prohibition in cases of private property in occupied territory.[93]

The unjustified appropriation must also be extensive. Similar considerations to those advanced in relation to the destruction of property appear applicable by analogy. The number of objects involved in the prohibited conduct, as well the scale of the appropriations, does not seem sufficient for the holistic evaluation imposed by the protective function of the Article, in coordination with relevant IHL provisions. The consequences for the victims must also be considered. This approach seems coherent with the orientation adopted by the ICC in the *Katanga* and *Bemba* cases, in which 'grave consequences for the victims, even if these consequences are not of the same seriousness for all victims involved' – eg assessing whether 'a large number of persons have been deprived of their property' – were considered essential indicators to evaluate the extent and gravity of the crime of pillage.[94]

In light of this consolidated jurisprudence, appropriation of land, property and objects indispensable for Bedouin communities in the West Bank therefore requires careful analysis as a potential international crime, given that the economic exploitation of the Palestinian territory is intertwined with the whole infrastructure of the Israeli occupation,[95] impacting a range of fundamental rights of the population, and deteriorating the living conditions of entire communities.

[90] ibid 135.

[91] ICTY, *Prosecutor v Mucić et al ('Čelebići')*, Trial Chamberm Judgment, IT-96-21-T, 16 November 1998, para 590.

[92] Dörmann (n 80) 83 and 89ff.

[93] See Werle, *Principles of International Criminal Law* (TMC Asser Press, 2009) 334.

[94] ICC, *Prosecutor v Katanga*, Trial Chamber Judgment, 7 March 2014, para 909; *Prosecutor v Bemba Gombo*, Trial Chamber Judgment, March 2016, para 117.

[95] See, inter alia, OHCHR, 'Israel's exploitation of Palestinian resources is human rights violation, says UN expert' (18 March 2019) www.ohchr.org/en/news/2019/03/israels-exploitation-palestinian-resources-

7.3.5. Destruction and Appropriation without Extensiveness: The Residual Applicability of Article 8(2)(b)(xiii)

When circumstances do not satisfy the requirement of extensiveness, it must be recalled that there is no reference to extensiveness in either Article 8(2)(b)(xiii) or 8(2)(e)(xii), prohibiting unjustified destruction and seizure/appropriation of protected property in international and non-international armed conflicts (IACs and NIACs). Given that 'there is no substantive difference between appropriation and seizure',[96] not taking into serious consideration this difference for a systematic reading of the RS would substantially construe an offence, that of Article 8(2)(b)(xiii), as a dubious duplication of the offence in Article 8(2)(a)(iv), equally applicable in IACs. The only possible reading of this three-fold criminalisation is that the statute intends to add a further layer of protection to property against unjustified destructions and appropriations not justified by military necessity in both IACs and NIACs, even in the absence of their extensiveness. This approach has been confirmed by the Office of the Prosecutor, which underlined the two different formulations in its Policy Paper on Cultural Heritage of 2021. After recalling that these crimes 'reflect the general prohibition of destroying or appropriating *any* property, provided it may be considered to be protected under applicable law', the document states that the extensiveness 'is to be assessed on a case-by-case basis – and may, in some circumstances, even be satisfied by a single act – but does not, *in any event*, apply to Article 8(2)(b)(xiii), which may be residually applicable'.[97]

This residual applicability thus assumes a rather non-residual and distinctive function that specifically punishes acts of unjustified destruction, or seizure, eventually targeting a small number of properties, or even a single property. This punishability assumes even higher importance in relation to the analysed prohibition to destroy, remove, compromise or deplete objects and resources indispensable for the survival of the civilian population (see section 7.3.4 above). Consequentially, where a Bedouin community survives by relying on a small number of tanks of water, or on a single set of solar panels, the prevention or punishment of their seizure or destruction remains crucial to give effect to the prohibition of Article 54(2) AP I. In this light, it is important to note that both institutional and NGOs reports have documented numerous seizures and demolitions of objects essential for water and electricity supply within Bedouin communities of the West Bank.[98] The well-documented, prolonged and regular instances of destruction of property in Bedouin communities in the last decade demands judicial scrutiny, especially given that these practices are part of a wider

human-rights-violation-says-un-expert. See also Human Rights Watch, 'Occupation, Inc. How Settlement Businesses Contribute to Israel's Violations of Palestinian Rights' (19 January 2016), www.hrw.org/report/2016/01/19/occupation-inc/how-settlement-businesses-contribute-israels-violations.

[96] Werle and Jessberger (n 83) 521.

[97] ICC, Office of the Prosecutor, 'Policy on Cultural Heritage' (June 2021) 19, para 54 (emphasis added).

[98] See Report of the United Nations High Commissioner for Human Rights, 'Allocation of Water Resources in the Occupied Palestinian Territory, including East Jerusalem' (15 October 2012), A/HRC/48/43. See also C Yeung, *The Sun Belongs to Everyone. Israeli Demolitions and Confiscations of Solar Panel Aid Projects in Area C of the West Bank* (Al Haq, March 2018), www.alhaq.org/The_Sun_Belongs_to_Everyone.pdf.

regime of the compression of fundamental freedoms contributing to the creation of highly coercive environments (see section 7.5.3 below), forcing victim groups into displacement.

7.3.6. Military Necessity as Legal Exemption, and its Requirements

A feature shared by the three offences against protected property, in line with many IHL and ICL prescriptions, is the reference to destruction, appropriation and seizures 'justified by military necessity', and as such not prohibited. Even beyond the provisions surrounding protected property, repeated references to military necessity,[99] with its indeterminacy as broad ground for varied exemptions,[100] generate vulnerabilities in the protective shield erected by IHL around civilians, particularly in occupied territory.

While it is undisputed that a *jus in bello* rule cannot be derogated by invoking military necessity unless explicitly set forth in the rule in question,[101] the problem of how, for what reasons, and to what extent derogations are allowed continues to challenge the effectiveness of this legal framework. In sum, military necessity exempts a belligerent from conforming its action to certain IHL prescriptions only to the extent that the derogatory measure is required for the achievement of a legitimate military purpose and is otherwise in conformity with IHL. As a consequence, four requirements are needed for military necessity to be operative within the boundaries admitted by the laws of war: 1) the action must be undertaken to achieve a specific purpose of strictly military character; 2) the action undertaken must be one strictly required for the attainment of that specific purpose; 3) the military purpose needs to be legitimate under IHL; and 4) the actions itself must be otherwise lawful under IHL.[102]

Since military necessity constitutes one of the basic rationales of the whole structure of *jus in bello* and its prescriptions, invoking military necessity as exception to legal provisions disrupts the fine balance between the laws of war and considerations of humanity, to the detriment of the latter. Without checks and balances, the concept of military necessity detaches from the texture of international law and becomes a meta-legal, *pass par tout* justification, dangerously available to powers inclined to alter the balance – normatively struck – by *jus in bello* between the competing paradigms of the legitimate necessities of war on the one hand, and of protecting civilians

[99] See eg MN Schmitt, 'Military Necessity and Humanity in International Humanitarian Law: Preserving the Delicate Balance' (2010) 50 *Virginia Journal of International Law* 795; H McCoubrey, 'The Nature of the Modern Doctrine of Military Necessity' (1991) 30 *Military Law & Law of War Review* 215.

[100] See the convincing systematisation proposed by AA Haque, 'Indeterminacy in the Law of Armed Conflict' (2019) 95 *International Law Studies* 118, 119.

[101] C Greenwood, 'Historical Development and Legal Basis' in D Fleck (ed), *The Handbook of International Humanitarian Law*, 2nd edn (OUP, 2009) 37.

[102] See similarly the scheme proposed by N Hayashi, 'Requirements of military necessity in international humanitarian law and international criminal law' (2010) 28 *Boston University International Law Journal* 39. The interpretation of these requirements does not preclude the author to cast doubts over the (more convincing) analysis of the legal implications of the ICJ Advisory Opinion on construction of the wall by Pertile (n 45) 149–50.

on the other. The following sections explain how this distortion manifests itself in radical terms in the infrastructure of the Israeli occupation, where discourses around necessity and security aggravate the fundamental disruption of the texture of IHL that lies at the very core of the prohibition and criminalisation of destruction and appropriation of property.

7.4. BACK TO THE LAW OF CONQUEST: DESTRUCTIONS AND APPROPRIATIONS OF THE ISRAELI OCCUPATION

7.4.1. A Curious Declination of Military Necessity (Framing Transferred Civilians as Auxiliaries for the Occupying Army's Hostilities)

Distorting military necessity far beyond the legal limits described above appears to precisely be the technique employed by the infrastructure of the Israeli occupation. Already in 1968–79, numerous orders of land requisition were issued and executed by the Israeli army, alleging the existence of the essential military needs evoked by the HR, and juxtaposing them to various 'security' needs.[103] In reality, these orders triggered an enduring policy of land-grabbing and population transfer which continues today, with more than 45,000 dunams of private Palestinian land requisitioned in the late 1960s and 1970s to make space for dozens of settlements.[104] This trend slowed down momentarily at the end of the 1970s, due to a jurisprudential shift of the Israeli High Court of Justice. In the *Elon Moreh* case, the Court held for the first time that military and security considerations ascribable to the HR could not justify the requisition of land to be used by Israeli civilians in the OPT, ordering the Israel army to dismantle the infrastructure laid down for the settlement object of the case, and to return the seized land to its owners.[105]

For a long time after that decision, land seizure orders based on alleged military and security needs were not used for the purpose of the establishment and expansion

[103] The notion of 'security' in the law of occupation deserves a separate analysis. However, in extreme synthesis, the value of 'public order and safety' for this legal framework is recognised in Art 43 of the Hague Regulations, which states that the occupying power 'shall take all the measures in his power to restore, and ensure, as far as possible, public order and safety, while respecting, unless absolutely prevented, the laws in force in the country'. The first issue, however, is that this provision wrongly translates the original French version of the Article, which referred to the need to ensure as far as possible '*l'ordre et la vie publics*', without mentioning the 'safety' found in the English translation (See Y Dinstein, 'Legislation under Article 43 of the Hague Regulations: Belligerent Occupation and Peacebuilding', Program on Humanitarian Policy and Conflict Research Harvard University, 1 Occasional Paper Series (20040) 2, www.hpcrresearch.org). The result of this translation is that very often Israeli laws have moved even further from the spirit of the provision, reinterpreting the 'safety' as 'security' of the occupation itself. The second, related issue is that the only provision acknowledging the security of the occupying power in the Fourth Geneva Convention is Art 64, concerning the duty to continue to apply the penal legislation in force before the occupation, and the provisions that can be enacted by the occupying authorities. The latter faculty, however, is not assigned to prolong the authority of the occupier indeterminately, but rather – and to the contrary – to 'enable the Occupying Power to fulfil its obligations under the present Convention' (see Art 64, Fourth Geneva Convention (n 37)).

[104] See N Al-Rayyes, *The Israeli Settlement Policy from the Perspective of IHL* (Al-Haq, 2000); Y Stein (ed), *Land Grab: Israeli Settlement Policy in the West Bank* (B'Tselem, 2002) 133.

[105] HCJ 390/79, *Duweikat et al, v Government of Israel et al* See also HCJ 606/78, *Ayub, et al v Minister of* Defence, et al (Beth El case), and HCJ 610/78, *Matawa, et al v Minister of Defence, et al* (Bekaot Case), 33(2) Piskei Din 113.

of settlements. However, by the mid-1990s, and after the Oslo Accords, new waves of requisitions and seizures of land by military orders were implemented, with a growth of so-called 'bypass roads', built in the OPT to connect settlements with each other, and with Israeli domestic territory subjecting Palestinians to a variety of restrictions and prohibitions to use them.[106] To enable this, demolitions of residential and non-residential structures in Palestinian communities, including Bedouin communities, rose in frequency and numbers on the basis alleged military needs.[107]

The shift produced by the *Elon Moreh* case, however, determined the emergence in the institutional infrastructure of the occupation of a new range of discourses legalising internationally prohibited appropriations of land. This primarily came in the form of the designation of 'state land',[108] drawing on the Ottoman Land Code of 1858 incorporated into Jordanian legislation, and the declaration of public land on the basis of Jordanian Land Law.[109] As leading experts noted, these provisions, 'due to the extensive or abusive way Israel has interpreted them and in conjunction with other policies', have been employed to appropriate land owned by Palestinians, to deprive them of their use, and to allow settlers to use this land.[110]

A closer analysis of the *Elon Moreh* case reveals that the shifting judicial approach only concerned the framing of the justifications for land-grabs used to support the settlement enterprise. In fact, even in this leading case, the HCJ carefully avoided clear guidelines to correctly interpret the concept of military necessity. The Court found that, based on the evidence provided, the army did not initiate the contested activities reviewed in the case, as would be expected if the relevant decisions were dictated by military necessity. Rather, the requisitions were approved by the Chief of Staff substantially ex post facto, because of political decisions whose 'driving force' was 'the powerful desire of the members of Gush Emunim to settle in the heart of Eretz-Israel, as close as possible to the town of Nablus'.[111] Despite these factual circumstances, the whole case revolved around a paradoxical debate over the admissible security functions of the transfer of Israeli civilians in the OPT (in itself unlawful under IHL).[112] Until that moment, the HCJ had followed the (revealing) orientation according to which:

> In terms of the purely security-based consideration, there can be no questioning that the presence in the administered territory of settlements – even '*civilian*' – of the *citizens of the administering power* makes a significant contribution to the *security situation* in

[106] See B'Tselem, 'Forbidden Roads, Israel's Discriminatory Road Regime in the West Bank', Information Sheet: (August 2004), www.btselem.org/download/200408_forbidden_roads_eng.pdf.

[107] See B'Tselem, 'House Demolitions: Demolition for alleged military purposes', statistics.btselem.org/en/demolitions/alleged-military-purposes.

[108] B'Tselem, 'Under the Guise of Legality. Israel's Declarations of State Land in the West Bank' (February 2002), www.btselem.org/download/201203_under_the_guise_of_legality_eng.pdf.

[109] See also A Amara, 'Civilizational Exceptions: Ottoman Law and Governance in Late Ottoman Palestine' (2018) 36 *Law and History Review* 915.

[110] T Boutrouche and M Sassoli, ''Expert opinion on the occupier's legislative power over an occupied territory under IHL in light of Israel's on-going occupation (Norwegian Refugee Council, June 2017) 30, www.nrc.no/globalassets/pdf/legal-opinions/sassoli.pdf.

[111] HCJ 390/79, *Duweikat et al, v Government of Israel et al (Elon Moreh)*, 1979, IsrSC 34(1) 1, translated in 19 *ILM* 148, 1980 at 169.

[112] 'Rule 130 – Transfer of Own Civilian Population into Occupied Territory' in Henckaerts and Doswald-Beck (n 35) 462.

> that territory and *facilitates the army*'s performance of its function. One need not be an expert in military and defence matters to appreciate that terrorist elements operate more easily in territory occupied exclusively by a population that is *indifferent or sympathetic to the enemy* than in a territory in which there are also persons *liable to monitor them* and inform the authorities of any suspicious movement. With such people the terrorists will find no shelter, assistance, and equipment. These are simple matters and there is no need to elaborate.[113]

Based on this, it appears that civilian citizens of the occupying power unlawfully transferred in occupied territory take on the function of auxiliaries of the army in the conduction of active hostilities; this develops a pseudo-legal discourse paradoxically based on the justification of an unlawful conduct, through an anti-juridical argument, making unlawfully transferred civilians functional to combat activities, indirectly endangering the civilians themselves. These original discourses have consolidated over time, allowing settler organisations to exercise growing pressures over Israeli state authorities to carry out appropriations and demolitions in area C, including in Bedouin communities (as seen in the Khan Al-Amar example in the introduction), as means to deny Palestinian self-determination.[114]

7.4.2. Presumption of Legitimate Necessity: Occupation as 'Zone of Reasonableness'

Despite the fact that these judicial views implied the involvement of unlawfully transferred civilians as intelligence-gatherers in the conduct of active hostilities, this approach was never explicitly ruled out by the HCJ. The Chief of Staff considered the requisition functional to the establishment of the Elon Moreh settlement as consistent with military necessity, asserting that a settlement on the relevant site would have served as a 'stronghold protecting freedom of traffic on the nearby roads at the time of deployment of reserve forces'.[115] The Court, however, declined to assess this justification, based on a presumption of correctness of the determination of the Chief of Staff. The judges stated:

> [W]e shall presume that the professional views expressed in the affidavit on behalf of the respondents, speaking in the name of those who are responsible for the preservation of security in the administered territories and within the Green Line, are the correct views.[116]

More recently, this presumption was reaffirmed in *Beit Sourik*.[117] In deciding the case, the HCJ contended that scrutinising matters of security and military needs

[113] Justice Vikton in HCJ 258/79, *Ayyub et al v Minister of Defense et al (Bet el)*, Piskei Din 33(2) at 119; transl by Stein (n 104) 48.

[114] See the inversions concerning 'Arab settlements' in the West Bank and references to Palestinian 'annexation' in the report by Regavim, 'The War of Attrition, The Palestinian Authority's Program for Establishing an Arab State in Area C', www.regavim.org.il/wp-content/uploads/2019/12/Fayyad-Report-2020.pdf.

[115] HCJ 390/79, *Duweikat et al, v Government of Israel et al (Elon Moreh)*, 1979, IsrSC 34(1) 1, translated in 19 *ILM* 148, 1980, at 154.

[116] Ibid 156.

[117] HCJ, *Beit Sourik Village Council v The Government of Israel et. al*, HCJ 2056/04, Supreme Court, 20 June 2004, translated at ihl-databases.icrc.org/applic/ihl/ihl-nat.nsf/46707c419d6bdfa24125673e00508145/09d47365bd007706c12575c20046ec2a.

was limited by their lack of expertise, only allowing the Court to assess whether the military commander's discretion in determining these needs was exercised within boundaries of reasonableness. According to the judges, the petition raised 'issues within the realm of military expertise'. They affirmed:

> We, Justices of the Supreme Court, are not experts in military affairs. We will not examine whether the military commander's military opinion corresponds to ours .... All we can determine is whether a reasonable military commander would have set out the route as this military commander did. ... In exercising judicial review, we do not turn ourselves into experts in security affairs. We do not substitute the security considerations of the military commander with our own security considerations. We take no position regarding the way security affairs are run. Our task is to guard the borders and to maintain the boundaries of the military commander's discretion .... However, we shall not substitute the discretion of the commander with our own discretion. We shall check the legality of the discretion of the military commander and ensure that his decisions fall within the 'one of reasonableness'.[118]

This 'zone of reasonableness' is theorised by the HCJ on the assumption of the possibility to strike, through a proportionality assessment, a balance between several contrasting instances, such as the security of the occupying army (and thus of the occupation itself), the rights of the unlawfully transferred population of the occupying power (carrying in 'their backpack' Israeli domestic law), and the humanitarian needs of the population under occupation, with a total absence/exclusion, in premise, of the right to self-determination (constituting a zone of 'unreasonableness' from the perspective of an occupying army's military commander). This approach carries at least two consequences: first, the parameters to assess the reasonableness of the commander progressively depart from the balance normatively struck by the law of occupation; second, the absence of self-determination from the balancing operation progressively facilitates the 'managerialisation' of the occupation as branch of the occupying power sovereignty ruling over the occupied population with the prerogatives of a government. As Koskenniemi argues:

> It is precisely this wiping away of any formal distinction between sovereignty, occupation, and (illegal) settlement – making them appear just factual contexts for balancing everybody's rights – that the turn to proportionality by the High Court achieves', with the consequence of increasingly 'characterizing occupation in managerial terms as regular 'government' and thus wiping out the sense of its exceptionality.[119]

In sum, presuming the exclusive competence of the military commander in determining military necessity, as well as limiting judicial scrutiny to the reasonableness of this determination, has allowed the ductile notion of 'security' to become a constant corollary of military necessity, functional to its deformalisation and its substantial expansion *a la carte* in the OPT, becoming alleged ground for thousands of appropriations and demolitions. This presumption, long-standing in the HCJ jurisprudence, has become the central mechanism according to which, as affirmed by Kretzmer:

> The Court has not seen itself as a body that should question the legality under international law of policies or actions of the authorities ... On the contrary, it has accepted and

[118] ibid 46 and 47.

[119] M Koskenniemi, 'Occupied Zone – A Zone of Reasonableness?' (2008) 41 *Israel Law Review* 13, 37–38.

legitimized policies and actions the legality of which is highly dubious and has interpreted law in favor of the authorities.[120]

7.4.3. The Vulnerability of Bedouin Communities in a Reality of Systemic Criminality

The combined effect of military orders defining security and military necessities under this judicial presumption, the security legislation enacted since 1967, and the multifaceted and oppressive regime of permits and authorisations to be granted by the Israeli military even to transport goods or build new structures on Palestinian lands,[121] has generated a constantly shifting framework in which the de facto occupying power defines the rights of Palestinians to use, move through and enjoy their public, private, movable and immovable property in occupied territory.[122] This misappropriation of sovereign prerogatives over property precedes and facilitates the material appropriation of the property itself. This factual reality therefore becomes theatre of large-scale and combined conduct consistently prohibited by IHL and criminalised by ICL, with numerus instances of seizures and requisitions followed by demolitions, or, in legal terms, appropriations followed by destructions, cumulatively violating the prohibitions analysed so far. Overall, the United Nations OCHA registered a staggering 5,361 demolitions and seizures between 2015 and 2022, falling entirely under the temporal jurisdiction of the ongoing ICC investigation.[123]

According to elements required for the configurability of the crimes in Article 8(2)(a)(iv) and 8(2)(b)(xiii) of RS, this factual reality appears to be a reality of systemic criminality,[124] in which an entire military and legal infrastructure constantly devises justifications for internationally prohibited conduct.[125]

The Bedouin communities present one of the highest profiles of vulnerability among all the victim groups impacted by the violations of the Israeli occupation.[126] Bedouin communities across the occupied West Bank, particularly in Area C, East Jerusalem and the area around Hebron, are at risk of forcible transfer. This risk is

[120] D Kretzmer, *The Occupation of Justice: The Supreme Court of Israel and the Occupied Territories* (SUNY Press, 2002) 163. See also D Kretzmer and Y Ronen, *The Occupation of Justice: The Supreme Court of Israel and the Occupied Territories*, 2nd edn (OUP, 2021).

[121] Planning and construction in Area C are governed by the Jordanian 'Villages and Buildings Planning Law no. 79 of 1966', as modified by the Israeli 'Military Order Concerning Towns, Villages and Buildings Planning Law (Judea & Samaria) (No. 418), 1971'. See also eg 'IDF Military Order 1797 Concerning the Removal of New Buildings (Judea and Samaria) 2018.

[122] See G Bisharat, 'Land, Law, and Legitimacy in Israel and the Occupied Territories' (1994) 43 *American University Law Review* 467.

[123] See eg OCHA, 'Peak in demolitions and confiscations amidst increasing denial of the right to justice' (8 December 2020), www.ochaopt.org/content/peak-demolitions-and-confiscations-amidst-increasing-denial-right-justice, and the updated 'Breakdown of data on demolitions and displacement', www.ochaopt.org/data/demolition.

[124] See A Nollkaemper and H Van der Wilt (eds), *System Criminality in International Law* (CUP, 2008).

[125] See the convincing elaboration based on Hart's category of the 'pathology of legal systems' proposed by V Azarova, 'The Pathology of a Legal System: Israel's Military Justice System and International Law' (2017) 44 *Questions of International Law: Zoom-in* 5.

[126] See UN OCHA database (n 58).

generated, inter alia, by sustained policies of unjustified destruction and appropriation of a variety of protected properties, included resources indispensable for the survival of the communities. Such policies contribute to, and indeed appear to be aimed at, the creation of dangerous, highly coercive environments, where deprival of means of subsistence and satisfaction of basic needs force victim groups to transfer. Such coercive environments ultimately result in displacing communities, without recourse to material deportations. As the UN Secretary General affirms:

> Forcible transfer does not necessarily require the use of physical force by authorities, but may be triggered by specific circumstances that leave individuals or communities with no choice but to leave; this is known as a coercive environment … Palestinians have been forced to move due to a coercive environment within Area C.[127]

According to OCHA:

> Israeli policies and practices applied in these areas create … a coercive environment, which generates pressure on Palestinians to leave their communities. These include the demolition and threat of demolition of homes, schools and livelihoods; forced evictions; denial of service infrastructure; access restrictions on farming and grazing land; poor law enforcement on violent settlers; promotion of 'relocation' plans; and revocation of residency rights, among others.[128]

This alarming context of civilian victimisation is additionally coupled with a consolidated unwillingness of the domestic Israeli justice system to put an end to the impunity for international law violations across the entirety of occupied Palestinian territory.[129] The traditional military or security considerations that are sanctioned by state policies and that underpin military orders, causing mass dispossessions, appropriations and demolitions, are nothing more than a vague and distorted resemblance – as demonstrated in this discussion – of the notion of military necessity set out in IHL. This complete detachment from the concept military necessity deriving from the law of occupation impedes – from the ICL point of view – the operativity of the grounds for excluding liability under Article 31(c) RS, referring to suspects who act 'reasonably to defend … property which is essential for accomplishing a military mission, against an imminent and unlawful use of force in a manner proportionate to the degree of danger to the … property protected.' This formulation indicates a construction of military necessity as the exemption from prohibited behaviours even stricter than in the IHL framework: this operates in a context of clear unlawfulness, under *jus ad bellum*, of the Israeli uses of force necessary to maintain territorial and population control against the cogent obligation to dismantle the settlements and allow Palestinian statehood and self-determination.[130]

[127] 'Human rights situation in the Occupied Palestinian Territory, including East Jerusalem' Report of the Secretary-General, A/HRC/34/38 (16 March 2017) paras 27–28.

[128] UN OCHA, 'Palestinian Bedouin Communities in the Central West Bank at Risk of Forcible Transfer' (January 2019), www.ochaopt.org/sites/default/files/wb_thematic_10_0.pdf.

[129] See B'Tselem and Palestinian Centre for Human Rights (joint report), 'Unwilling and Unable. Israel's Whitewashed Investigations of the Great March of Return Protests' 18–23, www.btselem.org/sites/default/files/publications/202112_unwilling_and_unable_eng.pdf.

[130] See Wilde (n 6).

Finally, considering the limited resources and necessary pragmatism in the case selection by the ICC, it must be emphasised that destructions and appropriations in Bedouin communities are overwhelmingly well documented by both governmental and non-governmental sources (including the UN), offering a uniquely robust body of evidence for investigations. Moreover, the (former) UN Special Rapporteur on the situation of human rights in the OPT highlighted in his final report the appropriation of land for 'military needs' as crucial mechanism to

> confiscate more than two million dunams of Palestinian land in the West Bank, which have been used to build settlements, Israeli-only highways and roads, recreational parks, industrial centres and military bases and firing zones, all for the purpose of cementing a permanent and immovable demographic presence.[131]

In sum, the thousands of appropriations and destructions of protected property characterising the last decades of occupation have not only consolidated practices repeatedly and on a large scale violating Article 8(2)(a)(iv) and 8(2)(b)(xiii), but have also instrumentalised these conduct to an overall regression of the occupation of Palestine, and of the Israeli infrastructure governing it, to pre-modern legal paradigms, in which occupation was still conceived as intermediate stage of control of territory and population preceding colonisation, conquest and definitive annexation (see section 7.2 above). These paradigms are ultimately considered admissible only under the colonial order of the international community, antecedent to the affirmation of self-determination as *jus cogens* principle, and to the emergence of the prohibition of the use of force against the territorial integrity and political independence of states.[132] It is not a coincidence that Israeli state representatives have recently affirmed that 'With regards to its status as a peremptory norm, Israel believes it is highly questionable whether the right to self-determination meets the standards for being recognized as a jus cogens norm'.[133]

7.5. CONCLUSIONS: CRIMES OF UNJUSTIFIED DESTRUCTION AND APPROPRIATION AS CRIMES OF COLONIAL CONQUEST SHOULD BE A PRIORITY FOR INTERNATIONAL CRIMINAL JUSTICE

Having traced the historical journey of the international legal protection of property in occupied territory in IHL and ICL, it is possible to conclude that this protection mirrors a defining process of legal modernity. This defining process is the shift of laws and customs of war from the Westphalian paradigm of legitimate conquest to the Enlightenment-inspired conception of war as relation of hostility between states, not peoples. At the same time, this defining process culminates in the contemporary

[131] 'Report of the Special Rapporteur on the situation of Human Rights in the Palestinian territories occupied since 1967', Human Rights Council – Forty ninth session (21 March 2022) A/HRC/49/87, 12.

[132] See inter alia O Corten, *The Law Against War* (Hart, 2010); WM Reisman, 'Coercion and Self-Determination: Construing Charter Article 2(4)' (1984) 78 *American Journal of International Law* 642.

[133] International Law Commission, 73rd session, Geneva, 18 April– June and 4 July–5 August 2022, *Peremptory norms of general international law (jus cogens), Comments and observations received from Governments*, A/CN.4/748.

Kelsenian ideal of prohibiting wars of conquest altogether, hence framing the legal regime of situations of occupation as a temporary 'state of exception'. Such exception appears indeed the ultimate, quintessential exception to the texture of contemporary international law, in that it severs the fundamental nexus between self-determination, authority and territorial control at the bases of any democratic legal order. Therefore, this exception *par excellence* can only exist as temporary anomaly, subject to strict limits.

In addition, the war crimes analysed seem characterised by a strong alignment between relevant treaty and customary prohibitions under IHL, and the boundaries of the corresponding crimes under ICL, with types of offence in some instances even stricter and more stringent. Through the lens of these legal frameworks, the Israeli practices in the last decades have not only been characterised by unique levels of systematicity, scale and impact on the fundamental rights of the Palestinian population, but they have also been progressively and explicitly detached from any justificatory claims based on legally admissible understandings of the concept military necessity.

These two features (magnitude and non-military purposes) are further aggravated by a third element: the instrumentalisation of these potential offences to the realisation of other, probable international crimes, such as the forcible transfer of Palestinian civilians,[134] and the transfer by the occupying power of parts of its own civilian population into the territory it occupies.[135] The relationship between the extensive destruction and appropriation of property, and the (forcible) transfer of civilians, appears to be a relationship between means and ends, both of international criminal relevance, as well as prohibited in IHL. From this point of view, the infrastructure of the Israeli occupation seems to have developed as a system overseeing a '*matryoshka*' scheme of realisation of intertwined serious violations, in which one international criminal offence anticipates and preludes to the subsequent, with the overarching rationality of settler colonial conquest and progressive annexation emerging increasingly clearly as the occupation continues. Meanwhile, the Israeli occupation, while perpetuating, has by far exceeded the limits of exceptionality, temporality, hostility and lack of sovereignty typical of the legal regime governing occupation, of which it maintains only a semblance. In fact, it is precisely through the commission of the crimes analysed that the hiatus between authority, sovereignty and self-determination admitted by the law of occupation has been exploited to build a regime of institutionalised oppression, discrimination and violence, aimed at denationalising Palestinians, 'de-Palestinising' Palestine, and maintaining perpetual control over the Palestinian territory as a whole via incremental annexation. Here, a concerning two-fold perspective of illegality emerges: not only the constant violation of fundamental *jus in bello* principles, but also the armed pursuit – through these violations – of outcomes that are manifestly illegal under *jus ad bellum* and Article 2(4) of the UN Charter, namely conquest by means of unlawful uses of force.

[134] See eg JL Aid, 'How Israel Legalizes Forcible Transfer: The Case of Occupied Jerusalem' (2017) 72 *Jerusalem Quarterly* 115.

[135] M Kearney, 'On the Situation in Palestine and the War Crime of Transfer of Civilians into Occupied Territory' (2017) 28 *Criminal Law Forum* 1.

Within such a macroscopic level of illegality, it is inevitable to conclude that the systematic appropriation and destruction of Palestinian properties targeting Bedouin communities urgently requires judicial scrutiny. At stake there is not only the right to justice of the Palestinian Bedouin victims and the interruption of a cycle of impunity nurturing dramatic spirals of violence, but also the very credibility of international criminal justice itself, which so far has fallen short of its minimal institutional responsibilities toward all Palestinians, as well as the range of world actors and human rights defenders convinced that a just and durable peace can only be based on international legality.

8

The Irrelevance of the Oslo Accords for ICC Jurisdiction Over (Alleged) Crimes Committed against the Palestinian Bedouin Community

GIULIA PINZAUTI

INTRODUCTION

THE INTERNATIONAL CRIMINAL Court (ICC) is regarded by many in Palestine and around the world as the appropriate forum to advance accountability for alleged crimes committed against the Palestinian Bedouin community in the West Bank. Although these alleged crimes are currently not included in the scope of the investigation, as defined in the Summary of Preliminary Examination findings (which sets out the conclusions reached by the Office of the Prosecutor at the end of the Preliminary Examination in the Situation in Palestine),[1] they fall within the scope of the Court's territorial, temporal and subject-matter jurisdiction. Indeed, the alleged crimes are Rome Statute crimes, that is, war crimes and crimes against humanity, that were allegedly committed on Palestine's territory – a state party to the Statute – following 13 June 2014. In line with relevant Appeals Chamber jurisprudence, the prosecution is required to investigate the situation in Palestine as a whole, thus including the alleged crimes committed against the Palestinian Bedouin community.[2] It would be particularly important for the prosecutor to do so in this situation in order to avoid separating the Bedouin community from the broader Palestinian polity.

One key legal issue that arises with regards to the prospects of bringing to justice those responsible for the alleged crimes at issue is whether the Oslo Accords that

[1] 'Situation in Palestine' (Summary of Preliminary Examination Findings), www.icc-cpi.int/sites/default/files/itemsDocuments/210303-office-of-the-prosecutor-palestine-summary-findings-eng.pdf.

[2] *Situation in the Islamic Republic of Afghanistan* (Judgment on the appeal against the decision on the authorisation of an investigation into the situation in the Islamic Republic of Afghanistan) ICC-02/17 OA4 App Ch (5 March 2020) 60.

were concluded in 1993 and 1995 between the Israeli Government and the Palestinian Liberation Organization (PLO) preclude the Court's jurisdiction over alleged crimes committed in Area C – the area of the West Bank that is under full Israeli civil and security administration, as explained in section 8.1 below – including those against the Palestinian Bedouin community. This chapter seeks to answer that question.

In its decision on the scope of the Court's jurisdiction over the State of Palestine in February 2021, the Court did not conclusively resolve the issue of whether and to what extent the Accords are relevant to its jurisdiction. Pre-Trial Chamber I affirmed, by majority, that the Accords 'are not pertinent to the issue of the authorization of an investigation' without elaborating at length on the basis for its decision.[3] It also appears to have deferred its consideration of the issue to later proceedings.[4] The majority seems to have followed the reasoning of the 2020 judgment in the *Situation in Afghanistan*, in which the Appeals Chamber held that the bilateral agreements between the United States and Afghanistan that limited Afghanistan's jurisdiction over US nationals for crimes committed in Afghanistan were not 'a matter for consideration in relation to the authorisation of an investigation'.[5] In that judgment, the Appeals Chamber further held that those agreements may affect the execution of cooperation requests under Part 9 of the Statute, and that under Article 19 of the Statute, states could raise jurisdictional challenges at the appropriate time.[6] Following the same line of reasoning, the Oslo Accords do not bar the prosecutor from investigating alleged crimes committed on Palestine's territory, but may have an impact on the proceedings at a later stage.

Following the Prosecutor's decision to deprioritise the investigation of the conduct of US troops and CIA operatives in Afghanistan, litigation in the situation in Afghanistan is not likely to provide any clarity on the effects of bilateral agreements on the Court's jurisdiction.[7] There is, however, reason to worry about the future of the situation in Palestine. In fact, the then presiding judge of Pre-Trial Chamber I has expressed the firm view that the Oslo Accords bar the Court's jurisdiction over alleged crimes committed by Israelis, as well as over crimes committed in Area C, and in East Jerusalem.[8] In his opinion, to investigate these crimes the prosecutor would need Israel's consent as the state having territorial or personal

[3] *Situation in the State of Palestine* (Decision on the 'Prosecution request pursuant to article 19(3) for a ruling on the Court's territorial jurisdiction in Palestine') ICC-01/18, PT Ch I (5 February 2021) 129.

[4] The PT Ch emphasised that its conclusions pertained to the initiation of an investigation, while reserving the right to examine 'further questions of jurisdiction which may arise' at a later stage of proceedings. ibid 131.

[5] *Afghanistan* Appeal Judgment (n 2) 44.

[6] ibid.

[7] Prosecutor Khan decided to focus investigative activities on alleged crimes committed by the Taliban and the Islamic State – Khorasan Province (IS-K) in Afghanistan, and to deprioritise other aspects of this investigation. 'Statement of the Prosecutor of the International Criminal Court, Karim A.A. Khan QC, following the application for an expedited order under article 18(2) seeking authorisation to resume investigations in the Situation in Afghanistan' (27 September 2021), www.icc-cpi.int/news/statement-prosecutor-international-criminal-court-karim-khan-qc-following-application. The bilateral agreements between the US and Afghanistan have no bearing on the Court's jurisdiction over alleged crimes committed by the Taliban and IS-K in Afghanistan.

[8] Kovács believes that 'the Prosecutor may exercise her investigative competences *under the same circumstances that would allow Palestine, as a State Party, to assert jurisdiction over such crimes under its legal system*, namely by duly taking into account the repartition of competences according to the Oslo Accords'.

jurisdiction.[9] If that position were adopted by the Court, it would preclude it from prosecuting the alleged crimes committed against Palestinians in Area C, including those against the Bedouin communities. Moreover, in their *amicus curiae* submissions in subsequent proceedings, some states parties and other interveners challenged the Court's jurisdiction over Israeli nationals based on the Oslo Accords.

Discussing the relevance – or rather, the irrelevance – of the Oslo Accords for ICC jurisdiction over alleged crimes committed in Palestine, including vis-à-vis the Bedouin communities in Area C, is thus important. This chapter argues that the Oslo Accords do not bar ICC jurisdiction over Rome Statute crimes committed in Palestine's territory. Section 8.1 will provide a short overview of the repartition of competences between Israel and Palestine as set out in the Oslo Accords. Section 8.2 will then explain how the Accords do not affect Palestine's jurisdiction to prescribe, and consequently the Court's territorial jurisdiction, while limiting Palestine's enforcement jurisdiction. Section 8.3 will argue that the Accords have an impact on ICC proceedings as far as complementarity and cooperation are concerned. Finally, the chapter concludes on why the ICC prosecutor should investigate the alleged crimes committed against the Palestinian Bedouin community in Area C, which fall within the ambit of the Court's territorial jurisdiction.

8.1. THE OSLO ACCORDS

The events leading to the signing of the Oslo Accords are well known: following secret negotiations which began during the first *Intifada* and the mutual recognition between the PLO and Israel, on 13 September 1993 Mahmoud Abbas on behalf of the PLO and Israel's Foreign Minister Shimon Peres signed the Declaration of Principles on Interim Self- Government Agreements (Oslo I) in Washington.[10] The Accord envisaged a gradual withdrawal of Israeli military forces and gradual transfer of powers during an interim period of originally five years.

Subsequently, in September 1995 the parties signed The Israeli-Palestinian Interim Agreement on the West Bank and Gaza Strip (Oslo II), which superseded all interim agreements previously signed. The West Bank was divided into three areas (A, B and C). In Area A, the Palestinians were to acquire control over civil matters, with responsibility for internal security and public order.[11] In Area B, Palestinians were to acquire control over civil matters and public order, whereas Israel retained the power to protect Israelis from the threat of terrorism.[12] In Area C, Israel had territorial jurisdiction, except for the functional jurisdiction of the Palestinian Council (which later became the Palestinian National Authority, or PNA) over Palestinians for 'civil powers and responsibilities not relating to territory'.[13]

See *Situation in the State of Palestine* (Judge Péter Kovács' Partly Dissenting Opinion) ICC-01/18-143-Anx1 (5 February 2021) 370.

[9] ibid 371.

[10] I Malik, 'Analysis of the Oslo Accords' (2001) 21 *Strategic Studies* 134, 135. For an analysis of the legal status of the Accords see the authorities cited in n 18.

[11] Arts XI(2) and XIII(1) Oslo II.

[12] ibid Arts XI(2) and XIII(2).

[13] ibid Arts XI(2), XIII(2)(8), XVII(2) and (4).

The Accords envisaged a gradual transfer of responsibility to the Palestinians regarding Areas B and C 'except for the issues of permanent status negotiation [including Jerusalem and the settlements] and of Israel's overall responsibility for Israelis and borders'.[14] Furthermore, Israel maintained control over external security.[15] On criminal matters, the Palestinian Council had jurisdiction over 'all offenses committed by Palestinians and/or non-Israelis' in the West Bank and Gaza, with the exclusion of certain territories, such as Area C.[16] Israel retained jurisdiction over offences committed by Israelis on Palestine's territory and over Area C.[17] Because of the Accords' repartition of competences in criminal matters between the Palestinian Council and Israel, some states, scholars and practitioners claim that the ICC lacks jurisdiction over alleged crimes committed by Israelis on Palestine's territory, which are not within Palestine's criminal jurisdiction domestically. However, as the following sections will illustrate, this interpretation is faulty given that ICC jurisdiction is not dependent on states parties' domestic criminal jurisdiction.

Whereas the precise legal character of the agreements is still debated, their legally binding character is not open to interpretation.[18] A statement made by the Palestinian President on 19 May 2020 – announcing that Palestine is absolved 'of all the agreements and understandings with the American and Israeli governments and of all the commitments based on these understandings and agreements, including the security ones'[19] – raised questions on the continued validity of the Accords. The PNA subsequently clarified that 'the Statement was not made as part of the record of [ICC] proceedings and did not in any way purport to, nor does it, legally affect the question presently before the Chamber'.[20] Furthermore, on 19 November 2020, it was reported that the PNA would resume civil and security cooperation with Israel.[21] Thus, despite violations of the agreements on both sides, neither party has

[14] ibid Arts XI(2)(c), XIII(2)(b)(8), XII(4)(a).

[15] ibid, Art X(4).

[16] Annex IV Art I.

[17] Annex IV Art I(2).

[18] Some authors consider the Accords as treaties between two states, to which the VCLT applies. See for example J Quigley, 'The Israel-PLO Interim Agreements: Are They Treaties?' (1997) 30 *Cornell International Law Journal* 720. Others argue that Palestine was not a state at the relevant time. Nevertheless, the Oslo Agreements can still be considered legally binding under the customary international law of treaties as agreements 'between other subjects of international law'. See Art 3 VCLT; O Kittrie, 'More Process than Peace: Legitimacy, Compliance, and the Oslo Accords' (2003) 101 *Michigan Law Review* 1661, 1675; GR Watson, *The Oslo Accords: International Law and the Israeli-Palestinian Peace Agreements* (OUP, 2010) 5758. Some authors claim that the Accords are legally void because the Palestinians' consent was coerced through the illegal use of force. R Wilde, 'Legal Opinion: Is the Israeli occupation of the Palestinian West Bank (including East Jerusalem) and Gaza "legal" or "illegal" in international law?' (29 November 2022), www.ucl.ac.uk/laws/sites/laws/files/ralph_wilde_opt_legal_opinion.pdf.

[19] Palestine News and Info Agency, 'President Abbas declares end to agreements with Israel, US; turns over responsibility on occupied lands to Israel' (WAFA, 19 May 2019), english.wafa.ps/page.aspx?id=cBrJbOa117154132029acBrJbO.

[20] *Situation in the State of Palestine* (The State of Palestine's response to the Pre-Trial Chamber's Order requesting additional information) ICC-01/18 (4 June 2020) 6.

[21] D Jacobs, J Kern and D Reisner, 'Implications for the ICC on the Resumption of Israeli-Palestinian Cooperation and the Relevance of the Oslo Accords in Current ICC Litigation' (*OpinioJuris*, 4 January 2021), opiniojuris.org/2021/01/04/implications-for-the-icc-on-the-resumption-of-israeli-palestinian-cooperation-and-the-relevance-of-the-oslo-accords-in-current-icc-litigation.

formally abrogated them. This chapter will proceed on the premise that the Accords are legally binding.

8.2. WHY THE OSLO ACCORDS DO NOT BAR THE COURT'S JURISDICTION OVER ALLEGED CRIMES COMMITTED AGAINST THE BEDOUIN COMMUNITY

As discussed in the preceding section, pursuant to the Oslo Accords, Israel (not Palestine) has exclusive criminal jurisdiction over conduct by Israelis in the Occupied Palestinian Territory. Likewise, Palestine's jurisdiction does not extend to Area C in the West Bank or to East Jerusalem. Importantly, this set-up was intended to be for a five-year period, although it has been extended over time.

Several influential voices (states, prominent academics and practitioners) interpreted these clauses in the Oslo Accords to have preclusive effect on the Court's jurisdiction over Israelis and over alleged crimes committed in Area C and in Jerusalem.[22] The background to this argument, in a nutshell, is that the prevailing interpretation of Article 12 of the Rome Statute is that it is premised on a delegation-based theory of jurisdiction.[23] Therefore, a state party like Palestine would not be able to delegate jurisdiction to the ICC if it does not have that jurisdiction domestically in the first place (*nemo dat quod non habet*). Aside from the fact that the delegation-based theory of jurisdiction is not universally accepted, those arguments misconstrue the principle *nemo dat quod non habet*, conflate the distinct notions of a state's jurisdiction to prescribe and its enforcement jurisdiction, and disregard the law of occupation.[24]

In a separate opinion appended to the Pre-Trial Chamber's decision of February 2021, Judge Kovács also reached the conclusion that the Accords preclude the Court's jurisdiction over those crimes that are excluded from the reach of Palestine's domestic jurisdiction, although he followed a different line of reasoning. In summary, he argued that the Court should have considered the Accords as part of the applicable law under Article 21(1)(b) of the Statute,[25] and challenged the transposition of the Appeals Chamber's reasoning in the *Afghanistan* decision to Palestine's situation.[26]

[22] See for example the following submissions in the *Situation in the State of Palestine* (ICC-01/18): Observations by the Federal Republic of Germany (16 March 2020) 26–28; Submission of Observations Pursuant to Rule 103 by the Czech Republic (12 March 2020) 12–13; Submission Pursuant to Rule 103 (Todd F Buchwald and Steven J Rapp) (16 March 2020) 25–26; Observations on the question of jurisdiction pursuant to Rule 103 of the Rules of Procedure and Evidence (Badinter et al) (16 March 2020) 51–56; Observations on the Prosecutor's Request on behalf of the Non-Governmental Organisations: The Lawfare Project, the Institute for NGO Research, Palestinian Media Watch, and the Jerusalem Center for Public Affairs (16 March 2020) 84–98; *Amicus Curiae* Observations of Prof Laurie Blank, Dr Matthijs de Blois, Prof Geoffrey Corn, Dr Daphné Richemond-Barak, Prof Gregory Rose, Prof Robbie Sabel, Prof Gil Troy and Mr Andrew Tucker (16 March 2020) 79–82. See also Y Shany, 'In Defence of Functional Interpretation of Article 12(3) of the Rome Statute. A Response to Yaël Ronen' (2010) 8 *Journal of International Criminal Justice* 329, 339–42.

[23] Shany (n 22) 331–32.

[24] Situation in the State of Palestine (Prosecution Response to the Observations of *Amici Curiae*, Legal Representatives of Victims, and States) ICC-01/18, 30 April 2020, 69ff.

[25] Kovács Partly Dissenting Opinion (n 8) para 285.

[26] ibid paras 360–61.

In his view, the proper approach to determine the extent of the Court's territorial jurisdiction was a harmonised interpretation of the provisions of the Accords and of the Rome Statute that would have allowed Palestine to comply with its international obligations under both treaties.[27] In practice, under this view the Court would also be bound by Palestine's domestic criminal jurisdiction – a view which is challenged in section 8.2.2. Kovács' remaining arguments will be addressed in section 8.3.

8.2.1. The Oslo Accords do not Constitute 'Applicable Treaties' under Article 21(1)(b) of the Rome Statute

I respectfully disagree with Judge Kovács' contention that the Court should have looked beyond the sources in Article 21(1)(a) – namely the Statute, Elements of Crimes and the Rules of Procedure and Evidence – to rule on the geographical scope of its territorial jurisdiction, and that the Oslo Accords constitute 'applicable treaties' under Article 21(1)(b) of the Rome Statute.[28]

First, as a matter of hierarchy of sources, the Court should not resort to the sources in Article 21(1)(b) (applicable treaties and the sources and rules of international law) 'unless it has found no answer in paragraph (a)'.[29] In the case at hand, the scope of the Court's territorial jurisdiction is clearly regulated in Article 12 of the Statute, which provides that the Court may exercise its jurisdiction if the state 'on the territory of which the conduct in question occurred' is a party to the Statute. Such is the case with the alleged crimes committed on Palestine's territory, including those against the Bedouin community. Therefore, there was no need to resort to Article 21(1)(b).

Second, the Oslo Accords have no bearing on the Court's jurisdiction even if they are binding on Palestine. The Court's jurisdiction in Article 12 is not defined by reference to states parties' domestic criminal jurisdiction pursuant to the international obligations they may have contracted. Whenever international obligations contracted by a state party are relevant for the law and practice of the ICC, the Statute expressly refers to such obligations. One example is Article 98, which refers to a member state's 'obligations under international law'. However, there is no such reference in Article 12. Thus, the Oslo Accords are not applicable in relation to the Court's jurisdiction.

In any event, according to authoritative commentators, 'applicable treaties' in Article 21(1)(b) of the Statute refers to those treaties of general application that form the basis for the definitions of crimes over which the Court has jurisdiction. Such treaties include, for instance, the Geneva Conventions, the Genocide Convention, the Convention on the Rights of the Child, the Vienna Convention on the Law of Treaties (VCLT), the UN Charter and treaties to which the Court is a party.[30] According to deGuzman, the provision should not be understood to include international agreements binding on the states that would normally have jurisdiction in given situations.

[27] ibid para 366.
[28] ibid paras 284–85, 308.
[29] W Schabas, *The International Criminal Court: A Commentary on the Rome Statute* (OUP, 2016) 519.
[30] M deGuzman, 'Article 21' in K Ambos, *Rome Statute of the International Criminal Court. Article-by-article Commentary*, 4th edn (Beck, 2022) 1129, mn 26; Schabas (n 29) 519–20.

In her view, given 'the ICC's wide-ranging jurisdiction ... this could contribute unnecessarily to the fragmentation of international criminal law',[31] and this argument is compelling. Following this line of reasoning, bilateral agreements binding on a state party, such as the Oslo Accords, do not form part of the applicable law under Article 21(1)(b).

For these reasons, the logical premise on which Judge Kovács' opinion is founded – that the Oslo Accords are relevant 'applicable treaties' to determine the scope of the Court's territorial jurisdiction – is flawed.

8.2.2. ICC Jurisdiction is not Dependent on States Parties' Domestic Criminal Jurisdiction

When a state accedes to the Rome Statute and then confers jurisdiction to the ICC through a referral (Articles 13(a) and 14 Rome Statute), the Court's jurisdiction over Rome Statute crimes committed on that state's territory is automatic. No further expression of consent is necessary to give effect to the Court's jurisdiction. As Stahn illustrated, there is also no requirement that the state in question has a parallel jurisdictional title in its domestic legal order.[32] In fact, as Schabas put it, 'Article 12(2) authorizes the Court to exercise jurisdiction over "the territory" of a state party and not over "the territory over which their courts exercise criminal law jurisdiction"'.[33]

If the Court's jurisdiction were dependent on the domestic criminal jurisdiction of the state concerned, this would create a very volatile situation for the Court, given that domestic law can change over time. This instability would seriously undermine the Court's function. Such an interpretation would also be at odds with the rationale of the principle of complementarity, according to which the Court can step in when a state party is unable to prosecute because it lacks the necessary domestic legislation.[34] This too suggests that the Court can exercise jurisdiction independently of a parallel jurisdictional title in the state concerned.

In this sense, the Court's jurisdiction is independent of the domestic criminal jurisdiction of the state party concerned. Any interpretation of the principle *nemo dat quod non habet* that presupposes that the ICC is bound by the domestic criminal jurisdiction of a state party is thus erroneous.[35]

[31] DeGuzman (n 30) Art 21 mn 26.

[32] C Stahn, 'Response: The ICC, Pre-Existing Jurisdictional Treaty Regimes, and the Limits of the *Nemo Dat Quod Non Habet* Doctrine – A Reply to Michael Newton' (2016) 49 *Vanderbilt Journal of Transnational Law* 443, 449.

[33] *Situation in the State of Palestine* (Opinion in Accordance with Article 103 of the Rules of Procedure and Evidence – Professor William Schabas) ICC-01/18 (15 March 2020) para 25.

[34] Stahn (n 32) 449.

[35] ibid 448–49; R Rastan, 'Jurisdiction' in C Stahn (ed), *The Law and the Practice of the International Criminal Court* (OUP, 2015) 156–57; *Situation in the State of Palestine* (Submission pursuant to Rule 103 – Professors Asem Khalil & Halla Shoaibi) ICC-01/18 (16 March 2020) para 4. *Contra*: K Ambos, '"Solid jurisdictional basis"? The ICC's fragile jurisdiction for crimes allegedly committed in Palestine' (*EJIL:Talk!*, 2 March 2021), www.ejiltalk.org/solid-jurisdictional-basis-the-iccs-fragile-jurisdiction-for-crimes-allegedly-committed-in-palestine.

In any event, there is also an alternative theory of ICC jurisdiction that is grounded on the right to punish (*jus puniendi*) of the international community and is thus entirely independent of any delegation by states.[36] Under this 'universalistic' view, ICC jurisdiction is inherently international in nature and does not derive from a bundle of delegated national jurisdiction titles. If one assumes that the basis of the Court's jurisdiction is *jus puniendi*, any bilateral agreements on the exercise of domestic criminal jurisdiction are clearly irrelevant for the Court's jurisdiction.

Judge Kovàcs, in his partly dissenting opinion appended to the Pre-Trial Chamber's decision on the scope of the Court's territorial jurisdiction in Palestine, held that the Court's jurisdiction mirrors Palestine's domestic criminal jurisdiction as defined by the various Israeli–Palestinian agreements dividing the exercise of competences between them.[37] He quoted a *dictum* in the *Rohingya/Myanmar* Jurisdiction Decision in which the Chamber (over which he presided) held that

> the drafters of the Statute intended to allow the Court to exercise its jurisdiction pursuant to Article 12(2)(a) of the Statute in the same circumstances in which States Parties would be allowed to assert jurisdiction over such crimes under their legal systems, within the confines imposed by international law and the Statute.[38]

However, when read in context, that paragraph does not suggest that the Court can only exercise jurisdiction if there is a parallel jurisdictional title in the state party concerned. Rather, the paragraph explains the reasons why the Court can exercise jurisdiction when only part of the relevant conduct occurs on the territory of a state party, similarly to what happens in domestic legal systems. This is far from asserting a requirement of parallel jurisdiction between the Court and the state party concerned. Any different interpretation would be legally unsound and should not be followed.

To conclude on this point, the fact that Palestine, by virtue of the Oslo Accords, cannot exercise its domestic criminal jurisdiction over Israelis and over crimes committed in Area C does not mean that the Court cannot investigate and prosecute such crimes.

8.2.3. The Oslo Accords Limit Palestine's Enforcement Jurisdiction but do not Affect its Prescriptive Jurisdiction

The arguments on the relevance of the Oslo Accords also overlook the distinction between prescriptive jurisdiction and enforcement jurisdiction. The capacity of a state, such as Palestine, to delegate its jurisdiction to the ICC is a manifestation of its capacity to make the law, that is its *prescriptive* jurisdiction.[39] O'Keefe describes

[36] *Prosecutor v Al Bashir*, Judgment in the Jordan Referral re Al-Bashir Appeal (ICC-02/05-01/09-397), 6 May 2019, 115; K Ambos, 'Punishment without a Sovereign? The *Ius Puniendi* Issue of International Criminal Law: A First Contribution towards a Consistent Theory of International Criminal Law' (2013) 33 *Oxford Journal of Legal Studies* 293; C Kreß, 'Article 98' in Ambos (n 30) mn 126–27.

[37] Kovács Partly Dissenting Opinion (n 8) para 370.

[38] Request under Regulation 46(3) of the Regulations of the Court (Decision on the 'Prosecution's Request for a Ruling on Jurisdiction under Article 19(3) of the Statute') ICC-RoC46(3)-01/18 (6 September 2018) 70.

[39] A Abofoul, 'The Oslo Accords and the International Criminal Court's Jurisdiction in the Situation in the State of Palestine' (*OpinioJuris*, 28 July 2020), opiniojuris.org/2020/07/28/the-oslo-accords-and-the-international-criminal-courts-jurisdiction-in-the-situation-in-the-state-of-palestine.

a state's jurisdiction to prescribe as 'a state's right under international law to assert the applicability of its law to given circumstances, whether by means of primary or subordinate legislation, executive decree, or judicial action'.[40] A state's prescriptive jurisdiction is plenary under customary international law, meaning that it is unqualified and absolute, with no limitations.[41] The Oslo Accords do not regulate Palestine's prescriptive jurisdiction (nor could they do so),[42] but rather its ability to exercise criminal jurisdiction over certain categories of persons (Israelis) and over parts of its territory (such as Area C).

The ability to conduct criminal proceedings is part and parcel of Palestine's *enforcement* jurisdiction. Enforcement jurisdiction 'refers to a state's right under international law to deploy investigative, coercive or custodial powers, whether through police or other executive action or through its courts'.[43] In the case at hand, the Oslo Accords undoubtedly limit Palestine's enforcement jurisdiction. In fact, they award exclusive jurisdiction over Israelis and crimes committed in Area C to Israel.[44] That a state cannot exercise its criminal (enforcement) jurisdiction by virtue of a bilateral agreement (or other international obligation) has nothing to do with the fact that the state lawfully possesses the underlying (prescriptive) jurisdiction under international law.[45] If anything, the Oslo Accords demonstrate Palestine's pre-existing jurisdiction to delegate the exercise of its criminal jurisdiction to other entities.[46] Indeed, if Palestine did not possess this jurisdiction in the first place, it could not have concluded the Oslo Accords. Any arguments that the Accords' references to 'criminal jurisdiction' (of the Palestinian Council and of Israel, respectively) mean jurisdiction to prescribe misapprehend the notion of prescriptive jurisdiction.[47] Moreover, as discussed in more detail in the next section, any interpretation granting Israel prescriptive jurisdiction over Palestine's territory would be inconsistent with the legal framework of the law of occupation. Under this body of law, Israel does not possess prescriptive jurisdiction over the occupied Palestinian territory, as that is a sovereign prerogative that rests with the representatives of the occupied people.

Furthermore, when the Accords state that Israel has 'sole' jurisdiction over offences committed by Israelis and in Area C,[48] that does not mean that they grant Israel exclusive jurisdiction over its nationals. While the Oslo Accords are binding on Israel and Palestine, they do not bind other subjects of international law, and cannot withdraw Israelis from the jurisdiction of other courts, whether domestic or international.[49]

[40] R O'Keefe, 'Response: "Quid," Not "Quantum": A Comment on "How the International Criminal Court Threatens Treaty Norms"' (2016) 49 *Vanderbilt Journal of Transnational Law* 1, 4.

[41] *SS Lotus (France v Turkey)* 1927 PCIJ Ser A No 10, 19.

[42] *Contra* Jacobs et al (n 21).

[43] O'Keefe (n 40) 4.

[44] Art I(2) of Annex IV to the Interim Agreement states that 'Israel has *sole* criminal jurisdiction' (emphasis added).

[45] O'Keefe (n 40) 5.

[46] Stahn (n 32) 451; *Situation in the State of Palestine* (Submission pursuant to Rule 103 – Professors Asem Khalil & Halla Shoaibi) ICC-01/18, 16 March 2020, paras 24–25.

[47] Jacobs et al (n 21).

[48] Art I(2), Annex IV, Oslo II.

[49] See *mutatis mutandis* B van Schaak, 'Can the Int'l Criminal Court Try US Officials?–The Theory of "Delegated Jurisdiction" and Its Discontents (Part II)' (*Just Security*, 9 April 2018), www.justsecurity.org/54620/intl-criminal-court-officials-the-theory-delegated-jurisdiction-discontents-part-ii (discussing how the SOFA

It has also been argued that, when states enter into bilateral agreements limiting their domestic jurisdiction, their jurisdictional competences remain intact (including their enforcement jurisdiction). The proponents of this theory view the effect of those agreements as to oblige the state on whose territory the crime is committed to refrain from exercising its enforcement jurisdiction in relation to a particular class of persons or geographical area.[50] Under this view, the Oslo Agreements would not even curtail Palestine's enforcement jurisdiction as such, but only limit its ability to exercise it with respect to Israelis and crimes committed in Area C.

In conclusion, any prior agreements potentially limiting the enforcement of a state's criminal jurisdiction domestically do not affect the Court's territorial jurisdiction, which is regulated by the Statute and not by bilateral agreements. For this reason, the Oslo Accords have no bearing on the Court's jurisdiction in the situation in Palestine. Palestine retains the right under customary international law to delegate its enforcement jurisdiction to another entity (in this case, the ICC) in respect of conduct committed on its territory.

8.2.4. Under the Law of Occupation an Occupying Power has Very Limited Prescriptive Jurisdiction Over the Occupied Territory

The Oslo Accords are best interpreted in their proper context: an agreement on the gradual transfer of power from Israel, the occupying power, to the occupied population, represented by the Council. Such transfer of power, and the ensuing distribution of jurisdiction between Israel and Palestine, occurred within the constraints imposed by the applicable law, namely the law of occupation.[51]

Under the law of occupation, the occupying power does not acquire sovereignty over the occupied territory, but is only an administrator for such time as the territory remains under occupation.[52] Sovereignty rests with the occupied sovereign, namely, in this case, Palestine and its people. As Dinstein put it, 'the sovereignty of the displaced sovereign over the occupied territory is not terminated. It is not even suspended.'[53]

One of the corollaries of the above principle is that plenary prescriptive jurisdiction over the occupied territory, which is an attribute of sovereignty,[54] rests with the representatives of the occupied people.[55] Such prescriptive jurisdiction is unaffected by belligerent occupation.[56] The law of occupation only grants the occupying power the ability to issue military orders when the need arises for the maintenance

between the US and Afghanistan is only binding on the parties and does not bind other domestic courts or the ICC).

[50] ibid.

[51] Prosecution Response (n 24) paras 69–70; *Situation in the State of Palestine* (Submissions Pursuant to Rule 103 – Robert Heinsch & Giulia Pinzauti) ICC-01/18 (16 March 2020) 63–67.

[52] Art 55 Hague Regulations. See also Heinsch & Pinzauti submission (n 51) 64.

[53] Y Dinstein, *The International Law of Belligerent Occupation* (CUP, 2009) 113.

[54] S Besson, 'Sovereignty' in *Max Planck Encyclopaedia of Public International Law* (2011) 118.

[55] Prosecution Response (n 24) para 70.

[56] H Jöbstl, 'An Unlikely Day in Court? Legal Challenges for The Prosecution of Israeli Settlements under The Rome Statute' (2018) 51 *Israel Law Review* 339, 351–52: 'A state retains such prescriptive territorial jurisdiction even when under occupation. The Oslo Accords cannot take away this inherent criminal

of security and public order, but without transforming 'the laws in force in the country'.[57] Other than that, the domestic jurisdiction of the occupying power does not and shall not apply in the occupied territory.[58] Thus, the occupying power has very limited prescriptive jurisdiction over the occupied territory. In contrast, the occupying power is responsible to 'take all the measures in his power to restore and ensure, as far as possible, public order and safety'.[59] In other words, the occupying power retains enforcement jurisdiction over the occupied territory for the duration of the occupation.

Against this backdrop, it is apparent that the Accords concern the gradual transfer of responsibilities and authority from Israel, as an occupying power, to the PNA. Thus, where Oslo II refers to a 'transfer' of jurisdiction from Israel to the PNA during the redeployment phases,[60] this term truly indicates 'a restoration of the full exercise of jurisdiction to the sovereign state, namely Palestine'.[61] It does not indicate that Israel has the sovereign prerogative of prescriptive jurisdiction over Palestine's territory. This is a prerogative that rests, and remains, with the occupied Palestinian people. In keeping with that, it was within Palestine's rights to refer the situation occurring on its territory to the ICC.

8.3. IMPLICATIONS OF THE OSLO ACCORDS FOR ICC PROCEEDINGS

The considerations above do not imply that the Oslo Accords have no bearing whatsoever on ICC proceedings in the situation in Palestine. To the contrary, the Accords – which have an impact on Palestine's ability to prosecute alleged Rome Statute crimes committed on its territory – are relevant in two important respects: complementarity and cooperation.

Regarding complementarity, the relevance of the Oslo Accords is that they render the Palestinian national judicial system substantially unavailable. As is well known, states have the primary responsibility for the investigation and prosecution of Rome Statute crimes, and the Court can step in only in case of inaction by the domestic authorities, or if the domestic proceedings resulted from the unwillingness or inability to genuinely carry out the proceedings.[62] The principle of complementarity is operationalised as an admissibility test in Article 17 of the Statute. The provision envisages the Court's jurisdiction over a state party's territory where the state is unable to prosecute due to the 'unavailability of its national judicial system'.[63] The admissibility assessment undertaken by the Office of the Prosecutor takes into

jurisdiction but merely oblige the State of Palestine not to exercise it with regard to Israeli nationals or conduct in Area C'.

[57] Art 43 Hague Regulations.

[58] Arts 54, 64 and 66 GC IV and Art 43 HR.

[59] Art 43 HR.

[60] Oslo II, Arts XI(2)(e) and XVII.

[61] Heinsch & Pinzauti submission (n 51) para 66.

[62] *Prosecutor v Katanga and Ngudjolo Chui* (Judgment on the Appeal of Mr Germain Katanga against the Oral Decision of Trial Chamber II of 12 June 2009 on the Admissibility of the Case) ICC-01/04-01/07-1497 (25 September 2009) (App Ch) paras 75–79.

[63] Art 17(3) RS.

account the limits on the exercise of jurisdiction by an occupied sovereign. Without full control over its territory, Palestine is unable to fulfil its duty to exercise criminal jurisdiction over those responsible for alleged Rome Statute crimes committed on its territory.[64] Moreover, the Oslo Accords limit the exercise of Palestine's enforcement and adjudicative jurisdiction to less than 40 per cent of its territory, thereby rendering it unable to genuinely prosecute.[65] The Accords also proscribe the prosecution of Israeli nationals by Palestinian courts, whereas territorial jurisdiction typically subsists irrespective of the nationality of the offender.[66]

Secondly, at a later stage of proceedings, the Accords may affect the execution of request under Part 9 of the Statute, as Palestine only has limited enforcement jurisdiction. The Rome Statute takes into account that states may have conflicting obligations on the strength of pre-existing agreements. Articles 97–98 address this situation. In particular, Article 98(2) provides that the Court shall not ask a state party to surrender a suspect if it has a prior undertaking not to do so. It is noteworthy that these provisions are enshrined in Part 9 of the Statute ('International Cooperation and Judicial Assistance'), rather than in Part 2 ('Jurisdiction, Admissibility and Applicable Law'). This means that for the drafters such agreements could create cooperation problems, rather than jurisdictional problems.[67] This argument further supports the interpretation that bilateral agreements limiting domestic jurisdiction do not affect the Court's jurisdiction, but only the obligation to cooperate with the Court and problems in relation thereto.

The ICC Appeals Chamber has confirmed the above interpretation. In the *Afghanistan* Appeal Judgment, it held that bilateral agreements limiting a state party's jurisdiction may have an impact on that state's ability to cooperate with the Court, but do not bar the Court's jurisdiction to investigate alleged Rome Statute crimes committed on that state's territory.[68] This judgment, albeit issued in a different context, is a highly persuasive authority, and the majority of Pre-Trial Chamber I in the Palestine situation correctly adopted the same line of reasoning when it held that the Oslo Accords 'are not pertinent to the issue of the authorization of an investigation'.[69] While the wording of Article 98(2) is reminiscent of status of forces agreements (SOFAs), given that it refers to 'sending State', the provision does not exclude other types of agreements from its purview. Authoritative commentators confirm this interpretation.[70] Although the content of the Oslo Accords is markedly different from

[64] Shany (n 22) 339: 'situations in which states (or quasi-states) lose control over parts of their territory represent a paradigmatic case for self-referral of situations to the ICC in so far as they reflect the "inability of the State genuinely to prosecute"'.

[65] Heinsch & Pinzauti submission (n 51) para 67.

[66] As well as the nature of the conduct. See O'Keefe (n 40) 5.

[67] Stahn (n 32) 451.

[68] *Afghanistan* Appeal Judgment (n 2).

[69] P-TC I Decision on the scope of the Court's territorial jurisdiction in Palestine (n 3) para 129.

[70] Kreß (n 36), mn 162 (arguing that the provision applies to agreements need to make use of the technical concept of a 'sending' and a 'receiving' state and give rise to the same conflict of international obligations); O'Keefe (n 40) 8 (arguing that although Art 98(2) refers to jurisdictional rights typically found in SOFAs, 'there is no reason why it cannot cover other agreements falling within the terms of the provision'); C Kress and K Prost, 'Article 98' in O Triffterer and K Ambos (eds), *The Rome Statute of The International Criminal Court: A Commentary*, 3rd edn (Beck, 2016) 2143. *Contra* Kovács Partly Dissenting Opinion (n 8) para 364 (arguing that the content of the Oslo Accords is very different from the content of the other kinds of agreements to which art 98 applies).

SOFAs, they likewise have the effect to limit the exercise of a state party's jurisdiction. Thus, there is no reason to exclude them from the scope of application of Article 98(2).

In his Partly Dissenting Opinion appended to the decision on the scope of the Court's territorial jurisdiction in Palestine, Judge Kovács expressed a different view on this point. He argued that 'the extrapolation of the *dicta* contained in Pre-Trial Chamber II's decision and in the Appeals Chamber's judgment [in Afghanistan] to the Oslo Accords is problematic'.[71] He disagreed with the majority that the Accord's impact is only to be dealt with at a later stage of proceedings when admissibility and cooperation are under scrutiny. He also submitted that the proper approach would have been a 'harmonized interpretation' of the provisions of the Oslo Accords and the Rome Statute, which would allow Palestine to implement its obligations under both treaties at the same time.[72] While undoubtedly well researched and extensively reasoned, Judge Kovács' dissent is unpersuasive for several reasons, outlined below.

8.3.1. The *Afghanistan* Appeal Judgment is a Highly Persuasive Authority

The *Afghanistan* Appeal Judgment, while not binding per se on the Palestine Pre-Trial Chamber,[73] provided an authoritative interpretation of the statutory provisions on territorial jurisdiction. Likewise, it authoritatively interpreted the provisions regulating cooperation problems in case a state party contracted conflicting obligations by virtue of pre-existing bilateral agreements limiting domestic jurisdiction. The majority thus decided to be guided by this decision in its reasoning.[74] Conversely, the two reasons provided by Judge Kovács for departing from the *Afghanistan* Appeal Judgment – namely, that the Oslo Accords are of a different kind, and that Palestine, unlike Afghanistan, is not a state – are unpersuasive.

First, Judge Kovács argued that the content of the agreements at issue in *Afghanistan* was very different from that of the Oslo Accords.[75] While it is a fact that the Oslo Accords are not SOFAs, the preceding section already explained that the scope of application of Article 98 is not limited to SOFAs. Second, Judge Kovács pointed out that the SOFAs at issue in the *Afghanistan* Appeal Judgment were contracted between two sovereign states. Instead, in his view Palestine is a 'special entity',[76] which he elsewhere defines as a '*nasciturus* state, recognized already as a full State by a great number of States, but not recognized as such by another number of States'.[77]

At first sight, Judge Kovács seems to raise a valid point. While some date Palestine's statehood to the mandate period,[78] many would argue that the decisive moment in

[71] Kovács' Partly Dissenting Opinion (n 8) para 364.

[72] ibid para 366.

[73] Under Art 21(2) RS the Court '*may* apply principles and rules as interpreted in its previous decisions' (emphasis added).

[74] P-TC I Decision on the Court's territorial jurisdiction in Palestine (n 3) paras 128–29.

[75] Kovács Partly Dissenting Opinion (n 8) 360.

[76] ibid 360.

[77] ibid 326.

[78] J Quigley, *The Statehood of Palestine* (CUP, 2010) 3–114; MM Qafisheh, 'Citizens of the State of Palestine and the Future of Palestinian Refugees: Legal and political scenarios, in idem (ed) Palestine Membership in the United Nations: Legal and Practical Implications (Cambridge Scholars Publishing, 2013) 45, 120 (dating statehood to the entry into force of the Lausanne Peace treaty).

Palestine's quest for statehood was GA resolution 67/19 of 29 November 2012, which accorded Palestine the status of non-member observer state in the United Nations.[79] Thus, one may argue that Palestine's statehood at the time when the Oslo Accords were concluded was uncertain, unlike Afghanistan's situation when it concluded the SOFAs with the US.

Nevertheless, the conclusion that Judge Kovács draws – that the uncertainty regarding Palestine's statehood excludes the Oslo Agreements from the purview of Article 98(2) – is open to challenge because at the time the Accords were concluded, Palestine already had at a minimum the sovereign prerogative of prescriptive jurisdiction. Even on the assumption that Palestine may not have been a fully fledged state by 1993–95, the very fact that the PLO as the legitimate representative of the Palestinian people concluded these international agreements with Israel demonstrates that at the very least Palestine already possessed the sovereign prerogative of prescriptive jurisdiction by virtue of its signature of the Accords.[80] This is sufficient to render Palestine's situation comparable to that of Afghanistan, as far as the conclusion of bilateral agreements is concerned. Other sovereign prerogatives may have consolidated over time, culminating with Palestine's collective recognition as a non-member observer state within the United Nations in 2012. This is consistent with the theory that the creation of states is a 'process'[81] and that there are some modes of creation of states that occur over time rather than 'at the stroke of midnight'.[82] This may well be the case when a territory gradually acquires statehood while under belligerent occupation. But what matters here is that at the time of conclusion of the Oslo Accords, Palestine had the sovereign prerogative to conclude agreements with other states limiting the extent of its domestic jurisdiction.

Thus, there are no valid grounds to distinguish Palestine's situation from Afghanistan's, contrary to what Judge Kovács argued. Therefore, the principle that was articulated in the *Afghanistan* Appeal Judgment – that bilateral agreement limiting domestic jurisdiction are relevant to cooperation rather than to territorial jurisdiction – also applies to the Oslo Accords in the Palestine situation.

8.3.2. The Court Correctly Determined the Scope of its Territorial Jurisdiction by Reference to the Rome Statute Only

As explained in Section 8.2.1, the Court's jurisdiction is regulated by Article 12 of the Statute. This provision makes no reference to states parties' domestic criminal

[79] D Akande, 'Palestine as a UN Observer State: Does this Make Palestine a State?' (*EJIL:Talk!*, 3 December 2012), www.ejiltalk.org/palestine-as-a-un-observer-state-does-this-make-palestine-a-state/; Situation in Palestine, Statement by the Office of the Prosecutor (3 April 2012), www.icc-cpi.int/sites/default/files/NR/rdonlyres/9B651B80-EC43-4945-BF5A-FAFF5F334B92/284387/SituationinPalestine030412ENG.pdf.

[80] See section 8.2.4.

[81] J Crawford, *The Creation of States in International Law*, 2nd edn (OUP, 2006) 255.

[82] ibid 349. For example, the grant of independence by the previous sovereign can take place through 'the gradual devolution of accretion of power in a local unit to the point where it is eventually seen as a separate state' (ibid 330). In this case, the acquisition of independence (and of statehood) may not occur at 'any clearly defined point in time' (ibid 349–50). Secession is another mode of creation that can occur over time. See for example the case of Guinea-Bissau (ibid 386). In practice, the distinction between devolution and secession may be artificial in some circumstances as elements of both processes can coexist (ibid 375).

jurisdiction pursuant to the international obligations they may have contracted. The consequence of this for Palestine's situation is that the Oslo Accords are not applicable by the Court in determining the scope of its jurisdiction, nor do they have a bearing on it. The problem is rather that Palestine has undertaken conflicting obligations through the Oslo Accords and by ratifying the Rome Statute. The former oblige Palestine to not exercise enforcement jurisdiction over Israelis, or over crimes committed in Area C and in East Jerusalem. The latter impose on it an obligation to cooperate with the Court, including for the execution of arrest warrants for the commission of crimes over the entirety of Palestine's territory, and irrespective of the nationality of the offender. Thus, in the future Palestine may well find itself in a situation in which it is faced with conflicting obligations under the Rome Statute and the Accords.

To solve this tension, Judge Kovács argued in his opinion that the Court should have interpreted the jurisdictional provisions in the Rome Statute in harmony with the rules of competence under the Oslo Accords.[83] Thus, in his opinion the Court could only investigate alleged crimes committed in Area C and in East Jerusalem subject to Israel's consent. This proposition is unconvincing for two main reasons.

First, as already explained, the Accords do not form part of the applicable law for determining the Court's jurisdiction under Article 21(1)(b) of the Statute. They are not applicable to determining the scope of the Court's jurisdiction even if they are binding on Palestine. Second, Judge Kovács' proposed 'harmonized interpretation' finds no basis in the VCLT or in international law insofar as it relates to two instruments with non-identical parties and that do not necessarily relate to the same subject matter.[84] Whether the rules on treaty interpretation codified in the VCLT apply at all to the interpretation of the Oslo Accords depends on their legal status as agreements between states (Article 2(1)(a) VCLT). In any event, given that the parties to the Oslo Accords and the Rome Statute are not the same, resolving treaty conflicts cannot disregard the principle that a treaty binds the parties and only the parties; it does not create obligations for third states. The implication is that it is not possible to reconcile the treaties by interpreting one (the Rome Statute) by reference to the other (the Oslo Accords) where this would affect the rights and obligations of the other states parties to the Rome Statute, unless their consent is also obtained.[85] By the same token, neither treaty can be invalidated, or subordinated to the other, by applying other principles of conflict resolution such as *lex posterior* (a later law repeals an earlier law) or *lex specialis* (special law repeals general law).[86] In any event, these considerations do not pertain to the opening of an investigation. If at a later stage of proceedings Palestine receives a cooperation request from the Court

[83] Kovács' Partly Dissenting Opinion (n 8) para 366.

[84] It is generally accepted that conflicts between treaties may be solved by way of a harmonising interpretation that gives 'the widest possible degree of application to both colliding provisions', even if this rule is not mentioned in the VCLT (N Matz-Lück, 'Treaties, Conflicts between, in *Max Planck Encyclopaedia of Public International Law* (2010) para 20). However, in the case at hand the treaties do not necessarily relate to the same subject-matter and have non-identical parties. These factors limit the operation of harmonising interpretations.

[85] S Ranganathan, 'Responding to Deliberately Created Treaty Conflicts' in C Tams et al (eds), *Research Handbook on the Law of Treaties* (Elgar, 2014) 447, 452.

[86] ibid 452–53.

that conflicts with Palestine's obligations under the Oslo Accords, the conflict will be solved pursuant to Article 98(2) of the Rome Statute. In contrast, Judge Kovács' proposed harmonised interpretation in practice has the effect of giving priority to the provisions of the Oslo Accords on the repartition of competences over the jurisdictional provisions of the Rome Statute. This approach finds no basis under the rules on treaty interpretation enshrined in the VCLT or in customary international law.[87] The majority of Pre-Trial Chamber I correctly determined the scope of the Court's territorial jurisdiction by reference to the jurisdictional provisions in the Statute only.

CONCLUSION

This chapter has argued that the Oslo Accords do not bar ICC jurisdiction over alleged Rome Statute crimes committed on Palestine's territory, including those committed against the Bedouin communities at risk of displacement in Area C. Under the jurisdictional provisions of the Rome Statute, when a state party confers jurisdiction to the ICC, the Court's jurisdiction over Rome Statute crimes is automatic over that state's territory. No further expression of consent is necessary. There is also no requirement that the state in question has a parallel jurisdictional title in its domestic legal order. By the same token, any prior agreements potentially limiting the enforcement of that state's criminal jurisdiction domestically do not affect the Court's territorial jurisdiction. If one assumes that the basis of the Court's jurisdiction is *jus puniendi*, any bilateral agreements on the exercise of criminal jurisdiction domestically have no bearing on the Court's jurisdiction. Even if one adopts the delegation theory, the arguments on the relevance of the Oslo accords conflate a state's jurisdiction to prescribe with its enforcement jurisdiction and disregard the law of occupation. However, these are distinct notions, relating to distinct competences. A state may undertake by treaty to refrain from exercising certain jurisdictional rights, such as the right to conduct criminal proceedings; however, it still retains this right under customary international law in respect of conduct committed on its territory. The Oslo Accords did not, and could not, strip Palestine of the (prescriptive) jurisdiction over its territory, but they only limited the exercise of this jurisdiction. In this sense, they do not affect the Court's jurisdiction over alleged Rome Statute crimes committed on Palestine's territory.

Accordingly, the alleged crimes committed against the Palestinian Bedouin community in Area C fall within the ambit of the Court's territorial jurisdiction. It is hoped that the prosecutor will undertake a comprehensive investigation of the situation as a whole, without overlooking the crimes committed against the Bedouin community. Failing to include these alleged crimes within the scope of the investigation would result in an artificial and unjustified separation of the Bedouin community from the broader Palestinian polity.

[87] Applying Kovács' harmonised interpretation comes closer to the application of the *lex prior* principle – a principle that has not found general acceptance in international law. Matz-Lück (n 84) para 17.

Epilogue

THE PAST, PRESENT and future forced displacements faced by Palestinian Bedouins across the West Bank – and by Palestinians elsewhere – have no legal basis in international law. Nonetheless, as the chapters in this book illustrate, these communities have been targeted in multiple ways by Israeli authorities and settlers in a climate of general impunity for those responsible for actions likely to amount to various international law violations, including the international crime of forcible transfer. Displacing Palestinian Bedouins results in harm at individual level for the families affected by evictions, home demolitions and destruction of property not justified by military necessity. At the same time, these violent actions result in collective harm for the communities, whose livelihoods and way of life is being irrevocably damaged by direct targeting and the imposition of the coercive environment of an expansionist settler colonial state. Furthermore, displacement and the risk of forced displacement of Palestinian Bedouins harms the Palestinian people as a whole, because the Bedouins are a group within the wider Palestinian people, who are all subjected to Israeli settler colonial policies and practices limiting their right to self-determination.

Driving the displacement of Palestinian Bedouins is the Israeli-imposed discriminatory permit and planning system in Area C of the West Bank. In a paradoxical misinterpretation of the international legal framework, the Israeli authorities view Bedouins – ie protected persons under international humanitarian law (IHL) – as illegal on the land; conversely, the Israeli State offers boundless protection to Israeli settlers and the settler project as a whole (now enshrined constitutionally[1]) despite the fact that settlements are illegal under international law, and residents of settlements reside unlawfully on occupied land. The displacement of Palestinian Bedouins allows for their land and associated resources to be taken over and reallocated for the benefit of Israel and Israeli settlements. This happens under the cover of the 1967 occupation of the West Bank, including East Jerusalem, and the Gaza Strip, which Israel has entrenched in virtually all aspects of life in a manner that blends military might with administrative absurdities.

The context in which the displacement of Palestinian Bedouins (and many more harms inflicted on Palestinians) occurs was assessed by the International Court of Justice (ICJ) in a landmark Advisory Opinion of 19 July 2024, which found that:

> The sustained abuse by Israel of its position as an occupying Power, through annexation and an assertion of permanent control over the Occupied Palestinian Territory and

[1] Israeli Knesset, *Basic Law: Israel – the Nation State of the Jewish People* (19 July 2018), Art 7: 'the state sees in the development of Jewish settlements as one of national value, and will act to encourage and advance its establishment and strengthening'.

> continued frustration of the right of the Palestinian people to self-determination, violates fundamental principles of international law and renders Israel's presence in the Occupied Palestinian Territory unlawful.[2]

The Advisory Opinion examines forced displacement of the Palestinian population 'commonly as a result of the demolition of their property or as a result of zoning and planning policies and the relocation plans associated with them'.[3] While the Bedouins are not mentioned by name it is clear that this analysis is applicable in full to their displacement. The Court notes how displacement can be induced by 'large-scale confiscation of land and the deprivation of access to natural resources divest[ing] the local population of their basic means of subsistence',[4] reported by many Bedouins (and discussed in this book).

A key consequence of displacement is the possibility for Israel – and Israeli settlers – to take over land emptied of Palestinian inhabitants and use it for its own benefit; wherever this occurs it may lead to annexation, violating the prohibition of acquisition of territory by force enshrined in Artice 2(4) of the UN Charter.[5] The link between displacement and annexation is understood in light of Israel's allocation of almost all of the land in Area C of the West Bank for its own use – settlements, military zones and nature reserves.[6] For Palestinians, including Bedouins, the long, complicated and expensive process for obtaining Israeli-issued building permits and their low approval rates results in many building without such permits; as the Court notes, 'Buildings lacking permits are subject to demolition, exposing their residents to the risk of eviction and displacement'.[7] In targeting Bedouin communities for displacement, Israel essentially targets the section of the Palestinian people who constitute the majority of Palestinian inhabitants in Area C, which Israel seeks to annex through force in contravention of international law.

The recent ICJ Advisory Opinion confirms the longstanding legal analysis of the context in which forced displacement of Palestinian Bedouins occurs: by continuing to occupy the land, Israel is violating a range of international legal norms through its policies and practices in the occupied Palestinian territory (OPT), including the inalienable right of the Palestinian people to self-determination.[8] For as long as there is impunity for international law violations affecting Palestinians, including for Israel's policies and practices driving Palestinian displacement, Bedouin communities will continue to be at risk of forcible transfer. While international law and its institutions do not have the ability to put an end to this harm, the Advisory Opinion should empower the rest of the international community to ensure no third state renders 'aid or assistance in maintaining the situation created by Israel's illegal presence in the Occupied Palestinian Territory'.[9] To uphold their duties under international law,

[2] International Court of Justice, Advisory Opinion: Legal Consequences arising from the Policies and Practices of Israel in the Occupied Palestinian Territory, including East Jerusalem (19 July 2024) para 261.

[3] ibid para 143.

[4] ibid.

[5] ibid paras 175 ff and 254.

[6] ibid paras 214 and 120.

[7] ibid para 216.

[8] ibid 243.

[9] ibid 278–79.

other states must take political, economic and diplomatic steps to ensure they 'do not recognize any changes in the physical character or demographic composition, institutional structure or status' of the OPT.[10] Thus, Israel holds primary responsibility for the forced displacement of Palestinian Bedouins, but international law is clear enough for the rest of the international community to act upon as well.

Alice Panepinto
22 July 2024

[10] ibid.

Index

www.ingramcontent.com/pod-product-compliance
Ingram Content Group UK Ltd.
Pitfield, Milton Keynes, MK11 3LW, UK
UKHW020844290926
15470UKWH00004B/1532

9 781509 977208